THE LIE THAT WOULDN'T DIE

THE LIE THAT WOULDN'T DIE

The Protocols of the Elders of Zion

HADASSA BEN-ITTO

Preface by
Lord Woolf,
Lord Chief Justice

Foreword by
Judge Edward R. Korman
United States District Court for the Eastern District of New York

VALLENTINE MITCHELL
LONDON • PORTLAND, OR

First published in 2005 in Great Britain by
VALLENTINE MITCHELL
Suite 314, Premier House, 112–114 Station Road, Edgware, Middlesex HA8 7BJ
and in the United States of America by
VALLENTINE MITCHELL
c/o ISBS, 920 NE 58th Avenue, Suite 300
Portland, Oregon, 97213-3786

Website http://www.frankcass.com

British Library Cataloging in Publication Data:

A catalogue record for this book is available
from the British Library

ISBN 0-85303-602-0 (cloth)
ISBN 0-95303-595-4 (paper)

Library of Congress Cataloging-in-Publication Data:

A catalog record for this book is available
from the Library of Congress

Printed in Great Britain by
MPG Books Ltd, Bodmin, Cornwall

Most members of my family perished in the Holocaust, their graves unknown and unmarked. Let this be their monument.

Contents

Preface

This is a remarkable book by a remarkable woman, Hadassa Ben-Itto. Because of her background she knows from personal experience the corrosive effect of anti-Semitism. This has caused her to devote her immense energy and talents in a personal crusade to combat its effect. In particular, she has attacked the poisonous lies that over the centuries have fuelled anti-Semitism.

As Hadassa Ben-Itto has been a distinguished lawyer and judge, it is not surprising that one of the principal weapons she has used, so effectively, in her campaign against anti-Semitism is the evidence she has collected that establishes beyond doubt the total inaccuracy of the most damaging lie of all, the *Protocols of the Elders of Zion*. This book is the product of her research. It demonstrates not only her total mastery of her subject, but also her ability to tell a most compelling story. Even when her material is largely based on the records of one of the trials that should have indelibly and permanently labelled the *Protocols* a forgery there is nothing turgid in her account. On the contrary, her account brings the proceedings to life. You are transported to the court in which the trial is proceeding and you feel you are witnessing at first hand what must be one of the most fascinating trials that have ever taken place.

This is a book you will find difficult to put down. When you do, you will be left amazed that it is possible that there are those who have so little regard for truth that they can still publish the *Protocols* without placing at the start and foot of each page in red ink 'This volume is a forgery, its contents are lies. It serves no purpose other than to demonstrate the lengths to which those who wish to damage the Jewish people will go to achieve their objective.' That the lie will not die does not detract from Hadassa's achievement. She cannot prevent the repeated publication of the calumny, but what she has achieved is that it is far more likely that the lie will be recognized for what it is. She deserves our applause.

Lord Woolf
Lord Chief Justice
London, August 2004

Foreword

For several years now my judicial responsibilities have included the negotiation and implementation of an agreement with Swiss banks concerning Holocaust era claims. In this context I sought a deeper understanding of the historic and political roots of anti-Semitism and their effect on the rise of Nazism. It was very clear that *The Protocols of the Elders of Zion* served as a poisonous wellspring for Tsarist pogroms and the Final Solution.

In February 1943, three and a half years after the Second World War began with Hitler's invasion of Poland, Nazism's end became predictable with the destruction of the German 6th Army at Stalingrad. The failure of Hitler's invasion of the Soviet Union was followed in May 1943 by the surrender of all Axis troops in North Africa after the rout of General Rommel. Yet I was particularly startled to read in the diaries of Goebbels under the 18 May 1943 entry: 'I have devoted exhaustive study to *The Protocols of the Elders of Zion*. In the past the objection was always that they aren't suited to present-day propaganda. In reading them now I find that we can use them very well. *The Protocols of the Elders of Zion* are as modern today as they were when they were published for the first time.' The entry then continues as follows: 'At noon I mentioned this to the Führer. He believed *The Protocols* were absolutely genuine ...' After a long recital of the Führer's fulminations against Jews and references to 'the Jewish peril', Goebbels quotes the Führer: 'There is therefore no other recourse left for modern nations except to exterminate the Jew ... The nations that have been the first to see through the Jew and have been the first to fight him are going to take his place in the domination of the world.'[1] For Hitler and Goebbels, the strength of the *Protocols* – 'The Lie That Wouldn't Die' – inspired them to ignore the writing on the wall and to prolong the war against the Jews and the predictable demise of the Third Reich.

The year 2005 marks the 60th anniversary of the liberation of Auschwitz, followed by VE Day – the military defeat of the Third Reich. This was also the time when we hoped and dreamed of 'Never Again'. To the shame of the Free World we are facing today a serious rise of anti-Semitism with ugly manifestations in countries where hundreds of thousands of Jews were murdered during the Second World War.

Hadassa Ben-Itto – a fellow judge – deserves great credit and recognition for the masterly and passionate exposition of the murderous fraud that was perpetrated by the authors of *The Protocols of the Elders of Zion. The Lie That Wouldn't Die*, the result of Hadassa Ben-Itto's prodigious research and powerful prose, should serve as a potent weapon in the struggle against the revival of virulent anti-Semitism at the start of the twenty-first century.

Edward R. Korman
Chief Judge
United States District Court for the
Eastern District of New York
New York, December 2004

Plates

Author's Note

This book is about a forged document that tells a dangerous lie about my people. Of all the libels that have served as a means of incitement against Jews, and as intellectual justification of anti-Semitism, the myth of the so-called 'Jewish Conspiracy' to gain domination of the whole world, as embodied in the forged *Protocols of the Elders of Zion*, is probably the most devious and, in the long run, the most dangerous.

The book tells the full story of those who forged the document, distributed it around the world and exploited it. It also pays tribute to those who exposed and disproved it.

For an entire century this lie has been published and disseminated in almost every language known to men in civilized countries, and time and again, for many decades, it has been challenged and exposed by honest journalists, by learned historians, by politicians and by diplomats, by religious leaders and former police agents, and most of all by courageous, responsible and unimpeachable judges in democratic countries. It has also been disproved by the horrible history of the twentieth century. Yet the lie endures and is still spreading its poison.

The story of the *Protocols* has been told numerous times in various languages in scholarly, well-researched accounts, which fill the shelves of libraries. Yet, although the *Protocols* have been, and still are, distributed around the world in hundreds of editions, in millions of copies, and now also on the Worldwide Web, the general public is not aware of the true facts of this dramatic story, for it appears that academic footnoted studies have a limited readership.

I am not a historian, and my involvement with the story of the *Protocols of the Elders of Zion* was personal, rather than professional. As described in this book, I became aware of the story by a chain of coincidences, and began my research as a matter of pure curiosity. As a judge I was particularly interested in the trials concerning the *Protocols*, which were mentioned, but not fully described, in former publications. As I became aware of the facts I felt duty bound to share them with the public. What began as a minor project, not supposed to interfere with my judicial duties, took on immense proportions, which created a personal dilemma. In order to follow the story as it developed I was compelled to retire before reaching compulsory retirement age, after having served 31 years in the Israeli court system.

As I followed the history of the *Protocols* I was astonished at the large number of people who had been involved in the story, in various capacities, and whose lives had been affected by it. Most of them had been mentioned in previous publications, but my curiosity about them remained unsatisfied. I decided to accumulate as much information as possible about each of the people who kept crowding my notes, and to bring them alive in my book. I was encouraged to do so by two people whose advice I sought.

Justice Haim Cohn was my friend and mentor for many years. One of the most outstanding jurists in Israel, he was the former attorney-general and minister of justice, deputy president of the Supreme Court and the author of many important books, including his famous study *The Trial and Death of Jesus*, which was translated into many languages. 'Follow the story wherever it takes you,' he advised. 'Write it as a judge, not as a historian.' In spite of his advanced age and failing health he later offered to read the manuscript, and wrote the introduction to the Hebrew version.

I received the same advice from a well-known historian, Professor Israel Gutman of the Hebrew University and of Yad Vashem in Jerusalem, one of the most reputable authorities in the field. Professor Gutman accompanied me throughout my research, discussing with me various aspects of the story. As I went along, I informed him of my sources, and he then read and approved the final manuscript. He also presented the Hebrew version at three public meetings.

Literally following the story, I traveled from one country to another, from St Petersburg to Berne, from Paris to London, from Johannesburg and Port Elizabeth to Washington, DC. I interviewed people, read as many available books as possible, in various languages, both for facts and for background material, combed public and private archives, and spent months studying the mass of documents accumulated both on my computer and on my microfilm screen.

I wrote the story as I found it, and used some license in describing events and persons in my own language, but all these events so described were taken from published sources, from documentary archives or from actual interviews.

It took me six years.

From 1933 the *Protocols* were used in Nazi propaganda around the world. As a judge I was particularly interested in the two major trials, both initiated in 1934 by Jewish communities in Switzerland and in South Africa, against local Nazi distributors of the *Protocols*.

From the beginning it was obvious that the Berne trial would be a focal theme of my book, but I could not have foreseen the unexpected sources that became available to me, one source leading to another. It began at a chance meeting with Odette, widow of Georges Brunschvig, a young inexperienced lawyer who had undertaken in 1934 to conduct in the City Court of Berne the most important historical trial concerning the *Protocols of the Elders of Zion*. This is when I first learned to my surprise that I could still interview, in 1988, witnesses who had lived through the Berne trial and remembered, after more than 50 years, details that were absent from all existing archives.

Throughout the years of my research I spent many days talking with Odette, rekindling her memory, recording her impressions, and rummaging through personal notes left behind by her late husband. It was through Odette that I discovered many other sources. The 800-page unpublished handwritten manuscript of Emil Raas, the law partner of Georges Brunschvig, provided invaluable insight into the conduct of the Berne trial. Emil Dreifus had miraculously kept for more than 50 years the newspapers that reported daily on the court proceedings, and supplied descriptions of the atmosphere and witnesses.

Willy Guggenheim, the secretary-general of the Jewish Community of Switzerland, put at my disposal the complete archive of Georges Brunschvig, which had been entrusted to him for safekeeping and had rested for many years in a cabinet in his office. It included a mass of documents, reports, minutes of meetings, correspondence and private notes accumulated by the lawyers for the plaintiffs in the Berne trial. It was through his efforts that the whole archive was microfilmed, and I am greatly indebted to Professor Dr Klaus Urner, director of the historical archive ETH (Archive für Zeitgeschichte) in Zurich and Dr Uriel Gast, the director of the Department of Jewish History, who mailed to me three microfilm cassettes that contained some 8,000 pages.

For long periods during the preparation of the book, the Wiener Library at Tel Aviv University was like a second home to me. Not only did I spend many weeks studying there the whole verbatim record of the Berne trial, but I could never have become so familiar with their vast material on the *Protocols* had it not been for the active assistance, freely offered, by the wonderful women in charge of the library, Miriam Broshi and Gila Michlovski. It is through them that I became acquainted with the documents of the Fryenwald Archive, which served to create a whole chapter in the book. All the facts about the Nazi defendants in the Berne trial, including their corre-spondence with each other, their tactics, their conspiratorial methods and their contact with the Nazi leadership in Germany, are fully doc-umented in this archive, which had been confiscated by the Swiss police after the Berne trial.

As described in the book, the full verbatim record of the South African trial in 1934 came into my possession privately, from the Port Elizabeth advocate Mr Jankelevich, in whose chambers it had been kept all these years. The rest of the information concerning the South African trial came from the library of the Zionist Federation in Johannesburg.

The records and background material of the appeal to the South African Board of Publications, in 1991, are in my possession as a result of my personal involvement in these proceedings. As president of the International Association of Jewish Lawyers and Jurists, I was consulted on the matter by our South African branch, and this is as good an opportunity as ever to convey my gratitude to the leadership of the branch and to the lawyers who volunteered their professional assistance, for the wonderful job they have done and for the materi-al they have put at my disposal.

The people who supplied the documents concerning the Moscow trial in 1991, and offered eyewitness testimony, remain unnamed at their request. They deserve all my gratitude.

Obviously the relevant period in Tsarist Russia was at the centre of the story. Many books describe the history of the period, but it took much more to describe the events that led to the publication of the *Protocols* and all the people involved in this saga.

The memoirs of Count Sergei Witte, the minister of finance in the Tsar's Cabinet, and of Paul Miliukov, the leader of the opposition, deserve special mention, as they brought to light many facts and episodes.

Dr Boris Moruzov, a historian who assisted me throughout my research, combed newly opened Russian archives and supplied and translated invaluable material. He also checked and re-checked Russian material derived from other sources, and the confusing spelling of Russian names.

The full story of the Russians figuring in the book, the forgers as well as the witnesses, came from those Russian archives and from documents in the private archive of Georges Brunschvig, as well as the testimony of witnesses at the Berne trial, and the published works of some of them.

The Last Tsarina, by Princess Katerina Radziwill, published in English in 1928, provided many colorful details noted by an eye-witness, which I used in my description of this woman, who had been so instrumental in revealing the truth about the forgery of the *Protocols*.

In order to recreate the atmosphere in Russia in those days, I read and used the fascinating memoirs of Maurice Paleologue, the last French ambassador to Tsarist Russia.

The London *Times* played a central role in the revelation of the truth about the *Protocols*, and the ongoing distribution of the facts around the world. The information concerning the role of their correspondent, Philip Graves, and of the London *Times* itself, came from the *Times* archive, which I inspected with the courteous assistance of the *Times* management. The personnel of the archive carried to my desk huge volumes filled with relevant documents and generously assisted in preparing photocopies. This is how I became acquainted with the full story of Philip Graves, his correspondence with the *Times* editor and management, the description of his meetings in Istanbul with the Russian refugee who wished to remain anonymous, his hope to receive the Nobel prize for his revelation about the *Protocols*, and his reluctance to testify at the Berne trial so as not to endanger his relatives in Nazi Germany.

The full details of the Ford story and the interviews of Katerina Radziwill and Henriette Hurblut came from the Library of Congress in Washington, DC, mainly from old copies of the *Hebrew American*. My friend Janet Terner deserves credit for her invaluable assistance in finding my way in the library and gaining easy access to relevant material. This is how I became acquainted with Mr Pipps, the editor of Ford's newspaper the *Dearborn Independent*, who opposed the publication of the *Protocols*, resigned in protest, and told the whole story in his own newspaper, *Pipps Weekly*.

It is there that I also discovered the facts concerning the appointment and report of the subcommittee of the Judiciary Committee of the Senate of the United States, in 1964, and their full report on the *Protocols of the Elders of Zion*, which is part of the congressional record.

From the beginning I was greatly fascinated with Maurice Joly, from whose book the *Protocols* were plagiarized. His own autobiography served as an invaluable source. I tried in vain to find the original record of his trial, but that particular courthouse had burned down. I did find a copy of the original prison record where he had served his sentence, with the assistance of Judge Miriam Ezratty, former first president of the Court of Appeal of France.

A most valuable source of information on current publications of the *Protocols* was the Project for the Study of Anti-Semitism of Tel Aviv University, headed by Dr Dina Porat, who offered ongoing advice and insight.

Professor Bernard Lewis, whose books and articles helped educate me on the situation in Arab and Muslim countries, willingly shared his personal experience during our walks on the Tel Aviv waterfront, affording me the privilege of learning the facts from one of the foremost experts on the subject. He also confirmed that the *Protocols* were currently sold in bookstores in Arab capitals, which he visited regularly.

Lest I omit the names of some of those who assisted me, and who all deserve my thanks, I shall not list them all. I shall only mention those who deserve special credit: Muzi Wertheim, for having confidence in me and in my project and for lending meaningful support; Ron Gazit, for being such a good friend and for closely accompanying the project, freely offering his advice, his support and his valuable time; Dr Gil Feiler, who introduced me to the world of computers and information data, combed the website, filled my disk with relevant publications and was never too busy to offer advice and assistance; Professor Ben Ami Shillony of the Hebrew University, who offered a personal story and checked the Japanese part; and my daughter Orly, whose judgment I value greatly as an intelligent critical reader, who read the full manuscript and offered moral support and helpful remarks.

In spite of all the assistance, this was a lonely job. I am very grateful to all my close friends and associates, too many to be individually named, who accompanied me on this long journey and never tired of listening to my reports, sharing with me the good as well as the bad times.

I wrote the book as a challenge to all those who unwittingly allow this and similar lies to be spread and to cause continuous harm. Many people have told me, time and again, that it is wrong to ban a book, any book, even a proven forgery. A lie, they say, should be confronted in the 'marketplace of ideas'. The facts described in this book should prove these people wrong. A deliberate lie is not an 'idea'. It may easily become a dangerous weapon. Those who exploit it don't belong in a genuine 'marketplace of ideas'. Unlike some weapons, a lie like the *Protocols* is never used in self-defense, so there is no reason for allowing it. It should be banned, as are other weapons that possess the potential of causing mass murder and destruction.

I belong to those who believe that lies and libels that set up a group of people as scapegoats, hate targets, potential victims of murder and extermination, should not be protected as free speech. This book challenges those who disagree with my view to present a viable alternative.

1 Encounters with the *Protocols*

This was my last day on the bench. Had anybody suggested five years ago that I would give up my judicial career to investigate a book, I would have ignored it as a bad joke. After 30 years in court, being a judge was as much part of me as being a woman. When I was not called by my first name, a common practice in our informal society, I was addressed as 'Judge' more often than 'Mrs'. Compulsory retirement was years away and voluntarily resigning my post would have seemed tantamount to living half a life. This was the very center of my existence. Yet here I was, on 31 October 1991, presiding over my last session in the District Court of Tel Aviv.

A crowd of black-robed lawyers, including some of my former law clerks, gathered from various courtrooms in the building to see me off. The court was packed as I announced my last judgments, trying to keep my voice as normal as possible. My best years had passed in this room. Here I had listened to witnesses and to counsel; I had watched a long procession of men and women in moments of strength and of weakness, of anguish and of joy; I had seen people with downcast eyes, either because they were not used to lying or because the truth was too difficult to tell; some had entered this room as prisoners, and left as free men; others came in free, surrounded by anxious families, only to leave with guards, through the inconspicuous side door leading to the cells. From this room I had sent men and women to be imprisoned for life. Mothers and fathers had learned here that they were to be robbed of the custody of their children.

I was part of this courtroom. I knew which window did not close all the way and which chair creaked. I could see the stain on the linoleum where a policeman had spilled a sack of confiscated hashish, and a spot near the witness stand where one day an old man had collapsed and died while being interrogated by an aggressive and persistent prosecutor. The panes of the windows were still criss-crossed with wide strips of cellophane, a compulsory precaution taken during the 1991 Gulf War, when Tel Aviv was the target of Iraqi missiles.

I was leaving part of myself in this room, but I was also taking away with me a strong sense of fulfillment. I was giving up my seat on the bench, but I would still be a judge, though self-appointed, out to discover the truth and to deliver judgment. I was about to put a book on trial, motivated mainly by a sense of anger.

I suddenly remembered how one day an American tourist had said to me 'I hear that you are in justice', as one would say 'in banking' or 'in insurance'. Yes, indeed, I thought, I was in justice, or at least I had always attempted to do justice, although, like all judges, I must have failed sometimes. Was I wrong or naive to abandon this courtroom looking for another kind of truth, seeking another kind of justice? Contrary to what others thought, it was not a difficult decision. Actually, there was no conscious decision at all, but a chain of events that inevitably led to the moment that was now upon me.

When friends inquired when this obsession had first taken hold of me, my standard reply was that it had all started 26 years ago in the delegates' dining room of the United Nations headquarters in New York.

THE UNITED NATIONS – 1965

Golda Meir, who served at that time as minister of foreign affairs, had invited me to join Israel's delegation to the United Nations for the twentieth session of the General Assembly, and to participate in the deliberations in the Third Committee, where matters of human rights were high on the agenda. That year we were discussing the final draft of the Convention on the Elimination of All Forms of Racial Discrimination, and apart from long committee sessions I was busy working on documents, preparing speeches and participating in delegation meetings. But business meals with other delegates were part of the agenda, not to be avoided. This is where contacts were established, information exchanged, deals made.

Lunch in the elegant delegates' dining room was a pleasant affair, and rules of etiquette were strictly observed. My guest that day was a diplomat from a friendly Latin American country, a perfect gentleman, his manners impeccable, though not stuffy, even when he symbolically kissed my hand, led me with a light but firm touch on my elbow to our assigned table, and succeeded in preceding the attendant by a split second in drawing out my chair. Where I came from manners like these existed only in the movies, but I liked it. What would have been utterly ridiculous in Tel Aviv seemed entirely proper in this isolated capsule where nothing looked like what it was, nothing was meant the way it sounded, meaningless speeches were made for the record, and matters of importance were discussed and concluded over a drink in the delegates' lounge, in corridors, and even in ladies' or men's rooms.

The twentieth session of the General Assembly was in full swing. During the previous six weeks the atmosphere of that particular Assembly had been established, the central issues defined, the ministers of foreign affairs had delivered their addresses and gone home, alliances had been formed and conflicts exposed. Inexperienced new delegates like myself had memorized the rules of procedure and, more importantly, the peculiar terminology and the unwritten code of behavior, polished to a fine art, that was imposed by former generations of diplomats on all those who were lucky enough to pass through the portals of this august institution, armed with a delegate's card and the various privileges that came with it.

Representing Israel, I had the additional burden of memorizing all the faces belonging to members of hostile delegations, to avoid the unpleasant experience of nodding to a delegate who looked through me as if I was air. This was particularly embarrassing in an elevator, where all present could not help noticing it. Members of Arab and Muslim countries were still at that time under strict instructions not to show recognition of Israelis whether by nod, smile or any gesture that could be interpreted as friendly, and not to mention the name 'Israel' when referring to one of our delegates. Nevertheless, they did refer to us constantly in their daily attacks in every committee room. Sometimes I was called 'the representative of occupied Palestine', or 'the delegate of the Zionist entity', and one day, when I appeared in a yellow suit, 'the lady in yellow'. The Hungarian delegate whispered to me, 'Did he mean the Yellow Star?' On one occasion I was called 'the delegate of the Elders of Zion'.

Although no other delegation suffered from similar breaches of UN etiquette, no chairmen of any committee bothered to remark on it. This behavior was part of the daily routine in the General Assembly. The popular joke circulating in the corridors described a daily morning meeting of Arab, Muslim and Eastern European delegates, in which at least one delegate was assigned in each committee to attack Israel, no matter what item was on the agenda. 'Free speech' in the General Assembly of the United Nations is carried to its most extreme limits, with no call for relevance and no right of interference.

My guest was an experienced diplomat, a member of the permanent delegation of his country. We actually had some legitimate business to discuss, part of the typical give and take between delegations – 'I shall vote with you on this item if your representative supports us on that one in another committee' – but the customary time for business talk was after dessert. He took a long time complementing me on my looks, my dress, my last speech, before turning to the more important subject of choosing the food and the wine. We were conversing pleasantly about our families, our work back home, our impressions of the Assembly, when he suddenly and very tactfully asked: 'Why did you omit any mention of the *Protocols of the Elders of Zion* in your reply to the Russian delegate, who was particularly nasty today? Wouldn't this have been a good opportunity to make some clear statement on this subject? I am surprised that the Russians, of all people, dare even mention this forgery.'

Most delegations never had the need to exercise their 'right of reply', but if you represented Israel you were compelled to do so daily. I made it a rule to limit my replies to matters concerning Israel and to ignore anti-Semitic utterances, although in the beginning those were the hardest to take. They ranged from accusations that the Jews were 'the money-lenders' of the capitalist world, 'manipulators of the press', the 'inventors of apartheid', 'publishers of pornography', to mention of the famous blood libels that accused Jews of murdering children to bake matzos for Passover, and the false quotes from the Talmud that supposedly 'ordered Jews to drink the blood of non-Jews'. The so-called 'Jewish Conspiracy' was often mentioned as if it were an indisputable fact.

I told my companion that it would be demeaning to honor such racist nonsense with a reply, because nobody in their right mind took it seriously. To my surprise, he disagreed. In his experience, he said, the most vile and false accusations, if constantly repeated and not challenged, filtered into the minds of people and formed their opinions.

'You Jews', he said, 'should have learned that lesson. You ignored Hitler's *Mein Kampf* at your peril. You, of all people, should never ignore anti-Semitic libels and, most of all, do not ignore the theory of the "Jewish Conspiracy" and the *Protocols of the Elders of Zion* – this book is dangerous.'

He informed me that the *Protocols*, as everybody referred to them, were being published in his country, that he himself had read them, and that many people believed they were true. I was ashamed to admit that I had never taken the trouble to read the *Protocols*, but promised myself then and there to do so.

When the General Assembly session ended, I returned to the court in Tel Aviv to resume my duties as a judge. It took more than 20 years, and many more encounters with the *Protocols*, for me to finally live up to that promise.

PARIS – 1972

On a rainy Sunday in March 1973 I was dining with a French lawyer in a Paris restaurant, discussing a new law that had been passed in France the previous summer. Since I had participated at the UN in the discussions on the final draft of the Convention Against All Forms of Racial Discrimination, I followed closely the process of its implementation, which called on member states to legislate anti-racist laws. In July 1972 the French Parliament had passed a law prohibiting incitement against a group of people on the grounds of their origin, or of their belonging to a particular ethnic group, race or religion.

We were discussing my confrontation with the Soviet delegation at the General Assembly, which had forcefully opposed the inclusion of anti-Semitism in the definition of the term 'racial discrimination'. In the mid-1960s the Soviet Union had already assumed an extreme anti-Zionist policy, not only suffering, but actually licensing and encouraging unrestrained anti-Semitism. Zionism and Judaism were interchangeable, in Soviet terms, and Jews were presented as the incarnation of all that was evil. The Soviet press had become the principal source of crude anti-Semitic propaganda.

The Soviets had strongly supported the adoption of the anti-racist convention at the UN, I told my friend, but the inclusion of anti-Semitism would immediately have labeled them as racists. With the growing part played by the Third World countries in the international arena, every member state in the

UN was most vocal in condemning racism. The Russians could live with being called anti-Semites, but to be marked as racists would have been intolerable.

They might have achieved a tactical victory, my friend said, but they could not prevent courts of law outside Russia from condemning anti-Semitism as a racial practice. Actually, he told me, a French court would have an opportunity to do so in a trial that was about to be held in Paris the very next day, the first trial under the new law. This might be the French equivalent of the famous Berne trial, he said, wrongly assuming that I was familiar with it.

This was when I first learned that in 1934 a Swiss court had ruled, in a trial initiated by the Jewish community against a local Nazi group, that the *Protocols of the Elders of Zion* were a crude forgery.

Coming back to the French trial, my friend told me that the accused, M. Legagneux, was the director of a bulletin entitled *Etudes Sovietique d'information* published by the Soviet Information Bureau in Paris, and was being sued by the International League Against Racism and Anti-Semitism, known as the LICRA, for having published an article on 22 September 1972 that accused Israel and Jews of the worst kind of racist and inhuman practices, misquoting and misinterpreting ancient Jewish writings. The article described how Jewish children were taught 'from the cradle' hatred of other peoples, and commanded to massacre non-Jews (Goys), under divine law. The Jewish conspiracy to dominate the world was being systematically implemented, according to the writer.

This theory was part and parcel of modern Russian anti-Semitism. The Ukrainian writer T. K. Kitchko had repeatedly warned that the Jews were creating a 'World Jewish power', and that soon the whole world would become a 'Kingdom of the Jewish Priests'. They were the hidden force that would soon dominate the universe. Kitchko was rewarded and given state honors for his achievement in 'public education'. Another book by Iurii Ivanov, the adviser on Jewish affairs at the Central Committee of the CPSU, entitled *Beware: Zionism*, had become known as the 'Soviet Protocols of Zion'. Ivanov's message was that the Jews were the worst racists, that they had collaborated with Hitler, and that their bankers had sentenced millions of poor Jews to be exterminated in the Holocaust in their pursuit of riches and power.

Parts of these anti-Semitic books, my friend said, read as if they had been copied from the *Protocols of the Elders of Zion*, a book often quoted by Russian people in authority. The so-called 'Jewish Conspiracy' was a wonderful common denominator, which offered easy explanations for otherwise embarrassing facts and situations in any given country. Now a court of law would decide whether they could spread this poison in France, he said with undisguised satisfaction. The Berne trial would surely be mentioned, he guessed. The *Protocols of the Elders of Zion* were not a direct issue in the case, but they were definitely part of it.

When I learned that Professor René Cassin would make a statement at the trial, I immediately canceled my plans for the next day. René Cassin, a famous legal philosopher, was acting at the time as a judge in the European Court of Human Rights, but he was best known as one of the drafters of the Universal Declaration of Human Rights and a winner of the Nobel Prize for Peace.

I always welcome an opportunity to visit the Palais de Justice. Used as I am to a bare and functional courtroom, I am awed by the palatial atmosphere created by the old tapestries on the walls and the heavy chandeliers hanging from the ceilings. Even the robes of the three judges seemed more elegant than ours, I thought, as they were ushered in by a liveried court attendant. The Berne trial and the *Protocols of the Elders of Zion* were soon placed on the agenda, as one witness after another described how the author of the Russian article had actually reproduced passages from the *Protocols*.

The impressive list of witnesses had drawn a large crowd and the court-room was packed. First Professor René Cassin. Then came Gaston Monnerville, former president of the French Senate, followed by well-known rabbis and historians, Catholic leaders and theologians. But the real surprise of the trial was delivered by a witness named Grigory Svirsky, a Soviet author, decorated nine times during the Second World War. He had been compelled to leave Russia because of state anti-Semitism. To the astonishment of the whole courtroom he produced and presented to the court a booklet that had been originally published in Tsarist Russia in 1906 by the Black Hundreds, a Russian anti-Semitic organization that had orchestrated pogroms against Jews. The court interpreter explained to the judges that the brochure displayed on its back page the address of the Novosty bookshop in St Petersburg where it could be purchased. The article at issue, the witness said, reading excerpts from the booklet, carried whole segments of a 1906 Russian publication of the *Protocols of the Elders of Zion*.

One after another the witnesses explained to the court not only that the text of the article was false, as were the original *Protocols of the Elders of Zion*, but that it fell within the definition of a racist publication, now prohibited by the new law.

The closing address of Robert Badinter, who represented the LICRA, was French *pledoirie* at its best. How was it possible, he asked, turning to the Russian defendant, that modern Soviet Russia was using in 1972 a text pub-lished in 1906 by the Okhrana, the Tsarist Russian secret police. 'We trace a curious path that began with the *Protocols of the Elders of Zion* and led to a French-language bulletin,' he said. 'It is sad that it should be from Russia that these things have come to us … Men have looked to Russia as a great country that overthrew tyrannical power, chose the path to socialism and set out on the march towards an ideal of a just and brotherly society. Decades passed and this same great country still claims to aspire to this ideal, nourishes this hope. Yet suddenly it rummages in dark places for the horrors it has condemned and dis-inters the most degrading of texts to be employed for its own purpose.'

When the judgment was delivered on 24 April 1973 I was back in my courtroom, and I learned of it much later when my friend sent me a book by

Emanuel Litvinoff entitled *The Paris Trial*, published in London in 1974. Litvinoff was an expert on Russian Jewry, who had testified at the trial. It included a brilliant introduction and the full verbatim record of the trial.

Quoting the various witnesses the court had stated that the article in issue contained passages from the *Protocols of the Elders of Zion*, 'an anti-Semitic publication compiled by the Russian Tsarist police, Okhrana, towards the end of the nineteenth century'. The defendant was found guilty of the offence of public defamation and sentenced to pay a fine of 1,500 francs to the state, and 1 franc to the LICRA (who had not asked for more). The court also ordered that the full verdict be published in the next issue of the Russian bulletin, and that excerpts of the judgment be published in six French newspapers or periodicals, selected by the plaintiff.

A short foreword on the first page of the book my friend had sent me was signed by the famous Russian ballet dancer Valery Panov, who had defected to the West. 'It is unbelievable', he wrote, 'that outworn prejudices should still be used to degrade human beings on the ground of race, religion or nationality ... one reads in these pages a confrontation between the sanity of civilization and old, malignant myths that have cost innocent human lives.' Panov concluded his short foreword with a message of hope. 'In Paris', he wrote, 'truth was vindicated and the lies that have haunted European history were exposed to the light of reason.'

I wondered if Maître Robert Badinter had ever discussed the Paris trial with the presiding judge, Simone Rozes, when they met in later years. Simone Rozes ended her judicial career 15 years later as president of the *Cour de Cassation*, the highest tribunal of France. By that time Robert Badinter was president of the constitutional tribunal of France, having become famous, before that, as the minister of justice who was responsible for the abolishment of the death penalty in his country.

THE UNITED STATES – 1985

I was having breakfast with Pacita in a downtown New York hotel when she suddenly exclaimed: 'This is your day, Hadassa, today we are going to the banks, we shall be discussing money!'

We were both part of a group of jurists from various countries, invited by the Unites States Information Agency (USIA) to witness American justice at work. For 30 days we were escorted from coast to coast and, as could be expected, some close friendships were formed. Spending long hours together, in the mini-bus that took us everywhere, in planes and at meals, I found myself more and more often sitting next to Pacita, a judge from the Philippines who served in a high-level Manila court. We soon started reserving seats for each other whenever possible. What we probably enjoyed most of all was a healthy sense of humor, which allowed us to share many laughs and got us through some pretty tedious sessions.

We soon started telling each other about our private lives, which couldn't have been more different if we had dwelt on different planets. What fascinated both of us was that we had almost nothing in common except our profession. We were both quite high-ranking women judges in courts of similar jurisdiction that operated under very similar systems of law, both rooted in the British tradition. Apart from that, we were strangers coming from different cultures, different religions and drastically different customs and ways of life.

Pacita was a Catholic, born and raised in the Philippines and married to a Chinese businessman. She lived in a compound surrounded by servants who waited on her hand and foot, and had a hard time doing without their services on this trip. I made her laugh, joking about her 'difficulties', and as I related to her my own circumstances in which personal servants were absolutely missing, her troubles assumed different proportions and she decided she could cope after all. We really had some very good times together.

On one occasion she confided to me that she had never met a Jew in person. 'But you don't look Jewish,' she said. She actually thought that all Jews had crooked noses, although she did not relate this astounding fact in a derogatory manner. She mentioned Barbra Streisand: 'Isn't she Jewish? She surely does have a crooked nose!'

On this particular morning she was beaming, proud of her ability to demonstrate familiarity with what she thought were Jewish characteristics. We were scheduled to meet directors of several banks to discuss ways of detecting the laundering of drug money through the banks. She was sure they would all be Jewish. Asked where she had acquired that particular notion, she answered with a serious expression: 'Haven't you heard about some book that was discovered and revealed how the Jews are in control everywhere, including all the financial institutions? Isn't this a part of some overall Jewish plan?'

When I named the *Protocols of the Elders of Zion* her eyes lit up in recognition, 'Yes, that's the book!' She was very surprised and a little disappointed that, of the five senior bank officials we met that day, not one was Jewish.

That evening, Pacita asked me about the *Protocols of the Elders of Zion*, and I was embarrassed to be so poorly informed. 'Then, how do you know the book is false?' she asked. As a judge, I knew I didn't have a valid or satisfactory answer, since I had never really studied the subject. Once again I decided to do so.

TEL AVIV – 1988

We had had a rainy week and Tel Aviv looked its best, washed and sparkling in the morning sun on a beautiful February day. I had just returned from my morning swim in the sea and was looking forward to an hour of relaxation, the best part of my hectic day. I settled down with a steaming mug of coffee to read the newspaper in silence. There would be noise soon enough when I left the privacy of my apartment to join the bustling morning traffic. A headline caught my attention: 'New edition of the "Protocols of the Elders of Zion" published'. This prompted a chain of associations diverting my mind from the article. More than twenty years had passed since the lunch at the United Nations, fifteen years since the Paris trial, three years since my encounter with Pacita. The *Protocols* had been quoted in my presence on various occasions, but I still had not laid eyes on the document. It was time I did so.

Two days later I spent the best part of the night reading an English edition of the *Protocols*, having learned at the university library, much to my surprise, that the book had never been translated into Hebrew, although it had appeared in almost every other language. Published by Small, Maynard & Company in Boston, the book was entitled *The Protocols and the World Revolution*. The fly-leaf announced that it included a translation and an analysis of the 'Protocols of the Meetings of the Zionist Men of Wisdom'.

They purport to be authentic protocols of meetings of a Jewish secret government, the 'Elders of Zion', but to my surprise I soon realized that these could not be actual minutes of meetings, but rather 24 lectures by a single person, addressing an unspecified audience. If they were actual minutes of meetings, as they were always represented, one would expect to find a date, a record of attendance, some kind of discussion, a resolution, but all these were absent. It appeared that this was an unnamed person, allegedly reading a carefully prepared text, to an anonymous audience, at an unknown location, on 24 undisclosed dates.

Later I learned that although the title of the whole document appeared to be part of it and was sometimes printed with inverted commas, it differed from one edition to another. Sometimes it was the 'Protocols of the Elders of Zion', sometimes the 'Protocols of the Meetings of the Learned Elders of Zion', sometimes the 'Protocols of the Meetings of the Zionist Men of Wisdom', and other numerous titles that could not possibly be an accurate translation of the title of an existing text.

In these lectures the unnamed speaker set forth in concise form a comprehensive program for the annihilation of all Christian states, proposing practical methods for achieving world domination by the Jews. International Jewry was described as a satanic sect, united in purpose, acting under the leadership of a group of elders, who lacked any moral consideration. Each protocol dealt with a more or less distinct part of one complete subject, and as a whole the 24 protocols described with great elaboration the means by which universal domination of the world was to be achieved. All governments were to be subjugated to the Jewish super-government, which would be an autocracy with a Jewish sovereign at its head.

In this edition the publisher had summarized the means by which this world domination was to be achieved:

1. The national power of non-Jewish states was to be broken down by the fomenting of internal revolutions through appeals to class hatred, and by pretended efforts to obtain greater freedom and privileges for certain classes of the people, using the words 'liberty, equality and fraternity' merely as catchwords to gain recruits for the Jewish cause. Autocratic governments, which alone are strong, must be weakened in the first instance by the introduction of liberalism, which would pave the way to anarchy.
2. All wars must be shifted to an economic basis, allowing no territorial advantages to result from war, and thus tending to make the Jewish control of wealth the determining factor in war.
3. Jewish international rights were to be strengthened at the expense of the national rights of the several Gentile nations.
4. The non-Jewish states were to be further weakened by promoting false and conflicting political policies, by obtaining secret control over the actions of public officials, by manipulation of the press, and by the gradual elimination of free speech.
5. The authority of governments where liberalism prevailed was to be weakened by the destruction of religion (other than the Jewish religion), since it was the conservative and moral force that made liberal governments possible.
6. In order to overcome the resistance of those states that were unwilling to make submission to the new Jewish power, there must be no hesitation in resorting to violence, cunning, hypocrisy, bribery, fraud, and treason, or to the seizure of the property of others.
7. The destruction of the social and economic structure of Christian states would also be brought about by the destruction of industrial prosperity, through speculation and constant strikes, throwing masses of workmen out of employment, artificially raising wages, thus increasing the cost of the necessities of life, and finally by bringing about a general economic crisis and the disorganization of financial systems. The financial strength of the various non-Jewish states would also be undermined by causing them to overburden themselves with foreign and national loans on an ever-increasing scale, which would ultimately lead to bankruptcy.
8. Upon the social and political chaos created by these various means a Jewish dictatorship was to be gradually built up, principally through the 'terrible' Jewish power of the purse and through the other great Jewish powers of control over the press and over the revolutionary movement.
9. During the period of transition from Gentile to Jewish political control in every state there would be secret government by the Jews, brought about through the manipulation of the press, the misleading of public opinion, mass terror, weakening the initiative of the Gentiles, misdirecting their education, and sowing discord among them.

As I read on, phrases and paragraphs leapt to the eye, totally devoid of reason, absolutely opposed to any Jewish tradition and teaching.

The best results in governing are achieved through violence and intimidation and not through academic discussion. Politics have nothing in common with morals. The ruler guided by morality is not firm on his throne. He who desires to rule must resort to cunning and hypocrisy ... according to the laws of nature, Right lies in Might ... violence must be the principle ... we must not hesitate at bribery, fraud and treason ... seizing the property of others ... our government must substitute for the horror of war less noticeable and more efficient executions ... he who desires to rule must resort to cunning and hypocrisy ... we plan to destroy all existing order and institutions, to lay hands on the law ... and to become the ruler of those who have voluntarily, liberally, renounced for our benefit the rights of their own power ...

I read on in total disbelief:

The power of the masses is blind, unreasoning, and void of discrimination, prone to listen to right and left ... Government must be concentrated in the hands of one responsible person ... God has given us, his chosen people, the power to scatter, and what to all appears to be our weakness, has proved to be our strength, and has now brought us to the threshold of universal rule ... 'The most important problem of our government', the speaker says in the fifth Protocol, 'is to weaken the popular mind by criticism; to disaccount it to thought, which creates opposition; to deflect the power of thought into mere empty eloquence ... to control public opinion it is necessary to perplex it by the expression of numerous contradictory opinions until the goys [an expression used for non-Jews] get lost in the labyrinth, and come to understand that it is best to have no opinion on political questions. This is presented as the first 'secret' of the ruler, the second 'secret' being multiplying popular failings, habits, passions, and conventional laws that no one will be able to disentangle himself in the chaos, and consequently, people will cease to understand each other.

Did anybody with a sane mind seriously print, and expect readers to believe, such silly statements, I wondered, realizing that indeed they did.

Protocol no. 6 heralded the establishment of great monopolies, reservoirs of huge wealth, upon which even the large fortunes of the Goys would depend to such an extent that they would be drowned, together with the governmental credits, on the day following the political catastrophe ... The Goys as landowners were harmful because they could be independent in their resources of life. For this reason, the speaker said in the sixth Protocol, 'We must deprive them of their land at any cost.' This was easily done, he explained – all one has to do is increase land taxes. 'At the same time,' he continued, 'it is necessary to patronize trade and industry vigorously, and

more important, to encourage speculation, whose function is to act as a coun-
terbalance to industry.' An alternative way suggested by the speaker to destroy
industry was 'to create among the Goys ... the strong demand for boundless
luxury'.

Wages would be raised, which, however, would be of no benefit to the
workers, 'for we shall simultaneously cause the rise in prices of objects of first
necessity, under the pretext that this is due to the decadence of agriculture,
and of the cattle industry'.

The Jewish plans should be secret, but in the event that they were discovered prematurely 'we have such a terrorizing maneuver in the West that even
the bravest soul will shudder. Underground passages will be established by that
time in all capitals, from where they can be exploded, together with all their
institutions and national documents.'

The detailed plan of action concerned the reorganization of politics, the
press, religion, the economy, taxation, the currency, the stock exchange, education, the law, the courts and the legal profession, the administration, ownership of property, the army and police, and succession to the 'throne'.

Fascinated and repelled, I could not stop reading.

> We will show our power in Europe by assassination and terrorism, and
> should there be a possibility of all of them rising against us, we will answer
> them with American, Chinese, or Japanese gun ... we will be surrounded
> by a crowd of bankers, by millionaires, because in essence everything will
> be decided by a question of figures ... when the King of Israel places the
> crown offered to him by Europe on his sacred head, he will become the
> Patriarch of the World ... the real Pope of the Universe ...

Suddenly reminded of anti-Semitic cartoons describing a huge snake
encircling the universe, I read the opening of the third Protocol: 'Today', the
speaker announced to his audience, 'I can tell you that our goal is close at
hand. Only a small distance remains, and the cycle of the Symbolic Serpent –
the symbol of our people – will be complete. When this circle is completed,
then all the European states will be enclosed in it as in strong claws.'

Protocol no. 10 described how the public would be brainwashed:

> It is important to know one detail in our policy. It will help us in dis-
> cussing division of authority, freedom of speech, of the press, of religion
> (faith), the right of assembly, equality before the law, inviolability of
> property and of the home, indirect taxes and the retrospective force of
> the law. All such questions should never be directly and openly dis-
> cussed before the masses. When it becomes necessary for us to discuss
> them, they should not be elaborated but merely mentioned, without
> going into details, pointing out that modern legal principles are being
> accepted by us ... we will not allow the formation of individual minds,

because the mob, under our guidance, will prevent them from distinguishing themselves or even expressing themselves. The mob has become accustomed to listen only to us who pay it for obedience and attention. We will thus create such blind power that it will be unable to move without the guidance of our agents, sent by us to replace their leaders ... To accomplish our plan, we will engineer the election of presidents whose past record contains some hidden scandal, some 'Panama' – then they will be faithful executors of our orders from fear of exposure, and from the natural desire of every man who has reached authority to retain the privileges, advantages, and dignity connected with the position of president ... The Chamber of Deputies will elect, protect and screen presidents, but we will deprive it of the right of initiating laws or of amending them, for this right will be granted by us to the responsible president, a puppet in our hands.

The eleventh Protocol described the exact process of legislation, and the twelfth opened with a redefinition of the term 'liberty'. From now on it will mean 'the right to do that which is permitted by law'. The speaker explained that in this manner 'liberty will be in our power'. He elaborated his plans for the press: 'We will shackle it and keep a tight rein on it. We will also do the same with other printed matter, for what use would it be for us to rid ourselves of attacks on the parts of the periodical press if we remain open to criticism through pamphlets and books?'

The Goys will see all world events through colored glasses because 'not one notice will be made public without our control', received through centralized agencies. 'Thought', the speaker promised, 'will become an educational instrument in the hands of our government, which will not allow the people to be led astray into the realms of fancy and dreams about beneficient progress.'

He described in detail how the press would be suppressed, by allowing only licensed and diploma-holding journalists, editors and printers to work, by placing stamp-taxes secured by bonds on each page of all printed material, and by forcing writers to publish only very long books, under penalty of double taxation, so that the bored readers would ignore them.

Most periodicals would be government owned, but they would include some contradictory views so as not to arouse suspicion, 'thus attracting to us unsuspecting enemies, and in this way they will be caught in our trap and made harmless'.

Religion would also be regulated. 'When we become rulers we will not tolerate the existence of any other religion except our own,' he promised in the fourteenth Protocol.

'Death is the unavoidable end of all,' he stated philosophically in the fifteenth Protocol, but 'it would be better to accelerate this end for those who interfere with our cause', adding that the wise men of old had ordained in their wisdom 'that to attain a serious object one must not stop at the means'.

Lawyers were dealt with in the seventeenth Protocol. After describing them in most derogatory terms the speaker revealed that their profession would be limited and converted into an executive public office. They would be deprived of the right to contact their clients, and cases would be assigned to them by the court. This would shorten legal proceedings, he said. The clergy would be dealt with in a similar manner.

After dealing with the reorganization of the police, the *Protocols* dealt with financial and economic matters.

In every Protocol the Goys were described as inhuman beasts, mere sense-less animals, which could easily be duped and ruled by the Jewish sovereign. Thus the whole economy, banks, stock exchange and other financial and credit institutions would easily be manipulated so that all financial and indus-trial enterprises would become dependent upon the new rulers.

The last Protocol dealt with the succession to the throne, to ensure that the future rulers would always come 'from the sacred seed of David'.

The book ended with a description of the king of Israel, whose 'mental capacity must be equal to the plan of rule herein contained'. People should know and love their sovereign, therefore he must not be influenced by his passions, especially by sensuality, which 'more than anything else, upsets mental ability and clearness of vision by deflecting thought to the worst and most bestial side of human nature'.

'Our sovereign must be irreproachable,' stated the closing sentence of the book.

I read it twice, unwilling to believe that these fanatical and insane allega-tions were ascribed to Jews, but I realized how uninformed readers might be impressed with its cleverness, its cold logic, its orderly arguments, its learned language. This was not something said about the Jews, this was allegedly said by the Jews. It also explained all the catastrophes happening in the world, providing the people and their leaders with a ready scapegoat.

Much later I learned that every edition of these *Protocols* was preceded by an introduction describing how the document had been 'discovered'. These stories, mentioning different sources, vouched for the authenticity of 'the Jewish plan', which was actually being implemented. Thus, wars, revolutions, economic crises, even the AIDS epidemic, can be explained as the realization of the Jewish Conspiracy.

As I read, my anger mounted. I felt personally assaulted by this lie, as if it were a libel directed at me. If there indeed existed a Jewish conspiracy, then I was allegedly part of it, I thought. A feeling of bitterness enveloped me. I sud-denly thought of my gentle grandfather, an Orthodox Jew in a little *shtetl* in Poland, and how he had taught me humility and respect for my fellow men. The demonic figure on some of the covers, complete with horns, claws and crooked nose, was the grossly distorted face of this good man, who perished in the Holocaust. He was depicted as a dangerous monster, robbed even of his right to be remembered as a victim.

Who would believe that the Jews were conspiring to take over the world? All we really wanted, I thought, was to be accepted as equals. We always tried to blend into any society in which we lived, to be admitted to their schools, to join their clubs, to be invited to their homes. We always tried to prove ourselves worthy by doing well, by acquiring an education, by contributing in the economic, social and cultural spheres. We tried to excel, but was it to take over, to rule over others?

I am not superstitious, and stories of supernatural events leave me cold. A coincidence is just that in my eyes and I do not look for other explanations. Yet at this point a very peculiar chain of events took place, as if an invisible hand were guiding me in one direction. I had the uncomfortable feeling that things were happening to me in a way that propelled me to probe into the history of the *Protocols of the Elders of Zion*.

BERNE – 1988

In April 1988 I was about to turn down an invitation to deliver a lecture in Berne, Switzerland, when I suddenly remembered the Berne trial, which had been mentioned in the Paris court. On a sudden urge, I decided to accept the invitation, as if it were an omen. It was at that event, which took place in a Berne hotel, that I was first introduced to Odette, whose late husband, Georges Brunschvig, had participated in the famous Berne trial concerning the *Protocols*.

Odette looked younger than her 70 years. Very thin, elegant, soft-spoken, with a twinkle in her eye and a firmly set mouth. I was surprised at the tears that welled up in her eyes at my mention of the Berne trial. Only much later did I realize that this event had been a focal point not only in her husband's career but also in his personal life, and in hers. Fifty-four years had passed since Georges Brunschvig confronted both German and Swiss Nazis in a Berne court. Fifteen years had passed since the Yom Kippur War, when he had suffered a fatal heart attack in the middle of an excited appeal to a Jewish audience in Zurich to assist Israel in its struggle for survival. Between these two events, Georges Brunschvig had pursued a brilliant career both as a lawyer and as an outstanding public figure.

We met in Odette's house, which had a special charm. She had lived in it since her wedding more than fifty years earlier, and it looked as if nothing in it had been changed since then. The only thing that looked out of place was a large television set. Fresh flowers were everywhere, and although everything was in its proper place, the atmosphere was warm, and I immediately had a sense of belonging, though I had never lived in a house like this.

As we talked about Georges and about the Berne trial, Odette climbed on a ladder and removed from a top shelf a small book in German, saying, as she handed it to me, 'This is the story in a nutshell.' Later that night I read all 72 pages of the booklet written by Emil Raas and Georges Brunschvig, entitled

Vernichtung Einer Foelschung (The Destruction of a Forgery) and published in Zurich in 1938. This was my first introduction to the story of the Berne trial and to the history of the *Protocols of the Elders of Zion*.

The next day we went to see Emil Raas, Georges Brunschvig's surviving partner. He lived in a charming house surrounded by a garden, its interior very similar to that of Odette's apartment. An old man in a wheelchair, partly paralyzed but completely lucid, greeted me. He was a big man with a still firm voice and a mastery of language fit for a courtroom. Odette told me that in his day he had been a great lawyer.

As soon as I mentioned the trial, he dropped his head and his eyes veiled. His plump hands rested heavily on the plaid coverlet concealing his semi-paralyzed legs. We waited in silence respecting his need for privacy as he gathered his thoughts. Slowly, hesitantly at first, pacing his words, each syllable taking on a life of its own, his deep voice carried us back to the Berne of 1933, to Nazi demonstrations, to a Jewish community faced with an impossible challenge, to consultations in smoke-filled rooms and to the charged atmosphere of a courtroom where the saga of the *Protocols of the Elders of Zion* had unfolded in all its historical dimensions.

Later, I climbed with Denise, Emil's wife, into their attic, where, following his instructions, we found the 800-page, hand-written manuscript of his full account of the trial. The manuscript had been completed on the eve of the Second World War but was never published.

'In those days,' Emil said dryly, 'there were more urgent matters on our agenda.' Jewish communities, he explained, could not spend money on the publication of books. Every penny was needed to help refugees fleeing from Nazi Germany. That is why they published only a small booklet, he explained, and the full manuscript was hidden away in the attic, completely forgotten.

I was to meet Emil again in a hospital room one year later, when we had, by special permission of his doctors, what turned out to be our final talk. With his family around him, Emil tried to recall every small detail about the trial, all of us acutely aware of the fact that for him time was running out.

Suddenly he said with a chuckle, 'I still remember the dramatic moment when Georges Brunschvig drew from his pocket a small volume, placed it on the judge's desk, and announced: This is the book from which the *Protocols of the Elders of Zion* was plagiarized.'

A few weeks later Emil Raas passed away, the last survivor of the historic Berne trial.

STOCKHOLM – 1989

I had a distinct feeling that I was being followed. It was Yom Kippur, the Jewish

Day of Atonement, and I was walking in the park with a journalist whom I had met the day before. It was he who noticed that the same car confronted us every time we approached one of the roads that criss-crossed the park. Four young men with crew-cuts were staring at me in an arrogant, almost challenging manner, which sent a chill up my spine. For me, one of the charms of visiting a foreign city is the complete anonymity that creates a feeling of delicious freedom. Somehow the repeated encounters with the men in the car made me uncomfortable. Suddenly I knew that I would not feel free again in this city. The next morning I learned how right I was.

I had come to Stockholm for a series of lectures and a meeting with members of parliament. As it happened, the trial of Radio Islam and its director, Ahmed Raami, was about to open, and I was introduced to the prosecutor, who had attended one of my lectures. As I expressed an interest in the approaching trial, he invited me to his office to explain the proceedings, and to the court, to attend the first session of the trial. This was no more than a routine courtesy extended to a visiting judge. Only later did I learn that one day after my visit to the Department of Justice, the court was petitioned by the defendant to discredit the public prosecutor 'as he is being instructed by an emissary of the Zionist government'.

Radio Islam was a licensed private radio station, directed by Ahmed Raami, who also served as anchorman. It was on the air all day and some nights, broadcasting almost exclusively anti-Zionist and anti-Jewish, Goebbels-type, propaganda. Whole passages from original Nazi pre-war propaganda were quoted daily. Shortly before my visit they had started broadcasting lists of Jewish businesses, mentioning names and addresses. Jewish families and firms felt threatened. Passages from the *Protocols of the Elders of Zion* figured prominently on each program.

When I arrived at the court with a volunteer interpreter, a few young men looked ominously familiar. They were handing out copies of the *Protocols* in front of the courthouse, and smiled viciously at me. Again I shivered. We waited in the small coffee shop, conversing with the witnesses for the prosecution. Among them was a Swedish bishop who had arrived from Boston, where he was teaching theology at Harvard, and Peer Ahlmark, a former deputy prime minister of Sweden, a non-Jew who maintained that anti-Semitism was a sickness of the Gentiles, and that therefore he was making it his business to fight it. To my surprise the prosecutor passed us without any sign of recognition. I learned later that he was on his way to the judge's chambers to discuss the motion for his dismissal for collaborating with the Israeli emissary. He explained that he could not be seen even to nod in my direction.

Suddenly I was approached by a medium-height, dark-haired man with an outstretched hand, who said he wanted to make my acquaintance. I did not understand the horror on the faces of my friends until the man coolly explained that he was the defendant, Ahmed Raami, and that he wished to have a picture taken with the envoy from Israel who had come to subvert

Swedish justice. A camera flashed in my face and he vanished. The photograph would probably be used in his propaganda, in some perverted context, my friends explained.

The motion for dismissal was denied shortly after the incident, and the trial began. The defendants had officially petitioned the Ministry of Justice to ban the Old Testament in Sweden as a racist book. The bishop was there to defend the Bible, and his testimony took all day. He was suffering from whiplash from a minor accident and sat very straight, his neck held tight by an orthopedic collar, his voice even and clear.

I sat in this sterile, elegant courtroom, facing the three judges and five jurors, holding in my lap a copy of the *Protocols of the Elders of Zion* in Swedish, which had been handed to me at the entrance. As the interpreter whispered in my ear, I found myself contemplating what would happen if this court decided that the Bible, the Old Testament itself, was indeed a racist book to be banned under Swedish law. The radio station preached that the plan elaborated in the *Protocols*, the Jewish conspiracy to take over the world, could be traced to the Bible and the Talmud. So, perversely, not only the *Protocols* but also the Bible was on trial in the Swedish courtroom, and so were the Jews.

Fortunately, the court convicted Ahmed Raami and closed down the radio station. The Bible was saved. When I visited Stockholm again in 1994, I learned that new editions of the *Protocols* were being distributed in Sweden.

JOHANNESBURG – 1990

I was drained and longing for the privacy of my room, impatient at the long wait for the elevator. Conventions often paralyze elevator service, even in big hotels like the Carleton in Johannesburg. This was the bi-annual convention of the Zionist Organization of South Africa, and I was the keynote speaker at the opening session.

I had arrived on a night flight from Zurich, and was still feeling the effects of the long flight. If the elevator didn't arrive soon, I was ready to drop into one of the chairs in the lobby and close my eyes. I was about to plead with the young woman who accosted me exactly as the numbers lighted above the elevator door announcing its approach, but it was too late. She was a journalist from Durban and invited me to join a group gathered at one of the tables in the lobby. She knew how tired I must be, she said, but I need only stay a minute, have a cup of tea and pose for a picture. One could refuse the tea, but not the picture-taking. This was a ritual I could not evade without being rude, so, with resignation, I submitted to my determined escort, who steered me energetically toward a far corner of the lobby. When she stopped to introduce me to a couple at another table, I was ready to protest. Instead, from sheer instinct and habit, I nodded and forced a smile to my face. This is how I met Dr Colin Jankelevich, a lawyer from Port Elizabeth, who would add yet another coincidence to the chain of events that was slowly injecting the *Protocols of the Elders of Zion* into my life.

He had heard I was interested in the *Protocols* and wondered whether I knew of the trial that had taken place in South Africa more than fifty years earlier. I assured him that I did, and was ready to move on, but he persisted: 'Do you need any material about this trial?' I told him that one of the judges had escorted me to the library that morning and had given me access to all available documents. Regretfully, I added, it happened so long ago that the court records were not available any more. 'Do you want them?' he asked innocently. 'I have a copy of the full verbatim court record in my office cabinet. It has rested there more than fifty years, left by one of the former partners.'

The journalist was surprised at the sudden change in my demeanor. Now I was ready not only to drink tea and pose for a dozen pictures, but, were it possible, I would have flown to Port Elizabeth that night. Instead, I flew home the next day to try a big fraud case. Three weeks later a heavy parcel was delivered to my chambers. The paper of the 800-page document was so fragile that some pages were virtually falling apart. A photocopy could not be risked, so Dr Jankelevich had sent the original, hoping I would put it to good use. I felt as if another commitment had been thrust upon my shoulders.

Two months earlier, I had learned that Georges Brunschvig had entrusted his full private archive concerning the *Protocols* and the Berne trial to his close friend Dr Willy Guggenheim, who had kept it intact in his office in Zurich all these years. The whole 8,000 pages of the archive were now on microfilm. With the arrival of the record from South Africa and the microfilm cassettes from Zurich, I felt that without making a conscious decision, I was being designated to 'do something' concerning the *Protocols*.

So, here I was, on 31 October 1991, terminating my judicial career to commence my own private inquiry into the *Protocols of the Elders of Zion*. Who had composed them and why? To what purpose? How had one booklet, called by some 'the greatest hoax of the century', survived for so long, and generated so much hatred? Forgeries had appeared on the public scene throughout history, but when exposed they had vanished into oblivion. Why not this one? What was it about this book that allowed it to emerge, thrive, nearly disappear, only to reappear again, chameleon-like, in new guise, from one generation to another, from one nation to another, from one social or political crisis to another? How had the myth been born? Who were the people who had concocted this brew? What was it that lent this particular document immortality, which made it immune to repeated exposure?

Where did one begin, I wondered.

I had an urge to begin with the Berne trial and follow in the footsteps of Georges Brunschvig, but Boris, the Russian historian whom I had consulted, was most insistent. 'You will never understand the story of the *Protocols*', he said, 'if you do not start in Russia, where they first made their appearance.'

2 The Romanov Dynasty and the *Protocols*

When Boris showed up at my house with an armload of books, I looked in vain for titles concerning the Jews in Russia. Instead they were all about the Romanov Dynasty. The Jews didn't compose the *Protocols of the Elders of Zion*, he said, they were only the victims. They were not the key to the story. If I wanted to learn about the *Protocols*, I should concentrate on the Romanovs.

Boris became my link to everything Russian in my quest to uncover the truth about the *Protocols*. He piled my desk high with history books and memoirs of Russian politicians. He found his way into obscure Russian archives that, fortunately, had been opened to the public for the past few years, but most of all he unraveled for me the intricate relationships and intrigues in the Russian capital of a hundred years ago, and it was he who accompanied me on my trip to Russia, where it had all happened.

I had been trained in the English legal system, and my approach had been to automatically exclude from consideration whatever seemed to be irrelevant material. I had reminded Boris that my purpose was to discover the origins of a book and trace its history, not to write a thesis on Russian history.

Not so, Boris had argued. The *Protocols* had not been composed in outer space. They were the product of a certain society at a given moment in time. It was impossible to understand their origin without considering the political and historical background during the reign of the last Romanov Tsar Nikolai II, and the intrigues and the mystical atmosphere surrounding the royal court. If I really wished to understand Russia in those years, I should concentrate on the Empress Alexandra, he advised.

Writing memoirs had been a favorite pastime in those days, Boris said with an apologetic smile, emptying two suitcases full of books. Fortunately, not only people in authority – politicians and diplomats, officials and policemen – were busy recording their past. It seemed as if every literate person wished to leave his or her mark. Those who did not write memoirs corresponded with each other and preserved their letters for posterity. And they all wrote well.

I soon learned that Boris was right. Empress Alexandra, her lady friends, her mystic advisers and mentors, all figured prominently in these records, not only as subjects of curious gossip but as decisive factors in Russian history, as phenomena influencing the fate of millions, and inevitably, leading to the downfall of the Tsarist regime.

It took great willpower to avoid getting entangled in the web of this fantastic period in history, with the large numbers of men and women who kept crowding my story, and concentrate on those who were linked, directly or indirectly, to the *Protocols of the Elders of Zion*.

On the night of 16–17 July 1918 Tsar Nikolai II, his wife, Tsarina Alexandra Fedorovna, and their children were murdered by the Bolsheviks in Ekaterinburg. When an examining magistrate was preparing the inventory of the house of Ipatiev, where the royal family had been held captive prior to their murder, he noticed in the room of the empress three books: the Bible, *War and Peace*, and the fourth edition of a book by Sergei Nilus, *The Great in the Small*, which contained the full text of the *Protocols of the Elders of Zion*. On 20 March, four months before her execution, Empress Alexandra had confided in a letter to her closest friend, Anna Vyrubova, that she was reading with interest the book by Nilus. On her window, it was said, the Tsarina had drawn the sign of the swastika. To fanatical Russians this was an omen, the true testament of the dead empress.

It was Sergei Nilus who had first published the full text of the *Protocols*, in 1905, as an appendix to the second edition of his book *The Great in the Small*, which had first been published in 1901. Translations of the *Protocols*, in every language, quote Nilus as their source. Actually they had been published before, in various forms, but never in a book. It was therefore Nilus who could rightly boast that he had been instrumental in launching the *Protocols of the Elders of Zion* on their grand world tour.

Since he had first published the *Protocols*, when Russia was in the grip of the first Bolshevik Revolution, Nilus kept warning his fellow Russians that it was all part of the Jewish conspiracy. A religious fanatic, he interpreted all political events in religious terms. Before the establishment of the Kingdom of Truth, through the second advent of Christ, the Antichrist must come hailed by the Jews as Messiah and by the world as sovereign of the globe. According to secret Jewish documents, Nilus asserted, the wise King Solomon, who had resided in the citadel of Zion in Jerusalem together with other Jewish wise men, had drawn up a scheme, as early as the year 929 BC, to conquer the world for the Jewish nation without bloodshed. As historical events developed, this plan was revised by successors, and had finally been completed at secret meetings of the Jewish Elders. The authentic protocols of these meetings, stolen from secret Jewish archives, and first published by him, should warn his countrymen of the approaching danger. In each new edition of the *Protocols* his message became more and more urgent. The symbolic serpent, which had been used for centuries to represent the Antichrist, was eating away all non-Jewish political forces in various countries, and was nearing its last stage, when it would accomplish its circular course and enclose all of Europe, and then the whole world, in its circumference.

On the fly leaf of the fourth edition of his book, published in 1917, on the eve of the Revolution, Nilus warned his readers: 'It is near, at the door, concerning something people do not wish to believe and which is so.' Indeed, Nilus is a key figure in the story, but it did not start with him. One could well say that the Russian chapter of the *Protocols* began when Prince Nikolai became the ruler of the mighty Russian Empire.

NIKOLAI AND ALEXANDRA

The body of Tsar Alexander III lay in state in the Winter Palace on 14 November 1894, where the royal family gathered, still shocked by his premature death. Mixed with their grief was extreme apprehension. These were dangerous times for Russia, and they all felt helpless with the sudden demise of a strong and mighty monarch. The next in line to hold the destiny of the empire in his hands was the young inexperienced Prince Nikolai. What policies would the new Tsar embrace, they all wondered. He was totally unprepared for the crown suddenly to be placed on his head, and they were not sure whether he had ever given it much thought.

Young Nikolai was immature and unfit for the position of the absolute autocrat ruler of 187 million citizens of the Great Russian Empire. His mind was fixed on Alix, later to become Tsarina Alexandra, whom he had met in the house of her elder sister Elizaveta, and with whom he had fallen madly in love. On 4 April 1894, she had agreed to become his wife after a long courtship, which had been opposed by his parents. He was devastated by his father's death, but on the following day, even before the Tsar's burial, he insisted on the conversion of Alix to the Russian Orthodox faith to pave the way for their wedding. They were married two weeks later and decided to make their home in Tsarskoe Selo.

Nikolai soon proved that the reactionaries had no cause for concern. He had been indoctrinated by Konstantin Pobedonostsev, a firm supporter of autocracy, Orthodoxy and nationalism, and strongly opposed to what he called western atheism. Even before Nikolai's birth, numerous attempts had been made on the life of his grandfather, Alexander II, who had finally been murdered on the embankment of the Catherine Canal in St Petersburg by members of the revolutionary group Narodnaia Volia (People's Will), on the first day of March 1881. Nikolai could still remember an attack on the Winter Palace that had frightened him as a child. He saw revolutionaries in every corner. A weak man who had grown up in the shadow of a strong father, Nikolai had not really been interested in the affairs of his country.

Listening to his new bride, Alexandra, and ignoring the prudent advice of his mother and other relatives, he decided to announce his policy without delay, even before his formal coronation. What better occasion than his first public audience, given soon after his wedding in the presence of nobility and of representatives of *zemstvo* from all provinces of the empire. They had all traveled to the capital to express condolences on the death of the Tsar, bearing gifts and congratulations for the young royal couple. With no thought for the consequences, Nikolai immediately made it crystal clear that he would follow in the footsteps of the worst of his reactionary predecessors, proclaiming: 'I want everyone to know that I will concentrate all my strength to maintain, for the good of the whole nation, the principle of absolute autocracy, as firmly and as strongly, as did my late lamented father.' Demands for a constitution, supported by the more prudent politicians, were dismissed by him as nonsensical dreams. The battle for the future of Russia was joined, crushing the hopes of liberals and kindling the fires of existing revolutionary groups.

The response was quick and unequivocal: before long the young prince found on his desk an open letter, signed by the Revolutionary Executive Committee of Geneva, which was also distributed all over the empire. They expressed 'a crushing feeling of betrayal' and promised that autocracy had dug its own grave. The reactionaries were gratified, their worst fears allayed. Alexander III had disliked minority nationalities, but most of all he had disliked Jews and had even condoned violence against them, yet he had no desire to use pogroms as an instrument of domestic policy. Now, with the declaration of the new monarch, the road was clear for unlimited atrocities soon to become a mark of the new regime.

It was against this background that the *Protocols of the Elders of Zion* made their first appearance in Russia, at the home of the Tsar's uncle, the governor-general of Moscow, Grand Prince Sergei Alexandrovich, and his wife Grand Princess Elizaveta Fedorovna, the Tsarina Alexandra's sister.

'She was a flower of exquisite loveliness when, at the age of 20, she married Sergei Alexandrovich, the fourth son of the Emperor Alexander II.' This is what the French Ambassador Paleologue wrote in his memoirs about the sister-in-law of Tsar Nikolai II, Elizaveta Fedorovna. Like her sister Alexandra she too was deeply religious – both had acquired their propensity for mysticism from their mother, Princess Alice, the daughter of Queen Victoria of England.

In 1891 Sergei Alexandrovich had been appointed governor-general of Moscow, where the couple moved from St Petersburg. He had soon blossomed as a protagonist of the reactionary crusade that was the hallmark of his brother Tsar Alexander III's domestic policy. One of his first acts had been to expel the Jews who had gradually made their way into Moscow, roughly driving them back into ghettos in the western provinces. Attempts by some senators to eliminate legal restrictions upon the Jewish population had immediately been quashed.

Soon after their marriage, in 1884, Elizaveta had embraced her husband's religion. Fervently adopting the mysterious rites of the Russian Orthodox Church, she had devoted herself with great enthusiasm to charitable deeds, founding and financing many charitable institutions. She stood by her husband despite his despotic nature, rude behavior and vicious brutality, and shared Sergei's uncompromising reactionary views and his unrelenting anti-Semitism.

Like others of her class, she had no qualms about the murder of Jews in pogroms. Yet she could be extremely merciful towards Christians, as she proved many years later when her husband was blown up by a terrorist bomb. On the eve of his funeral, after spending five days in solitary prayer, she went to visit his murderer, offering to plead for his life if he repented. When she later learned that he had been hanged in the night and buried beneath the prison wall, she prayed for his soul. It had never entered her mind to plead with her husband for the lives of innocent men, women and children who had perished in brutal pogroms; she had never thought of praying for the souls of Jews.

Philip Petrovich Stepanov was a welcome guest in the house of Grand Prince Sergei. He was especially friendly with Grand Princess Elizaveta and forever grateful to her for having arranged the appointment of his niece, Elena Aleksandrovna Ozerova, as lady in waiting to her sister, Empress Alexandra. Yet he had a special reason for paying them a visit one day in 1897. Carefully extricating from his briefcase a thick sheaf of papers, he presented to the prince with a conspiratorial air a manuscript entitled 'Subjugation of the World by Jews', declaring dramatically that they were holding in their hands evidence of a Judeo-Masonic conspiracy to dominate the world. This was the first appearance of the document later known as the *Protocols of the Elders of Zion*. There were 24 protocols, he explained, minutes of meetings of a secret Jewish government, on dates unknown, at undisclosed venues.

The print, done by Stepanov in hectograph jelly, was not easy to read, but it was better than the handwritten version he himself had received from his neighbor in the government of Tula, Alexei Sukhotin, a retired army major, who also served as marshal of nobility in the district. Sukhotin had told him in secret that a Russian lady of his acquaintance maintained that she had found the document at the house of a Jewish friend in Paris, and had secretly translated it into Russian and brought it with her.

In spite of the poor print, Sergei immediately recognized the potential of such a document in his constant persecution of the Jews. This was an opportunity not to be missed. Without any attempt to verify the story or the document, the head of his household was immediately summoned and ordered to assist Stepanov in the printing of the manuscript. They soon reproduced the first known printed brochure of *The Ancient and Modern Protocols of the Meetings of the Elders of Zion*. Stepanov saw to it that the pamphlet appeared on the desks of various officials in the government administration in St Petersburg, who, to his chagrin, completely ignored it. Most people took it to be another example of anti-Jewish propaganda periodically distributed by the secret police. Not so Witte, the minister of finance.

SERGEI IULIEVICH WITTE

The *Protocols of the Elders of Zion* were associated in my mind with secret police agents, backroom forgers, religious fanatics and initiators of pogroms. It had never entered my mind that they could have been fabricated for any other reason than to embarrass the Jews and incite hatred. The idea that somebody would go to all the trouble of inventing such an elaborate concoction for the sole purpose of undermining the policies of one of the most important political figures in Russia seemed preposterous. If this were a real trial and somebody had tried to introduce Witte into the evidence, I would have told him to stick to the relevant facts and stop clouding the issue. Yet I soon learned that judges who had dealt with the *Protocols* in real court proceedings had all faced the same dilemma, and sooner or later realized that in dealing with this book they were compelled to deal with history. Historians were key witnesses in all these trials, and the political reality at each stage of the story was a central issue.

The minister of finance, Sergei Iulievich Witte, read with growing concern the typed booklet that had been hand-delivered to his office. Normally he would have ignored it as he had no interest in anonymous documents, but his assistant had marked it for his attention, adding that it had been widely distributed to senior government officials. After careful examination he ordered his assistant to commission Henry Sliosberg, a well-known and brilliant Jewish lawyer, to submit an appraisal of this astonishing document.

Although his name was not mentioned in the manuscript, Witte, with his keen intellect and deep understanding of the undercurrents influencing Russian internal and external politics, felt that if made public, the document would not only serve as a potent tool in the ongoing persecution of Jews, but also threaten him and his policies. Both issues caused him profound concern. Keenly aware of the Jewish problem in Russia, he had tried to discuss it with the late tsar, Alexander III, for whom he had had great admiration and a relationship much closer than the one he had with the present tsar, Nikolai II. In one of his conversations with the late tsar he had advocated liberalization of the laws against Jews, when the emperor suddenly asked him whether it was true that he was in sympathy with this race. 'The only way I can answer this question', he had replied, 'is by asking your majesty whether you think it possible to drown all the Russian Jews in the Black Sea. To do so would, of course, be a radical solution of the Jewish problem. But if your majesty recognizes the right of the Jews to live, then conditions must be created that will enable them to carry on a human existence. In that case, gradual abolition of the discriminatory laws applying to Jews is the only adequate solution of the Jewish problem.'

Actually Witte was no great lover of Jews. His main concern was the fact that the treatment of the Jews in the empire was causing great harm to Russia. This conviction grew throughout his career, but even when he became chairman of the Council of Ministers, his attempts to change the official anti-Jewish policy of the tsar were totally disregarded.

But at that particular moment, in 1898, Witte was not worried about the Jews. His concern was about himself. On his appointment as minister of finance, on 30 August 1892, he had found himself in charge of an empty treasury and a collapsing economy and had to print money to pay the salaries of the army officers. Since then he had been trying to save thee conomy of Russia by transforming a mainly agricultural society into a modern industrial empire. The country was racked with famine and social unrest was brewing. In order to succeed he had to radically change the composition of Russian society with its 80 per cent of illiterate *moujiks* who lived off the land. To build an industry the country needed a network of functioning railways and a radical change of its monetary system. It was time, he decided, to adopt the gold standard, as most European countries had done. He was painfully aware of the fact that in the period of transition the realization of his plan would bring misery to millions of Russians and encounter strong opposition.

At the close of the century he could feel justly proud. He had succeeded in filling the cash reserves by selling natural resources such as coal, iron, steel and cotton. He had increased industrial production and had started implementation of an ambitious plan to build a railway network. Twenty-five hundred kilometers of rails in six years were quite an achievement, he thought. True, small industry and farmers had not yet adjusted to these changes, and they were paying a heavy price. In 1898 a deep depression caused massive unemployment and a collapse in the stock exchange as well as the collapse of two banks. The adoption of the gold standard meant that five million farmers had to give up agriculture. If one took into account their families, one was speaking of some 25 million people!

This is why Witte was so appalled on reading this strange document: it was uncanny how some parts of this so-called 'plan of the Jews to dominate the world' so closely resembled his own plan. One of his boldest and most criticized steps had been the adoption of the gold standard in January 1897. Opponents of his requested foreign loans were spreading stories about the unreliability of the Russian economy and the possibility of the collapse of the gold standard. It could surely not be a coincidence, he thought with horror, that the anonymous speaker was telling the Elders in Protocol no. 20: 'You are aware that the gold standard has been the ruin of the states that adopted it, for it has not been able to satisfy the demands for money, the more so that we have removed gold from circulation as far as possible.'

He did not believe for a moment that the document was authentic. How could one speak of 'Jewish power' when five million Jews were living in the Russian Empire in appalling conditions, prey to discrimination both by law and in practice, in daily danger of pogroms and massacres? True, Jews in Western countries had more influence. He himself was negotiating loans for Russia with Jewish banks. But a Jewish conspiracy? If the Jewish bankers had so much power, if they had a secret government, why would they have to beg him to intervene with the tsar to alleviate the suffering of their brethren in Russia? He knew that the revolutionary winds blowing in the empire were caused by the unbending stubbornness of a regime that held so many millions in a state of virtual serfdom, not something engineered by international Jewry. He was honest enough to admit that if there were Jews in the ranks of the revolutionaries, it was not as part of an overall international intrigue, but because they had been pushed beyond the limits of human endurance. All they really wanted was to be equal citizens, a goal they could never achieve in the present regime.

Who had concocted this document, he wondered; and for what purpose? The Black Hundreds did not need it to incite their disciples to pogroms, not something so elaborate! A few speeches blaming the Jews for all their troubles were enough to start a pogrom. 'Beat the Jews and save Russia', their monstrous but effective slogan, had the desired impact on the masses. This must have been created for a more sophisticated purpose, he mused. Every Russian anti-Semite who read the *Protocols* would be convinced that Witte was adopting in Russia the plot of the Elders of Zion. Could it have been done to discredit him, to advocate that he was a tool in the hands of the secret government of international Jewry, cooperating with Jewish financiers, manipulated by them and assisting them to bring about the enslavement of all Christians to the king of Israel? How devious, he thought. Was he being paranoid? Knowing his enemies and their expertise in forgeries and intrigue, this possibility could not be ignored, he decided.

Looking at the book with distaste, he could almost detect the fingerprints of the Okhrana. For some time his opponents had been linking his name with that of Jewish bankers abroad, spreading wild accusations that went so far as to imply actual treason. If his enemies succeeded in convincing the tsar that his policies were treasonous, and that he was conspiring with others to undermine the tsar's autocratic regime, he would be in real danger. He was conscious of the fact that the new tsar was not a fan of his and was using him out of sheer necessity. This was to prove a continuous pattern in their relationship. Witte's strength of character, experience and talents secured him an outstanding place among the political leaders of the empire, and he had saved the tsar more than once from the consequences of his imprudent policies. Yet deep down he knew that the emperor hated his penetrating and acid intellect, in contact with which he always felt himself inferior and disarmed.

Sliosberg submitted his well-written learned opinion a few weeks later, stating that the so-called 'Jewish Conspiracy' was a lot of nonsense, one of many periodic anti-Semitic inventions. In his opinion the *Protocols* were definitely a crude forgery, virtually ignored by both official and aristocratic Russian society. Although he had his suspicions, he had not succeeded in revealing where, when and by whom the document had been fabricated.

Sliosberg's opinion only added to Witte's anxiety. The Jewish lawyer agreed with the minister that the document had probably been fabricated not only to incite against the Jews, but mainly to undermine Witte's financial policy.

Witte's suspicions were well founded, Sliosberg wrote. It was no coincidence that so many points in the so-called 'Protocols' were identical with the measures initiated by the minister in his financial and agrarian reform. The Jews only served as a tool.

But pressing matters on his agenda soon occupied Witte's mind. He heard nothing of the *Protocols* till 1903, when they made their appearance in a series of articles in the anti-Semitic newspaper *Znamia* (The Banner), edited by Pavel Krushevan.

KRUSHEVAN AND COMPANY

'Personally I have nothing against the Jews,' Minister Wentzel Von Pleve told the Chairman of the Committee of Ministers. 'I know we are following an essentially wrong policy, but I am committed to pleasing Grand Prince Sergei Alexandrovich and his majesty, the tsar.' What a surprising admission, Witte thought, from the man in whose time and by whose instigation pogroms in Jewish towns and settlements raged with particular violence, the author of the slogan 'We must drown the revolution in Jewish blood.' The initiative never came from the people, he knew – it was always orchestrated from above, well planned and meticulously prepared. Nothing in Russia was possible without official sanction, often with the active blessing, always with the unqualified approval, of the tsar. The terrorist brigades known as the Black Hundreds, so nicknamed in the beginning because of their small numbers, enjoyed the favor and the full protection of the royal court. Created during the reign of Alexander III to assist in the struggle against the Revolution, they came to regard themselves as true patriots, defenders of the Russian state, Church and tradition. In time their numbers grew and they enjoyed the legitimacy of a political party calling itself the 'True Russians'. From 1907 they gained representation in the state Duma, where they served as a recognized political party until the Revolution. Led by unscrupulous political adventurers, goading and exploiting the low instincts of the ignorant mob, they assassinated known radicals and liberals and indiscriminately massacred Jews in the most brutal pogroms against Jewish communities. Any opponent of the extreme rightist policies of the court, or even a loyal monarchist, who dared support liberalization of internal policies, as did Witte, was immediately accused of acting in the service of the Jews. Pavel Krushevan was one of the leaders of the Black Hundreds. *Znamia* was their newspaper.

Of the hundreds of pogroms that occurred in the Russian Empire, none aroused such an uproar around the world as did the pogrom that took place in the capital of Besarabia in Easter of 1903. The Kishinev pogrom cost the small Jewish community 45 lives, with hundreds of men, women and children injured, hundreds of houses and shops plundered and destroyed, synagogues desecrated and scrolls of the holy Torah torn and defiled. The intensive anti-Jewish propaganda preceding the pogrom, the wild accusations of ritual murders and the organized inhuman brutality of the attack left no doubt in world opinion that this atrocity had been orchestrated by official circles and approved by the palace.

Witte was especially interested in the fact that the existence of a Jewish conspiracy had played a central part in preparing the pogromchiks for the massacre, substantiated by a document entitled 'The Rabbi's Speech'. Mention was also made of the *Protocols of the Elders of Zion*. Four months after the pogrom, from 28 August till 7 September *Znamia* carried installments of the *Protocols of the Learned Elders of Zion*.

The use made by Krushevan of the 'Rabbi's Speech' should have served as a warning that the *Protocols* were not far behind. The allegation of the existence of a Jewish conspiracy to dominate the world, which worked so well in Kishinev, had not been born with the *Protocols*. Thirty years earlier, during the 1870s, Russian anti-Semites had published in St Petersburg and in other Russian cities various editions of a pamphlet entitled *In the Jewish Cemetery in Prague*. It was the reproduction of a chapter by the same name from *Biarritz*, a novel by Sir John Retcliff, published in Germany in 1868, which did not purport to be anything but pure fiction. The author had good reason to hide behind the respectable English name: he was Herman Goedsche, a former German civil servant, who had been dismissed from service in the postal office after having tried to incriminate and discredit the German democratic leader, Benedic Waldeck, by producing forged letters as proof of Waldeck's participation in a conspiracy to assassinate the king and overthrow the constitution. Goedsche, who was blessed with a vivid imagination, became a journalist and a writer, prudently publishing his books under the English pen name. In one fictional chapter he dramatized an old myth concerning a Jewish plot to dominate the world, a myth that, like the blood libels and other libels against the Jews, had never been substantiated. Nor did Goedsche treat it as anything but pure fiction, a figment of his imagination. His dramatic description of the midnight scene at the Prague cemetery was chilling. In his novel, one after another, the representatives of the twelve Jewish tribes, including the ten lost ones, arrive at the ancient Prague Jewish cemetery clad in long white mantles and gather round the tomb of a rabbi. They meet once a century to plan the final Jewish triumph over Christendom and indeed over the whole world, and to report their achievements of the previous century. They report their plans concerning the gold concentrated in Jewish hands, their influence on the stock exchange, and the control they are gaining over the working masses, the economy and the press. They conspire to undermine the Christian Church, to foster revolution against the ruling classes, to infiltrate government circles, and to control the press. They even discuss how to corrupt and defile Christian womanhood.

After each representative has spoken, they all swear an oath to a golden calf that emerges from the rabbi's grave, surrounded by a ball of fire. Satan is also present, speaking to them from the grave while they kneel in a circle.

This chapter ignited the imagination of Russian anti-Semites. They first published it in its original form as pamphlets, which appeared in various Russian cities from 1872. In 1881 the speeches delivered by Goedsche's white-clad fictional representatives of the twelve tribes were transformed in France into one speech, presumably delivered by a flesh-and-blood chief rabbi to a secret assembly of Jews. Proof of its authenticity was offered by an 'English diplomat' who 'vouched' for the document and whose name was non other than Sir John Retcliffe. *The Rabbi's Speech* was soon published as an authentic document in Russia as well as in other countries, a forerunner of the later fabricated, much more detailed and sophisticated *Protocols of the Elders of Zion.*

It was this 'speech' that was used by Krushevan and his friends in the Black Hundreds to inflame and incite the pogromchiks in Kishinev. When the *Protocols of the Elders of Zion* were published in *Znamia* four months later, the ground had been well prepared.

But newspapers are a perishable and fleeting commodity. To obtain a more lasting effect, it was necessary to lend to the document the respectability of a printed book. It was time for full and lasting public exposure. Two years later the *Protocols of the Elders of Zion* were first published in book form by Sergei Nilus.

PAVING THE WAY FOR NILUS

Walking in the royal gardens of Tsarskoe Selo it was easy to imagine how Sergei Nilus had walked on these same paths with the Tsarina's lady in waiting, Elena Ozerova. He might even have proposed to her in the shadow of one of the magnificent sculptures at which Boris and I were now looking. It seemed incredible that the fate of a book, which has been printed in every language, its world distribution not much less than that of the Bible, should have depended on a chain of events that were completely irrelevant to its subject matter.

Boris had insisted that we visit Russia. 'Places are as important as books,' he used to say. 'You have to see with your eyes where things happened in order to reconstruct the past.'

If he had had his way we would have gone to Russia in the winter. 'In summer you don't see the real Russia,' he had repeated again and again. 'You have to walk in the snow, gaze upon the white-encrusted plains, blow on your hands to keep them from freezing and watch the people bundled up in their heavy coats and fur hats. Russia in summer is just like any other country.' But I could still remember the freezing winters in the little town in Poland where I was born, my nose numb, my small feet slipping on the ice on my way to school. Forty degrees centigrade below zero had no appeal for me, so we went in the summer.

In a city that hosts some of the most spectacular palaces in the world, the Catherine Palace in Tsarskoe Selo is one of the most impressive. Built by the famous Italian architect Count Bartolomeo Francesco Rastrelli for Empress Elizabeth in the middle of the eighteenth century, it was named after her mother, Ekaterina I, wife of Peter the Great. Its blue and white facade, its rows of brown sculptures, its gilded and olive details, all sparkling in the bright sun, are a feast for the eye. The richly decorated rooms, the long halls, the impressive gallery and chapel, crowned with gold domes, make it hard to tear oneself away. Russian tsars, their families and court entourage, actually lived amidst this splendor, I thought.

'But not Nikolai and Alexandra,' Boris reminded me. 'They chose to live in the adjoining Alexander Palace, much simpler and much more frugal.' Indeed, Boris explained, pointing out the adjoining unadorned building, the empress had insisted on a very simple apartment within this palace as living quarters for her family. When she was not ill, which she was most of the time, Alexandra used to spend hours at prayer in the family chapel. The lavish royal entertainment bestowed on the nobility by her predecessors was almost entirely discontinued, a permanent source of bitter criticism among them.

We were walking in the magnificent royal gardens, the lawns and bushes trimmed to perfection, the flowers in full bloom, the white sculptures proudly glimmering in the sun. 'How is it possible', I asked Boris, 'that for more than two decades the fate of the great Russian Empire was decided by a sickly and fanatical woman, acting under the spell of mystic charlatans and fanatics? How did some insignificant women whom she had chosen as her companions worm their way onto the central stage of Russian politics?'

Boris and I speculated that if two Montenegrin princesses had not introduced a magician called Philippe to the royal couple, there probably would have been no reason for Grand Duchess Elizaveta Fedorovna to introduce Sergei Nilus to the niece of Stepanov, Elena Alexandrovna Ozerova, and the *Protocols of the Elders of Zion* might have vanished into oblivion along with other political forgeries such as the *Testament of Peter the Great* and the *Memorandum of General Tanaka*. The famous testament of the Russian tsar purported to be a warning to the world of Napoleon's plan to dominate Russia and the whole of Asia; the Japanese memorandum appeared to contain a plan for the conquest of Europe by Japan. When exposed as forgeries, these two documents vanished from the world scene, as did also the *Monita Secreta*, another proven fabrication implicating the Jesuits. This too was an invention of so called 'protocols' of secret instructions purporting to be composed by the superiors in the Jesuit order, instructing their subordinates to put into practice 'the shameful and Machiavellian policies of the Society of Jesus'. That the *Monita Secreta* was a brazen invention was admitted even by adversaries.

The Protocols of the Elders of Zion, the crudest forgery of them all, was fated to gain immortality by a chain of events in which a central role was played by a bizarre religious fanatic, favored by a Russian grand princess in her attempt to discredit a foreign fake healer who was bewitching a powerful monarch by hypnotizing his wife in nocturnal spiritualist seances.

I had set out to investigate the story behind a book, but as I did so, a procession of people started crowding into the story, forcing themselves upon me. These men and a surprising number of women had all played a part in the saga. The story of the book, I soon discovered, would become the story of the people who had inspired, created, distributed and exploited it, as well as those who had finally exposed it.

Reading the *Protocols* for the first time, Tsar Nikolai II had been fascinated. As was his custom, he scribbled enthusiastic remarks on the margin of the copy delivered to him, marveling at the great precision of the program, convinced that 'everywhere one can recognize the directing and destroying hand of Judaism'. This document would serve as his handbook for politics, he exclaimed. It was his minister of the interior, Stolypin, who made him change his mind. Approached by the Union of the Russian People, which needed his authorization for mounting a major anti-Semitic campaign using the theme of the *Protocols*, Stolypin, who had his doubts, assigned two officers of the corps of gendarmes to conduct a secret inquiry. He was soon able to report to the tsar that they were dealing with a forgery. In a rare gesture, the tsar ordered in another marginal note 'Drop the Protocols. One cannot defend a pure cause by dirty methods.'

This would probably have been the end of the matter had not Ozerova, with the help of Princess Elizaveta, succeeded in obtaining the permission of the censorship committee to publish the book by Nilus which contained the full text of the *Protocols of the Elders of Zion*. It is this book that became the source of all publications of the *Protocols*, in every language.

The grand princess was very worried about her sister. Since Alexandra's coronation there seemed to be a growing lack of warmth between them. Like many others in the Russian ruling circles, Elizaveta watched with deepening concern how the empress surrounded herself with fanatical women, to the exclusion of all the rest of St Petersburg society, and how she fell under the spell of unscrupulous magicians, who were using her to gain and wield power in the royal palace. It was after the tragic events of the first day of September 1902 that she decided she must act.

In the spring of 1902, the tsar and his entourage were overjoyed to learn that the empress was again with child. They all hoped that this time it was going to be a son, the next tsar of Russia. They also prayed that a male child would have a curing effect on the poor tsarina, who had become totally immersed in religious mysticism. She had given birth to four daughters, but Russia needed an heir and as long as she did not deliver one she would continue to feel inadequate, a virtual failure. This time there would be a son, promised her French adviser, Philippe, whom she had installed in a room next to her own. She had absolute confidence in him and even related to her husband how Philippe had given her an icon with a little bell 'which warns me when evil people are around and prevents them coming closer to me'.

It was early summer when court circles noticed with joy that the empress had grown considerably stouter, and had begun to wear loose garments. They even stopped criticizing her for ceasing to appear at court functions. Any day the cannons of Petropavlovsky Fortress would announce to the nation the birth of the imperial son, as was the ancient custom. Russia was holding its breath. Professor Ott, the court *accoucheur*, with his assistants, came to stay in the palace at Peterhof, ready for the great event. Still the empress stayed in her rooms, announcing that she would call for the doctor when the time came. As the days passed, everybody became more and more nervous. Finally, Professor Ott deemed it imprudent to wait any longer. He asked her majesty's permission to examine her, and she could no longer refuse. Emerging from her room he wore a shocked expression, worried as to how he would break the news to the tsar. There was going to be no heir this time: Alexandra was not even with child. It was a classic case of phantom pregnancy. The international press reported that the strange phenomenon had been invoked by the hypnotist Philippe during prolonged nocturnal seances with the tsarina. The royal empress of the Russian empire had become the laughing stock of Europe, but the enamored tsar would not tolerate any criticism of his beloved wife or Philippe. So they all kept quiet, but in secret, behind the scenes, they looked for ways to save their majesties from the spell cast upon them. That was when Elizaveta conceived the idea of installing Nilus in the royal court as the official religious adviser and confessor to the tsar. She had just read his book *The Great in the Small*, which had been published the previous year, and it touched upon her deep religious convictions. Nilus might be the right person to discredit Philippe and replace him in the royal palace. Acting as matchmaker, she introduced Nilus to Ozerova, whom she had helped install in the palace as a lady-in-waiting to the empress. She regretted having waited so long: she should have acted as soon as she realized the danger from the unnatural liaison between her sister and the two Montenegrins. She hoped it was not too late.

TWO MONTENEGRINS AND ONE FRENCHMAN

Militza and Anastasia, daughters of Prince Nikolai of Montenegro, had been prudently placed by their father in the Smolny Institute, which allowed them, on graduation, to come out in St Petersburg society. In recognition of the attachment the Montenegrins manifested to Russia, Tsar Alexander III had toasted the prince at a public dinner, calling him his friend, and showing some attention to his daughters. This proved sufficient for members of the imperial family to come forward as suitors. With the manipulative assistance of their father, the two young ladies were soon married to two second-rate dukes, the sons of the tsar's uncle. The two Montenegrin princesses were on their way to becoming a driving force in the empire.

Their opportunity came when the emperor died and Princess Alix married Prince Nikolai. She was a foreigner in St Petersburg, to be officially crowned only two years later, after the intricate preparations for the official coronation ceremony were completed. In the meantime, the dowager empress and the grand duchesses of the court were cordial but reserved. The two Montenegrins began their campaign by bestowing on the young princess love and admiration. They were the only ones who curtsied to her as if she were already crowned empress. They clung to her day and night, waiting on her hand and foot, displaying their unlimited devotion. When it appeared that the princesses, who were avid spiritualists, also shared a mystical streak with the future empress, they became her close friends for life. It was the sisters from Montenegro who introduced the empress to a series of miracle workers and mediums, and in other ways involved her in the bizarre occultism that pervaded the court and high society at the time. One such occultist was Philippe Vachat of Nizier.

A former butcher boy from Lyon, Philippe believed he was endowed with mysterious powers. At the age of 23 he had opened his own consulting room, where he treated his patients with psychic fluids and invoked supernatural forces. He soon built up a lucrative practice, charming his patients with his simple ways, his gentle manner and his seemingly unselfish care. Denounced as a fake healer by the doctors of Lyon, he was twice convicted and fined, but that only increased his reputation. His consulting room, at No. 35 rue de la Tête-d'or, was initially crowded with simple folk but they were soon joined by growing numbers of nobility, society women, and men of all professions. His neighbors were particularly intrigued by the appearance in their quarter of two elegant ladies, connected – as Philippe's cook proudly boasted – to the imperial court. The two Montenegrin princesses decided to introduce Philippe to their imperial highnesses, the tsar and tsarina, who were paying a royal visit to France in 1900, and had been received with much pomp and grandeur.

A secret Russian agent in Paris, Manasevich Manuilov, was assigned to accompany Philippe to meet the royal couple. He traveled to Compiègne, where their majesties were staying at the time, and received Philippe at the doors of the local palace, where he was instructed to question him before conducting him to the imperial apartments. Manuilov encountered a heavily built fellow with a big moustache, dressed in simple black but spotless clothes. He appeared quiet and grave, rather like a schoolmaster in his Sunday best. There was nothing remarkable about him except his eyes – blue, penetrating, half concealed by heavy eyelids, but every now and then with a curious, soft light shining in them. Round his neck hung a small, black, silk triangular amulet, the contents of which he refused to reveal.

This meeting, instigated by the Montenegrin princesses, was to have a far-reaching effect on the Russian royal court. It was also destined to play a role in the history of the publication of the *Protocols of the Elders of Zion*.

As the princesses had suspected, the sovereigns were immediately hypnotized by Philippe, and as they had hoped, the 51-year-old French occultist could hardly refuse a royal invitation to make his home in Tsarskoe Selo, with an elegant house at his disposal, assured of royal patronage. A convicted fake healer and former butcher boy could hardly aspire much higher.

The empress was fascinated by this man. He held her completely in his power, practicing on her his brand of hypnotism and prophecy. The practice of occult sciences had always been popular among Russians. Spiritualists, fortune-tellers and high priests of mysticism and magic had habitually found a sympathetic welcome on the banks of the Neva. No wonder that the French fake healer immediately won the full confidence not only of the empress but also of the tsar, who was soon following his advice on everything, including matters of state.

Testing his power over the tsar to the limit, Philippe insisted that he be made a 'doctor of medicine'. His persistence paid off when, on orders of his majesty, and against his better judgment, Witte applied to the war minister, General Kuropatkin, to have Philippe appointed medical officer of the Reserve. As a result, the St Petersburg Military Medical Academy was forced to bestow on the Frenchman, in secrecy, the degree of doctor of medicine, in flagrant violation of the law, granting him the rank of councillor of state. Like all secrets in the capital, this one was also soon exposed, and St Petersburg society amused itself in drawing rooms with stories describing how the 'saint' paid a visit to a tailor and ordered an army physician's uniform.

When Philippe finally fell from grace and was compelled to return to France, he could not have known that his presence in the palace had played a role in the saga of the *Protocols of the Elders of Zion*. After living out his days in shabby retirement in his country house at Arbresle, he died on 2 August 1905, barely three months before the *Protocols* were first published by Nilus.

Elizaveta's efforts to replace Philippe in the palace by Nilus had failed, but her matchmaking efforts were more successful. Nilus did marry Ozerova, both of them enjoying the patronage of the grand princess. It was through her contacts in the royal court, and the support of Grand Princess Elizaveta that Ozerova succeeded in her efforts to obtain the permission of the censorship committee for the publication of the *Protocols* as part of the second edition of her husband's book *The Great in the Small,* in spite of the former veto of the tsar. On 28 September 1905 the committee reversed its former decision to prohibit the publication of the *Protocols*, and allowed Nilus to print his book. They had serious doubts as to the authenticity of the document, but the head of the press department urged them to return the approved manuscript without delay, 'in order to pass it on to her majesty's maid-of-honor'.

Ozerova received the approved manuscript on the eve of a most fateful day, when the tsar, faced with a general strike of the workers, was pressured into signing the famous October Manifesto, granting his citizens constitutional rights. But it was too late. The first Revolution of 1905 was at the door and the Black Hundreds, acting under the protection of the secret police, were blaming the Jews. On 16 October the *Protocols* were quoted in a public sermon delivered by

Metropolit Vladimir of Moscow, and, on his orders, repeated in sermons in 368 churches.

The time was ripe for more pogroms. The Revolution was to be presented as part of the Jewish plot. Nilus could not have hoped for a better promotion of his book. The first edition, published in 1901, was hardly remembered. Only a limited number of readers were concerned with the coming of the Antichrist. The second edition, now including not only the full text of the *Protocols*, but also the story of their alleged origin, would become famous around the world, the most quoted source of an international best-seller.

The censorship committee could not have known that their approval of this book was to turn its author into an international figure, a household name in anti-Semitic movements around the world, for years to come.

SERGEI NILUS

His marriage to Elena Ozerova was the best thing that ever happened to Sergei Nilus. The daughter of the former Russian ambassador to Athens, the sister of the administrator of the Anichkov Palace, a maid-of-honor to the empress, she could have hoped for a better match. Not only did she find herself married to an unstable dreamer, the father of an illegitimate son, but she was also compelled to suffer the presence in their home of his former lover, Nataliia Komarovskaia. It was Ozerova, with her extensive contacts, who opened the doors for Nilus to St Petersburg high society. Although they all lived on her pension from the palace, she always behaved like a submissive wife, walking one step behind her overbearing husband.

When they met he was 40 years old and his prospects were poor. He had absolutely no source of income and no definite plans. His future looked bleak indeed. Yet, as a young man, his prospects had been excellent. He was well educated, having graduated with honors from the Moscow law school, fluent in French, English and German, and familiar with modern foreign literature.

Descendants of a Swedish prisoner of war, the family had settled in Russia and owned lands in the province of Drell. They were well respected and Sergei's brother, Dmitrii, served as president of the Moscow District Court. Sergei himself was appointed by the Ministry of Justice as investigating judge in the Kavkaz, on the Russian–Persian border. This post and the revenue from his lands could have made his life secure, both socially and financially, but his wild character and his quarrelsome behavior soon caused his dismissal from his post. His total lack of administrative qualities and the mismanagement of his lands turned him into an impoverished landowner. He became estranged from his own family, severed relations with his brother Dmitrii, whom he called an atheist. Dmitrii considered him a lunatic.

Suddenly there was nothing for him in Russia. Accompanied by Nataliia Komarovskaia, he moved to France, where their son was born out of wedlock. They lived on the income from his lands, now better administered by his representative in Russia.

In 1894 Nilus suffered a mental breakdown and, embracing extreme fanatical religious mysticism, became obsessed with the dangers facing the world with the imminent coming of the Antichrist. In 1900 the administrator of his properties informed him that he was facing financial ruin. With no secure income he could not remain in France and was forced to return to Russia, blaming his misfortunes on the financial policies of Witte, whom he considered a traitor, 'the invention of the Jews'. 'In ten years Witte had succeeded in changing the character of Russia,' he proclaimed, 'the Russian people had lived off the land, and now, thanks to this traitor, they depend on industry, they will become enslaved by the Jews!'

A staunch supporter of total uncompromising autocracy, Nilus was vehement in his opposition not only to the revolutionary winds blowing in the country, but also to any suggestions of liberalism or constitutional reform. Witte was considered an enemy, and the Jews were denounced as revolutionary murderers, disciples of the devil. Not only did he oppose any liberalization of the anti-Jewish laws, but he was a staunch supporter of the Union of the Russian People and of the anti-Jewish practices of the Black Hundreds. His extreme religious fanaticism went hand in hand with his right-wing political convictions. They both became a major theme in his writings.

This was the man whom Grand Princess Elizaveta had tried to install in the palace as the tsar's confessor. She would have succeeded had it not been for the fact that the Church hierarchy refused to ordain him as a priest because of his unorthodox love life. His marriage to Ozerova, which was part of the plan, was not enough to lend him the respectability of a married man. His union with Komarovskaia and his illegitimate son were obstacles the clergy refused to overlook.

Disappointed, Nilus settled with his wife in the famous monastery Optina Pustyn, taking in his former lover, who was now crippled and ill and had nowhere else to go. It became a classic *ménage à trois*.

THE YEAR OF THE *PROTOCOLS*

The publication of the *Protocols* could not have occurred at a more propitious time. In the history of nations no one year resembles another. One year may pass unnoticed, while another is crowded with events that make history: 1905 was such a year. It started with a massacre and it ended with a pogrom.

On 9 January, later known as 'Bloody Sunday,' shots were fired into a crowd of 140,000 workers who were peacefully marching to the Winter Palace in St Petersburg to petition the tsar for a constitution. Thousands, including women and children, were killed or injured. In quick retribution Grand Prince Sergei, the tsar's uncle, was blown up by a terrorist bomb on 17 February. The victim had been carefully chosen. Sergei was one of the most hated members of the royal family. He was quarrelsome and despotic by nature, rude and offensive in his behavior even towards his wife, Elizaveta, and vicious and cruel to his victims. His murder should have served as a danger warning to the tsar, yet he was reported to have played social games after dinner that same evening.

Witte was again at the center of the political arena. Having failed to prevent the war with Japan he had resigned his post as president of the Council of Ministers, but he was not allowed to live in retirement for long. In all of Russia the tsar could not find a better candidate to conduct negotiations with the Japanese when the United States offered to lend its auspices to the peace talks to be held in Portsmouth. Witte sailed for America in July 1905, and in an admirable feat of diplomacy succeeded in accomplishing his mission. On 5 September 1905, at 3 p.m., the peace treaty with Japan was signed in Portsmouth and a celebration was held in a church, attended by ministers of various creeds, including Jewish rabbis. The tsar had no choice but to show his appreciation. On 9 October he informed Witte that he was to be awarded the rank of count of the Russian Empire, 'in spite of all the base intrigues conducted against me by a host of bureaucrats and courtiers, whose vileness was only equaled by their stupidity', Witte later wrote in his memoirs.

The country was in turmoil. What had until then been isolated acts of terrorism escalated into a full-scale countrywide upheaval that marked the first Russian Revolution. The response of the authorities was quick and merciless. Thousands were arrested, many of them exiled; newspapers and periodicals were closed; print shops stopped working; demonstrations and meetings were banned and trade unions were disbanded.

The stabilizing hand of Witte was badly needed and he was again appointed president of the Committee of Ministers, a post he voluntarily gave up six months later, convinced that he was losing the favor of the tsar, who would listen only to the most extreme uncompromising supporters of total autocracy. In his stupidity the emperor ignored the fact that in Witte he had his most valuable supporter. Though advocating liberalization of internal policies, Witte was in favor of preserving the empire. Describing the events of that fateful year, 1905, when revolutionary winds were blowing, he wrote in his memoirs: 'It was clear to me that in our enthusiasm for political emancipation, we Russians had lost all respect for our glorious history and its product, the great Russian Empire. The radicals confused emancipation from the misrule of bureaucrats and courtiers with emancipation from all the traditions of our historical existence.'

April 1905 also marked the return to Russia of Pavel Miliukov, one of the principal architects of the liberal policy and one of the founders of the liberal Kadet party, later to become the minister of foreign affairs in the provisional government. A brilliant speaker, a historian and a political analyst, Miliukov was driven by events from scholarship to revolutionary politics. Expelled from Moscow University for a year in 1881, he was finally exiled from Moscow in 1895 'because of his harmful influence on students', spending the next ten years in and out of prison and also abroad.

In the bitter controversy between leaders like Miliukov and Witte, who hoped to save the throne of the autocratic dynasty by constitutional means, and the right-wing extremists, who opposed all reforms advocating merciless suppression of any demands for liberalization, the Jewish problem was a crucial issue. Setting the Jews up as perpetual scapegoats, depicting them as arch-anarchists, leaders of the Revolution, the greatest danger to the throne and to the autocratic regime, was part of the planned policy of the right-wing leaders, sanctioned by the emperor. 'Drowning the Revolution in Jewish blood' was part and parcel of their program. The Black Hundreds were the champions designated as exponents of this policy, with no means too cruel or too inhuman in their drive to achieve the final goal. The Jews had to be portrayed as a force to be feared, a force that manipulated Russian liberal leaders and fostered revolution. The Kadet party, led by Miliukov, was referred to as 'Kike-Freemason'.

The visit to the Unites States had confirmed Witte's belief that in order to save Russia, the Jewish problem must be solved. Ignoring warnings that the Jews might harm him, he used his first day in America to visit, unguarded, the Jewish quarter in New York, and met with Jewish groups wherever he went. Communication was easy as many spoke Russian, having fled from the pogroms. To the astonishment of his security agents, not only did he emerge from these meetings unharmed, but he learned that these Jews still considered themselves Russian patriots. Russian soil, they told him, held the bones of their ancestors, and so Russia would forever remain their fatherland. They had become American citizens, they said, but they could never forget Russia. 'We do not love the Russian regime,' they told him, 'but we love Russia above all else.'

Finding himself again in the role of president of the Committee of Ministers, Witte decided to use his authority to stop the mistreatment of the Jews, but he was defeated at every step. One day he learnt from a private communication that under his very nose, in the basement of the Department of Police, presses seized in raids of revolutionary underground print-shops were being used by a secret autonomous special section, headed by Captain Komissarov, to turn out anti-Semitic material, inciting to pogroms. Whole bales of such literature had already been dispatched to various cities and many more were printed daily.

Careful not to give Komissarov an opportunity to cover his tracks, Witte dispatched his secretary in his own carriage to bring him to his office without delay, not allowing him even to change from his citizen's clothes to his official uniform, as protocol demanded. But even in his civilian clothes Komissarov was an impressive figure – tall, dark, with a medium-size beard split in the middle, carefully combed hair above a high forehead, and horn-rimmed glasses ordered from the most expensive optometrist in town.

Witte knew that Komissarov held an important position and was in line for promotion. If he denied the existence of the printing press it would be difficult to prove him a liar. So he had planned his approach very carefully. Pretending to be interested in Komissarov's clandestine activities, he inquired how the operation was proceeding, revealing enough details to show he was fully informed. Taken by surprise, the captain admitted to the facts, upon which Witte immediately instructed him to destroy the entire supply of pogrom literature and either demolish or throw into the Fontanka river all the printing presses, and never again engage in such activities.

This would serve as a warning, Witte thought, but he soon realized that it was but an isolated gesture in a sea of anti-Jewish activity, initiated from above. When he loyally reported the matter to the emperor, his majesty was silent, appearing to be familiar with all the details.

Witte soon realized that in his attitude toward the Jews, as in other respects, the emperor's ideals were basically those of the Black Hundreds, of whom he wrote in his diary:

> Most of their leaders are unscrupulous political adventurers, with not a single practical and honest political idea, and all their efforts are directed toward goading and exploiting the low instincts of the mob ... It is the embodiment of savage, nihilistic patriotism, feeding on lies, slander, and deceit, the party of savage and cowardly despair, devoid of the manly and clear-eyed spirit of creativeness. The bulk of the party is dark-minded and ignorant, the leaders are unchanged villains ...

The message was clear: The treatment of the Jews was out of bounds even to the president of the Committee of Ministers.

Witte soon learned that he had undertaken an impossible task. Describing the situation in his memoirs, he wrote:

> A general feeling of profound discontent with the existing order was the most apparent symptom of the corruption with which the social and political life of Russia was infested ... all the ills came to afflict the land at one and the same time and such terrible confusion resulted that one can truthfully say that Russia's soul cried out in agony for relief from the torment of chaos. The universal exclamation was: 'we can live like this no longer'!

He had one ambition left. Before resigning, he proposed obtaining a big loan to save the dwindling economy. He soon put together a syndicate of French, Dutch, English, German, American and Russian banking firms to handle the loan. Attempts by Germany to thwart his efforts were soon twisted by his opponents, who claimed that the Jews were obstructing the loan – an allegation later found to be totally baseless. In fact a Jewish group headed by the Rothschilds declined to participate in the loan unless the Russian government enacted legal measures tending to improve the situation of the Jews in Russia, a condition that was not even seriously considered. The loan was finally obtained in April 1906. It was the largest foreign loan in the history of modern nations.

On 14 April Witte tendered his resignation to the tsar, writing: 'I am unable to defend ideas that are out of keeping with my convictions, and I cannot share the extremely conservative views which have lately become the political credo of the Minister of the Interior.' One of the important political problems on which he disagreed was the treatment of the Jews.

Soon after his retirement, while spending a vacation abroad, Witte was warned not to return to Russia as his life might be in danger. His opponents were accusing him of being a supporter of the Jews. He knew that there was no worse accusation in those days. 'Russian Jews never had as many enemies as they have now,' he wrote, 'nor was the outlook for the Jews ever more somber than it is at the present. Such a state of affairs is highly unfavorable to the pacification of the country. It is my profound conviction that as long as the Jewish problem is handled in an unstatesmanlike, vindictive and non-humanitarian fashion, Russia will remain in a state of unrest and upheaval.'

Indeed, the forgers of the *Protocols of the Elders of Zion* could not have planned for them to be published at a better time. A scapegoat on whom all misfortunes could be blamed was urgently needed. What better scenario than a secret government of the hated Jews convening in a foreign land to plan the destruction of the Christian world? The autocratic regime paled in comparison to what awaited them in the future, when the Jewish king mounted his throne and enslaved them all. Participating in pogroms, the Russians were told, they were not murdering defenseless victims but were fighting the ultimate enemy, who must be totally destroyed.

But the *Protocols*, created to serve the powers of darkness at the helm of an empire fast approaching its self-imposed doom, were destined to outlive the empire. They would survive to fire the imagination of prejudiced bigots who believed in apocalyptic prophesies.

In the words of Christopher Sykes (in an article published in the periodical *History Today* in 1967), 'Nilus thought he had dropped a high-explosive bomb; in fact he had set a delayed-action land-mine.'

3 The *Protocols* on Trial

Georges Brunschvig had no premonition that particular July morning that his offer to run an errand for his mother would change his life. A young lawyer, aged 25, he had just moved his law office from his parents' home to the prestigious Marktgasse in Berne. Still, he persisted in stopping by his parents' home every morning, a pattern he would follow for the rest of their lives. The family spoke French since his father, a native of Avanche in the French part of Switzerland, had never completely mastered the German language. His father's family traced its origins to Alsace, while his mother's family came from Endingen, a little Swiss village where Jews had lived for 350 years. His parents chose to make Berne their home so that their children would have the chance of a better education. Still, his father insisted that he complete his studies in French at the University of Dijon after graduating from the law faculty at the University of Berne.

They usually discussed family matters over a quick cup of coffee in the morning, so Georges was surprised on that particular day when his father abruptly changed the topic to the Nazi rally that had taken place on 13 June in the Berne casino. Anti-Semitism had never been a subject much discussed in his family, although they were aware of its existence, as were all Jews in Europe. Georges had never recounted to his parents a number of minor anti-Semitic incidents in his past. The first one had occurred at the age of 8, when a classmate refused to pair with him for a walk to the park because he was a Jew. The teacher had reacted by pairing him off with a Jewish boy. The incident remained vivid in his memory and still rankled. He would never forget the teacher's silence.

Fourteen years later, in 1931, when he reported for reserve duty at his new army unit, he was surprised by his commanding officer's cool reception. When he set off with his comrades to the local bar that evening, he overheard the captain, the son of a diplomat, and himself a lawyer, complain bitterly because a Jew had been assigned to their unit. When his presence was noticed the officer apologized, blaming the incident on alcohol, but Georges knew his Latin and the phrase *in vino veritas* immediately flashed through his mind. He had just been promoted to lieutenant and hoped for a better start on assuming his duties as a Swiss army officer.

At the university, he had not felt any discrimination personally, and he soon made a name for himself as an excellent student. But two of his Jewish friends were discreetly asked to withdraw their applications to join the student club. He still regretted that he had not reacted because he didn't want to jeopardize his position. But all this was in the past.

In the excitement of establishing his own law firm, he had not given much thought to the Nazi rally. But his father's worried expression seemed so out of character that he promised to look into the matter. An opportunity to do so presented itself that same morning.

He had stopped at the pharmacy owned by a family friend. While waiting for his mother's prescription to be filled, he noticed that his friend was unusually preoccupied. The pharmacist confided that at the community board meeting held the previous evening they had debated the possibility of initiating legal proceedings against the leaders of the National Front for distributing copies of the *Protocols of the Elders of Zion* at the casino rally. They knew that across the border Hitler was using the *Protocols* in his campaign against the Jews. They also knew how the *Protocols* had been used to incite the mob in Russia's pogroms and how they were being published all over Europe to promote anti-Jewish feeling. Like most Jews, they had never read the book, although it was available in Switzerland. This was the first time, however, that it had been publicly offered for sale at a mass rally, its text quoted through loudspeakers in speeches blatantly intended to incite the crowd. In an epilogue to this German edition of the *Protocols*, the editor, Theodor Fritsch, asserted that this document proved that the people should not suffer the presence of Jews in their midst any more. It was the duty of all nations, he proclaimed, to eliminate the very existence of this dangerous race.

Even after full emancipation was granted to Swiss Jews in 1866, discriminatory practices and vilification, rooted in a long history of prejudice, remained a part of Jewish life in Switzerland. In the past there had been blood libels, and Jews, falsely accused of spreading the plague, had been burned at the stake. But that was long ago. By the present time, the Swiss brand of anti-Semitism had become more subtle and discreet, even though now and again the calm was broken by reports of tombstones being desecrated in Jewish cemeteries. The representative bodies of the Jewish community routinely protested against particularly disturbing outbursts of Jew hatred in the press or public institutions and the distribution of anti-Semitic material, but never mounted an aggressive campaign, fearing that it might harm the balanced existence with which they had learned to live.

The increased activity of anti-Semitic groups since the 1920s was a source of concern and became a permanent agenda item for the board of the Jewish community. The news from neighboring Germany and the emergence of the new Swiss Nazi party, the National Front, publicly committed to following in the footsteps of Adolf Hitler, dictated the need for a new policy. The participants at the previous evening's meeting had agreed to explore the possibility of legal proceedings against the publishers and distributors of the *Protocols*, but they doubted whether they could find a lawyer who would willingly risk involving his practice in that kind of litigation.

Georges' visit to the pharmacy that particular morning appeared to be a lucky coincidence. It was well known that the newly founded partnership of Georges Brunschvig and Emil Raas was not yet over-burdened with work. Would they consider representing the community in such a lawsuit? The pharmacist asked whether Georges would permit the suggestion to be presented to the board.

Georges had never read the *Protocols*, and it surely raised doubts in his mind whether it would be to his benefit to identify his new law firm with a Jewish issue. His family was not orthodox, neither keeping a Kosher kitchen nor observing the strict rules of the Sabbath, but they did observe the Jewish holidays and kept seats in the synagogue where they all attended the services on the high holidays of Rosh Hashana and Yom Kippur. Georges had studied Hebrew in *cheder* once a week and with a private tutor for his Bar Mitzvah, but in general, his Jewishness did not occupy him much. He was first and fore-most a Swiss citizen and proud of it. Now, remembering the promise to his father, he decided to give the offer some thought and to talk to his partner. But first he had to consult Odette.

She had just turned 17 and he was about to propose to her. He was fairly certain she would accept, but protocol must be observed. Since Odette's father had died when she was 3 years old, Georges presented himself to Odette's mother, bearing the customary bouquet of flowers, to formally ask for her daughter's hand in marriage.

Odette had known him all her life. They shared similarities in their backgrounds; her paternal grandfather came from Endingen, and her grandmother's family originated in Alsace. The families had been friends for years and Georges had begun courting her when she was 12 and he was 19. Her classmates joked about the serious young man who would meet the little girl in pigtails after school and carry her books. Just a few weeks earlier he revealed to her that he had decided even then that she would be his wife, and offered as proof a letter he had written, which had been stamped at the post office. The letter was a proposal of marriage written to her on her twelfth birthday. This romantic gesture would melt the heart of any girl, let alone one who had loved him as long as she could remember.

The critical decision turned out to be an easy one after all. Both Georges and Emil had purchased copies of the *Protocols* and were so shocked by what they read that they became convinced this was a challenge they could not refuse. Odette immediately concurred and felt proud and intrigued, not yet realizing that this commitment would postpone her wedding for many months and change her life.

THE INNER CIRCLE

Georges was the youngest member of the team that assembled a week later in the community boardroom. Their leader was Saly Mayer, from St Gallen, the president of the Schweizerische Israelitische Gemeindebund, the Swiss Jewish community, usually referred to as the SIG. They were joined by Dr Wiener, a Jewish historian from Germany, who researched, collected and systematically recorded every document concerning anti-Semitism he could find. There was also Professor Matti, Georges' teacher, a prestigious scholar, the only non-Jew among them, who agreed to act as attorney of record for the SIG. Georges was to represent the Jewish community of Berne and was awed at the opportunity to collaborate with his former professor. Emil Raas was assigned to work behind the scenes and, at the same time, keep their fledgling private practice going.

Listening to their colleagues on the committee, Georges was worried and so was Professor Matti. They suspected that a judge would not be satisfied with analytical opinions of historians. In a court of law one needed live witnesses, but where would they find them? Not long afterwards, they were introduced to Dr Juris Boris Lifschitz. Born in the Ukraine, Lifschitz had been sentenced to death by a firing squad for opposing the tsarist regime, but had miraculously been liberated. This small, rotund, chain-smoking man, now in his fifties, was an outstanding criminal lawyer, educated in philosophy as well as jurisprudence, and a Hebrew-speaking scholar of the Bible and the Talmud. He would turn out to be the answer to their prayers, although they did not yet fully realize it. Lifschitz would become their link to Russia.

They had undertaken a tremendous assignment. They needed to study all the facts, collect the necessary documentary evidence and find witnesses. But the critical question was whether they had a legal basis for the lawsuit. This was to be their first stumbling block. It also proved to be an opportunity for Georges to quickly gain the respect of his colleagues. It was he who stumbled onto an obscure, little-used paragraph in the local laws of Canton Berne, and it was he who suggested what first seemed to the others to be an impossible legal maneuver.

How does one sue the publishers of a book? How does one legally stop its publication? They knew that some cases concerning the *Protocols* had been initiated in other countries, one even in Basle, Switzerland. But in all these cases the individuals proved that they had been personally libeled in context with the *Protocols*. No such luck here. They would study these cases in due course, but first they had to find an applicable paragraph in the law.

How does one get a court to condemn a book? The law did not prohibit the spreading of lies and libels against the Jews. Georges walked the streets and tossed in his bed, trying to find a solution. He spent long, seemingly fruitless hours at the library in search of an answer. Then, as so often happens, an idea suddenly took form in his head, which at first he hesitated to present to his colleagues. A local Berne law, passed on 10 September 1916, prohibited the publication of 'obscene literature' (*Schundliteratur*), and was originally intended to prevent pornographic publications. But there was no definition of the term *obscene literature*. Could one not argue that certain printed material might be construed as 'politically obscene?'

When Georges first presented his idea, his colleagues were dubious, since this was clearly not what the legislators had in mind. But, Georges argued, it is the courts that interpret the written law and a brave judge might be convinced to broaden the interpretation. At worst, should their case be thrown out of court at the very beginning, their arguments would be published and they might receive some positive publicity. From a strategic point of view, if they were lucky, the judge might reserve his decision on the legal issue to the end of the trial. Then, even if he decided that there was no legal basis for their claim, there was still the possibility that he would condemn the book on the facts. All they really hoped for was an objective, unbiased forum, to say that this was not a factual book, that it was totally false and a vile fabrication. The conviction of these particular defendants was of secondary importance.

Without any real alternate strategy available, they decided to proceed. Lifschitz remembered that the famous Russian author Maxim Gorky had called Nilus' book 'obscene' and warned that it was liable to soil the hands of whoever touched it. Gorky had been one of the few Russians who raised his voice to condemn the hate literature published against the Jews as part of a broad conspiracy to exterminate them. If need be, they could quote Gorky. They could hardly foresee that some 42 years later, in October 1975, the American Senator Patrick Moynihan would stand before the United Nations General Assembly in New York and call the resolution equating Zionism with racism 'an obscene resolution'.

On 26 June 1933, they filed their complaint in court, and prayed for a fair, imaginative, open-minded judge. The judge assigned to the case was Walter Meyer, a practicing Christian, who had never heard of the *Protocols* and who had never before tried a book.

What would I have done in his place, I wondered. It must have crossed his mind, I mused, that his courtroom was being used for a purpose that was more historical than legal. He must have realized that he had been handed a political bombshell, and that his judgment could have far-reaching consequences. He could have dodged the issue by throwing the case out of court and he would have been on firm legal ground, since the use of a legal clause intended to prevent the publication of pornography was, in this case, clearly unorthodox. Surely he would be upheld on appeal. Was he intrigued by the challenge, I wondered; did he consider the high profile of the case, which was already gaining attention in the press?

Judges do not reveal their innermost thoughts. Their final decisions alone are in the public domain. They publish their reasons, not their motives. It was probably Judge Meyer's basic fairness and his experience on the bench that dictated his decision to conduct the trial on the merits of the case. Defining the issue, he knew that in the last analysis he would have to decide on the authenticity or falsehood of this astounding document. He would not conduct a political trial, he decided. He would examine the witnesses, appoint experts and hear arguments. He would be scrupulously fair to both sides, but he would not allow his courtroom to be turned into a political circus.

The first court session was set for 16 November. They had less than five months to get ready and they had not even started. It was now time to earnestly study the facts, collect evidence and, most important, find witnesses. They were confident that the defendants would not be able to present even a scintilla of evidence of any alleged *Jewish conspiracy*. There would be no positive proof that the *Protocols* were indeed authentic records of secret meetings. But they were also aware of the impact of a printed document. They could not completely disregard existing anti-Jewish prejudice. Even if, legally, the burden of proof rested on the shoulders of the publishers and distributors of the document, they must volunteer to prove the forgery. If a judge were to rule that the document had been forged, he would have to know with certainty when, where and by whom it had been done, and he would need to learn it from reliable witnesses. It was therefore imperative that they prove the forgery. But how?

Meanwhile, Saly Mayer, forever practical, reminded them that this was going to be an expensive enterprise, and they would also need to raise some funds. It was decided that Wiener and Lifschitz would collect the evidence and study the historical background, Brunschvig would study the various trials connected with the *Protocols*, and Mayer would contact Jewish organizations and communities to ask for financial assistance. Impressed with Georges' performance and enthusiasm, they decided that before beginning his research, he would be their emissary to the Jewish community in France.

Georges felt greatly honored to be entrusted with this mission, and besides, what young man would not he happy with a trip to Paris! What a pity that Odette could not join him. He promised to take her to Paris for their honeymoon.

It is difficult to judge who was more astonished, the French delegation, which hardly expected such a young and inexperienced lawyer, or Georges, who was invited to a private dining room in a famous restaurant and confronted by ten elegant, self-important men, most of them wearing some decoration on their lapels.

Georges put on his best performance but soon realized, as they nodded their heads with condescending smiles, that it was all in vain.

Yes, they fully respected and admired the activities of the Swiss Jewish community, which had every reason to feel threatened by their northern neighbor. But France was different, they assured him. There was no virulent anti-Semitism and no threat from the National Socialist ideology. The French made fun of Hitler's ramblings, they said, and the story of a so-called *Jewish conspiracy* was a forgotten myth. They concluded that raising the issue would only serve to publicize it.

Georges could hardly swallow the excellent food. As he was not yet fully familiar with the story of the *Protocols*, he could not confront them with the role France had played both in the fabrication and dissemination of that document, but he felt in his heart that they were wrong. As they were speaking, he became painfully aware of the fact that the small Swiss Jewish community could rely only on itself, while the Nazi Front could expect both material and financial help from Germany, with the recent election of Hitler as Chancellor of the Reich. But they accused the Jews of being supported by an international cabal. What irony, he thought.

As we were examining Georges' personal notes in his old study, Odette told me that in later years her husband had mentioned this meeting in Paris many times, wondering how many of those ten French Jews had survived the Holocaust. They had felt so safe!

ALIBI FOR MURDER

To his great surprise, Georges could not find any court judgment directly concerning the *Protocols*. With his limited resources he had to rely on information gathered by his associates, but the only trials they uncovered had ended with an agreed settlement. One such trial had been instigated by Asher Ginzburg, better known by his Hebrew name, Achad Ha'am (one of the people), against Graf Rewentlau, who had named him in print as the author of the *Protocols of the Elders of Zion*. Actually, Rewentlau had merely copied the 'research' of a certain Madame Lesley Fry (also known by her married name, Shishmarev), published in April 1921 in Paris in the anti-Semitic journal *La Vieille France*. In her article 'Achad Ha'am and Zionism – On the Authenticity of the Protocols' she maintained, in all seriousness, that he was to be blamed for the First World War, the widespread demoralization, Bolshevism, total rule by Freemasons, and the attempt of the Jews to finalize their world domination. Achad Ha'am was described as the prophet of the Jews, a hater of all humanity, who lived frugally in London supervising his 'Cohanim', who were busy executing his plan.

Dr Wiener explained to Georges how ludicrous this allegation was. Achad Ha'am had been an opponent of Theodor Herzl, the founder of the Zionist Movement, an extremely non-political person who had advocated the establishment of a 'spiritual center', as opposed to a political one, for the Jews in Palestine.

On 19 March 1923, eight days before the date set for the opening of the Rewentlau trial in a Berlin court, the defendant had offered to settle the case. He announced that he regretted his 'mistake' in copying the French journal's claim that the plaintiff was the author of the *Protocols of the Elders of Zion*, a claim that he could no longer support. He undertook to pay all trial costs, 150,000 marks, and to publish a retraction in the Nazi newspaper.

Concentrating on the Berlin trial, Georges completely ignored the mention of Madame Fry. He had no way of knowing that at that very moment this woman was actively assisting the Swiss Nazis in preparing the defense for the Berne trial.

Another case had been uncovered closer to home. In 1929, Dr Markus Ehrnpreis, Chief Rabbi of Sweden and a Zionist leader, had sued, in a Basle court in Switzerland, the Nazi organization called the Iron Broom, which, in similar fashion, had maintained that Dr Ehrnpreis was one of the authors of the *Protocols*. In preliminary proceedings, the court had ordered all existing copies of the *Protocols* to be confiscated and destroyed. This case had also been settled with a retraction by the defendants.

Georges thought he had exhausted the subject of the trials when his eye fell on a footnote in one article that mentioned a trial, which also seemed to relate to the *Protocols*, if only indirectly. Desperate for any relevant material, he reached for the reports of another German court. What he read made him sick with fear and apprehension.

On 24 June 1922, the famous foreign minister of the Weimar Republic, Walter Rathenau, was assassinated after leaving his home in Grunewald. Several months later, in October 1922, Ernst Techow, a 20-year-old student, who had been the driver of the get-away car, went on trial as an accomplice to the murder. The actual assailants, an officer named Erwin Kern and an engineer named Herman Fischer, had committed suicide.

Techow's defense was clear and simple: they had executed the Jew Rathenau because they believed he was a member of the Council of the Elders of Zion, whose aim was to dominate the world. In killing him, Techow argued, the murderers had actually performed a public service by eliminating a member of a group that constituted a danger to the civilized world.

The German judge called Rathenau's murder 'a sacrificial death', and expressed the hope that it would 'serve to purify the infected air of Germany, now sinking in moral sickness and barbarism'. In his outspoken judgment, he called the *Protocols* 'a vulgar libel, which sows in confused and immature minds the urge to murder'.

How had the assassins linked Rathenau to the *Protocols of the Elders of Zion*, Georges wondered. The answer soon became clear.

It had all started at an international conference in Vienna in 1922, where Rathenau quoted a passage from a Christmas article he had written years earlier, on 25 December 1909, for the Viennese *Neue Freie Presse*, entitled 'Unser Nachwuchs', which he later included in his book *Zur Kritik Der Zeit*, published in 1912 in Berlin.

Only a few months earlier, in February 1922, he had accepted the post of foreign minister in the Weimar Republic, ignoring repeated warnings from his mother and his friends, who suspected that his life might be in danger due to anti-Semitic protests against his appointment. He refused to be swayed from his decision and felt confident, since he had held important public office before. At the outbreak of the First World War in 1914, he had resigned his post as head of A.E.G., the largest electronics firm in Germany, to assist Germany first in the War Office and later as economic ad-viser and negotiator on the war reparations in 1919. Through these efforts and a series of books and articles he had published, which were translated into many languages, he gained an international reputation.

Facing the assembled audience in Vienna, he repeated his former warning that Europe's economy was controlled by an elite closed group of financiers. The critical passage was innocent enough. It read as follows:

> In the field of industrial operations wherein each foolish word, each failure can cause ruin, where the public rules by virtue of its control of the stocks and bonds and controls all policies – in this field an oligarchy has come into being, as inaccessible to the outsider and the uninitiated as old Venice. *Three hundred men*, who all know each other, control the economic fate of the European continent and they choose their successors from their own circle.

When his original article and the book had been published, the story of the alleged *Jewish conspiracy* and the *Protocols of the Elders of Zion* had not yet been shared by the Russian Jew-baiters with their partners in other European countries. But when Viennese newspapers reported Rathenau's public address in 1922, with headlines shouting: 'Three hundred men control Europe', young hotheads who had been conditioned for the last two years by repetitious warnings that the Jews were planning to overtake the world saw their chance. The statement by one of the most prominent Jews of his time was tantalizing bait that could be easily used by anti-Semites. They saw their chance and took it.

Little did Rathenau know that by publicly repeating the long-forgotten passage, he was signing his death warrant. The Three Hundred soon became Three Hundred Jews, and, soon thereafter, they became the secret Jewish government, The Elders of Zion.

The German Supreme Court in Leipzig called the *Protocols* 'the Bible of the Rathenau murderers', and stated that: 'Behind the Rathenau murder was fanatical anti-Semitism, which found expression in the libelous legend about the Elders of Zion. This has engendered murderous instincts in the hearts of men.'

In 1922, when Rathenau was assassinated, the German general public knew that it had lost a great leader. Over a million people showed up at his funeral in Berlin. It was said that the German Republic buried him as the Romans buried their dead emperors. But a little more than ten years later, the memorial sign that had been put up at the spot where the murder had taken place was removed by order of the political authorities. At a mass meeting of jurists, a high government official of the Third Reich declared, amidst loud applause, that those who had hitherto been looked upon as murderers would henceforth have their names inscribed as heroes in the Fatherland's roll of honor.

Although there was absolutely no mention of Jews in Rathenau's entire article, the press had clearly abetted this interpretation by alluding to the Three Hundred sometimes as 'Three Hundred Men', sometimes as 'Three Hundred Jews', sometimes as 'Three Hundred Bank Directors' and sometimes as 'Three Hundred Elders of Zion'. It was these distorted interpretations of the innocent words of a great statesman that set him up as a so-called Elder of Zion, and as such, a legitimate target for extermination.

A few weeks after he had found the judgment, Georges was holding an English edition of the *Protocols*, translated by Victor E.

Marsden, formerly the Russian correspondent of the *Morning Post* in London. In 1925, just three years after the outspoken judgment of the German judge, Marsden wrote in his introduction: 'Who, it may be asked, are the *Elders of Zion*? What are their names?' He called them the 'Hidden Hand', and maintained that Walter Rathenau had doubtless been in the possession of the names of the Elders, he 'being, in all likelihood, one of their chief leaders himself'. According to Marsden, The Three Hundred were 'three hundred Jews', and the Learned Elders were 'their General Officers'.

Until now Georges had not grasped how dangerous the *Protocols of the Elders of Zion* really were. Pogroms in Russia were associated in his mind with a different culture and time. They were remote and only relevant to Switzerland as a general warning. But now he was confronted with an actual victim in his own back yard – the first Jew whose blood had been spilled in Germany in a direct link to the *Protocols of the Elders of Zion*.

Pushing aside the pile of library books, Georges started making notes. They would have to explain to the Swiss judge how, instead of traditional religious anti-Semitism that vilified the Jews as Christ-killers, there now existed a form of political anti-Semitism, based on the so-called Jewish conspiracy theory, which depicted the Jews as the greatest danger to world order.

In the early 1930s, as new movements called Fronts began to appear throughout Europe, their main activity was anti-Semitic propaganda. The Jews were the scapegoats blamed for all the current troubles, such as unemployment and inflation. The members of these organizations were in the main young, but they had highly positioned sympathizers, generally army officers and politicians, who envisioned themselves at the forefront of this 'New Europe'. They spoke at public meetings, while the young members served as ushers, resplendent in a kind of uniform of black trousers and white shirts. They used the Nazi salute or something very similar. Nazi parties were openly surfacing in many other parts of the world.

Georges suspected that the Nazis would seize the opportunity to use the Berne courtroom proceedings for their propaganda.

The judge must be made to realize that allowing the publication of the *Protocols* in Switzerland could be tantamount to condoning political assassination. He must convince him that what was happening in neighboring Germany had a direct influence on their own country.

He thought he had exhausted the list of trials. He told his colleagues that he could find no judgment concerning the *Protocols*, and he was not interested in studying more legal proceedings that ended with a settlement. He hoped there would be no offer of compromise this time, he said. Personally he would resolutely oppose any kind of settlement. They needed nothing less than a binding decision by an independent court.

No fear, Lifschitz said, waving his cigar, there will be no offer of retraction this time. With Hitler's rise to power in neighboring Germany, the tactics had changed swiftly and dramatically.

Dr Wiener, who had been studying in a corner the list of trials Georges had prepared, looked up with astonishment. He had just realized that Georges had limited his research to Europe. There was no mention of Henry Ford. What about Ford's two trials, he asked quietly. He reminded them that Ford's version of the *Protocols*, a brochure entitled *The International Jew*, was on sale in every kiosk in Berne, in some of them distributed free of charge. Did they know that this brochure had been translated into 17 languages?

There was a good chance the judge would see it, maybe read it. He would surely ask himself why such an outstanding industrialist had published the *Protocols of the Elders of Zion*.

As much as he did not wish to burden Georges with more work, he must insist that he learn all the facts of Ford's involvement in the matter of the *Protocols*. Fortunately, Wiener said, he had in his archive all the relevant documents.

He was as good as his offer, Georges thought, when he found on his desk one week later a thick portfolio labeled 'Henry Ford and the *Protocols of the Elders of Zion*'.

'Here goes another weekend,' he said to Odette, who had made other plans for both of them.

HENRY FORD'S PRIVATE WAR AGAINST THE JEWS

The year was 1918; the great world war that had claimed millions of victims, disrupted the life of nations, and irrevocably changed the order of things was finally at an end.

On a rainy day in November Henry Ford was driving to Dearborn, his old home town, accompanied by Edwin Pipp, editor of the *Detroit News*. They were on their way to buy a newspaper.

It had not been easy to lure Pipp away from the only newspaper on which he had ever served, where he had worked his way up to the post of editor-in-chief. He was a man of honor and vision, an excellent editor, and Ford decided that Pipp would edit the weekly he was about to acquire.

There was little Ford could not get if he set his heart on it. He used all his charm with Pipp, presenting compelling arguments: the world was in turmoil, he argued, man had his brother man by the throat, or was sticking bayonets into him, or putting dynamite under him, or shooting flames of poisonous gas at him. There was great need for kindliness, he said, and they were going to try to make the world kinder, to spread the gospel of tolerance.

Pipp felt inspired: Ford's words lifted him up above the sphere of a routine existence, opened new vistas. He felt that with this man he could indeed fly high and give vent to his secret aspirations to make a real change in the world. He knew that Ford did not limit his activities to making cars, but this was the first time he was exposed to Ford's electrifying personality and to his ideas. 'I want Dearborn to become known the world over as the place where kindliness is practiced, where the brotherhood of mankind is preached,' Ford declared. The kindly feeling was to include every race and every creed the world over.

This was heady stuff, and Pipp fell easily under Ford's spell. He had but one condition: he must have Billy. Billy had been with him every day that he worked on a daily newspaper, he said; his work was among the finest bits of writing done in America the past 20 years. 'I want his splendid writing in our pages,' he told Ford.

Billy was William Decameron, and Ford had no problem hiring him away from the *Detroit News* too. He told Pipp to go get him, and so Billy came aboard.

Ford had decided some time ago that he needed a newspaper to spread the ideas for which he was becoming known. His mind was set that the base of his journalistic venture must be in the town of his birth, the town that he was planning to make famous. And now the local weekly, the *Dearborn Independent*, was up for sale.

Later, Pipp often wondered at what point he had realized that things had gone sour. He had not been aware of Ford's obsession with the Jews, but it soon became a major issue in their relationship. In the beginning he and Billy were of one mind: 'We did not agree with the Ford notion regarding the Jews before going on the paper, we did not agree with it while on the paper, and we have not agreed with it since,' he later told a friend. His admiration for the man was such that he did not blame him. He was convinced that it was all the fault of Ford's private secretary, Ernest Liebold.

Long after he had resigned from the paper over the Jewish question, Pipp remembered vividly the strange meetings they used to hold. Liebold would tilt back his chair, unbutton his coat, put his thumbs into the armholes of his waistcoat, expand his chest and declare: 'Mr Ford, YOU don't have to think as other men think; YOUR thoughts come to you like a flash, from a subconscious mind, and you have your problems solved.' Ford would straighten up, his shoulders going back a bit, his chin raised, his eyes sparkling. A look of satisfaction would spread over Liebold's countenance. It was the look that comes to a man's face when he feels that he has put something over.

With Liebold the Jews were an obsession. No subject came up in their editorial discussion into which Liebold did not bring the Jews. And Ford would eat it up, in spite of protests from all others who were present. Pipp felt nauseated at these meetings, and Roland, who was associate editor and special writer on the paper, could not contain his anger and used to speak against it fiercely, while Billy would dish up his biting bits of sarcasm, and give vent to expressions of uttermost disgust.

'Oh, the pity of it all!' Pipp would later cry out to Billy, whom he still considered his ally and his friend.

'I recall one occasion,' Pipp later recounted, 'when Roland got back from Mexico. Liebold had been to Mexico before, as Ford expected to start a tractor plant there, and so there was a sort of general conference about it. Roland reported that there was a change of attitude, especially between the Catholic clergy and others. Liebold had a ready explanation, with the Jews at the bottom of it. According to him, the Jew money-lenders of Europe induced the Pope to order his priests in Mexico to do "so and so", and he proceeded with stuff so sickening that one could not listen it out in patience.'

Oh, the hopelessness of it all, Pipp thought. Ford became more and more resentful of any expressions of sanity that might counteract the poison that was being fed to him and that he so readily swallowed. He really believed that the thoughts which Liebold had implanted in his mind had come to him suddenly, from some supernatural source. Liebold called it a 'subconscious mind'. Ford, in plainer terms, called it a 'hunch'.

But Pipp knew that Ford's hunches did not come in 'uncanny' fashion from a 'subconscious' mind. They came from a mind very conscious of what was being done. Flattered by Liebold and at the same time manipulated by him, Ford developed a dislike for Jews, which grew stronger and more bitter as time went on. One way and another, the feeling oozed into his system until it became a part of his living self.

The anti-Jewish tirade in the *Dearborn Independent* started on 22 May 1920, and continued throughout 91 issues of the weekly. The first article proclaimed the message in clear terms:

> There is a race, a part of humanity, which has never yet been received as a welcome part, and which has succeeded in raising itself to a power that the proudest Gentile race has never claimed – not even Rome in the days of her proudest power.

When the first article was still at the printer, and Pipp realized he was powerless to stop it, he submitted his resignation. He did not know that his good friend, Billy Decameron, would sell his integrity and swallow his nausea in order to replace him as editor-in-chief of the *Dearborn Independent*. When he realized that Billy was fully cooperating with Liebold, he was sick to his stomach. Billy was now calling Ford's hunches 'his uncanny way of divining the truth'.

Pipp was so devastated by his short-lived association with Ford and by the betrayal of Billy Decameron that he decided to start his own newspaper, and never again allow himself to be subordinated to another owner. The responsibility would be his and the paper would carry his name: *Pipp's Weekly*.

He reacted to the 'Jew' articles in the *Dearborn Independent* by publishing a series of 'open letters' to Henry Ford. He was sure that if he wrote personal letters they would not even reach Ford's desk, he explained, so he must react publicly. In these open letters, Pipp explained how Ford's newspaper had adopted the theme of the *Protocols of the Elders of Zion*, never bothering to substantiate it with any real proof. He wrote bitterly:

> They assert an international conspiracy and, asked for proof, rail out against the movies. They would have us fear the downfall of our nation as a result of Jewish domination of international affairs and, asked for proof, talk about the 'oriental' mind. They say they are not anti-Semitic and hire detectives to hunt the country over for anything they can run down against any Jew or Jews, individually and collectively, and find that an

owner of a show play once sold theater tickets on the streets of New York. They charge an international conspiracy and, asked for proof, assert that Irvin S. Cobb got his start in life through the financial help of a Jew in Paducah, Kentucky...

At that time, the prevailing thought was that the *Protocols* were a co-production of the Russians and the Germans, as they were so widely distributed in Germany. The true facts about the origin of the document were to be revealed a few months later. Pipp declared that he had no prejudice against Germany, being himself of German origin on both sides of his family. But facts are facts, he wrote, 'the Germans were and are a great nation for propaganda. During the war their printing presses were as busy as their guns. Since the war Germany has turned many of those presses toward the Jew. The Jew is denounced and reviled much after the same fashion that he is being assailed here, only they have gone further in Germany...'

Explaining in his paper why he had resigned from the *Dearborn Independent*, he wrote:

> The stuff against the Jews was being written. It was being read, passed around, re-read, re-written and read again ... the Jews are being blamed for everything. If the wind blew the smoke in the window from the west that was the fault of the Jews; and if the wind blew the dust in from the east that, too, was the fault of the Jews ...'

No honest sane man could live with this, he declared.

In the meantime the articles and editorials in Ford's weekly continued. They accused Jewish leaders, such as Louis Marshall and Louis Brandeis, of using Presidents Taft and Wilson as their puppets. Other prominent Jews were accused of instigating the First World War for the benefit of Jewish bankers, and of fomenting the Russian Revolution to promote racial imperialism. The paper denounced the Jewish conspiracy for corruption on Wall Street, in labor, and on the ball-field. Jews were also allegedly responsible for the Civil War and the assassination of Abraham Lincoln. What Jews could not achieve by money, media or manipulation, they would achieve by pandering to the sexual perversions of the powerful and prominent, the paper warned, claiming their facts came from the plans of the Jewish secret government set out in the *Protocols of the Elders of Zion*.

Ernest Liebold, who was in charge of the campaign, hired spies and private detectives to gather dirt on prominent Jews. The *Protocols* quickly became the cornerstone of Ford's anti-Semitic campaign. Everything was blamed on the Jewish conspiracy, including jazz, short skirts, rolled-down stockings, rising rents, the Bolshevik Revolution, the deterioration of American literature, social conduct, and whatever else came to mind. Later the articles were published in a pamphlet under the title *The International Jew*, or sometimes *The Eternal Jew*, then translated and distributed around the world. The national sales force and assets of the Ford Motor Company were deliberately being used to spread Jew hatred.

In December 1920, the quadrennial convention of the Federal Council of the Churches of Christ in America, attended by delegates representing 30 denominations and 50,000 churches, adopted the following resolution:

> Whereas, for some time there have been in circulation in this country publications tending to create race prejudice and arouse animosity against our Jewish fellow-citizens and containing charges so preposterous as to be unworthy of credence, be it resolved that the Federal Council of the Churches of Christ in America, impressed by the need at this period of our national existence for unity and brotherhood, deplores all such cruel and unwarranted attacks upon our Jewish brethren and in a spirit of good will extends to them an expression of confidence in their patriotism and their good citizenship and earnestly admonishes our people to express disapproval of all actions which are conducive to intolerance or tend to the destruction of our national unity through arousing racial division in our body politic.

On 12 November and again on 10 December 1920, the Jewish journal The *American Hebrew* challenged Ford, suggesting that they present him with 50 names of American leaders from whom he was invited to pick a jury of twelve. They invited Ford to present to this jury his proof of a Jewish world conspiracy. Should the findings of the jury fail to substantiate his charges, he would be bound to admit publicly that he was mistaken and to reveal the influences brought to bear upon him to print the articles in his publication. The decision of the jury was to be published in as many dailies in the United States as the jury may select.

Ford could have saved himself much embarrassment, and the Jews much aggravation, had he responded to the challenge, but he kept silent.

American Jews meanwhile began refusing *en masse* to purchase any vehicle bearing the Ford emblem. In early 1921, the Jewish community in Connecticut held a 400-car parade honoring Albert Einstein and Chaim Weizmann; the parade rules included the proviso 'Positively no Ford machines permitted in line'.

On 16 January 1921, a protest was issued. It was prepared under the initiative of the eminent American author John Spargo, and signed by 119 distinguished Americans, led by Woodrow Wilson, William Howard Taft, William Cardinal O'Connell and others, who protested the introduction into American national life of 'a new and dangerous spirit'. They condemned the anti-Semitic campaign as subversive of American ideals and as 'un-American and un-Christian'. They said that American citizenship and American democracy were challenged and menaced.

Ford's only answer was a statement that he was not attempting to engender race hatred, but to awaken the 'boob Gentiles' against the alleged 'machinations of the Jew'.

When the truth about the forgery of the *Protocols* surfaced, the editor of the *Dearborn Independent* took care not to vouch explicitly for their authenticity. In consultation with Liebold, he devised a tactic of comparing the document with actual events, thus leading the public to draw the desired conclusion, a tactic that later became known as 'the Ford tactic'.

How ingenious, Georges Brunschvig thought, as he studied the Ford file; ignore the authenticity of the document, avoid confrontation with proof of the forgery, and use old anti-Semitic themes to implant in people's minds the idea that the Jewish plan was really being implemented before their very eyes. He had no way of knowing that the defense in the Berne trial was planning to use this same technique in the Swiss courtroom.

The anti-Jewish campaign of the *Dearborn Independent* stopped in January 1922, as suddenly as it had begun. Many speculated that the reason for this move was Ford's ambition to run for president, an ambition encouraged for some time by leading papers such as the *New York Times* and the *Wall Street Journal*. Like many politicians before and after his time, Ford could not ignore the Jewish vote. When his political dream evaporated, he resumed attacking the Jews in April 1924.

On 31 March 1927, the 63-year-old Henry Ford appeared on foot, dazed and bleeding, at the gatehouse that guarded the driveway to his mansion at Fair Lane. He claimed that he had been involved in an accident while driving his Model T. But there were those who strongly suspected that Ford had staged the crash, risking serious injury, by driving himself off the road, to avoid an appearance in court a few hours later, in answer to a subpoena issued at the request of the lawyer of Aaron Sapiro. Sapiro was something of a hero to fruit-growers in the farm belt of California. In 1919, he had devised a plan to refine business and marketing procedures of cooperatives so that farmers could control the market. By 1925, the 'Sapiro Plan' had been adopted by 90 associations in 32 states, as well as in Canada, with a total membership of 890,000 farmers. The value of farm products handled amounted to some $600 million annually. Back in 1924, Sapiro became the target of anti-Semitic attacks in the *Dearborn Independent*, which cried, 'A band of Jewish bankers, lawyers, moneylenders, advertising agencies, fruit pickers, produce buyers, professional office managers, and bookkeeping experts … is on the back of the American farmer.'

Much to Henry Ford's surprise, Sapiro sued for libel. Convinced that nothing was printed without Ford's personal involvement, he chose to name him, not the newspaper, as defendant. He did not count on the editor, William Decameron, willing to perjure himself. In March 1927, Decameron took the stand and testified under oath that he had never discussed any article on any Jew with Mr Ford, that he had never sent his employer an advance copy of the magazine, and that he had never even seen Henry Ford read any of the articles. Decameron maintained this curious position for five whole days.

Having no other proof of Ford's personal involvement, Sapiro's lawyer decided to subpoena Ford himself. But the game was far from over. On his lawyer's advice, Ford used every trick to avoid service of the subpoena. Eventually the server threw it on Ford's lap through the open window, when he stopped his car at an intersection. Ford suffered severe loss of face when the judge summarily rejected his lawyer's argument that the service of the subpoena was faulty, claiming that the document had not actually landed in his client's lap, but slipped to the floor of the car between his knees.

The judge probably resented Ford's attempts to manipulate him, and had his suspicions when Ford's lawyer marched into court on All Fool's Day, 1 April 1927, and presented a doctor's certificate confirming that his client had suffered severe injuries in an accident the previous evening. The judge was compelled to grant a continuance but immediately set a new date.

Having exhausted all the tricks in his lawyer's bag, Ford gave instructions to settle the case. Attacking the Jews was one thing, but perjuring himself in court was out of the question. He was tired of the courts and of the public attacks against him and decided to use this opportunity to settle both claims, that of Sapiro and another one started by Herman Bernstein.

Bernstein was an American journalist, special correspondent of the *New York Times* and the *New York Sun,* a recognized authority on Russia and Russian literature as well as on Jewish matters. He had translated and introduced in America some of the most important works of Leo Tolstoy, Maxim Gorky and Anton Chekhov. He had participated in the famous voyage of the Peace Ship *Oscar II,* organized by Ford. Ford later maintained that it was during this voyage that Bernstein had handed him the *Protocols of the Elders of Zion,* drawing his attention to the book.

I had often wondered what makes a good trial lawyer. Some lawyers come to court well prepared, having studied all the relevant material, having coached their clients and their witnesses, having spent long hours preparing the cross-examination of adverse witnesses, meticulously researching material for their legal arguments, and yet something was clearly missing in their presentation of a case. What is it that separates these lawyers from the really great ones? After many years of watching lawyers in the court arena, I am convinced of the absolute necessity for a trial lawyer to put himself in the judge's place. How true the saying that it is not enough 'to know your case'; you must also 'know your judge'.

The way Georges Brunschvig prepared the Berne case for trial definitely places him in this elite category.

Georges was sure that the name Henry Ford would be one of their biggest obstacles. The man was a living legend; his personal story was famous all over Europe, as were his new Ford automobiles. Surely such a man could not be completely wrong, the judge might feel. It was not only the conscious but also the subconscious that often played a part in a court decision. How would they convince the judge that a man like Ford could stoop to such depths and make such plainly ridiculous allegations. One good example, Georges thought, was the incredible allegation that Herman Bernstein was the source from whom Ford had received the *Protocols of the Elders of Zion.*

As early as February 1921 Herman Bernstein published a book entitled *The History of a Lie – The Protocols of the Wise Men of Zion*, in which he presented the known facts and documents proving that the *Protocols* were completely false. True, at that time the whole truth had not yet been revealed. It was only later in that same year that Princess Radziwill, Armand du Chayla and Philip Graves published their sensational information and discoveries. But Bernstein was familiar with the writings of Herman Goedsche and he had in his possession a copy of the 'Rabbi's Speech'. He was confident that these documents had been used by the forger of the *Protocols*, and in his book he quoted passages from these sources, comparing them to similar passages in the *Protocols*.

In the foreword to his book, Bernstein called the *Protocols* 'a cruel and terrible lie ... an old weapon exhumed from the scrapheap of Russian autocracy ... for the purpose of defaming the whole Jewish people'. Describing, three years after the First World War, the political background that lent prominence to this false document, he wrote:

> In the war's aftermath the Jews are being blamed by the minions of autocracy and reaction for all the ills that have befallen mankind. Some blame them for the war, and others for the peace. Some attack them for the defeat of the German military machine, and others for the victory of the allies. In Germany they are attacked by Junkers for having opposed the submarine warfare and thus assured Germany's defeat; while in some of the allied countries the Jews are denounced for constituting 'the brains of Germany'. All the revolutionary leaders of Germany are credited to the Jews, and bolshevism, which has as little in common with Judaism as it has with Christianity, is branded as a Jewish movement; and there are Jew-baiters who in their blind madness have gone so far as to declare that ex-Kaiser Wilhelm was not only influenced by the Jews but is himself of Jewish descent, and for this reason did not defend Germany as loyally as he should have done. He conspired against the Hohenzollern dynasty and undermined it. He destroyed his own throne because he was serving the secret Jewish world organization.
>
> On such absurdities have people been fed since the armistice, in civilized countries by anti-Semitic agitators and their dupes, while Jews have been slaughtered in the Ukraine, in Poland and in Hungary.

It was this man who was supposed to have furnished Henry Ford with a copy of the *Protocols of the Elders of Zion*.

The *Dearborn Independent* did not mention, or quote, Bernstein's findings.

At a meeting of their group, Georges wondered aloud why the Jewish community in America had not undertaken the costly conduct of a trial and, instead, had left Herman Bernstein no choice but to sue Ford personally. Lifschitz explained that according to Anglo-Saxon law, an individual may be compensated for a libel uttered against him, but there was no way to seek compensation for libels perpetrated against a group or a nation or a people, unless the plaintiff could prove that he himself had suffered damage as a result of the publication. In European countries, which have adopted the French model, a group could sue for libel, and it could do so in criminal proceedings. That was why Bernstein decided that it was his duty to avail himself of the exceptional situation created by the 'private' libel uttered against him, to prove the falsity of the allegations made against the Jewish people. He sued Henry Ford, seeking $200,000 in compensation.

On 30 June 1927 Henry Ford signed a letter of apology and retraction, its phrasing agreed upon at a meeting convened in the house of Bernstein's lawyer, Edwin Untermeyer, at Greystone, Yonkers. Ford was represented by his agent Harry Bennet and by three lawyers: Clifford B. Longley of Detroit, De Lancey Nicoll, Jr. and Martin C. Ansorge of New York.

The plaintiffs had been advised by leaders of the Jewish community that Ford was seeking a truce. They drove a hard bargain. They had waited seven long years for this moment. Ford was constantly consulted over the phone and when his representative told him the situation was pretty bad, he retorted: 'I don't care how bad it is, just settle the cases!'

On 7 July 1927, Ford released to the press his long and detailed apology and pleaded for forgiveness for the wrongs he had done to the Jewish people. It contained the following passage:

> I deem it to be my duty as an honorable man to make amends for the wrong done to Jews as fellow-men and brothers, by asking their forgiveness for the harm I have unintentionally committed, by retracting so far as lies within my power, the offensive charges laid at their door by these publications, and by giving them the unqualified assurance that henceforth they may look

to me for friendship and goodwill. Needless to say that the pamphlets which have been distributed throughout the country and in foreign lands will be withdrawn from circulation, that in every way possible I will make it known that they have my unqualified disapproval, and that henceforth 'The Dearborn Independent' will be concluded under such auspices that articles reflecting upon the Jews will never again appear in its columns.

Shortly afterwards, Ford's advertising agencies were instructed to spend about 12 per cent of the Model A's $1.3 million introductory advertising budget on Yiddish and Anglo-Jewish newspapers. The new Chevrolets were now on the market, and the Jews, who had boycotted Ford's cars, would now put money in his pockets.

Ford also directed that five truckloads of *The International Jew* be burned, and he ordered overseas publishers to cease publication of his book, revoking their rights. But it was too late. The Ford books had been widely distributed all around Europe and it proved impossible to destroy them, let alone prevent their publication and sale. Ford's letters to publishers and distributors in other countries were mostly ignored. One of these letters was addressed to Theodor Fritsch in Leipzig, the German translator of the book and owner of *Hammer Verlag*, which published the German translation. The letter revoked and terminated any rights to publish *The International Jew* in any language, forbidding its publication anywhere under the name of Henry Ford. Fritsch promptly ignored Ford's instructions, claiming that his signature had been forged. No action was taken when the book was later distributed in every school and public institution in Germany, bearing the photographs of Ford and of Hitler, side by side, or distributed, free of charge, in kiosks in Switzerland.

But the plaintiffs, Sapiro and Bernstein, kept their part of the bargain. As part of the settlement, Ford agreed to pay them large sums of money to cover costs and compensation, on the condition that the sums were not to be disclosed. He knew he was dealing with honorable men. Indeed, the sums have remained secret to this day.

Bernstein, who had also received a personal letter of apology from Ford, considered the matter closed. In 1935 he published another book, *The Truth About the Protocols of Zion – A Complete Exposure*, which included new facts that had been revealed since the publication of his first book in 1921. Ford's apology, which had been published in a 1928 edition of his first book, was now absent. The Ford episode was not even mentioned.

What a forgiving people we Jews are, Georges mused. In spite of all he had done to them, the Jews in America were ready to vindicate him and take his forced apology at face value. On 23 May 1929, a testimonial dinner was held in honor of David A. Brown, publisher of *The American Hebrew*, in tribute to his humanitarian services. Henry Ford attended and posed for a photograph with the honoree. The caption under the picture, published in the Jewish journal, stated: 'Mr Ford's presence at that function, amidst Jewish spokesmen of the highest type, attested his inherent friendship for our people.'

Hitler used Ford's book throughout his reign of terror, and kept Ford's photograph on his desk. He once told an American reporter: 'I regard Heinrich Ford as my inspiration.' Passages from Ford's book *The International Jew* were actually incorporated in Hitler's *Mein Kampf* and served as the credo of the Nazis. There is no evidence that Ford tried to intervene, even when Germany was still accessible to Americans. Editions of Ford's book still appear periodically in various countries.

Ford's apology should indeed be presented to the Berne court, Georges decided, but he knew it had little probative value. Little by little, the size of his task became clearer in his mind. There were no real precedents, he realized. It was up to this small group in Berne to prove for the first time in a court of law that the *Protocols of the Elders of Zion* were a blatant forgery, which actually threatened Jewish lives everywhere.

How dare he, a young inexperienced lawyer, presume to represent the Jewish people. What if they failed? Wouldn't the lawyer be blamed? How would he live with himself if the judge were to rule in favor of the defendants? What if the court ruled that the *Protocols* were authentic? Who had empowered them to risk a possible judgment that could be used against Jews around the world?

He thought about Professor Matti, unquestionably a brilliant jurist, but could a non-Jew realize the full responsibility and the danger to his people? His mother had once told him that no man could ever understand the pains of childbirth. This must be experienced to be understood, she had said. Was it the same with anti-Semitism, he wondered. Was not the emotional involvement emanating from personal experience, fundamentally different from the intellectual understanding? One thing became certain in his mind: he could not turn back. He wondered when he would again sleep peacefully, free of nightmares.

It was at the first preliminary session of the trial, on 16 November 1933, that the plaintiffs learned that their prayers had been answered. They had been assigned a fair-minded, unbiased judge. Georges had his first encounter with the defendants: Herr Silvio Schnell, publisher of the *Protocols*, Herr Georg Haller, editor of the Nationalsozialistisher newspaper *Eidgenosse*, and its publisher Herr Theodor Fischer, and the architect Walter Aebersold, a prominent member of the National Front.

They started by denying personal responsibility, shifting it from one to another. Haller said that it was not he but Theodor Fischer from Zurich who was responsible for publications such as the newspaper *Eidgenosse*. Aebersol maintained that it was Silvio Schnell who was responsible for the distribution of the *Protocols of the Elders of Zion*.

One of the defendants, Dr Meyer, looked distinctly uncomfortable, the judge noted. He was not surprised when later in the day, as soon as the court session had ended, this defendant submitted to the court a formal statement that he had severed all ties with the *Eidgenosse* and had never participated in the process of its editing or distributing. The newspaper was not connected with the *Protocols*, but had been included in the complaint because of an article it had published, warning all blonde Swiss maidens about the filthy Jews, who were all presented as potential sexual offenders. The judge decided to clarify this immediately. If any defendant had been included by mistake he should be excused at this stage.

He began by questioning Theodor Fischer, but soon realized that he could not expect much cooperation.

J: Could you please tell me who ordered the distribution of the *Protocols of the Elders of Zion* at the meeting in Berne on 13 June?

F: No.

J: Is it correct that the meeting was arranged by the National Front?

F: Is that so? I have no idea.

J: Is the *Eidgenosse* the newspaper of your Front?

F: *The Bund Nationalsozialistischer Eidgenosse.*

J: Are you the publisher of this newspaper?

F: Yes.

J: Who ordered a certain number of issues for distribution at the 13 June meeting?

F: We usually send a certain number of issues to Berne.

J: To whom are these issues addressed?

F: They are sent for sale on the street.
J: But to whom are they addressed?
F: To the local group.
J: Who actually receives it?
F: The postal authority.
J: (in a resigned tone) I cannot summon a postal authority.

Aebersold denied membership of the group at the relevant time.

The only one who proudly admitted to having distributed the *Protocols of the Elders of Zion* was Silvio Schnell.

Nobody would be excused at this stage, the judge announced.

Professor Matti spoke first, making it very clear that the plaintiffs would not enter into political discussions. They were only interested in proving that the defendants published false and obscene material, in contravention of an existing law. The court would render a great service to humanity by stating the falsehood of the *Protocols,* and to make it completely objective he suggested that non-Jewish experts be appointed. Georges Brunschvig concurred.

The defendants demanded immediate dismissal of the complaint. The judge was not competent to rule on the issue of the authenticity of the *Protocols,* their lawyers said. This was a matter for historians, not for jurists. They also argued that the paragraph concerning obscene literature did not apply.

Both arguments were rejected by the judge. He would allow evidence and later rule on the issue of the authenticity of the *Protocols.* The interpretation of the legal paragraph was a matter to be decided in the final judgment.

Brunschvig and Matti could hardly contain their joy.

The judge then announced that he would appoint a court expert and invited the litigants to appoint their own experts. He had already formulated the questions the experts would have to answer:

1. Are the *Protocols of the Elders of Zion* a forgery?
2. Are they a plagiarism?
3. If they are, what was their source?
4. Are they 'obscene literature?'

The lawyer for the defense, Dr Ursprung, wished to be heard on the matter of experts.

U: The expert should be an Aryan, not only a Christian, for this is a question of race rather than religion.

J: I shall appoint a person who has some knowledge of the matter

U: Yes, but not a Jew.

J: Would 14 days be enough for you to find an Aryan expert?

J: The litigants have 14 days to appoint experts. I shall appoint an independent expert, whose qualifications will be expertise rather than race. I shall find a scholar who will give his opinion without hatred or discrimination.

The stage was set for the Berne trial and the rules were defined. They could not have guessed that it would take the court 17 months to announce its judgment. That same evening the group met in Professor Matti's office to discuss strategy. They decided to start compiling a list of possible witnesses. Lifschitz suggested that they start with three names: Katerina Radziwill, Armand du Chayla and Philip Graves. Preparing their testimony was the next assignment for Georges Brunschvig.

4 Unmasking the Myth

KATERINA RADZIWILL

Three years after the Revolution, Katerina Radziwill still felt that her stay in New York was temporary. Like many of her compatriots who had escaped to the West, she kept alive the hope that all was not lost, that one day soon Russia would awaken from the Bolshevik nightmare. Although the Romanov dynasty was gone for ever, somehow Russia would find a way to establish a sane political system that would enable all of them to go home. She missed her beloved, glorious St Petersburg, where she had enjoyed a civilized existence of tea parties, dinners, concerts, the ballet and theater, breathtaking ceremonies, good conversation, and, yes, delicious gossip and political intrigue. But in her heart, she knew that it was gone for ever. The Russia she loved was no more.

She often thought that nations, like men, sometimes experienced a premonition of what was about to happen to them. She remembered the premonition that hung in the air of festive Moscow on that sunny Sunday following Bloody Saturday in May 1896. The young Tsar Nikolai II had just been crowned, and the glorious ceremonies and processions that drew masses of Russians from all parts of the empire, plus members of the nobility, diplomats, journalists and hordes of guests from around the world, were still in full swing. Gala performances and huge balls were yet to be held, the ladies getting ready to parade the dresses that had taken months of preparation by expert seamstresses both at home and abroad. She could still recall in detail all the outfits she herself had spent so much time designing, the silk, velvet and the gold lamé; the intricate embroidery that went into the bodices, the jewelry removed from the vaults, ready for public display.

She had been promenading with friends on that fateful Sunday, fascinated by the endless procession of elegant carriages. Suddenly they noticed on the shoulder of the road a long line of carts carrying what turned out to be injured men and mutilated bodies for burial. Cries of women and children filled the air. There had been no official announcement, but it was quickly revealed by word of mouth that a terrible disaster had caused the death of thousands, and injury to many more, on the Khodynka Field. Originally an area that served as a training ground for the Moscow Garrison, it had been poorly prepared to handle the half a million citizens who had assembled for the popular festivities. They packed into an impossible mass, and in their eagerness to gain access to the promised gifts and refreshments, trampled each other to death.

Journalists, officials, politicians and diplomats, all hurried out to Khodynka to report and to assist. The widower empress and many other ladies did not even stop to change their outfits as they rushed to the hospitals to offer help in caring for the wounded. Not so the royal couple. Their majesties, the newly crowned Tsar of All the Russias Nikolai II, and his wife, now officially the Empress Alexandra Fedorovna, decided on a policy of 'business as usual'. The planned festivities continued, the tsar and tsarina attending the balls, one hosted by the French ambassador and the other by the tsarina's sister Elisaveta Fedorovna, the wife of the tsar's uncle, Grand Prince Sergei Alexandrovich, governor-general of Moscow. A gala performance at the Bolshoi theater played to a house packed with nobility. It was this Bloody Saturday and the days that followed that marked in the memory of the princess the beginning of the end. She remembered a man standing beside her in the street as they watched the ongoing festivities, whispering in her ear: 'Look at them, they are beginning to climb the road of their future Calvary!'

These events, as fresh in her mind as the day they happened, suddenly brought to consciousness the decision she had to make. On an impulse she rose and, fishing a crumpled piece of paper out of her purse on which a friend had scribbled the telephone number of *The American Hebrew*, called this Jewish weekly in New York. At a party the previous week she had divulged to a circle of friends her astounding revelation. She had no idea what to do with the information she possessed. Going to the press was not a solution that came easily to the mind of somebody who had grown up in a dictatorial autocratic monarchy, like tsarist Russia.

She had spent most of her life in a society that at best tolerated, and at worst instigated, active anti-Semitism. General Cherevin, head of the Okhrana, the empire's secret police, the body most responsible for the suffering imposed on the Jews, had been one of her closest friends, as were other Okhrana operatives whom she had known in France. She had been a welcome guest at small parties in the famous salon of Juliette Adam in Paris, where she came to know Edouard Drumont, the champion of French anti-Semitism. There she witnessed many heated discussions concerning the Dreyfus affair throughout the late 1890s, but seldom took part in them. She wondered how many active Jew-baiters had been welcome guests in her own salon, which had operated during various periods in Berlin, Paris and St Petersburg. Hating the Jews had been routine in tsarist Russia. Discrimination against various groups was part of life; the pogroms had happened far away from the capital. She herself had never witnessed one. They had been mentioned in whispers but never discussed at dinner tables. The Jews were simply not her concern.

Her indifference toward anti-Semitism had begun to change during her stays in England and in America where she had met some Jews, and was surprised to realize that they were not regarded as inferiors. On the recommendation of a close friend, she had even entrusted her health to a Jewish doctor in whom she now had full confidence. She knew very little about Jews and she was not sure she wanted to become involved in publicly defending them. But still, there was that nagging feeling which wouldn't leave her. She felt that by suppressing the proof she possessed she would somehow become an accessory to a crime, the consequences of which could be very dangerous. And, of course, she had to admit to herself, she was also not averse to publicity.

She was beginning to make a name for herself in the West as a writer on matters Russian and European. The previous year she had published her book *Secrets of Dethroned Royalty*, and she was already planning a major work, to be published seven years later under the title *The Last Tsarina*, which dealt not only with Empress Alexandra Fedorovna, but with the whole period that marked the closing chapter of Romanov dynasty rule.

She knew she possessed exclusive information on a matter that was raising much excitement in the press. Going to press was not a solution that came easily to mind of somebody who had grown up in a dictatorial autocratic monarchy such as tsarist Russia, but she felt she had no choice. Making her decision she called the editor of *The*

American Hebrew, a Jewish weekly published in New York, and arranged to meet him the very next day, 20 February 1921.

Katerina Radziwill had been a princess in her own right even before her marriage to Prince Radziwill in 1872. Her nondescript husband was better known as the brother of Anton Radziwill, the famous friend of Bismarck, who had taken part in the German-French war. She came from an old aristocratic family and her father had served as adjutant-general to the tsar. She was a great beauty and a famous adventuress, the subject of much juicy gossip. Married to an insignificant man, she was known for various liaisons with men of power. The most notorious, no doubt, was General Cherevin, head of the secret police, the Okhrana, during the rule of Tsar Alexander III. The general was her ticket to St Petersburg high society. She had tried to meddle in politics, but after the general's death she had lost most of her influence and some scandalous gossip had surfaced that compelled her to leave Russia. In her prime, she had been a famous hostess and had entertained many men of power. She had been the recipient of many secrets. Her outstanding memory and the notes she kept served her well in her new role as an author.

Preparing for her meeting with the editors of *The American Hebrew*, she realized that she might be disbelieved, as she had no proof, no document, only memory. But she could produce a witness. She suddenly remembered Henriette, whom she had met by chance some time ago in New York, but never bothered to look up again. They had been quite friendly in those days in Paris, when they had been part of the crowd that gathered around some of the Okhrana agents operating in the French capital. They were drawn to this group for different reasons. While she was nurturing a personal relationship with Golovinskii, the assistant to the famous Piotr Rachkovskii, the Okhrana's chief agent in Europe, Henriette Hurblut, was there for ideological reasons.

Descended from a French mother and an English father, Henriette Hurblut was married to an ultra-conservative American. She and her husband agreed on political matters, and a close liaison with the Russian agents was what they needed to nurture their extremist outlook. On many occasions Henriette appeared unaccompanied either at Golovinskii's apartment or at the small intimate gatherings hosted by Princess Radziwill at her house on the Champs Elysée.

Golovinskii had always been welcome at these gatherings, entertaining Radziwill's guests with amusing stories. They were all familiar with his occupation and were thrilled when he lowered his voice, pretending to take them into his confidence, as he recounted stories of espionage and international intrigue.

The princess had become Matvei Golovinskii's friend innocently enough. His mother had been a large landowner in the Ufa river region in the southern Ural Mountains, where she had also possessed property at that time. Thus, when he called on her one day in Paris, she received him socially as an emissary of his mother, not yet aware of his service in the Russian secret police. A close relationship developed.

One day stood out distinctly in her memory. She and Henriette were part of a small, intimate group having tea in his apartment. Putting on his most clandestine expression, Golovinskii made them swear to absolute secrecy. He then ceremoniously unlocked a drawer and proceeded to remove a simple notebook of the kind commonly used by students. She immediately noticed that it had a blue ink stain on its cover page, and wondered who had been so sloppy and what could possibly be the importance of such a stained, shabby specimen. The inside pages, which she remembered very clearly, were yellow-tinged and covered with handwritten text. What surprised her most was the fact that the writing had obviously been done by various hands. It also puzzled her why a Russian agent would show them a manuscript drafted in the French language.

This strange, crudely drafted document, together with the secretive behavior of their host, had aroused their curiosity immensely. With great drama, Golovinskii boasted, a mischievous smile washing over his face, that this fabricated manuscript, which he and his colleagues were forging on behalf of Rachkovskii, would implicate the Jews in an international conspiracy and would one day revolutionize the world. It was to be called the *Protocols of the Elders of Zion*. This was but the first measure to fight this conspiracy, he proclaimed, the objective being the wholesale expulsion of the Jews from Russia.

She remembered how she and the other guests had laughed at the whole affair, but Golovinskii had been quite serious and seemed very proud of his achievement.

At the time, she had no idea that Golovinskii's concocted forgery was connected in any way to another document that General Cherevin had entrusted to her years ago, and which had been lost together with all her possessions in Russia. She later learned that Sergei Nilus had incorporated Golovinskii's manuscript in his famous book, published by the press of the Red Cross in Tsarskoe Selo.

She had dismissed and all but forgotten the incident, until she learned, a few years later, that such a document had indeed surfaced in Russia and was being used for anti-Jewish propaganda. She had not been surprised, since forgeries were often used by the Okhrana for their unholy purposes. In her circle nobody took such forgeries seriously; they were seen as good fodder for inciting the Cossacks and the *moujiks* against the Jews. So much for Golovinskii's boastful scheme of revolutionizing the world, she had thought. But that was then, before the Revolution. And now, in America, quite a few years later, she suddenly noticed the *Protocols of the Elders of Zion* displayed prominently in bookstore windows, in English. She also heard people discussing his document at social gatherings and noted that it was being debated in the press.

To her utter amazement, she realized that the book was now considered to be authentic, that people were actually talking about the Jewish conspiracy, even quoting from these *Protocols*. In Russia, she mused, the book had passed almost unnoticed, and, as far as she knew, had since been entirely forgotten.

In preparation for her appointment, she decided to read the *Protocols*, a friend having furnished her with a copy. As she read she was again convinced that she was dealing not with one but with two forged documents, and that she was probably the only living person who had held both documents in her hands. She felt again she had an obligation to reveal the truth.

The editor, Isaac Landman, and his assistant were at first skeptical. Katerina Radziwill's story was completely new. Two important books about the *Protocols* were about to be published, but they did not contain the information she was supplying. In America, Herman Bernstein, the well-known writer and diplomat, was publishing *The History of a Lie*, which would prove that Russian agents had based their forgery on a fiction composed by the German writer, Herman Goedsche, posing as an Englishman. And in England, the well-known Jewish scholar Lucien Wolf was about to publish *The Myth of the Jewish Menace*. Was it possible, the editor must have asked himself, that these important writers, who had done so much research, had no inkling of the facts the princess was now disclosing?

Indeed, some versions mentioned that the manuscript of the *Protocols* had been prepared in France, but it had not even been published in that country until 1920, as a translation from the Russian. Why would anyone go to the trouble of forging a document in

French if it was not intended for publication in that language? Why would Russian forgers not use their own language? Who would believe that Russians in Paris had forged a document in French to be published in Russia in the Russian language? It all seemed illogical and unrealistic. This was a very complicated text, and it was inconceivable that some Russian agents had written it in a stained exercise book in different handwritings. From what she told them about Golovinskii, it stretched the imagination that he could have participated in the fabrication of such a complicated manuscript. After all, he was surely an agent, not a writer.

They knew that if the Jews were suspected of publishing false unsubstantiated information, it would only serve as oil on the wheels of the anti-Semites, who were even now having a field day with this document. Yes, they were intrigued by her story, but they would need some corroboration. Too much was at risk.

Yet the story could not be ignored. This was not a silly woman with an over-developed imagination. She was sitting upright in her chair, her hands clasped in front of her. Her hair was piled high on her head in the current fashion. She was wearing an elegant simple suit, her neck adorned by a single string of pearls. She was so sure of herself, so confident in her demeanor, so dignified in her behavior, so persuasive and, most of all, so knowledgeable in describing the intricacies of pre-revolutionary Russian politics and intrigues, that little by little she won their confidence. They came to realize that this was indeed explosive, first-hand information.

There was no way of corroborating the first part of her story about the document, which had never been mentioned before, so their strategy was to concentrate on Golovinskii's tea party.

They would find Henriette Hurblut, and if their stories matched, they would publish Princess Radziwill's complete account.

Four days later, on 25 February 1921, the full interview with Princess Radziwill appeared in *The American Hebrew*. In it the Princess revealed, for the first time, that the *Protocols of the Elders of Zion* had their beginnings in Russia in 1884, many years before their publication by Nilus. They had originally been created to serve a political purpose following the assassination of Tsar Alexander II, and were again dragged out for public display for similar political ends on the eve of the first Russian Revolution in 1905.

This beautiful, elegant woman told the most amazing story in a forthright manner, concentrating on the essentials:

After the assassination of Alexander II, his son and successor, Alexander III, took very much to heart the fact that the murder of his father had been planned and executed entirely by Russians belonging to the better classes ... The inner clique of the ultra-conservative party, however, made every effort to convince Alexander that the assassination of his father was accomplished not at the hands of Russians, but through the machinations of the Jews, who, they said, were planning a general conspiracy to destroy all the monarchs of the earth. It was General Orzhevskii, then the head of the Third Section of Police of the Russian State Department, who was determined to convince his emperor of this by fraud and forgery. Years afterwards, for the poor, weak Nikolai II, this forgery was developed into the *Protocols of the Elders of Zion*. Orzhevskii, in pursuance of his bold stroke, sent agents to Paris to prepare the fake documents. They did their work with care and cunning. They searched old books, compiled citations from Jewish philosophers and ransacked the records of the French Revolution for abstracts of the most inflammatory speeches. All this and more they did with the sole object of attempting to prove that the Jewish people were a gang of murderers, aspiring to overthrow the Russian social order, of which Alexander II was the head. General Orzhevskii of the Third Section had no personal connection to the tsar. Realizing this he attempted to reach the emperor through the person of General Cherevin, the head of the Okhrana, whose duty it was to guard the person of the emperor. Cherevin, however, refused to lend himself to the plot and as a result, perhaps, Orzhevskii soon resigned his post. The Paris report, that is, the draft of the forgery, remained in the archives of the Third Section. General Cherevin also, I know, retained a copy, which he included in his memoirs. The original manuscript of this book he left in his will to Tsar Nikolai II. A copy he gave to me. I was one of his closest and dearest friends. And once again, following the Japanese War and at the beginning of the first Russian Revolution [1905], Russian secret agents and police officials, with Grand Prince Sergei at their head, attempted to allay the fears of their emperor, this time Nikolai II. Anything to prove that the Russians were not dissatisfied with his rule was demanded. Someone then recalled the old Orzevskii document, stored in the archives of the Third Section. It was brought forth and read. It would do.

Agents were dispatched to Paris with instructions to develop and enlarge the original into a better and more modern form. I recall the men who took up this task. There was the too-famous Rachkovskii. He was the head of the Russian secret police in Paris. Manasevich-Manuilov was another. This man later yielded a great influence on Prime Minister Sturmer. He was also one of those who used the infamous Rasputin for their own special aims and ambitions. Then there was also Matvei Golovinskii.

At this point, the princess recounted her meeting with Golovinskii in Paris. It was only last night, she confessed, that she had actually made the connection between the Orzhevskii document and the Golovinskii manuscript, and everything suddenly became very clear to her.

The editors, mesmerized by her story, believed her now, but they also felt it imperative to find Henriette Hurblut, knowing that their readers would lack the advantage of being exposed, as they had been, to the electrifying, creditable presence of the Princess.

When they did locate her, Henriette Hurblut was initially unwilling to discuss the subject. An admitted anti-Semite, she would not even consider the thought of being seen in the offices of *The American Hebrew*. Finally she relented, reluctantly agreeing to see them at her home. She was anti a lot of things, she told the interviewers, but principally she was anti-Jewish. Her home was adorned with pictures and paintings of many notables; among them there was a large photograph of Count Spiridovich, the unabashed Russian anti-Semite who had recently come to America.

Not surprisingly, given her avowed sentiments, Mrs Hurblut was not too communicative. But, she agreed that if she found herself in a position to shed light on the origin of a base forgery, she would not withhold her corroboration of the truth.

'Yes,' she said, after the facts disclosed by Princess Radziwill had been communicated to her, 'I recall the incident perfectly. I have known for some time that the *Protocols* and the Orzhevskii manuscript are one and the same, and I can substantiate Princess Radziwill's account in every detail.' She had never seen the original Orzhevskii document, but suspected that Golovinskii was enlarging it and using it in his new fabrication, as Princess Radziwill had explained.

With that, she felt she had divulged enough to satisfy her sense of honor, and wanted them out of her house as quickly as possible. But they would not settle for a general statement of corroboration and pressed her for more details from her own experience. She resisted at first, but their questions brought to mind long-forgotten events. As these memories rose to consciousness, she smiled, and began recalling the image of the Russian secret service agent, proudly parading about in the homes of the nobility as the hero of a cleverly devised plot, one calculated to deceive his emperor and destroy the Jews.

'Golovinskii was very proud of his "work",' she reflected. 'He never hesitated to boast about it. He would come to the home of Mme Radziwill in the Champs Elysée from the Bibliothèque Nationale, where the compilation was made, carrying the sheets of the document with him.

'I remember when he showed us the completed document. It was written in French, but in different handwritings. It was on a yellowish paper and bound with a white ribbon. There was a big blue inkspot on the first page.

'I am anti-Semitic, you know,' she now declared. 'When I heard and read about the *Protocols of the Elders of Zion* I got a copy at the time. I had not connected this book with my friends in Paris. But the minute I opened the book, "Ha, ha!" I said, "here is my old friend Golovinskii." There is no doubt about the identity of the Golovinskii document and the *Protocols*.

'We, Katerina Radziwill and myself,' she added, 'we know that the so called *Protocols of the Elders of Zion* are nothing but a crude forgery. We know that they were fabricated for the sole purpose of inciting feelings against the Jews. We never doubted that this "outstanding document" had been invented by the functionaries of the Russian Okhrana with full cooperation of the "pogrom-provocateurs". So, Princess Radziwill and myself were not surprised and not astounded ... we were familiar with the ways of the Okhrana.'

As was made perfectly clear, she was no lover of Jews. To her mind, the Jews were bad enough, but forgeries of this kind were not needed. They would only discredit those, who like herself, believed the Jews were a negative element in society.

Three weeks after the publication of the interview with Princess Radziwill, on 15 March 1921, *The American Hebrew* published the interview with Henriette Hurblut.

ARMAND ALEXANDER DU CHAYLA

Almost two months later, Armand Alexander du Chayla was also faced with a difficult decision.

He had been lucky to have a home to come back to, after the termination of his 'Russian period'. Unlike some of his Russian compatriots, who hoped that their exile from Russia was only temporary, he knew in his heart that his return to France was probably permanent. He would have liked to share their hopes, recalling with fondness his love for the Russian people, and his service in the Russian army, which had brought him into close contact with men of all classes and all parts of the empire. Nevertheless, his knowledge of Russian culture and religion, subjects on which he wrote and lectured, his intellectual disposition and innate sense of honesty all combined to prevent him from entertaining false hopes and optimistic dreams.

He had mixed feelings about the new regime in Russia. He was not a socialist and opposed many aspects of Soviet rule, but he had to admit that it as also doing some good for the Russian people, who had suffered terribly under the tsarist regime.

He had left France, his country of origin, when he abandoned the Catholic faith to embrace Russian Orthodoxy. He loved Russia with all his heart and had hoped to be part of it for ever. He had fought and been decorated as a captain in the Russian army, and proudly carried with him the cross of St George, awarded him for outstanding service. In the army, he had risen from being the commander of a transport division of infantry in 1914 to become head of a political department responsible for diplomatic relations in the headquarters of the Donau Army, where he had been at the start of the Revolution in 1917. After his evacuation from the Crimea, he spent four desolate months in Constantinople, and was then ready, at the age of 36, to begin a new chapter in his life.

He was strolling in the Place Bellecour in Lyon, on a beautiful spring morning, when he noticed a book displayed in the window of a large bookstore. A sense of total disbelief enveloped him and he found himself walking into the store, where he immediately purchasd the book.

Returning home by the shortest route, he spent the rest of that glorious morning examining a document that he had hoped never to see again. He did not actually need to read the so-called *Protocols of the Elders of Zion*. He had read the document in Russia some twelve years earlier, and although he was aware of its French origin, he had no idea it had ever appeared in print in the French language. From his research and military experience he knew it was propaganda meant for consumption by ignorant Russian *moujiks*. He also knew that it had been fabricated by cynical *agents provocateurs* of the old Russian regime and exploited by mystics and occultists who had abounded in Russia at the time. It seemed incredible that this scandalous fabrication would now be published in France and presented as authentic to an unsuspecting public.

The publisher was one Msgr Jouin, whose long introduction du Chayla now read with growing astonishment. It dealt with the 'history' of the document and discussed the character of the 'famous Russian' who had first revealed and published it.

'A famous Russian, indeed!' du Chayla exclaimed to himself. Through his mind flashed the image of Sergei Nilus, as he had first seen him 12 years before in the monastery Optina Pustyn, a tall, wide-shouldered, typical Russian. Although he was only 45 years old, his beard had already turned gray. Du Chayla could never forget Sergei's characteristic appearance – the high boots, the Russian peasant shirt with its high collar unbuttoned on the left and gathered at the waist with a colorful cord-like belt embroidered with words from a prayer. He vividly recalled the blue, deep-set, piercing eyes, with their mystic, somewhat veiled look. What an impressive hulk of a man, he had thought at the time. He now remembered him fondly, with even a feeling of nostalgia, although they had clashed on almost every subject, their discussions always turning into heated argments.

Nilus was indeed an 'authentic' Russian of the kind that was not so rare in those days, he thought. He was a simple soul, with strange beliefs, unshakable prejudices, unlimited love for his motherland, and a total, uncritical, unswerving dedication to its royal ruler. Beyond that, he had been possessed by a fervent, mystic religiousness divorced from any modern concept, but which did not prevent him from partaking freely in the joys of the flesh. He tried not to label this impassioned Russian as a mere fanatic, but in his heart he knew that the man had been completely out of touch with reality, that his confused ramblings occasionally bordered on insanity. Still, he could never forget the warm hospitality of the man's household, where he had always been welcome on a cold night, or the memorable walks they had taken together along the banks of the Zhizdra. As they crossed the rich forest terrain, du Chayla could never successfully catch up with Nilus, who strode ahead waving his arms and talking animatedly, unconscious of the fact that his guest was trailing behind. Once in a while, when he would stop to let him catch up, Nilus would flash him a big smile and continue his argument as if there had been no interruption. The two women who accompanied them always lagged far behind.

His sense of nostalgia was probably directed to that period in his life rather than to the man Nilus. What a wonderful time he had had in Optina Pustyn. He had been invited to lecture on the Russian religion in the Academy of Sciences in St Petersburg and was doing research on the subject. He remembered that it had been the late Mitropolits Antonii from St Petersburg who had advised him to do his research at Optina Pustyn, the famed monastery near the city of Kozelsk, in the district of Kaluga. The nine months he had spent there, beginning in January 1909, were among his most instructive and enjoyable. His meetings with Nilus at the time, though frequently irritating or downright disturbing, were part of the fond memories he carried away with him from the monastery. Now, in reflection, he could reappraise the man in a more benevolent light than he had ever done in the past.

Optina was at that time a center of spiritual and intellectual life in Russia. Du Chayla had great respect for the elders of the monastery. They had nothing in common with some swindlers who posed as 'elders', such as the infamous Rasputin, and others who contributed so largely to the downfall of the last tsar. The real elders were well-educated men, great spiritual leaders, filled with love for their fellow men, who preached tolerance and understanding and were not afraid to stand up to officialdom. It had been the spirit of these elders and the still existing tradition of Church culture, that had drawn to Optina Pustyn Russian intellectuals interested in religious research. The correspondence between the elders and authors such as Gogol and Dostoevsky were still preserved among the precious books and documents in the monastery's renowned library. Father Ambrosji, one of the best-known Optina elders, famous for his mystic teachings, had been immortalized by Dostoevsky in the figure of Father Zosima, the colorful character in *The Brothers Karamazov*. Tolstoy had lived there briefly and became so fascinated by the monastery that he planned to spend there the last days of his life, doing menial work, on the condition that he would not be required to officially enter the Church. At 82, feeling he was about to die, he made his daughter promise to help him fulfill this last wish. Forewarned that his move to Optina was opposed by official circles who were on his track, he secretly traveled to the provinces with his daughter, hoping to evade his pursuers, but fell mortally ill at the station of Astapovo.

There, in the station master's house, he died at 6 a.m. on 20 November 1910. On the daughter's insistence no final rites were administered.

These and other stories ran through du Chayla's mind as he recalled his years at Optina Pustyn.

On arrival at the monastery, he had found some 400 inhabitants leading simple lives, who alternated between working the fields and receiving religious and spiritual instruction from the elders. The main buildings were built of stone, and consisted of six churches, a hotel, a house for visiting pilgrims and a hospital. The villas surrounding the main buildings were occupied by laymen who sought to be associated with the monastery for one reason or another. Archimand Xenophont, the chief administrator, had shown him the villa he would occupy for the duration of his stay and introduced him to Nilus, his next-door neighbor.

His Russian had still been imperfect, so he had been pleased to meet a man who spoke such fluent French and gratefully accepted an invitation to tea that same evening. The spacious ten-room villa that stood in an orchard was home to the Nilus 'family' of three, consisting of Sergei, his wife Elena Alexandrovna Ozerova, and Nataliia Komarovskaia, with whom Nilus had cohabited for many years before his marriage and who was now too sick to live alone. They all lived in four rooms of the villa on Ozerova's pension from the Imperial Palace, which also supported the hostel that occupied the rest of the villa and served as a home for cripples, and mentally ill people, who came there in hope of a miraculous cure.

The family rooms were furnished in traditional style, the walls hung with autographed paintings of grand princes. The large library was filled with books on many subjects and a private chapel served for family prayers. The villa's special atmosphere was indelibly imprinted on du Chayla's mind. He fondly remembered his contacts with that bizarre household, which he was eventually compelled to sever on later visits to the monastery due to Nilus's extreme intolerance of anybody who did not share his views.

From their first meeting, they had disagreed on almost every subject. They were both deeply religious, but each of them regarded religion from vastly different viewpoints. Nilus, dedicated to his anarchistic ideals, preached the negation of all modern culture, opposed all scientific methods of research, adopting and promoting instead the most primitive 'moujik' interpretation of orthodox religion.

Modern culture, to him, was a desecration of everything that was holy, a harbinger of the coming of the Antichrist. Du Chayla's methods of research were repugnant to him but, conscious of the respect the elders of the monastery displayed towards this stranger, he curbed his intolerance during du Chayla's initial stay in the monastery and instead, argued with him endlessly, hoping to convert him to his own way of thinking.

And now he had to make a decision. The book he was still holding in his hands was, to du Chayla's knowledge, a crude forgery that had caused great misery to the Jews in Russia. It was well known in Russia that the Okhrana had used the *Protocols* to promote pogroms with the full consent and encouragement of palace circles. Yet St Petersburg society had ignored the document, not even bothering to discuss it seriously. How puzzling, he thought, that a document he knew to have been composed in France, in the French language, was now being presented in France as a translation from the Russian.

The conflict that stalled his decision lay in the fact that he had enjoyed this man's hospitality, had been befriended by the women of the household, and according to his code of ethics, it would be unthinkable to publish information related to him in private while visiting them. But from the moment he had laid eyes on this book, he knew in his heart that he could not keep silent. He might be in a unique position to publish the truth. The famous words of Aristotle sprang to mind: *Amicus Plato, sed magis amica veritas* (Plato is a friend, but the truth is a greater one). He had to reveal the truth, he decided – he had a moral obligation to do so.

It had been on his second visit to Nilus's villa that the question of the Jews had first come up in their discussions. They were strolling in the forest when they encountered a man out walking with his friend. The man was asking Nilus for directions as the women caught up with them. Ozerova immediately volunteered that the man had been seen talking to a Jewish chemist from the town of Kozelsk. Nilus blanched and then burst out with the most outrageous denunciation of the Jews. He refused to believe that the Jew had been strolling innocently in the neighborhood of the monastery on a Sunday afternoon. 'He must be spying on us,' he exclaimed. This had been the first of their frequent and almost violent arguments about the Jews. Nilus maintained that they were the incarnation of the Antichrist, the most dangerous enemies of mankind, on the verge of causing the destruction of the Christian world. When du Chayla reminded him that the Jews were actually victims, persecuted in many countries, discriminated against and sometimes massacred in pogroms in Russia, his only answer was, 'You are blind, they must have got to you too, to make you promote their cause.'

Two days later, Nilus had asked him whether he had read the *Protocols of the Elders of Zion*, published in the second edition of his book. When he had answered in the negative, Nilus immediately grabbed the book from a shelf and, since they had been conversing in French, started translating passages from the *Protocols* into French.

This conversation stood out distinctly in du Chayla's mind. He had tried, in vain, to discuss the matter sensibly. He had declared that such a 'document' did not surprise him, that he had encountered similar anti-Semitic theories in the writings of the Frenchmen Edouard Drumont and, even more extreme, the mystic Leo Taxil, who a few years back had 'led by the nose' the whole Catholic world, including Pope Leo XIII. With that, Nilus exploded, the veins popping out on his neck, his voice thunderous; he would make him change his mind, he shouted. A few days later, one of the hostel residents handed him a note from Nilus summoning him for an 'urgent meeting' that same afternoon.

They had met in the study, where he was informed that the women were occupied with their evening prayers. Dusk had set in, but the falling snow that covered everything in a pure white blanket lent some light to the room, which was pleasantly cozy and warm. In the fading light he immediately noticed a large parcel wrapped in black cloth in the center of the desk. The cloth had been decorated with a large triple cross, embroidered in white. The words 'In this sign shalt thou conquer' were embroidered in color. A small paper icon representing the Archangel Michael had been pasted on the cloth.

The atmosphere was reminiscent of a spiritual event, a religious ceremony. Nilus dramatically crossed himself three times before the large icon of the Holy Mother of Smolensk, a copy of the famous painting that stood in front of the Russian army as it prayed on the eve of the Borodin battle. With considerable aplomb he unwrapped the parcel and ceremoniously removed a notebook bound in beautiful leather. Later he would explain that the leather binding and the cloth cover had been prepared in the monastery workshop in his presence. He would never allow the document to remain there unattended, firmly convinced that 'the Jews would surely steal it'. The embroidery had been done by his wife under his careful supervision.

He had brought the parcel that day from its hiding place at the home of the monk Daniil Bolotov, a portrait painter, who lived half a kilometer from the monastery. Daniil was in his debt, and he could trust him infinitely, he explained.

At Sergei's instigation, Daniil had prepared a painting depicting the royal couple and the young tsarevich, threatened by devils with horns, tails and hoofs, being saved by a local idiot, Mitia Kozelskii, one of the hostel inhabitants, believed to have powers of exorcism. The canvas, delivered to the royal palace by friends of Nilus, had made such an impression on the tsar that Mitia was soon presented to court, his patron, Nilus, traveling with him first class to interpret Mitia's incomprehensible mumblings. St Petersburg society referred to Mitia as 'that little imbecile'. Both Mitia and Daniil were indebted to Nilus for their success in St Petersburg circles. Daniil was now one of the most popular portrait painters of the nobility. Whom better could Nilus entrust with his treasure?

'Here it is!' Nilus had exclaimed on that day. 'The Magna Carta of the Kingdom of Antichrist!' He had opened the notebook and pushed it in du Chayla's direction. 'Read,' he demanded, 'read and you will believe!'

The first thing du Chayla had noticed was a blue or light violet ink-stain on the cover. He remembered thinking that somebody had spilled ink and attempted unsuccessfully to absorb it. The paper was yellowish and quite thick. It was immediately apparent that the text had been written in different hands, each one in a different kind of ink. 'Yes,' Nilus was quick to explain, 'at meetings of the *Kahal*, the secret Jewish government, various persons probably performed secretarial duties, that is the reason for various handwritings.' That, in his opinion, was abundant proof that the manuscript was an original, but Nilus was inconsistent on this subject, maintaining on another occasion that it was a copy.

Sitting in his armchair in Lyon, du Chayla relived that strange event. He had spent two and a half hours reading the full document from beginning to end, with mounting disbelief and consternation. What utter nonsense, he had thought. Noticing the frequent orthographic faults in French, he concluded that it had definitely not been written by a Frenchmen. When he finished reading, Nilus had immediately retrieved it, ceremoniously rewrapped the notebook in its special cloth cover, and locked it in his desk drawer.

Nothing was said for a while, as the women had returned and

Ozerova was serving tea, a procedure not to be interrupted. Besides, du Chayla did not know whether Madame Komarovskaia had been privy to the secret of the *Protocols*. But Nilus could not wait to hear his opinion.

Well,' he exclaimed, 'now do you believe, you doubting Thomas? Now that you have seen and read these *Protocols*, tell me your impression. Please don't fear, there are no strangers here. My wife knows everything, and as far as Madame K. is concerned, we actually have to thank her that the plans of the enemies of Christendom have been revealed.'

He was intrigued to learn what role, if any, Komarovskaia had played in all this. It seemed impossible that this sensible woman, who could hardly move due to her illness, could have infiltrated the *Kahal* of the Zionist Elders. 'Well,' Nilus expounded, 'Madame K. had lived abroad for many years, mainly in France, where she received the *Protocols* from a Russian general and, in turn, entrusted them to me. This general had succeeded in removing the *Protocols* from the Masonic archive.' Asked whether the name of the general was secret he replied, 'No, it was General Rachkovskii, a good man, who has contributed much to undermine the plans of the enemies of Christ.'

This name was not new to the listener. He had heard it from Jesopoff, the student who had instructed him in Russian when he was still living in Paris. Jesopoff had related how Rachkovskii, the head of the Russian secret police in that city, used to harass Russian immigrants. Nilus was not too happy to learn that his guest was aware of Rachkovskii's real function, and countered: 'This man's contribution to the fight against the Freemasons and the Satanic sects is invaluable. He does it at great sacrifice.'

As to the *Protocols*, du Chayla recalled how upset Nilus had become when he had said that he did not believe in the existence of Elders of Zion. It all stemmed, he had observed, from the same 'kitchen' of cooked-up tales dealing with the unmasking of the Devil and other mystic prognostications let loose on the public around the end of the century.

Nilus's face had darkened. 'You are directly under Satanic orders,' he had thundered. 'The greatest strength of Satan lies in the fact that he not only uses people to influence world events, but also makes them deny his very existence. What will you say when I show you how the secret sign of Antichrist materializes everywhere, when I prove to you that this Satanic plan is being implemented before our very eyes?'

At this point Nilus had retrieved his book from the shelf, spread out a map on the table, and opened a file that contained scattered pages. From his bedroom he brought a small chest, which du Chayla jokingly referred to later as 'the museum of Antichrist'. He then started reading excitedly both from his book and from his file, quoting indiscriminately from prophecies of Orthodox as well as Catholic saints, and the encyclicals of Pope Pius X. After reading for a long while, he opened the box to present the *corpus delicti*. He fished within the jumbled disarray in the chest to locate and show du Chayla various pieces of cloth, India rubbers, kitchen utensils, badges of various technical institutes, as well as a monogram of the Empress Alexandra Fedorovna and a cross of the Légion d'Honneur. All these seemingly ordinary objects represented, in the words of Nilus, 'the seal of Antichrist'. Sometimes it was portrayed as a triangle, other times as two triangles superimposed on each other. In Nilus's sick fantasy, rubbers made by Treugolnik, the combination of the stylized initials of the empress 'A' and 'TH', the five-cornered star of the Légion d'Honneur, all resembled three-edged crosses that stood for the sign of the Antichrist and the emblem of the Elders of Zion. Any resemblance of a manufactured token or emblem to the three-edged star was enough to gain the item entrance into his 'museum box'.

With great anxiety and anguish, appearing to be enveloped in mystic terror, Nilus revealed that the sign of the expected 'Son of Evil' had already contaminated everything, appearing even on Church ornaments and in the icons of the new monastery chapel.

The hour was past midnight and du Chayla was exhausted. Observing Nilus, he felt as if they were on the brink of an abyss, where, at any minute, reason might give way to madness. He tried to calm his host, reminding him that in the *Protocols* there was nothing even remotely resembling the 'sign' he spoke of. He told Nilus that this 'sign' was nothing new, that it had been mentioned by every mystic or occultist beginning with Hermes Triswegist and Paracelsus, and what was more relevant, it had been used and mentioned by Papus and other non-Jews. It was not even considered an anti-Christian sign.

Nilus had made frantic notes in his journal, and it soon became clear not only that there was no chance of convincing him, but that he was preparing new arguments that could raise his abnormal anxiety to new heights. There was no point in arguing with a lunatic, du Chayla concluded.

He later learned that Nilus had ordered from Moscow a large

number of books dealing with secret cults, and in 1911 a new edition of his book appeared, with a foreword containing more secret occult material and pictures from books by authors mentioned by du Chayla in their earlier discussion. The title contained phrases such as 'we are near the approaching Antichrist' and 'the kingdom of Satan on earth'. On the cover there was a picture of the King of Spades with the caption 'behold the Antichrist'.

Visiting Optina Pustyn at a later date, du Chayla had again encountered Nilus. It was a time marked by court proceedings against the former director of the police department, Lopukhin, and many tactics of the secret police in the old regime had been publicly revealed and widely discussed. He recalled asking Nilus if he would now agree that the *Protocols* were probably another one of Rachkovskii's forgeries. Still wrapped up in his bizarre fantasies, Nilus responded by reminding him of a quotation from St Paul: 'The power of God works through human weakness.' God had his own ways of speaking to men, Nilus declared. Even if the *Protocols* were a forgery, he said, 'is it not possible that God has chosen to reveal the truth to us mortals through this document? Has he not chosen Bala'am's ass to deliver prophesies? And may he not have chosen a liar to deliver a message of truth?'

Their last meeting took place on yet another of du Chayla's visits to Optina Pustyn. It was summer and the windows were wide open, allowing a pleasant breeze filled with the aroma of ripening fruit into the stuffy apartment. Nilus was bent over his desk, where the latest edition of the newspaper *Znamia* was spread out alongside a map of Europe. The Young Turks' revolution had just broken out and the army of Mahmud-Scheche-Pasha had marched from Saloniki against Constantinople. On the map of Europe du Chayla noticed the drawing of a frightful snake worming its way through most European countries. Various dates of conquest were marked, the latest one in Constantinople, on the route to Jerusalem. A very disturbed Nilus murmured that the snake was nearing its final aim. He retired to his private chapel to pray for the victory of the Sultan over the Young Turks. The late Orthodox father, Varsonofii, who had also been present, tried in vain to convince Nilus that Abdul-Hamid had rightly been punished for his mass murders of Christians, but he only succeeded in arousing Nilus's anger.

Du Chayla never saw Nilus again, but he learned later that soon after their last meeting in 1910 his ramblings had become too embarrassing to the Church. A bishop had been dispatched to Optina Pustyn to conduct an inquiry, which ended with Nilus being forced to leave the monastery and never return. He wandered from one monastery to another, sometimes finding temporary refuge on the estates of friends. Years later du Chayla heard of Nilus again from the head nurse with whom he had become friendly when he was hospitalized in the White Cross Hospital in the Crimea. A former palace maiden in St Petersburg, she told him that Nilus had stayed in a women's hostel in the Pokrov monastery in Kiev in 1917–18, and had ended up in Berlin in 1918–19. Although he had no way of knowing it, Nilus had actually returned to Russia and while du Chayla was struggling with his conscience in Lyon, Nilus was living with his wife in a house in the south of Russia, which he shared with the former hermit Seraphim. Later, evicted by the Bolshevik authorities, Nilus was twice imprisoned and died of heart failure on New Year's Day 1930, at the age of 68. Ozerova outlived him by eight years, and died of cold and hunger in the Kola Peninsula on the Arctic Ocean, her place of exile.

Back in Lyon, du Chayla noticed that the sun had set while he was enveloped in his memories. He had thought that the episode of Nilus was a closed chapter in his life. Well educated and speaking many languages, the man remained in his memory a curious relic of the old regime, who even in his day had not been taken seriously except by those who exploited him for their own ulterior motives. Was it possible that this man, almost single-handed, had succeeded in letting loose on the world this bizarre fabrication called the *Protocols of the Elders of Zion*? Was it possible that he was being presented in the West as a genuine Russian authority?

This would not only harm the Jews, du Chayla thought, but also expose Russia to ridicule. On 12 May 1921, he published his remarkable experiences in the first of five articles in the Paris newspaper *Dernières Nouvelles*, entitled 'S. A. Nilus and the Zionist Protocols'.

PHILIP GRAVES

'If you only stay here long enough you will meet many men who matter, and you may find the key to many strange secrets.' This is what a friend told Philip Graves, who was less than enthusiastic when, for the second time, late in 1919, he was appointed correspondent of *The Times* of London in Istanbul. During the war he had served in

Egypt, Arabia and Palestine as an intelligence officer with the rank of captain. He was a particularly valued member of the *Times* staff due to his work first in the Arab bureau in Cairo and then (in the company of his consular uncle, Sir Robert Graves), in the political mission under Sir Gilbert Clayton at Bir Salem, General Allenby's G.H.Q. in Palestine. After the armistice, Graves had returned to Turkey, still in a military capacity, and stayed there until demobilization, late in 1919.

He did not appreciate being posted to Turkey again, but on 12 July 1921 his friend's prophesy came true. This was a date he would not forget to his last days. It was the beginning of a chapter that was to become the peak of his career.

It was on this day that he received by messenger a thick envelope to which a card and note were attached, both bearing the name Mikhail Raslovlev in bold letters. This was also the signature name on the note, which was written in French. The writer informed Graves that he was in possession of irrefutable proof that the book called the *Protocols of the Elders of Zion*, formerly published in Russia in 1905, which was then making such a big impression on the European public, was a complete forgery. To attract Graves' attention, the writer noted that the book, which had been the subject of an article in *The Times* of London on 8 May 1920, was an audacious plagiarism of a French book published in the 1860s and probably completely forgotten. 'It is a small political treatment', he wrote, 'which the perpetrators of the plagiarism have appropriated to suit their anti-Semitic views, but have done so in a superficial manner, copying whole passages verbatim from the original French book ...'

Convinced that a revelation of such a mystery would be of interest to the whole world, Raslovlev inquired whether Graves would like to acquire a copy of the French book, on terms that should be discussed. To substantiate his claim, the writer had attached a few printed passages in French from both books, which seemed to be identical. He invited Graves to contact him at his club the very next day.

Both the letter and the attached passages were enough to arouse his interest. He remembered the article in *The Times* the previous year, but he had never read the *Protocols*, which had appeared in England in a booklet entitled *The Jewish Peril*. *The Times* had described the contents of the book in detail, remarking that indeed 'some of the features of the would-be Jewish programme, bear uncanny resemblance to situations and events now developing under our eyes'.

At the time he had been especially intrigued by the last passage in the article:

> The trouble is that all this fosters indiscriminate anti-Semitism. That the latter is rampant in Eastern Europe ... that its propaganda in France, England, and America, is growing, is also a fact. Do we want and can we afford to add exacerbated race hatred to all our political, social and economic troubles? If not, the question of the *Jewish Peril* should be taken up and dealt with. It is far too interesting, the hypothesis it presents is far too ingenious, attractive and sensational, not to attract the attention of our not too happy and not too contented public. The average man thinks that there is something very fundamentally wrong with the world he lives in. He will eagerly grasp at a plausible working hypothesis. Have we been struggling these tragic years to blow up and extirpate the secret organization of German dominion only to find beneath it another more dangerous because more secret? Have we, by straining every fibre of our national body, escaped a *Pax Germanica* only to fall into a *Pax Judaica*?
>
> The Elders of Zion as represented in their *Protocols* are by no means kinder taskmasters than Wilhelm II and his henchmen would have been ... An impartial investigation of these would-be documents and of their history is most desirable ... They appear to have been written for Jews by Jews. If so, in what circumstances were they produced and to cope with what inter-Jewish emergency, or are we to dismiss the whole matter without inquiring and to let the influence of such a book as this work go unchecked?

Was it possible, Graves wondered with mounting excitement, that he was on the brink of discovering the true facts? Was it plausible that a major scoop would be handed to him by some obscure Russian refugee on a hot summer day in Istanbul? Stranger things have happened, he mused. He would definitely meet the mysterious Mr Raslovlev in his club the next day. Indeed, he would have called him immediately, but there was no address or telephone number.

Graves had followed the publication of the *Protocols* in Europe with some interest. He knew that Russian refugees, including former officers in the White Russian army, had carried copies of the *Protocols* to various countries, and that for at least the last two years the book had been distributed in many languages around all of Europe. The passages in French in Raslovlev's message had actually been copied from Jouin's French translation of the *Protocols* published in France in 1920. It had been preceded by German translations that sold very successfully in Germany. *The Jewish Peril*, to which *The Times* had referred in its article, was an anonymous translation of the *Protocols* that had appeared in England early in 1920. It had been followed by an editorial in *The Spectator* calling the *Protocols* 'one of the most remarkable productions of their kind'. Could it be that he was on the threshold of uncovering the true story behind this doubtful document?

The meeting the next day took place in a clandestine atmosphere. Raslovlev met him at the entrance of the club, exactly at noon, motioning with his hands and speaking in whispers. He gratefully accepted Graves' invitation for lunch, but insisted on a dark corner. He asked not to be mentioned by name throughout the conversation, although he was known to the staff of this club. 'Walls have ears,' he whispered. Throughout lunch he cast nervous looks in all directions. Graves was surprised that his guest spoke English.

As soon as they had been served, Raslovlev explained that, for him, this was not a purely business transaction. 'Had it been so,' he said, 'I would certainly have applied to one of the Jewish organizations in Constantinople, who, no doubt, have greater interest than *The Times* in purchasing the French book, and using it as a weapon against certain people and newspapers. But I would not like to give a weapon of any kind to the Jews, whose special friend I never have been... I have kept this secret for a long time in the hope of using it one day or other as proof of the impartiality of the political group to which I belong, and it is only a very urgent need of money that persuaded me now to change my mind.'

He had not brought the book with him. It was too dangerous, he said, but if Graves was interested and vouched for its safety, he would have it delivered to his home after the meeting, together with a copy of the *Protocols of the Elders of Zion*, in English, so that Graves could examine them together and draw his own conclusions. He had no idea who had authored the French book or what its title was, since the flyleaf was missing. But he was sure it contained no mention of Jews. For all he knew, it might be the only existing copy. The foreword mentioned Geneva and the year 1864, he stated, and assured Graves that the identical passages from both books were but examples, there were many more of the same kind.

Although he showed some reluctance, Raslovlev finally agreed to divulge what he had kept secret throughout the whole conversation. When Graves insisted that he had to know how the book had come into his possession, he revealed in a whisper that he had received it from a former colonel of the Okhrana, but would under no circumstances reveal the officer's name. He explained that he was hoping to return to Russia as soon as this Bolshevik Revolution was over. He was a respected landowner of two estates in Russia and proprietor of a townhouse that alone cost him £2,000, he boasted. He would not like to be accused of selling secrets to assist the Jews. Mentioning names could prove dangerous for him, that was why any transaction with *The Times* must be kept secret.

He was not proud to raise money in this way, Raslovlev confided, but he was in debt. He needed £300, but would not like it to appear as coming from the sale of the document. He preferred to regard the money as a loan for a certain period, hoping to pay it back on the return of civil peace in Russia.

Intrigued and excited, Graves promised complete secrecy and agreed to contact *The Times* without delay. He even risked advancing the man 160 lira out of his own pocket, as he suspected that Raslovlev's need for immediate cash might tempt him to offer the book to somebody else. To this token of confidence Raslovlev responded by revealing his address: rue Sextime 33, Istanbul.

The two books were delivered by messenger to his apartment one hour later. Before settling down to examine them, Graves decided he needed more information. The Russian spelling of the man's name and his address were enough to enable him to make some inquiries. Within a few hours, through his good connections, he received the information he sought and conveyed it that same evening in an urgent letter to H. Wickman Steed, the editor of *The Times*. He noted his discovery that Raslovlev was working for the American Red Cross in Istanbul.

In his letter he described the circumstances in which the book had been delivered to him, and the 'curious discovery of this Russian Orthodox man' that the *Protocols* were a plagiarism 'from a book published in Geneva, in French, anonymous, the title missing, date of introduction Geneva 15 October, 1864'. 'This book', he wrote, 'is a series of dialogues between Montesqieu and Machiavelli, the latter does most of the talking. A great many of the resemblances are extraordinary (examples follow).'

He further explained in his letter that Raslovlev, being a member of a monarchist group, did not wish to damage his reputation by selling political information, and therefore proposed the arrangement of a loan. 'Meantime he is much in debt and I have decided on my own responsibility to advance him 160 lira (receipt herewith).' He concluded by urging the editor to reply immediately by telegram, adding: 'I feel this may be a very big scoop for *The Times* ... the *Protocols* is largely a paraphrase of the Geneva book; the latter is in much better French! Mr Raslovlev got the Geneva book from a Russian ex-Colonel of the Okhrana who attached no importance to it. I think that the *Protocols* should be exposed by non-Jews ... Raslovlev thinks the *Jewish Peril* lies in the materialism of the Jews rather than in their revolutionary idealism.'

A whole week passed, his tension mounting with each passing day. He was anxious that his superiors not underestimate this extraordinary information, although he sensed that tingling feeling that always preceded the publication of a scoop. He worried whether Raslovlev would be patient enough to wait. He rationalized to himself that such decisions took time, there were proper channels that had to be followed.

Finally, on 20 July, a telegram from the manager of *The Times* arrived: 'Re your letter July thirteenth, we accept proposal, sending loan, arrange book conveyed by trusty messenger, advise when dispatched.'

The Times insisted on a legal document, and it was not until the second day of August that a formal memorandum of agreement was signed between Philip Graves, acting on behalf of *The Times*, and Michel S. Mikhailoff Raslovlev. They had agreed not to deduct the advance from the sum of the loan and delivered £337, to be repaid in five years. As guarantee, Raslovlev 'charged' his house in the town of Atkarsk in the district of Saratov. The book 'from which document or book of the so-called *Protocols of the Learned Elders of Zion* have been plagiarized' was transferred to *The Times*, with full rights to use and publish it, or any material in it, for the period of five years. Raslovlev, for his part, undertook not to make any use of said material, or the information in it, for the said five years. On repayment of the loan at the expiration of this period 'the said document shall be returned to Raslovlev with the full copyright'.

Graves did not wait for the signed document. On 25 July he dispatched to London the first of three articles, which, years later, he hoped would earn him the Nobel Prize. The articles were published in *The Times*, with Philip Graves' byline, on 16, 17 and 18 August, under the title *Truth about the 'Protocols' – a Literary Forgery*. In the preface to the first article *The Times* wrote: 'In the following three articles, the Constantinople correspondent of *The Times* presents for the first time conclusive proof that the document is in the main a clumsy plagiarism.'

Though not spelled out in the written agreement, the secrecy promised to Raslovlev was maintained by referring to him as 'Mr. X'. The plagiarized book was kept anonymous, referred to as 'the Geneva document'. Hoping to obtain more information about the book or its author, Graves described it in detail:

> A small volume in French, lacking the title page, with dimensions of 5½" by 3¾". It had been cheaply rebound. On the leather back is printed in Latin capitals the word 'Joli'. The preface, entitled *Simple avertissement*, is dated Geneva, October 15, 1864. The book contains 324 pages of which numbers 315–322 inclusive follow page 24 in the only copy known to Mr. X, perhaps owing to a mistake when the book was rebound. Both the paper and the type are characteristic of the 'sixties and seventies' of the last century. These details are given in the hope that they may lead to the discovery of the title of the book. Mr. X believes it must be rare, since, had it not been so, the *Protocols* would have speedily been recognized as a plagiarism by anyone who had read the original.

In the third article Graves dealt with Nilus, 'the first publisher of the *Protocols*', and the various versions of the origin of the *Protocols*, which, to his mind, proved the forgery. 'One is struck', he wrote, 'by the absence of any effort on the part of the plagiarist to conceal his plagiarisms. The paraphrasing has been very careless; parts of sentences, whole phrases at times, are identical; the development of the thought is the same. There has been no attempt worth mentioning to alter the order of the Geneva Dialogues.'

In this article Graves also added another dimension to the dramatic events connected with the publication of the *Protocols*.

> Mr. X, the discoverer of the plagiarism, informs me that the *Protocols*, shortly after their discovery in 1901, four years before their publication by Professor Nilus, served a subsidiary purpose, namely, the first defeat of Monsieur Philippe, a French

hypnotist and mind reader, who acquired considerable influence over the Tsar and the Tsarina at the beginning of the present century. The Court favourite was disliked by certain great
personages, and incurred the natural jealousy of the monks,
thaumaturgists, and similar adventurers who hoped to capture
the Tsar through the Empress in their own interest, or in that of
various cliques. Philippe fell from favour, to return to Russia
and find himself once more in the Court's good graces at a later
date.

In conclusion, Graves wrote:

1. The *Protocols* are largely a paraphrase of the book here provi-
sionally called the *Geneva Dialogues*.
2. They were designed to foster the belief among Russian conserva-
tives, and especially in Court circles, that the prime cause of discontent among the politically minded elements in Russia was not
the repressive policy of the bureaucracy but a worldwide Jewish
conspiracy. They thus served as a weapon against the Russian liberals, who urged the Tsar to make certain concessions to the intelligentsia.
3. The *Protocols* were paraphrased very hastily and carelessly.
4. Such portions of the *Protocols* as were not derived from the
Geneva Dialogues were probably supplied by the *Okhrana*, which
organization very possibly obtained them from the many Jews it
employed to spy on their co-religionists.

So much for the *Protocols*. They have done harm not so much, in
the writer's opinion, by arousing anti-Jewish feeling, which is older
than the *Protocols* and will persist in all countries where there is a
Jewish problem until that problem is solved; rather, they have done
harm by persuading all sorts of mostly well-to-do people that every
recent manifestation of discontent on the part of the poor is an
unnatural phenomenon, a fictitious agitation caused by a secret society of Jews.

Concurrently with Graves' third article, on 18 August *The Times*
published an editorial that stated: 'The fact of the plagiarism has now
been conclusively established, and the legend may be allowed to pass
into oblivion ...'

Seventy-three years later, in October 1994, I was sitting in the *Times* archives
in London, examining the original correspondence between Graves and his

editor, and the agreement signed by Raslovlev, in a file graciously put at my disposal by the managing editor. What would the writer of that editorial have thought had he known that this so-called 'legend' not only had refused to pass into oblivion, but was flourishing and enjoying a new revival around the world.

5 Defending a Lie

VON ROLL AND TOEDLI: A PAIR OF SWISS NAZIS

In a way a trial is like a show put on for the benefit of the court, but the judge is never allowed to look behind the scenes. Listening to witnesses and to counsel in my courtroom I had often tried to imagine the drama that preceded the trial: the investigation in closed police facilities; the coaching of witnesses; the conferences in counsel's chambers in which tactical decisions were made. I used to wonder which witness had been manipulated; what fact or item of evidence had been suppressed; what argument had been discarded; how strategy had been planned. If there was one thing I missed during my long years on the bench, it was the drama played out behind the scenes of a trial.

In the process of studying the Berne trial, I was therefore intrigued by the fact that I was able to study not only the court record but also the private documents of both the plaintiffs and the defendants.

We would probably never have had access to the secret documents of the defense in the Berne trial had it not been for a law enacted by the Swiss legislature on 21 June 1935, exactly five weeks after the judge announced his judgment. This 'Espionage Act' made it an offense punishable by imprisonment to transmit communications concerning the political activities of persons or political organizations to a foreign government, authority, party or similar organization, to the disadvantage of Switzerland, one of its citizens, or inhabitants.

It was this new law that prompted the authorities to investigate Swiss citizens who had been manipulated by Nazi Germany in the conduct of the defense in the Berne trial, and who were now suspected of having supplied foreign political organizations with information prejudicial to the safety of individuals living in Switzerland. It was in the process of investigating these offenses that the Swiss police searched the homes of persons involved in the trial and seized the documents that comprise the Freyenwald Archive, so called because most of the documents were found in the home of Dr Hans Jonak von Freyenwald. Three years later, in 1938, von Freyenwald edited a German edition of the *Protocols* entitled *Der Jüdische Antichrist und die Protokolle der Weisen von Zion* (The Jewish Antichrist and the Protocols of the Elders of Zion), with an introduction written by him.

The Swiss historian Friedrich Külling called his book on anti-Semitism *Bei*

Uns Wie Überall? (Here Like Everywhere Else?). I had spent many vacations in Switzerland, and I had thought I had the correct impression of this beautiful country with its polite, though detached, hotel managers and innkeepers. I had never associated this pastoral paradise with the European brand of crude anti-Semitism. Studying the history of the Jews in Switzerland and the documents in the Freyenwald Archive I experienced a rude awakening. Indeed, 'in Switzerland like everywhere else', I realized.

Who were the Swiss citizens behind the defense of the Berne trial? Two key figures were Ubald von Roll and Boris Toedli. They first met in 1933 at a National Front meeting, and they both attended the public rally that was held on 13 June in the Berne casino. They had both supervised the distribution of hundreds of copies of the *Protocols of the Elders of Zion*. This was the thirteenth edition of the German version of the *Protocols* issued in Germany by Theodor Fritsch. In his foreword Fritsch stated: 'One thing is clear. Jews should not be suffered among us any longer. The civilized nations are honor bound to get rid of this nasty race, who, by their very presence, contaminate everything around them.'

This was the real thing, von Roll and Toedli felt. The Nazi movement in Berne was on the move. Discussing future plans for the party they still formally addressed each other by their last names. Toedli, who was the senior of the two, spoke at length about his philosophy concerning the Jews, and his words were music to von Roll's ears. He could not have found a better collaborator. They decided to cooperate, not yet aware of the future controversy that would turn them against each other.

A few months later, the Jewish community filed its complaint in court, naming as defendants a number of members of the National Front and of the Union of Swiss National Socialists: Silvio Schnell, Johan Konrad Meyer, Georg Bernhard Haller, Ernst Walter Ebersold and Theodor Fischer. But the individual defendants were only straw figures, as Ubald von Roll later confided in a letter to his friend Princess Karadja; it was the Nazi party that lurked in the shadows and it was von Roll who carried the full moral and legal responsibility for the trial *vis-à-vis* the National Front. In reality, as it turned out, it was not even the trial of the National Front; Boris Toedli would turn it into the case of the German Nazi party. It was only after the trial that the full extent of the German Nazis' involvement was revealed and their tactics and manipulations exposed.

On 13 November 1936, Boris Toedli was arrested by the Swiss

police, who had previously searched his home at 21 Gewerbestrasse, Berne, and seized his files, which contained incriminating letters. He was charged with an offense against the new Espionage Act.

In his interrogation Toedli freely admitted his anti-Semitic feelings and his hatred of Jews. 'My aim in life', he said, 'is to fight communism, Jewry and Freemasonry.' On a different occasion he confessed that he was a sympathizer of the NSDAP and the present German regime, 'for I am a fanatical opponent of Bolshevism and Jewry. It is they who are responsible for the present world crisis.'

Toedli had been born in Kiev to Swiss parents who came from *Altstätten*, in the canton of St Gallen. In 1917 he voluntarily joined the White Russian army and was promoted to the rank of officer. He lost his hearing in a bomb explosion and was later taken prisoner by the Bolsheviks. After contracting typhoid, he was freed and decided to settle in Berne. His parents, who had owned a furniture business, lost all their property during the Russian Revolution. In the Russian tradition in which he was brought up, Toedli automatically blamed the Jews.

Asked why he had sought assistance from German Nazi headquarters in Erfurt in conducting of the defense in the Berne Trial, Toedli replied: 'We here in Berne are not as informed about the Jewish problem as are the professionals in Erfurt ... The Jews are the real traitors of our country ... I confirm that I am a Jew-hater and regret that these people live in Switzerland ... I am an anti-Semite out of personal experience, which explains my behavior. My family lost everything in Russia, and the Jews are to blame, not the Russian people.'

Toedli played an active part in international agitation against Jews, participating in various anti-Semitic organizations. He not only kept in constant touch with Nazi officials in Germany, but also was given far-reaching powers in Europe by the 'Führer' of the All-Russian Fascists, whose headquarters was in Charbin, China. On 25 February 1935 he issued the following document to the White Guards, the Swiss chapter of the Russian Monarchist organization, under the heading 'We are Russians – God is with us.'

DIRECTIVE NO. 1

1. As of today I am temporarily assuming the position of head of department of the Russian Monarchist organization in

Switzerland (according to the resolution of the Supreme Council of the Monarchist organization of 24 February 1935.

2. As my personal assistant I am appointing the co-fighter Wladimir Alexandrovitch Kunz, who will also fill the post of secretary of the Swiss chapter; I hereby order him to take up his post immediately.

Chief of the Swiss chapter of the Russian Monarchist organization
Boris Toedli

This was the first of many directives ordering members of the White Guards to perform duties ranging from the gathering of information to the 'liquidation' of individuals in various countries. Fortunately Toedli meticulously kept and filed all correspondence with his colleagues in capitals around the world, making it easy for the authorities to substantiate the charges against him.

Facing his interrogator, Toedli patiently explained, in all seriousness, the plan promoted by a Pan-Aryan world organization that aimed to rid all countries of their Jews. At that time the plan for the total extermination of the Jews had not yet been finalized – this was to come a few years later – so Toedli explained that they wished to secure a state for the Jews, and as Palestine was partly inhabited by Arabs and therefore could not absorb all the Jews of the world, the island of Madagascar would be ideal for that purpose. Although officially charged with a serious offense, Toedli was not worried, as he explained to a friend in one letter: 'To be confronted with such charges is of no real concern to me, since Fleischhauer promised to intervene on my behalf with Himmler.' Fleischhauer was the head of the German Nazi headquarters, the Weltdienst, in Erfurt.

Toedli also remembered that a similar investigation had been initiated against him on a former occasion, about which he had written to one of his collaborators: 'Concerning the "Nazi" propaganda you must not worry. About ten days ago I was invited by the chief of police, who informed me that the investigation cleared me of any political propaganda activity except that concerning the Komintern. The chief of police told me that he himself was an anti-Semite. So all my worries were in vain.' The Berne police were quick to deny this charge.

Fleischhauer was the first to congratulate him: 'I am happy to hear', he wrote, 'that the police visited you and confirmed that you did not commit any offense against the law. Please tell them again and again that we are not a German but an international organization, only temporarily situated in Germany for security reasons.'

In the beginning, Toedli was more than willing to collaborate with Ubald von Roll in assisting in the conduct of the defense in the Berne trial, but they only became involved many months after the trial had officially started. Initially, the defendants did not attach much importance to the impending trial. Some of them did not even bother to obtain representation by counsel. It was only when they realized that both the plaintiffs and the judge took their tasks seriously and that the trial might be a boon to Nazi propaganda that they became active. The burden was placed on the shoulders of Ubald von Roll, who by then had become the official leader of the Berne chapter of the National Front. Toedli was appointed his deputy.

Ubald von Roll had gained attention at the rally in the Berne casino, where he had delivered a short speech offering to dedicate himself to 'the cause'. This speech, and the fact that he had been one of the organizers of the rally, gained him the appointment of Gauleiter of the Bernese chapter of the Front. He was a student, supported by his father, and he felt a little guilty at having rashly offered to work for the party full-time. He tried not to dwell on the approaching meeting with his father, when he would have to report on his studies in order to collect his monthly cheque. This young generation would teach their elders what was really important for the future of their country, he told himself.

The contact with Toedli seemed most beneficial, although it was not easy talking to a man who was almost deaf. Toedli seemed to know so much about Jews, he thought. His international contacts would serve them well in their future endeavors. Toedli's contacts with the Germans would indeed turn out to be crucial to the trial.

ENTER THE GERMANS

Almost a year had passed since the first preliminary session in the Berne trial, but the defendants had still not found an expert. Not that they hadn't tried. They had suggested to the court one name after another, but the court clerk's letters to their candidates either met with refusals or were not even answered. The lawyers met numerous times in the judge's chambers, the defendants using every possible tactic to gain one postponement after another. Finally Judge Meyer's patience was exhausted. He appointed Carl Albert Loosli as court expert, and noted the appointment of Professor Arthur Baumgarten as expert for the plaintiffs. The defendants had run out of names. They could find no expert who would be willing to support their case. On 8 August 1934, the judge wrote to the experts appointing them officially and ordering them to submit their opinions by 15 October. He set a date for the trial – 29 October 1934.

On 19 October, ten days before the opening of the trial, von Roll wrote a letter to 'The Brown House, Munich', concerning the trial of the Zionist *Protocols*. No address was necessary. The Brown House was Hitler's headquarters.

He was most pessimistic about the outcome of the trial, von Roll wrote, as their lawyer had made numerous mistakes, and had also, in the meantime, left the movement. He begged for a supply of both material and funds. The Jews were going to produce witnesses from all over the world, he stated, people of great importance, and the defense did not have any evidence to confront all this testimony. He wondered whether the Brown House could furnish the defense with an expert witness and with funds. The Jews were planning a death blow to the Nazi movement, he warned.

On 2 November his letter was officially acknowledged by none other than Hitler's deputy, Rudolf Hess. It would be referred to the legal department, Hess wrote.

But the Brown House would not become officially involved in the Berne trial. This role fell to its subsidiary in Erfurt, the Weltdienst, headed by Ulrich Fleischhauer. It was Boris Toedli who had made the contact with this group, as he had by then become responsible for the publishing house of the Weltdienst, the U. Bodung Verlag. This publishing house was founded in 1919 by Fleischhauer, a retired *Oberstleutnant*, who had commanded an artillery regiment in the German army in the First World War and had been severely wounded. In 1933 he had moved to Erfurt, where he had founded the Weltdienst, a center for the dissemination of anti-Semitic propaganda, aiming to establish a liaison with anti-Semites in various countries. The Erfurt center, financed by the German government, strived to establish an international counter-organization to combat 'International Jewry'. Their publication, also called *Weltdienst*, openly proclaimed its intention 'to deal with the machinations of the Jewish underworld'. All their publications, including an anti-Semitic lexicon entitled *Sigilla Veri*, were translated into many languages and distributed in various countries. Fleischhauer was also the founder and head of the

Pan-Aryan Union, an international organization of anti-Semites, which held yearly secret congresses in Erfurt under his presidency.

I had started out to study allegations of an international Jewish conspiracy. Instead I was confronted with evidence of an international network of individuals and organizations bound together by one common agenda: their hatred of Jews and their aim to implicate the Jewish people in every possible crime and present them as the greatest danger to world peace in general, and to the well-being of the peoples of all Christian countries in particular.

Seek as I may, I could not find in their correspondence any trace of an honest attempt to find out the truth. Jewish guilt was never questioned: it was taken for granted. Historical events were not researched: they were automatically interpreted in a way that implicated the Jews. There was no attempt to find honest evidence for the trial; instead, all the planning was aimed at manipulating the facts and inventing tactical methods to subvert the truth.

They could have found no better weapon than the *Protocols of the Elders of Zion*, and no more suitable organization to support their case than the German Weltdienst in Erfurt. Indeed, the Berne trial was a godsend to Ulrich Fleischhauer. He had found a public arena in which he could confront the Jews and prove to the leaders of the Reich his worth to the common cause.

On 22 October 1934, Fleischhauer wrote to von Roll offering his assistance in the trial and promising that he was familiar with all matters concerning Jews. Even in this first letter the roles were immediately defined. Fleischhauer did not propose to play second fiddle, and made it clear that he meant to establish himself in a leading role; he demanded a stenographic verbatim record of all court proceedings up to that date and added: 'Please tell "Judentum" that these proceedings will only reveal to the world the truth about the Jewish power and will bring everything into the daylight, which the Jew usually tries to avoid. Make them see how stupid this trial is, it will only make a lot of Aryans see the light about the Jews.'

So began the close, and sometimes tortuous and traumatic, collaboration between the defense in the Berne trial and the Nazi Weltdienst in Erfurt. Fleischhauer was to gain center-stage.

ERFURT TAKES OVER

It would be run as a clandestine operation, because the Jews were everywhere, Fleischhauer decided. A secret code was composed in Erfurt and no names or addresses or meeting places were to be mentioned in writing. The list of code-names grew as time went on and more names were added. In the end there were 28 names on the list. The more important participants in the project rated more than one code-name, so von Roll was 'Harzer' or 'Hoche'; Toedli was 'Tauber' or 'Heberling'; Fleischhauer was 'Slacher' or 'Düring' or 'Flache'. As leader he needed better protection, so he rated three code-names. Money was to be deposited anonymously, so that there was no record of its German origin.

The Berne–Erfurt partners were relatively safe with the Swiss postal service, so they felt free to correspond, using their code-names. Meetings were few and took place in predetermined obscure locations in back alleys and railway stations. Almost every letter from Erfurt included a warning about the need for extreme secrecy.

More than fifty years later, when I visited Emil Raas in a Berne hospital, he became so agitated by the mention of Fleischhauer's name that the doctors almost stopped my interview with him. When describing the trial he struggled to find the right words, then exclaimed with a tremor in his voice: 'You must understand, it was not only the *Protocols* that were on trial, it was the whole monstrous, abhorrent issue of anti-Semitism. We were confronted with the sick, perverted mind of Fleischhauer, who made this his life's work.'

It took no time at all for von Roll to realize his mistake. Not only were the Germans calling all the shots and taking over the Swiss case, but they had no idea how a Swiss court operated. Inexperienced as he was, von Roll knew enough to realize that in a Berne court you needed real evidence: you could not get away with Nazi slogans alone. As suspicion and mistrust between him and Fleischhauer mounted, he tried to establish other contacts and recruit witnesses and raise funds through anti-Semitic organizations in other countries. His most valuable contact was Princess Karadja, the mother of the Rumanian consul-general in Berlin, an elderly, wealthy aristocrat, residing in Villa Lux, in Monti, Locarno. The princess was well connected and had many friends in anti-Semitic groups in Europe. She herself had established an Anglo-American operation calling itself the Aryan Protection League, to which von Roll appealed for support.

Although she had dedicated herself to building an international anti-Jewish league, and was ready to support any anti-Semitic cause, Karadja persistently strove to disassociate herself from any secret or underhand activity. 'I wish to build a "facade", all white and bright and shining. There must be nothing suspicious about it, nothing secret,' she wrote to von Roll. She was aware of the tactics used by anti-Semitic organizations against Jews, but she herself wanted no part in such methods. 'I am the left hand,' she wrote, 'and do not want to know what the right hand does.' She did not wish to know anything of 'destruction', she wrote; those who concerned themselves with 'that' must keep their intentions secret. The 'facade' could take no responsibility for the actions of the various groups.

But this idealistic vision of 'a shining white spotless facade' did not prevent Karadja from enthusiastically supporting the various groups that constituted the 'right hand' and did the dirty work. She not only organized and financially supported anti-Semitic groups in many countries, but also actively pulled strings in all directions to further their efforts. In spite of her advanced age, she not only corresponded with the Weltdienst, but traveled to Erfurt and discussed in her letters every little detail concerning anti-Semitic activities around the world, as well as the personal matters of those involved.

A close relationship developed between von Roll and Karadja, and she addressed him as 'dear friend', although he always respectfully addressed her as 'Your Highness'. Karadja was the only person with whom he could be completely honest, describing, in long letters, the difficulties confronting the defense in the trial and his complicated relationship with the Germans in Erfurt. They were taking over the Swiss trial, he repeatedly wrote; they had no understanding of the workings of Swiss democracy and a Swiss court; they did not realize that the defense must use only clean witnesses – a person such as Julius Streicher, the famous editor of the German anti-Semitic journal *Der Stürmer*, was out of the question. Fleischhauer was too much of a Prussian officer, he wrote.

Another close and valuable contact was the writer Lesley Fry, who had formerly implicated Ahad Ha'am in the composition of the *Protocols*, and continued to pose as an expert on the document. Her real name was Shishmarev. Her code-names on Fleischhauer's list were Madame Laurier and Madame Gordon.

For a time von Roll was hopeful that she would be the perfect expert witness for the defense. He was deeply impressed by her 30-page 'research' on the *Protocols*, which had appeared in the anti-Semitic journal *La Vieille France* under the title, 'Ahad Ha'am and Zionism – on the Authenticity of the Protocols'. Not bothering with any serious research, he had no idea that Rewentlau, who had quoted her, had been compelled to apologize in a German court and pay damages to Ahad Ha'am when he could not substantiate her allegations. But it was not her unfounded theories that finally persuaded the defense team to abandon Fry's candidacy as expert. The decision was taken at one of their rare meetings to discuss trial strategy. They were well aware of the numerous versions concerning the origin of the *Protocols*, which appeared in various editions. They must stick to one version, the lawyers insisted. They had no proof of the authenticity of the *Protocols*, but they must at least present a viable theory. That was easy, von Roll said. The most popular theory was that the document had been adopted by the Jewish leadership at the first Zionist Congress in Basle in 1897. According to this version, the public sessions of the Congress, pretending to deal only with the establishment of a Zionist movement, were but a facade. In reality, the Jewish leadership conspired in secret meetings to plan their domination of the whole world, in accordance with a plan presented by the founder of the movement, Theodor Herzl.

They immediately realized their predicament. They could not use Lesley Fry as an expert, for she was on record with a list of compelling reasons why Herzl could not have been the author of the *Protocols*. Not only were the dates wrong, she had written, but the *Protocols* were originally written in Hebrew and Herzl did not write Hebrew. He had also not reached the rank of *Gaon*.

In the process of my investigation of the history of the *Protocols*, it soon became clear that I was not dealing with just one false theory and one forged document. In their efforts to lend credibility to the forgery, a web of lies was woven. The false and completely unfounded allegations of Lesley Fry served as a good example: not only had the *Protocols* not been originally composed in Hebrew, but surprisingly, they have never seen light in that language. There is no 'rank' of *Gaon* in Jewish tradition. This title had been awarded to heads of Jewish academies in various countries of the diaspora between the sixth and the thirteenth centuries. Since then it has been used as an honorific title for any scholar with great knowledge of the Torah.

In his letters to Karadja, von Roll poured out his doubts and his disappointment with the tactics of his collaborators. He felt that they were not speaking the same language. It was he, more than the others, who was worried about the outcome of the trial, but he realized that Fleischhauer and his colleagues were not even making preparations to convince the judge. They were planning to use the court to speak to the public at large. They would be playing to an international audience, represented by hundreds of journalists. They would have at their disposal the front pages of every newspaper in Europe. The world was suffering from economic depression, and scared of the threat of communism. Public opinion in the Europe of 1934 was receptive to allegations against the Jews; they were preparing to try their case not in a court of law, but rather in the court of public opinion, where rules of evidence did not apply and where you could lie with impunity as long as you did so in an effective manner, tuned in to the needs and the prejudices of your audience. They did not even try to find evidence of the authenticity of the *Protocols*. They had no doubt that the *Protocols* were false. In his letters he raged at their lawyer. He should have made an effort to prevent the judge from ruling that he would consider the authenticity of the *Protocols*.

Discussing plans for the defense, he wrote to Karada: 'We shall only try to prove that the forgery is not provable ... it looks as if it is almost impossible to prove the authenticity of the *Protocols* ... we are not expecting a positive result under the existing circumstances, as the assessing of the evidence is in the hands of the judge alone.' Although the atmosphere in Berne was not friendly to Jews, he wrote, in Switzerland even the most prejudiced judge could not sweep clear evidence under the table. Their best bet was to establish the existence of an international Jewish plot to dominate the world. Why not try to get the support of Henry Ford, he suggested. Maybe they should use Ford's approach, pleading that the *Protocols* must be true because they were actually being implemented on the world scene.

Another one of his suggestions was to emphasize the high cost of the trial to the Swiss taxpayer: 'You know how sensitive the Swiss are about money.'

In the meantime Fleischhauer kept pushing them from across the border. The trial was of great moral and psychological importance. It must be won 'so that no Jew would ever dare institute similar proceedings'. 'The Jews are trying to cut our throats,' he warned.

It was only to his patroness in Locarno that von Roll admitted to having sleepless nights, worrying over the outcome of the trial. Realizing that Toedli was actually working for the Germans, he wrote to her in despair, 'I am trying to guard against us becoming a chapter of the German National Socialists.'

But it was too late. Von Roll was becoming too inquisitive and Fleischhauer started to prepare the ground for his dismissal. When von Roll demanded information about the 'international committee' in the name of which Fleischhauer was raising money abroad, the

Oberstleutnant finally exploded: 'I am shocked and I can't find the proper word to describe your demand,' he wrote. 'I have lived through many events in my life and I can't find a "parliamentary" expression for your outrageous request. Why do you need this information! You should be happy that there is a committee to deal with the trial, it takes care of all the matters with which I, as a professional expert, cannot deal. I have met in my life many people and I have dealt with many matters, but I have never encountered anything like this. You will not get from us the name of the head of the committee or the names of its members. I shall also report your request at the next meeting of the committee!' Von Roll had become too much of a liability. On 11 November 1935, a report went out to Erfurt stating that von Roll had been fired from his post as Gauleiter of the National Front in Berne. Boris Toedli was appointed in his place.

Full discipline was established. Every member of the team was scrutinized. Suspects were immediately reported. A 45-year-old secretary in the Weltdienst in Erfurt, by the name of Rantzau, was reported to Germany, and her name was immediately put on a list of people to be deported to a concentration camp. The unfortunate woman had repeated, in the presence of Toedli, a forbidden joke, in which the testament of Goebbels was opened after his death and found to include the results of the upcoming referendum. This was enough to denounce a devoted employee and send her to an almost certain death.

DEFENSE TACTICS

One of the most difficult questions defense lawyers are asked by laymen is 'How can you defend a guilty client?' They are invariably ready with the standard reply: they do not presume to judge a client, that is the province of the court, they explain; the lawyer only represents the client, and sees to it that all his rights are preserved and that his version of the facts and his arguments are properly presented to the court. The moral issue involved in helping put a rapist or a murderer back on the street is conveniently wrapped up in layers of formulas, which lawyers repeat, but with which most of them are uncomfortable.

The moral issue will probably never be settled. As long as innocent people are in danger of being convicted of crimes they did not commit, all defendants must rightfully be represented by counsel. So it becomes a question of ethics. Where does one draw the line? What would a lawyer definitely refrain from doing in the service of a client?

It appears that, like their clients, the defense lawyers in the Berne trial were not bothered by ethical considerations. No attempt was made to find out the truth about the *Protocols*. There was little chance of finding witnesses for the defense. Instead, there was a concentrated effort to discover incriminating material against the leaders of the Jewish community involved in the trial and against their witnesses. But even before the full list of witnesses was available, there was one man who would have to be discredited at any cost. In the eyes of Fleischhauer he was their most dangerous opponent, for he was not even Jewish. So letters went out to every possible address to find compromising evidence implicating the court-appointed expert Carl Albert Loosli.

CARL ALBERT LOOSLI

'Had anybody told me a few months ago, that I shall feel obliged to publicly deal with the Jews and with the so-called Jewish question, I would probably have been shocked. Yet, today, to my utter astonishment, as a citizen of good conscience, I feel duty bound to do exactly that.' So begins the book published by Carl Albert Loosli in Berne, Switzerland, in 1927.

From early childhood he had been raised to hate Jews. Anti-Semitism was part of his upbringing. At the age of 5 he was told in detail how the Jews had crucified the savior. So impressed was he with the description of the role of the Jews in the crucifixion of Jesus Christ, as described by his pious mother on every occasion, that his nanny found him one day laying out his wooden blocks in the form of crosses all over the floor of the living room. He enthusiastically explained to her that he proposed to beat the bad Jews with these wooden crosses. His parents repeated the story to all their friends, who praised him and patted his head. Whenever he refused to eat smoked ham, which he loathed, his mother threatened that people would think he was a Jew.

There was only one Jewish family in their village. They were quite well off, making a good living as horse traders. He could still remember their spacious farmhouse with its red-painted wood and yellow grillwork. The boys called it 'the Jew-house' and never hid in its yard when they played hide-and-seek, but on the rare occasions when they approached it to retrieve a ball mistakenly thrown in that direction, they would never come away without receiving an apple or a pear or a piece of cake. They enjoyed the food, but were somehow convinced that it had a peculiar Jewish taste.

He was friendly, but never close, to the two Jewish sons of this family, one of whom was his classmate. When the Jewish boys spoke French between them, their parents having originated in France, he and his friends were convinced they were speaking Hebrew, which created an atmosphere of mistrust, as if they were discussing clandestine matters.

It was only much later, in his student years, that he encountered other people of Jewish origin. In those years Loosli had already developed a mind of his own, unwilling to accept without question the prejudices prevailing in the society in which he lived. His intellectual curiosity and his inborn honesty made him take a second, unbiased, look at his Jewish fellow students. Most of them were at that time of Polish or Russian origin, poor devils, as he thought of them, hardly the image of the wealthy blood-sucking Jew. Although some of their ways were strange to him, he had to admire their good manners, their hard work, and their dedication not only to their studies but also to any cause they idealistically supported. Out of an inborn curiosity, he would sometimes accept an invitation to one of their bare rooms, where they would hold arguments late into the night on matters of general importance, as if they had no problems of their own. He always came away with the feeling that they were ready to give their lives for an ideal, which some of them later actually did. He envied them their dedication, which he could not share.

In years to come, as an art dealer and critic, he often expressed to his Aryan friends his preference for doing business with Jews, who, in his experience, were more ready to remove from an exhibition, and from the market, a painting that was labeled as a forgery, thus suffering considerable loss. Invariably his friends admitted the facts concerning an individual Jew, but they often added that 'He was honest, in spite of his Jewish origin.' They would hold on to their prejudices concerning Jews in general. Loosli could not, in good faith, take a similar stand.

One day, in 1924, a friend handed him the German edition of the *Protocols of the Elders of Zion*, published by Alfred Rosenberg. He had read in some paper that a document existed concerning a Jewish conspiracy to dominate the world. At the time he had ignored it as a lot of nonsense. But holding the book in his hands he started reading it out of sheer curiosity. After a few pages he felt like throwing it away, but was prevented by his sense of respect for anything in print. It was such crude and vulgar nonsense, surely no more than an idiotic joke! By this time Loosli had made a name for himself as a serious historian, a writer and an art critic. When his friend insisted that many people believed that the *Protocols* were authentic and that local anti-Semitic groups treated them as their Bible, he decided to read the book to the end. Some time later he bought a newspaper in a kiosk and was handed Henry Ford's book *The International Jew*, which was being distributed free of charge. He hoped to find in Ford's book support for his belief that the *Protocols* were mere trash. He forgot about it for a while, for, after all, what did he care about the Jews?

When he finally read Ford's book, he was astounded at the fact that Ford actually accepted without challenge the contents of the *Protocols* and promoted their publication around the world. He had never heard of Philip Graves and had not read his articles in *The Times* of London, but he had a vague memory of something similar to the *Protocols*, and suddenly remembered the book by Maurice Joly, which he had come across years earlier when studying the period of Napoleon III. He compared the two books, realized the extent of the plagiarism, and became very angry. He was convinced that the *Protocols* were forged, and maintained that its distributors, like Henry Ford and Alfred Rosenberg, were accomplices to the forgery, and deserved to be tried by a Swiss court. It was at this point that he decided that his duty, as a decent Swiss citizen, was to expose the forgers and the liars. He decided to write a book about the Jews, about Judaism and about the evil of anti-Semitism. Examining the state of the Jews in his own country he learned for the first time that the Jews had been given full citizen rights in Switzerland on 29 May 1874, and he wondered how it was possible that they were still being discriminated against by some segments of society 50 years later. How was that possible in a country where there was statistically only one half Jew for each hundred Aryans?

He had long been an admirer of Henry Ford. He had read his autobiography and was intrigued by the American fairy tale in which a poor mechanic had succeeded in becoming the world's most famous multi-millionaire. He had considered Ford a man of vision, a model for young people everywhere, the embodiment of everything good this century had to offer. On reading *The International Jew* his disillusionment was therefore devastating. How could such a man be so blind, so misled? There was not even one Jew per thousand people in this world, and most of the Jews were poor and miserable: how could a secret Jewish government be said to lead the whole world by its nose? How could 300 Jews, who constituted the alleged Jewish government in Ford's book, initiate wars and revolutions? How could they manipulate the economy, the banking world and the stock exchange when they could not even succeed in protecting their own people from misery and from persecution?

In the eyes of Ford, he mused, it was not the German Emperor Wilhelm who had promoted the German dream that caused the big war; it was not the German firms, such as Krupp, that had been interested in opening up new markets for their products; it was not the Germans who had torn Alsace-Lorainne from their French neighbors: it was the Jewish newspapers that were responsible for all that. It was Jews who were behind the murder of the Austrian crown prince in Sarajevo that triggered the war; it was Jews who had drawn Jew-less countries such as Japan and Montenegro into the war; it was Jews who were behind the Chinese declaration of war against Germany, in a country free of Jews. It was Jewish journalists who had drawn the long-hesitant US government into the war. How could a man like Henry Ford believe such utter nonsense?

One of the things that angered Loosli most was Ford's statement that the Jews, who had promoted the war in the first place and were the sole reason for its outbreak, did not take part in the patriotic efforts of their countries during the First World War. The man should have at least researched his facts, Loosli thought. There was ample proof of Jews' patriotism in every one of their adopted countries. In Germany alone 100,000 Jews had fought in the war, 12,000 Jews had been laid to rest in military graveyards, and 35,000 still proudly carried on their uniforms the Iron Cross, the most important decoration for bravery under fire. The same was true in other countries involved in the war.

He had set out to write a book about the Jews, but soon found that he was arguing with Henry Ford. Loosli's disillusionment with the man who had written such unfounded nonsense, yet whose book had found its way into the homes and the hearts of so many Europeans, was boundless; he perceived it as a personal affront, an insult to man's intelligence.

Like other non-Jews before and after his time, and indeed many Jews, Loosli believed he could confront the issue of anti-Semitism armed with facts and figures. He wrongly thought that he could expose anti-Semites such as Henry Ford and show them up for what they were. He was naively sure that once the readers saw how wrong and unfounded Ford's allegations were, they would laugh him out of all the kiosks and bookstores. Was it not the Aryans who, for a thousand years, had tried to force their religion on others by means of brutal force, even torture and murder? Was it not the planting of the cross in foreign lands that had brought in its wake death and extermination to so called 'non-believers'? Was it not the Aryan nations that had conquered foreign lands and by foul means enslaved whole populations? Was it not the Aryans who had labeled others 'inferior races', ruthlessly robbing them of their lands and of their freedom, and even of their right to their own God? How could they blame all that on the Jews, who were the victims?

He remembered with shame how he had been taught that the Jews were all bad, so he called his book *Die Schlimmen Juden* (The Bad Jews). But the sarcasm was lost on his readers. His book enjoyed a brief spark of life, when readers at first mistakenly thought it was another book exposing the Jews. When the true nature of the book became known, it sank into oblivion. Loosli learned that anti-Semitism had no rhyme or reason. It was just there, and confronting it with logical arguments was like beating your head against a stone wall. Long after his own book was forgotten, Ford's was re-published in many translations and distributed around the world, even after his famous apology and his formal undertaking to remove it from the market.

In 1934 Loosli was appointed by Judge Meyer as court expert in the Berne trial. The judge did not want to appoint a Jew, and there were not many non-Jewish candidates in Berne who were able and willing to undertake such a mission. Loosli gave his consent after much hesitation. He knew from bitter experience that it was fruitless to confront the anti-Semites in the so-called 'marketplace of ideas'. This was not about ideas, this was about prejudice, he now realized. He had learned that the Fords of this world could not be confronted in a bookstore. Could they be beaten in a court of law? It was not the Jews who would be on trial here but a forged document, he said to himself; he would not be confronted with bigots, the defense would have to produce an expert, if they could. A Ford would not be allowed to testify in a court of law. Little did he know that instead he would be confronted with Ulrich Fleischhauer.

Ubald von Roll had read Loosli's book. He knew they would be facing a formidable, non-corruptible expert. He wrote to Princess

Karadja in desperation seeking ways to meet Loosli's expertise, the contents of which he could well guess. Again it was Erfurt who had the answer: Loosli must be discredited.

On 28 November Fleischhauer wrote to Schnell, 'You all have to start working hard! I urgently need information about persons named Loosli so that we can identify "our" Loosli. Our "friend" C. A. Loosli, is he the only one or are there others? Did our L. visit Algiers in 1906?'

This demand for information about a visit to Algiers became an obsession with Fleischhauer, to be repeated in many letters. 'You have no idea what wonderful material I have from Paris, which will be useless unless I have your information about Algiers,' Fleischhauer wrote. Four days later Toedli informed Fleischhauer, using the codename Düring, that he was sending him a list of all the Looslis in the telephone book, but still had not found any information about a visit to Algiers.

He was greatly disappointed when Toedli finally informed him that 'their' Loosli had never lived in North Africa.

In later years, whenever Loosli's name was mentioned, Georges Brunschvig used to recount to his friends a little anecdote. On the evening of 26 October 1934, three days before the opening of the Berne trial, he had been working very late in his office. He was tired and discouraged and hoped to rearrange his material and his thoughts. When the telephone rang he considered ignoring it, but the caller was persistent and on the seventh ring he picked up the receiver. An excited Jewish owner of a small business was on the line, complaining that anti-Semitic books were being publicly displayed in the Werdt-passage in the center of Berne. Georges tried to calm him and promised to deal with the matter immediately. It was a short walk from his office on the main street and it would do him good, he decided, striding resolutely in the direction of the Werdt-passage. He was astounded to see whole rows of Loosli's book *The Bad Jews*, published in 1927 by the Pestalozzi-Fellenberg publishing house, filling the center of the bookshop window. Suddenly his spirits rose. If a Swiss shopkeeper foresaw a possible profit, it was a sign that the city of Berne was taking notice of the trial. The trial was about to open and the owner of the store was trying to benefit from the publicity, displaying the book with a red jacket as the first revelation in the Berne trial.

They had a forum and the public would be listening. It was up to him and to his colleagues to make the most of it.

It was scary, but it was also exhilarating for a young lawyer on the threshold of his career. Most of all it was a privilege from which no responsible Jew could walk away.

Standing in front of the bookstore, in the cold but clear autumn evening, after long months of excruciating work and many fears and disappointments, Georges Brunschvig knew that he must win this trial. He dare not fail.

6 Difficult Decisions

Georges Brunschvig read and reread the articles of Radziwill, du Chayla and Philip Graves. He could not wait for scheduled meetings of the group to give vent to the turmoil in his head. He could think of nothing else, for the phenomenon he encountered undermined all his beliefs, all his convictions. He had decided to study law as a means of serving the cause of justice. He believed that prejudice and hatred stemmed from ignorance. Wrong ideas were based on wrong facts, he thought. Give people access to the truth and they will draw the right conclusions, he believed. The law, for him, was an instrument, a way of revealing facts in their proper perspective, supported by a respected, unbiased, voice of authority. How else did you confront lying witnesses, false Messiahs, religious fanatics and crooked politicians, who spread lies to enhance their illegitimate aims? The law, for him, was not an academic exercise, it was a means of promoting justice, of building a better society. Some of his friends told him that he was naive. The law was a profession like any other, they argued. It was a way to make a living; a lawyer represented the subjective truth of his client, they maintained, not the ultimate truth.

Studying his long career at the bar, one noticed that, unlike most of his colleagues, Georges Brunschvig never lost this 'naivety'; all his life he insisted on representing clients in whom he believed, causes that he could, in good faith, support. How did he succeed in maintaining this moral attitude, how did he become such a famous lawyer without acquiring a touch of cynicism, friends often asked Odette and Emil Raas. It was the trial of the *Protocols* that shaped not only his career, but also his life, they both agreed unequivocally. They remembered how he had insisted that they read the articles of Radziwill, du Chayla and Philip Graves; he made them sit up late at night, quoting to them from a book by Benjamin W. Segel, a well-known journalist and historian, *The Protocols of the Elders of*

Zion – The Greatest Lie in History, published in Germany in 1924. Segel's book, he told them, was widely approved and admired in scientific circles for its precision, its wit and its wealth of accurate and well-researched material. He also had in his possession two books in English. Fortunately they all knew English, so he made them read these books as well. One was by a well-known British scholar, Lucien Wolf, entitled *The Truth About the Forged Protocols of the Elders of Zion*, and the other, by Herman Bernstein, the man who had sued Henry Ford, *The History of a Lie – The Protocols of the Wise Men of Zion*, both published as early as 1921, even before the full truth about the *Protocols* emerged.

How was it possible, he asked again and again, keeping them awake late at night in a smoke-filled room, how could it be that all these facts, revealed in important newspapers and learned books, were completely ignored by publishers and distributors of the *Protocols of the Elders of Zion*; what made liars immune, he wondered; what about the intelligentsia, what about academic circles, he asked.

The intelligentsia mostly kept its silence. Some, such as the German author Thomas Mann, to whom Segel had sent his book, praised him for his work, and were sure that this was the end of this particular infamous libel. Others were less confident.

Professor Hans Delbrück, of the University of Berlin, wrote to him on 27 August 1925: 'You demand too much of German science. Science can only fight on a scientific basis; against stupidity even Gods fight in vain.'

A LAWYER'S TACTICAL DILEMMA

There was no doubt in Georges' mind that Princess Radziwill, Armand du Chayla and Philip Graves should be invited to testify at the Bern trial. Not only did each of them possess first-hand authentic and unique information, not only were they non-Jews who could not possibly be accused of subverting the truth, but most importantly their stories, drawn from personal experience, supported and corroborated each other and offered logical answers to obvious questions any judge might ask himself or herself: Who composed the *Protocols*? When? Where? For what purpose?

He carefully listed the points on which their case might benefit from the testimony of these witnesses:

1. All three witnesses stated that in spite of the fact that the *Protocols* were first published in Russia, they had been prepared in France.
2. Both Radziwill and du Chayla revealed that the *Protocols* had been composed in the French language, both of them having seen the original manuscript.
3. Although they had seen the manuscript on different occasions, in different countries and in the possession of different persons, both Radziwill and du Chayla, independently of each other, identified the document as being written in different hands, in a notebook that had a blue ink-stain on its first page.
4. Both Radziwill and du Chayla linked the fabrication of the document to agents of the Russian secret police in Paris: Radziwill having actually seen the manuscript in the hands of one of the forgers, who had confessed that he was working in the service of the chief Russian agent in Paris, Rachkovskii, and du Chayla having heard from Nilus that the document in his possession had been indirectly sent to him from Paris by the same General Rachkovskii.
5. Before the revelation of Philip Graves many questions concerning the *Protocols* did not seem to have a logical answer. Inevitably one wondered why Russian agents preparing a forged document to be published in Russia, did so in the French language; du Chayla, who had seen the French manuscript, also wondered why the document contained identifiable parts that were well written, while others were in poor French, obviously composed by a different person, not of French origin; finally, the document as a whole was too complicated, too ingenious, to have been composed by a police agent.

The answers to all those questions were fully supplied by Philip Graves. Almost two-thirds of the *Protocols* had been copied verbatim from the well-written *Dialogues in Hell* by Maurice Joly. Adapting the book to suit their purposes by deleting any reference to Machiavelli or Montesqieu, omitting any mention of an allegorical dialogue, and presenting it as a political document containing real minutes of meetings of a secret Jewish government, was much easier if done in French and then translated as a whole into Russian. Now it became clear why the parts composed by the forgers were inferior to those written by Maurice Joly.

It was not enough to present Joly's book to the court, Georges decided. Philip Graves must describe the dramatic manner in which he had received the book and the information from the Russian refugee, and, most important, the fact that the informant had received it from a retired colonel in the Russian secret service. He may even be induced to reveal the name of his informant.

6. The testimony of Princess Radziwill was fully corroborated by Henriette Hurblut, an admitted anti-Semite who had no reason to lie in favor of the Jews. Not only did her testimony fully support the details supplied by Radziwill, but she also added an important detail that served as a link to the testimony of Philip Graves. Although there was no chance that Hurblut would agree to testify at the trial, Georges hoped that Radziwill would be able to remember this missing detail that she herself had not mentioned.

Hurblut described how Golovinskii had prepared the forgery in the Bibliothèque Nationale in Paris, a detail that at the time seemed of no consequence. But, with mounting excitement, Georges now knew the importance of this seemingly marginal item. He had asked a friend in Paris to find him a copy of Maurice Joly's book, but was informed that it had not been on sale ever since it had been banned by the court at Maurice Joly's trial in 1865. Only one copy could be found in the Bibliothèque Nationale. On examining this copy, his informant had noticed various passages marked in pencil. At his request the friend compared these passages to the ones copied by the forger into the manuscript of the *Protocols*, and found them to be identical.

The forger had been so sure of himself that he did not even bother to erase the pencil marks, Georges thought. One could not pray for a better clue at a crime scene.

The testimony of these witnesses, Georges thought, was a boon from heaven, the answer to a lawyer's prayers. For the first time he felt not only hopeful but even confident that they had a good chance of winning the case, but he must find a solution to one problem that was at the back of his mind, and must now be dealt with.

In compiling his list of witnesses a trial lawyer often faces a difficult dilemma. Witnesses are not perfect and memory often plays strange tricks. An honest, truthful witness may be mistaken about one fact, which can be easily disproved, supplying the opposition with a golden opportunity to try to discredit his whole testimony. Witnesses have been known to cling obstinately to a mistaken detail, putting their true version in jeopardy.

Reading the testimony of Princess Radziwill, Georges immediately realized that she had made a glaring mistake. Describing how Golovinskii had come to call on her in Paris, she had added, 'I am now referring to the years 1904 and 1905.' On that occasion she had not even realized that Golovinskii was in the service of the Okhrana, Georges thought. She did not mention when Golovinskii showed her and her friends the manuscript of the *Protocols of the Elders of Zion*, only that it happened 'one day'. Obviously it had happened considerably later, as they had already become friends and were visiting each other. She was also aware at that time of his true work, and he mentioned quite freely the names of his collaborators.

In another passage of the interview, she said, 'Later, I heard that this same manuscript was incorporated by Sergei Nilus in his famous book.'

Had she paused to think, she would have realized that the episode in Paris, when she saw the forged document, must have occurred much earlier than she thought, for the manuscript to have reached Russia, been translated into Russian, and incorporated in a book that was published in 1905. By then Rachkovskii had been recalled from Paris and was back in Russia.

Actually, Georges suspected that the document had been fabricated some time before the turn of the century. Passages from the *Protocols* had been published in the newspaper *Znamia* in 1903, and he was fairly certain that the document had been in the possession of Nilus even before that time.

In his heart Georges felt that the princess had made an honest mistake. She had lived in Paris at different periods and had spent many years in that city; she was testifying from memory more than twenty years after the event she mentioned; she had no reason to invent such a fantastic story, which was fully corroborated by Henriette Hurblut; had she invented the story she would surely be careful about her dates. But would the judge agree? Would he not discard her whole testimony as unreliable? Would this not taint and harm their case? Was it a risk worth taking?

Presenting his dilemma to his colleagues, he insisted that the princess must absolutely be invited to testify, but suggested that they should not risk exposure by the opposition. They should volunteer to expose the discrepancy themselves.

They never foresaw that the witnesses, who had so readily and courageously exposed the truth 13 years before, would now hesitate to testify to the same facts in a court of law. So they were unpleasantly surprised when both Princess Radziwill and Philip Graves declined their invitation. The princess mentioned 'personal reasons', the nature of which she never disclosed, but she sent a sworn affidavit confirming all the facts published in her interview with *The American Hebrew* in February 1921. They decided to present the affidavit to the court and explain the discrepancy in dates. As it turned out, the defense did not even try to use the mistaken date in order to discredit the princess, not choosing to confront any matters of substance. Instead, they tried to discredit the princess by digging up scandalous gossip, to picture her as a loose woman who should not be believed.

The refusal of Philip Graves to testify in person was much more frustrating. Here was a journalist who had gained fame and prestige as being the first person to reveal the truth about the *Protocols of the Elders of Zion*. Through him *The Times* was identified everywhere as the newspaper devoted to fight this dangerous libel. How was it possible that this man would suddenly shy away from repeating his story in open court? Who or what scared him?

It was Saly Mayer who had sent the invitation to Philip Graves, forwarded by the Board of Deputies of British Jews in London. The sworn affidavit sent by Graves, which laconically confirmed that his account of the affair of the *Protocols*, which he had helped to expose, was true, came as a shock. Philip Graves was to be a central witness; they had hoped that his oral testimony would be dramatic and convincing. They had also hoped that he would present to the court the relevant documents from the archives of *The Times*, and that he would, for the first time, reveal the identity of his Russian informant. Having to settle for a sworn affidavit was a severe blow.

Like Georges, I too wondered what lay behind Philip Graves' refusal to testify, and decided to investigate.

On a sunny day in October 1994, I was sitting in the archive of *The Times* in London, reading, with mounting astonishment, the documents that told the full story of the involvement of Philip Graves and *The Times* in the matter of the *Protocols of the Elders of Zion*. I had thought that the role of *The Times* in the story of the *Protocols* had been limited to the publication of the Graves articles in August 1921. I had no idea that their involvement in the matter had continued for more than a decade, that it had become a source of income, and that, at a certain point, it had become a source of embarrassment. I was also not aware of the long arm of Hitler, who, as early as 1933, succeeded in causing apprehension at a prestigious British newspaper and fear in the heart of an otherwise courageous first-rate English journalist. The documents revealed the real reasons for Philip Graves' refusal to testify at the Berne trial, but more than that, they described the atmosphere prevailing in Europe at the very beginning of the Nazi regime in Germany, and the part played by the *Protocols of the Elders of Zion* in the Nazi propaganda machine.

A JOURNALIST'S MORAL DILEMMA

On 4 June 1953, one day after Philip Graves died at the age of 77 at his home in Ireland, *The Times* published a long obituary honoring him as one of its foremost correspondents. After describing his family history and listing the many posts he had occupied, *The Times* wrote: 'One of the pieces of historical research of which Graves was proud was his work in helping to prove that the *Protocols of the Learned Elders of Zion* were forgeries, at a time when they were being widely exploited for anti-Jewish purposes.'

Indeed, it was not only Graves who had reason to be proud of his revelation. *The Times* too had gained much prestige and credit by being the first to publish the dramatic truth about the *Protocols*. They also made a considerable profit, exceeding by far their initial investment in the loan granted to Raslovlev.

As soon as the Graves articles were published, in August 1921, they began to be in great demand. *The Times* printed the articles in a pamphlet and initiated a sales campaign promoting it around the world. It was reprinted in thousands of copies and sold in England for £1 each. The rights for publication in the USA were sold to E. Marshall in the beginning of September 1921, for $150. Rights were also sold to many other countries.

As early as 31 August the assistant manager of *The Times* reported that the *Protocols* pamphlets were 'selling quite well'.

On 8 September the manager of *The Times* wrote to Itamar Ben-Avi at the *Palestine Weekly* offering to sell the publishing rights in Palestine 'at a reduced price'. He also wrote to Poland saying there should be a good sale in that country, 'which could continue for years'.

On 24 October Mr Barker of the French Times Agence Continental wrote, in answer to a demand for £100 for the French rights, 'I am sorry to say that after having seen the principal papers and publishers here, nobody seems to want it.' They were not interested in the subject, he wrote, adding: 'The French are a funny lot!'

The five years mentioned in the agreement with Raslovlev had long expired, and the rights should have reverted to him on repayment of the loan. But the Russian refugee had vanished, leaving no forwarding address. Not that *The Times* had given up on the loan. Unaware of the fact that Hitler would precipitate a revival of the *Protocols*, they had thought, on the expiration of the five-year period in 1926, that they had exhausted the market as far as the sale of the *Protocols* pamphlet was concerned. They now decided to find Raslovlev and hold him to his obligation. They thought they had no more use for the Joly book. *Times* correspondents were instructed to search for Raslovlev, careful not to expose his identity. Publicly he was still referred to as 'Mr X'. The correspondent in Paris, Mr Barker, was the one who finally discovered him, living in a non-descript apartment in the French capital. On 27 January 1927, Barker presented Raslovlev with the demand to repay the loan.

Raslovlev was shocked. Indeed, he wrote to *The Times*, he had hoped at the time that the Bolshevist regime would not last and he would get his property back and repay the loan, for he was most interested in acquiring this rare document for his personal library. He reminded *The Times* that they knew quite well why the agreement had been made in the form of a loan. Now that he had no access to his property in Russia and funds, he suggested that *The Times* retain full ownership of Joly's book at the price of the loan, or that they extend the loan.

The Times chose the first alternative, and was thus in a position, as full owners of the Joly book, to continue the sale of their pamphlet when the *Protocols* were adopted by the Nazi propaganda machine, gaining renewed popularity in many countries.

By this time Philip Graves had become so identified with the exposure of the truth about the *Protocols* that even Jewish leaders sought his advice and assistance. On 11 September 1933, Neville Laski, chairman of the Joint Foreign Committee of the Board of Deputies of British Jews and the Anglo-Jewish Association, wrote to Graves quoting a letter by one Pierre van Paassen to Doctor Rubinow, in answer to a suggestion to investigate a rumor about the *Protocols*, not divulging the source of the rumor. According to the letter, Count Zu Rewentlaw, the man who had been sued by Achad Ha'am and retracted his allegations concerning the origin of the *Protocols*, as far back as March 1923, was the animator of the idea. He had already written extensively on anti-Semitic subjects and was now 'what you may call "the Nazi expert" of the anti-Jewish branch in the German administration.' According to this information the *Protocols* were to be preceded by a book written by Herman Goering, entitled *An appeal to English-speaking People*. The publication of the *Protocols* was to be postponed until they saw what reaction Goering's book produced. But by all appearances the *Protocols* were to be utilized, van Paassen wrote:

> I hear many grave things, I am afraid a new wave is coming. If the Soviets break off commercial relations with the Reich, Hitler will take it out on the Jews, as he imagines or pretends to think that this would be a Jewish counter-measure, and from what I hear, and I don't like to say it to a Jew, the worst is yet to come. The Jews have simply to make up their minds in America to get all Jews out of Germany. If this is not done they will be systematically starved and done away with. We must abandon hope that Hitler will relent!

Graves immediately sent the letter to his manager, but times had changed. An element of fear and apprehension had spread in Europe. In his letter to Graves of 14 September 1933, the manager of *The Times*, discussing the plan to publish again the *Protocols* pamphlet, advised caution: 'If we proceed with the project of a new edition of our pamphlet,' he wrote, 'it might be wise for us not to give it too much, or perhaps any, publicity in the columns of *The Times*, in view of the possibility of reprisals against us in Germany.'

The pamphlet was, indeed, published again, and it sold quite well. On 20 December 1933, the South African Jewish Board of Deputies asked Graves for the pamphlet for the purpose of reprinting it 'in order to counter a country-wide campaign to disseminate the *Protocols of the Elders of Zion*, especially within the Afrikaner section of the population'. The Board of Deputies in London had supplied 1,400 copies, and *The Times* agreed to sell them 400 more. The Board of Deputies could not have known that a few short months later they would need all available material concerning the *Protocols of the Elders of Zion*, in order to confront a hideous libel invented by the Nazi Front called the Grey Shirts, in a court of law in the small town of Grahamstone, in what came to be knows as the 'South African trial of the *Protocols*'.

Finally, even the French became interested. In March 1934 *The Times* was asked for permission to translate the pamphlet into French by Dr Brutzkin of the World Union of the Medical Advisory Bureau in Paris, which dealt with preserving the health of the Jews.

The *Protocols* were enjoying a new revival and the *Times* pamphlet was selling quite well, but, like the manager of *The Times*, Philip Graves was also trying to avoid unnecessary publicity and exposure. Asked to write an adaptation of his original articles, he flatly refused. He also refused to reveal the name of Raslovlev without his permission.

The reason for his refusal to testify in the Berne trial now became clear. In a memorandum to the editor of *The Times*, dated 28 February 1935, Graves informed him that he had sent a sworn statement to the lawyers in Berne 'to the effect that my account of the affair of the *Protocols* which I helped to expose, as you will remember, was true.' Further in the memorandum Graves' private dilemma was exposed:

> Meantime, as enclosed shows, one Dr Fleischhauer, professional anti-Semite and probably a Hun, has made statements impugning my personal character and veracity and implicitly accusing *The Times* of either having been deceived by me or having shared in the deception. So far I have declined to give the name of the Russian who collaborated with me in the matter, which is regarded as suspicious by the anti-Semites ... The Nazi champion also says that the copy of the book which I sent to *The Times*, and which I presume is in its possession, did not exist. Well, we ought to have it ... I cannot help thinking that if there is any doubt about the verdict and if it is admissible by the Swiss code, the ends of Justice might be served [here the following words were deleted: 'and my own reputation incidentally cleared'] if *The Times* consented to send the documents in its possession connected with the case to the Swiss court for confidential study, not of course for any public discussion, and on that condition. These documents would of course be returned ... I do not want to appear over-fussy as far as I myself am concerned, but I have step-relations, whose connection with me is unfortunately known in Bavaria. They have had a bad time already. One because his grandmother was a Jewess, the other because his wife's sister married a Jew and he himself as an ex-Guards officer, was always a strong Bavarian monarchist. The German embassy, which is full of Nazi agents, knows of my connection with these people and I am rather afraid that if Fleischhauer and these people get off with it and go on publishing stuff in the anti-Semitic press to the effect that the exposure of the *Protocols* was a fake done by me with corrupt

motives, this may react a bit on my step-relatives, who are decent people. On that account I would like to ask whether, should Swiss legal procedure permit it, *The Times* would consent to put the documents connected with the exposure of the *Protocols* into court. The Jews can probably help themselves; but my luckless Bavarian step-relations might not be able to if the Nazi crowd, knowing the fact of my connection with them, were able to publish statements, such as the attached, without any sort of denial. I quite see that there can be no question of polemics between *The Times* and the anti-Semitic rags of Germany and it is not in the least what I suggest. But I think that if the Swiss judge had the chance of examining the documents concerned, justice might be expedited and risks eliminated.

As to his request not to reveal the identity of Raslovlev, he explained:

So far I have declined to give the name of the Russian who collaborated with me in the matter, which is regarded as suspicious by the anti-Semites. My reason is this. I do not care to give the name of a third party in this matter without his permission, and where that Russian whose very name I cannot spell now, has gone, I do not know. I suspect he has gone back to Russia and on that account it will do him no good to have been mixed up with a correspondent of *The Times* in 1920 when Constantinople was full of anti-Bolshevik Russians.

On 24 April the editor of *The Times*, Wickham Stead, wrote to the manager of the paper about the request to have Graves submit a letter to the Berne court, suggesting that they find out if the book by Maurice Joly had reached the British Museum any time after 1864 and therefore the value and the importance of Graves' discovery would be beyond question, yet he maintained that 'It is not his discovery but the existence of the Geneva book [as Joly's book was still called], many years before the *Protocols* can have been issued or fabricated, that should form the main count in whatever trial may be pending in Berne.'

The considerations he suggested were these:

1. No lives should be endangered. They felt they had a moral, if not a legal, obligation to shield Raslovlev, though they did not know whether he was alive or whether his life might be endangered.
2. He was aware of the importance of the fact that the source was a

Russian ex-colonel, but it must be remembered that the colonel had not been named.

3. As Graves was anxious to shield his relatives, 'full weight should be given to the danger they may be in, but on the other hand, if it is merely a matter of sentiment ... I think we should not allow sentiment to stand in the way of our rendering what may be a very important service. If, from the standpoint of the Paper, it is desirable that it should not be dragged into a private lawsuit, it is, on the other hand, desirable that its action in being the first to expose a peculiarly damnable swindle should be widely known and recognized. As things stand today militant anti-Semitism may spread from Germany to other countries, particularly to the United States, and we may not be altogether immune from it here, as the tactics of Oswald Mosley suggest. Therefore it might be well if *The Times* were on record as having sought to vindicate the truth as soon as its attention was drawn to it by the vigilance of a member of its foreign staff.'

Finally, a compromise was reached between *The Times* and the Board of Deputies: in addition to the affidavit Graves had already sent to Bern, photocopies of various documents were delivered to Neville Laski on the condition – confirmed in a letter by Laski to *The Times* on 26 April 1935 – that they should not be produced by the Jewish community of Switzerland in the trial, of their own motion. It was desirable, they agreed, that the court in Bern should use some means analogous to a *subpoena duces tecum* on *The Times* to provide the production of the original documents and the book, so that *The Times*, so far as possible, could maintain the attitude of impartiality in the interests of truth emerging in this trial.

Neville Laski wrote further: 'You also press upon me, and I recognize to the full, the desirability of protecting, particularly as we do not know whether the Russian individual is alive or dead, the safety of this individual, which might be endangered if he is alive and his name were disclosed.'

Unhappy with the compromise, but feeling bound by it, the team in Berne decided not to subpoena *The Times* or Philip Graves. They did present to the court Philip Graves' sworn affidavit, but made no use of any of the *Times* documents.

I remembered Emil Raas's description of how, in a dramatic gesture, Georges Brunschvig had presented Judge Meyer with Maurice Joly's book. Emil could not remember how Georges had got hold of it.

Years later I was presented by Odette with an original copy of Maurice

Joly's book, which she had found in Georges's private library. A small brown book, bound in leather, printed in Brussels in 1864 by 'A. Mertens et Fils' of 'rue de l'Escalier, 22'. No name of the author on the fly-leaf. Instead, it says 'Par un Contemporain' – by a contemporary. But after these words, somebody had scribbled with a soft pencil the words '(Maurice Joly)', in beautiful unidentified handwriting. The introduction, also unsigned, less than two small pages long, is entitled 'Simple Avertisement'. It explains that although the book is composed as fiction, it may be applied toany government, but applies, in particular, to one certain political system. The words 'Genève, le 15 Octobre, 1864', printed at the bottom, reveal where and when Maurice Joly had composed these pages. Now it is clear why the book was sometimes erroneously referred to as 'the Geneva book'.

I do not know, to this day, where this copy came from. The court archives in Berne do not exist, so there is no way of confirming my guess that Georges may have retrieved the book from the court files after the termination of all the court proceedings; but nobody knows how Georges had originally obtained it.

I cherish this rare copy, which is still in my possession. It has 324 pages of text, divided into 25 'dialogues'; I remember that the forgery contains 24 so-called 'Protocols'.

The printer was not very careful, I note, as the last page, entitled 'Errata' lists no fewer than 14 corrections.

I sometimes look at the book wondering how such an intelligent, well-written book, composed by a concerned French citizen who wished to expose a corrupt dictatorial regime, could have been exploited by crude forgers to cause my people so much pain and suffering. I also wonder how Maurice Joly would have reacted had he known how his book was used. But Maurice Joly was long dead.

It was only when the appeal against Judge Meyer's judgment was pending in the Supreme Court in Berne that Philip Graves was finally ready todisclose the name of his informant. On 28 April 1937, he wrote to the manager of *The Times*:

> At the time I thought that the disclosure of Raslovlev's former association, however slight, with a member of the staff of the 'Capitalist-Imperialist' *Times* might do him no good with the *Ogpu* [military intelligence service]. Now, however, it looks as if the situation in Russia is greatly changed. Most of the leading Communists have been killed or are doing hard labor, and it is very likely that the present Russian Government would not show any hostility to a man because he had formerly been cooperating with me for a short spell ... and I am inclined to think that, assuming that my Russian informant has returned to Russia ... it might serve the interests of justice if *The Times* agreed to

give this person's name, on condition that the Jews interested in the trial were able to obtain a promise from the Russian embassy that my informant in Constantinople, if living in Russia, would not be regarded or treated with hostility on account of the service which he rendered more than 15 years ago.

Indeed, if Raslovlev had returned to Russia, which was most doubtful, he was at no risk at all. At that time the authorities in Russia were cooperating fully with the lawyers in the Berne trial and allowing their representative to examine and copy any relevant documents in the official archives.

But Graves had other reasons for his change of attitude. He realized by now that, try as he may, he could not disassociate himself from the *Protocols of the Elders of Zion*. At the end of his letter he wrote:

Might I add a personal reason which induces me to express the hope that *The Times* might see its way to supplying the material to the parties interested, through Mr Neville Laski. Statements have been made several times in the Nazi papers to the effect:

1. That the *Times* correspondent in Constantinople was really Mr Lucien Wolf.
2. That the *Times* correspondent at Constantinople was a man of straw who was paid or persuaded by the Jews to take the credit of an unreal discovery.
3. That the *Times* correspondent at Constantinople was of Jewish origin.

He added:

The first two allegations are more comic than important; as for the third, however, it might put German friends and relatives of mine into a difficult position. My stepmother is German, and I am again through her family connected further back with the von Ranke family of Bavaria. One of them, who had the misfortune to have a Jewish maternal grandmother, though she made haste to be baptized, lives in continual fear of losing his scanty pension. Another who is a good friend of mine is under suspicion as a Bavarian Monarchist, and I have been rather afraid lately that if my relationship with these people was known to the Nazis, the fable of Jewish extraction might be worked to their great disadvantage. This gives me a reason for hoping that *The Times* might be able to stretch a point in this affair and allow a larger disclosure than in the first trial.

I have spoken to the Editor on the matter. He says that for his part he has no objection provided that it does not involve *The Times* in any difficulties.

I might add that so far the Jews who brought the action in Switzerland appear to have behaved quite honorably with regard to the material which they were allowed to see.

The matter of the *Protocols* continued to be a focal point in Philip Graves' life. The importance he attached to his involvement in the matter is clear from a letter he wrote to the editor of *The Times*, Mr Dawson, on 18 February 1939. He had conceived the idea, he said in the letter, of writing a book on the *Protocols of the Elders of Zion*, and their exposure by himself in 1921. After describing again all the facts of the matter and the history of his revelation, he mentioned that the pamphlet published by *The Times* had sold extremely well 'and is now sold out', adding 'I had no royalty from *The Times* and took no commission from the vendor.'

He continued:

Some time ago, I remember that you told me that you regarded the discovery by *The Times* of the forgery as in some respects unfortunate. I quite see that in the present state of feeling in a great part of the continent, *The Times* might wish to be disassociated from this publication in the future, not on account of any sympathy whatever with the prevailing anti-Semitism, but because the connection of *The Times* with the exposure makes it hard to persuade many important people in Germany and elsewhere that *The Times* is not Jewish influenced or Jewish run.

In any case *The Times* has now made all it can be expected to make out of the discovery. I have conceived the idea, perhaps foolishly, of writing a book on the subject that might be eligible for the Nobel Prize. Quite obviously this would be impossible and indeed undesirable were the book still the property of *The Times*. I also feel that the book would be of interest and perhaps of a little value to my family. I would therefore be glad to know whether the proprietors of *The Times* would give me an option for two years on the book and such relevant documents as guarantee its authenticity, on the condition that on its surrender to me, or within a period to be fixed hereafter, I should pay *The Times* Publishing Company a sum equal to that which they paid for the book.

On 28 February 1939, J. S. Maywood, of the *Times* staff, wrote to assistant manager, Mr F. Philippe Bishop:

> In a book on anti-Semitism written by the late Count Coudenhove I find the following passage: 'It ought to be made clear to all those who know the *Protocols* that the publication is a plagiarism of fatal world importance. The work of enlightenment is not only a duty to the caluminated Jews, but also to truth, for it is no exaggeration to say that the so-called *Protocols of the Elders of Zion* are both one of the most insolent forgeries of all times and one of the meanest calumnies which have ever existed in universal history.'
>
> This, I feel, provides the key to Graves' idea of writing a book on the subject; and if, as he suggests in his letter to the editor, that it would be unwise to do so while the book remained the property of *The Times*, then there is good reason for suggesting that for the purpose of his book he should consult the copy in the British Museum, for he mentions also, the documents proving its authenticity.

On 10 March 1939 Mr Bishop informed Graves of their decision:

> At the request of the Editor I put before the Board yesterday your letter of 18 February. The matter was fully discussed and in result the Board instructed me to say that there would be no objection to your making use of the books and papers connected with the *Protocols of the Elders of Zion* which are now in our possession. The Board decided, however, that they should remain the property of *The Times*.'

Philip Graves did not avail himself of the permission granted by *The Times* to use their material for his book. The Second World War, which broke out a few short months after the permission had been granted, may have placed other more important matters on the agenda of a busy foreign correspondent of a big newspaper.

Most of these facts were unknown to Georges Brunschvig and to his colleagues on the team. In any event, they could not have revealed to the court any information received from London, bound by their promise to honor the agreement reached with *The Times*. Indeed, as

Philip Graves mentioned in his letter to *The Times*, 'the Jews who brought the action in Switzerland appear to have behaved quite honorably with regard to the material which they were allowed to see'.

They were, indeed, honorable men, I muse, confronting adversaries devoid of honor and of any moral considerations.

Actually the name of Raslovlev was not revealed to the lawyers in Berne. It remained secret till 1978, when Colin Holmes, a lecturer on economic history at Sheffield University, who researched the matter in the *Times* archives, found the receipt Raslovlev had signed for the loan he had received from *The Times*, and made his discovery public.

THE *MORNING POST* – HOW TO MAKE MONEY BY BLAMING THE JEWS

I often pondered what I would have felt were I in the shoes of Judge Meyer. As issue after issue of the *Protocols* was added to the growing pile of books on my desk, I wondered how a judge, with his limited access to historical material, could divorce himself completely from the sheer impact of publications in so many languages: surely he must have been aware of the numerous introductions to all these publications, comparing, in all seriousness, current historical events with actual items which were part of the devious so-called Jewish conspiracy. How could he rule on the evidence presented in court, ignoring all the publications promoting the *Protocols*, including articles published in respectable newspapers?

Judge Meyer must have been aware of German anti-Semitism, but what about German historians and scientists, what of German writers and intellectuals? How was it possible that all through the 1920s, before the Hitler era, faced with a massive amount of publications and articles even in respectable newspapers, repeating the story of the *Protocols*, blaming the Jews for the World War, and warning of the Jewish conspiracy, the spiritual leaders of German culture kept their silence. Didn't it make him wonder?

The lawyers in Berne had the same misgivings, but they were particularly worried about the impact on the judge of publications in British newspapers, for British fairness was taken for granted in Switzerland.

True, *The Times* was now on record claiming unequivocally that the *Protocols* were a forgery. The *Spectator*, which had on 20 May 1920, described the *Protocols* as 'brilliant in [their] moral perversity and intellectual depravity', and had, on 16 October 1920, called for the appointment of a Royal Commission to inquire into the subject, suggesting re-examination of the admission of Jews to British citizenship, did not repeat its claim after the revelation of Philip Graves. But it was the *Morning Post* that had mounted the most persistent anti-Jewish campaign based on the *Protocols*, the British equivalent of the campaign led in America by Henry Ford's *Dearborn Independent*.

Why would a British newspaper adopt the *Protocols* as a major feature, lending its pages to the most virulent attack on Jews, refusing to retract its policy even in the face of the public sensational revelations of Philip Graves?

Studying the strange affair of the *Morning Post* Georges Brunschvig suggested to his colleagues that they must be prepared with a full brief on the matter, in case the opposition decided to refer to it in an attempt to influence the court and the press.

Unfortunately their brief was incomplete, as they did not have access to all the relevant material. It was only much later, years after the Berne trial, that the full behind-the-scenes facts were revealed and made public.

The Berne lawyers could not have known that it was pure greed that motivated the editorial board of the *Morning Post*. All they knew was that in the summer of 1920 this newspaper published a series of 17 articles, based on the *Protocols of the Elders of Zion*, followed, in August 1920, by a book entitled *The Cause Of World Unrest*, to which almost all the staff of the *Morning Post* contributed. They repeated the theory that all political unrest was artificial, the product of the Hidden Hand, of a formidable sect, the Jews, those ancient enemies of the human race, who throughout their worldwide dispersion had secretly preserved their old political organization, and were still using it with deadly persistency to overturn the established Christian order of things and to found in its place a universal Jewish dominion under the scepter of a Sovereign of the House of David. The Jews were, in short, *The Cause Of World Unrest*. The *Protocols of the Elders of Zion* were presented as proof.

Like America, Britain, too, was gripped by a 'red scare' in the wake of the Russian Revolution. Although the vast majority of the Jewish community in England was completely unsympathetic to Bolshevism, it was enough to mention some prominent names of Jews who were supporters of the Russian Revolution to give credence in the eyes of the public to the fantastic allegation that the Revolution was part of the Jewish conspiracy, and that the Jews were therefore a threat to British society.

But, fantastic though it may seem, the Jews were also accused of collaborating with the Germans, and as early as 1918 rumors of a German–Jewish–Bolshevik conspiracy were circulated in England, emanating from an anonymous booklet entitled *England Under the Heel of the Jew*. It promoted the idea that Jews and Germans were behind the Bolshevik Revolution, and were collaborating in gaining domination of international finance, banking and business. Anti-German feelings, which were still strong in the wake of the war, combined with the fear of Bolshevism, turned out to be a potent tool fully exploited not only by anti-Semites but also by diplomats and even by the responsible press.

Both *The Times* and the *Morning Post* had right-wing correspondents in Russia. The *Times* special correspondent, Robert Wilton, who had been brought up in Russia, declared in a book published in 1920 that the Bolsheviks were Jewish agents of the Germans. But it was the correspondent of the *Morning Post* who became obsessed with the *Protocols of the Elders of Zion* and after returning to England dedicated all his remaining years to their promotion.

Victor E. Marsden was an Englishman married to a Russian. His vivid descriptions of the events in Russia earned him the anger of the Soviet authorities. Suspected of the murder of a captain by the name of Cromie, he was arrested and thrown into the famous Peter-Paul prison in St Petersburg, where he was subjected daily to threats of execution. He believed that a Jew had murdered the captain, and blamed the Jews for his troubles. When he was finally released and allowed to return to England, he was a wreck in body and in mind. On his return journey he carried with him not only a burning resentment of the Jews, but also a copy of the *Protocols of the Elders of Zion*, which he swore to make public in his home country, if it was the last thing he did.

Losing no time, Marsden immediately started his translation of the *Protocols*, his mastery of both Russian and English coming in handy. He worked in the British Museum, comparing his copy of the fourth edition of the Nilus *Protocols* with the first edition deposited in the museum in 1906, and composing not only an introduction, but also a summary placed at the head of each one of the 24 protocols.

It was a long and tedious job, as his ill health did not allow him to work more than one hour a day. His translation of the *Protocols* was finally published in London in 1925 by the British Publishing Society, and was on sale for many years.

The anonymous composer of the preface to Marsden's edition maintained that 'this work was carried out at the cost of Mr. Marsden's own life's blood'.

In his introduction Marsden referred to Sergei Nilus as 'Professor Nilus', and quoted Henry Ford, who had said in an interview published in the *New York World* on 17 February 1921: 'The only statement I care to make about the *Protocols* is that they fit in with what is going on. They are sixteen years old, and they have fitted the world situation up to this time. They fit it now.'

'Indeed they do!' declared Victor Marsden.

He also maintained that there was a strong presumption and ample proof that the *Protocols* were issued at the first Zionist Congress held at Basle in 1897 under the presidency of the Father of Modern Zionism, the late Theodor Herzl.

It was this man who prepared the ground for the immense involvement of the *Morning Post* with the *Protocols of the Elders of Zion*. His connection with the paper was not severed on his return to England, and his prestige was such that when his health improved slightly he was assigned the important post of special correspondent in the suite of HRH The Prince of Wales on his empire tour. Marsden's views on the *Protocols* carried much weight with the editorial staff, but they did not wait for his translation, which was published only in 1925. Actually, the *Protocols* had preceded him and had arrived in England immediately after the Revolution, carried by Russian intelligence officers. An anonymous typewritten translation, which omitted anti-British passages, was circulated among politicians, highly placed civil servants and editors of newspapers. Even before the *Protocols* were published under the title *The Jewish Peril* early in 1920, a copy found its way on to the desk of the *Morning Post*'s editor, H. A. Gwynn, in the autumn of 1919.

Intrigued by the document, realizing its potential, Gwynn was nevertheless doubtful of its authenticity, and sent it for evaluation to various people, among them the owner of the paper Lady Bathhurst, the poet Rudyard Kipling, Sir Basil Thompson, head of the Special Branch of Scotland Yard, and Leon Maxse, a right-wing political journalist.

In spite of his anti-Semitic views, Rudyard Kipling indicated that the document was a forgery. 'The typed stuff is some sort of fake,' he wrote, 'a concoction of German Philosophy twenty years ago.' Sir Basil Thompson considered the document 'mere moonshine'. Leon

Maxse was emphatic in maintaining that it was 'a hoax' and advised against publication, warning that serious consequences might arise should it be published. But Gwynn chose to adopt Marsden's belief in the *Protocols*, putting his reputation on line.

From late October 1919 until the summer of 1920 a heated debate went on in the *Morning Post* about the publication of the *Protocols*. It was mostly an argument between the editor, Gwynn, and the business manager, Henry Peacock, who, uncharacteristically, chose to intervene in editorial policy. Both these gentlemen wrote long memorandums to Lady Bathhurst in an attempt to influence her, as she herself had serious doubts about the authenticity of the document and hesitated to agree to publication.

Henry Peacock urged her to refrain from publication. 'Men of the world will regard these articles as mere midsummer moonshine,' he wrote. 'They remind me of the absurd attacks made by zealous Roman Catholics from time to time on Freemasonry, and I regard them as having just as much foundation.' He quoted George Saunders, who had served as their expert on other occasions, as completely denying the authenticity of the *Protocols*; Sir William Tyrrell, director of the Department of Political Intelligence at the Foreign Office, wrote: 'A rapid glance at the *Protocols* confirms my impression that they almost verge on lunacy.'

Peacock was convinced that the *Protocols* were false, explaining that 'if a gathering of great international Jews with the knowledge of generations of their predecessors to help them in this formidable conspiracy could not turn out anything better than these documents, it seems a rather poor tribute to the genius and intellect of the Jewish race ... Frankly I believe we have stumbled on a mare's nest.'

He stated frankly that he was no lover of Jews and that they might have well deserved their persecution in Russia. It was not so much a dedication to honest journalism, he confessed, as a fear of the Jews, who were 'good haters', that prompted his opposition to the publication of the articles, which were even then in preparation.

But Gwynn had set his heart on the publication of the articles. He had good business reasons. In the spring of 1920 the paper was in need of a major feature.

At the end of the war the average daily sales of the *Morning Post* had been reduced by 10,000 copies, compared to sales at the opening of the war. In the beginning of 1920 they had hit on a bit of luck: they succeeded in acquiring, for the price of £1,500, what was

considered by some as 'the scoop of the century' – the letters of
Kaiser Wilhelm II to Tsar Nicholas II, which later became known as
the *Willy Nicky Letters*. When the letters were serialized in the
Morning Post, daily circulation grew by 7,000.

Soon afterwards they published the *German Spy Articles*, which
had an even wider popular appeal, and raised sales to their highest
point yet.

Gwynn believed that this was the winning formula – all they
needed now was another winning feature. In the existing anti-
German and anti-Bolshevik atmosphere, a document placing the
blame for all international unrest squarely on the shoulders of the
Jews would surely be a feature to beat all other features, evidence of
the biggest and most dangerous conspiracy in human history.

It was now a question of who won the race *vis-à-vis* Lady
Bathhurst. To Peacock's memorandum Gwynn responded with one
of his own. They should not fear the Jews, he wrote, 'We have had
the reputation of being anti-Jew for three years and we have flour-
ished!'

> I consider the *Protocols* a most masterly exposition – very high-
> falutin' of course, as would be natural in an oriental race – a dis-
> tinct programme intended to achieve the aim of the political
> Jew, which is the domination of the world ... You cannot point
> to a single revolution, since the French Revolution, in which the
> Jews have not played the principal part.

To allay the fears of Lady Bathhurst he promised that the articles
would not be a reprint of the *Protocols* but would only set forth the
theory of the conspiracy, ending with extracts from the *Protocols*;
they would not vouch for the absolute authenticity of the *Protocols*
and it would be up to the Jews to disprove their truth; he would get
'a splendid phalanx of historians' to support the articles; he intended to get the editors of other newspapers, both in London and in
the province, to agree to simultaneous publication so that the
Morning Post would not be alone in taking the blame. He assured the
owner of the paper that leading American newspapers would pay
handsomely for the reproduction of the articles.

In the end Gwynn prevailed, although he did not obtain the promised historians or the simultaneous publication by other newspapers.
The articles prepared by Colvin Grant were published. Not only did
the daily circulation increase by 10,000 copies, but the 17 articles

were followed, in August 1920, by a pamphlet called *The Cause of World Unrest*, to which most journalists of the *Morning Post* contributed, the introduction composed by Gwynn himself.

In 1921 the famous Jewish scholar Lucien Wolf, in his book *The Myth of the Jewish Menace*, said in response to the theory supported by the *Morning Post*:

> I confess to a feeling of shame at having to write this pamphlet at all. That reputable newspapers in this country should be seeking to transplant here the seeds of Prussian anti-Semitism, and that they should employ for this purpose devices so questionable and a literature so melodramatically silly, cannot but cause a sense of humiliation to any self-respecting Englishman.

The *Morning Post* folded in 1937 without ever having retracted the lie it had helped spread.

Studying the matter Georges Brunschvig was awed, realizing once again what formidable opponents he was going to face in that courtroom.

THE SYMBOLIC SERPENT

Closeted in his office, late at night, Georges spread out on his desk cartoons that decorated the covers of editions of the *Protocols* in various countries. Most of them presented an ugly and distorted image of a Jew, with a crooked nose, bulging eyes, wearing a skullcap on his head, and embracing the globe with claw-like hands. This one image, Georges recognized, succeeded in a most ingenious manner in conveying the whole message of the *Protocols*: it portrayed the ugly Jew enveloping, in a vicious vise, the whole world. Then there was the symbolic serpent. In many cartoons a menacing snake wound its way around the globe, choking the whole universe. He was reminded of du Chayla's description of his last meeting with Nilus, when Lifschitz translated for him from the Russian what Nilus had written on the coming of the Antichrist, who, springing from Jewish blood, will become Emperor of the World.

How will this be achieved? By means of the artfulness of the symbolic serpent. The tail of this serpent rests in Zion; the body, however, head forward, glides over the entire world. As the serpent insinuates itself into the bosom of the various states, it gnaws and eats away all non-Jewish political forces through constitutional liberalism and economic upheavals. The serpent had already passed seven stages on its way through universal history. At first, it began gnawing at the grandeur and power of Greece in the time of Pericles. The seventh halting-place was in St Petersburg in 1881, when Tsar Alexander was murdered. With the return of the serpent's head to Zion, the symbolical serpent would have accomplished its circular course round the world's history. It had already enclosed all of Europe in its circumference, and, through Europe, the rest of the world. The return of the serpent's head to Zion would take place only when the political powers of all European countries had been destroyed by the destruction and devastation the Jewish people always and everywhere brought about, through moral decomposition and depravity, foremost in which decline were liberal institutions.

Nilus did not invent the snake, Lifschitz told him. A man by the name of Butmi, a notorious Black Hundred writer, had also published the *Protocols* in Russia in 1906 and again in 1907, claiming to have obtained them from an independent source. His 1907 edition contained a note by an unnamed man who claimed to have translated the *Protocols* from the French on 9 December 1901. This man, too, mentioned: the political plan, conceived 929 years before the birth of Christ, by Solomon and the Judean Sages ... to conquer the world peacefully for Zion, with the cunning of the Symbolic Snake, whose head should be composed of the Jewish Government initiated in the plans of the Wise Men (always masked even to their people), and the body – the Jewish nation.

Georges had read the *Protocols* from cover to cover, including the introduction by Nilus, and he could not remember having noticed any mention of the symbolic serpent. How could he have missed it? He and Emil Raas now studied again the German as well as the English and the French editions – all translations of the fourth edition of the Nilus book – looking for a reference to the famous snake. To their utter amazement they realized that the European publishers had completely omitted these and similar passages from their text, fearing that such fanatical ramblings would be too much for their readers. What was good for Russian peasants, immersed in mythological horror-stories, might repel the German, English and French public. How else could they present Nilus to civilized Western society as a sane philosopher?

Translators in other countries followed suit. It was only Russian readers who were exposed to the full Nilus theory.

How ingenious, Georges thought, and how appropriate. No rules of copyright exist where a forgery is concerned. Each country may adopt its own version of the document.

But somehow the Russian-invented snake did reach the Western European public. It was a godsend to cartoonists and, though absent from the written text, it made its appearance on the book-covers of the *Protocols* and in the anti-Semitic press, leaving its mark, in a much more forceful manner, on the imagination of the public. Georges realized that even if the *Protocols* were to be declared a forgery by every court in the world, even if they were to be banned everywhere, the images in the cartoons, depicting an awesome snake encircling the globe, or wrapped around a huge cross, or worming its way through the map of Europe, dragging behind it a Star of David, would be forever stamped on people's minds.

How right he was, I thought 60 years later, examining cartoons published in the anti-Semitic press spread out on my desk. The same cartoons, the same Jew with the crooked nose, the same snake and the same message.

What is to stop them, I thought. What indeed?

7 The Witnesses

The lawyers in the group, Georges Brunschvig, Professor Matti and Boris Lifschitz, were worried. Their colleagues were confident that the experts, Loosli and Baumgarten, would convince the court of the falsehood of the *Protocols*. Hadn't the lawyers told them that the burden of proof rested on the shoulders of the defendants? There was no way, they maintained, that the defendants would supply any reliable evidence to substantiate the authenticity of the *Protocols of the Elders of Zion*.

But the lawyers knew that a courtroom is not an academic seminar. A judge might be bored by an historical expertise. What wins cases, even without juries, they argued, is the drama of a trial, the impact of live witnesses. They were sure that their opponents would supply enough drama with their unfounded but picturesque allegations. The sheer amount of the publications of the *Protocols* around the world and the support of respectable newspapers and leaders in various communities were powerful weapons in the hands of the defense. Add the existing prejudice against the Jews and you may well ask yourself what local judge would stick his neck out and declare a book published in every language, for the last 30 years, to be a forgery. An academic expertise was not enough, they felt, they needed live witnesses, authentic documents.

How would a small group in Berne, with limited funds, find material hidden in Russian archives? The Russians who might possess relevant information about the forgery had probably fled Russia after the Revolution. Who were they? Where do they live now? Would they remember? Would they be willing to testify?

It was at one of their morning meetings that a radiant Saly Mayer surprised them by reporting that he had good news and bad news. 'The bad news first,' he announced. 'In answer to our request for financial support by Jewish organizations, the Joint has sent us only $1,000. This is the bad news. But they have offered help, which might be worth much more.' They were indeed in need of some good news, Professor Matti whispered, as if to himself.

It was thus by sheer coincidence that they established contact with Alexander Tager, who was to become central to the preparations for the trial.

The American Jewish Joint Distribution Committee (better known as the Joint) was founded in 1914 to help Jews in need. After the Revolution they maintained firm contacts with the Soviet authorities to facilitate relief work among the Jews in Russia. Under an agreement reached with the authorities in 1922, the Joint contributed to the efforts of settling Russian Jews on the soil in the Ukraine and then in the Crimea. In 1924, with full Soviet support, the American Jewish Joint Agriculture Corporation (Agro-Joint) was founded to serve as the Joint's agent in this work. Alexander Tager, the legal representative of Agro-Joint in Russia, succeeded in building up and maintaining a close relationship with the authorities.

Like other Jewish organizations, the Joint became worried about the *Protocols of the Elders of Zion* as soon as they were published in the West. They had been corresponding with various officials in Russia since 1921, in an effort to obtain relevant material. Like other representatives of the Joint, Tager was also asked to assist in this effort and became quite familiar with the subject. The Joint officials had suggested to Saly Mayer that he contact Tager, and he could now inform his colleagues that the Moscow lawyer agreed to assist them in conducting research in Russian archives, collecting available information from official sources and supplying names of possible witnesses.

This was indeed great news. Tager became the most valuable source of material and information presented in the Berne trial. Unexpectedly, the Soviet authorities not only allowed him access to archives and to other sources of information. They were also ready, he informed Lifschitz, to lend original documents for presentation to the Berne court.

This called for a small celebration, Lifschitz announced, so they decided to drink a glass of schnapps, in spite of the morning hour.

SERGEI SVATIKOV

One of the first names supplied by Tager was that of Sergei Svatikov, professor of law and philosophy from the Universities of St Petersburg and Heidelberg, now living in Paris, where he was well known in the circles of Russian emigrants.

Georges Brunschvig was again dispatched to Paris. Remembering his former visit to the French capital, and his disappointment with the leaders of the Jewish community, he could only hope for more success this time.

Lifschitz had already contacted Svatikov, and reported that he was not only willing, but eager to cooperate. Now Georges was on a train to Paris planning the interrogation of a possibly important witness. He had never done this before and as the train neared its destination, his nervousness mounted.

They met in a pleasant Paris coffee house on a nice sunny day, and the older man, sensing the young lawyer's tense mood, took charge of the conversation. Lifschitz had prepared him to expect a young lawyer, brilliant, he said, but, alas, quite inexperienced. So he suggested that they first have coffee and become acquainted. 'My story is long,' he said, 'and it would take more than one meeting to tell it all.' At his suggestion they conversed for an hour, discussing the trial in general, and decided to meet again at his Paris apartment. 'You will need a better place than a coffee house to make your notes, and we both need a more private place,' he said. 'You are dealing with dangerous opponents,' he warned. 'They might even have you under surveillance.'

George came with a prepared list of questions, as he had been taught in law school. Always come prepared, his professor repeated many times – prospective witnesses do not know what is relevant, one must lead them through their story, and one must be well prepared.

As soon as their meeting commenced, however, Georges felt instinctively that the routine procedure was not proper in this case. This man not only had relevant information, he had authority and experience. He had a presence. So Georges wisely decided to let Svatikov tell his story in his own way.

They were both seated at a large round table, with only Georges' notebook and pen resting on the colorful tablecloth. Not a rich apartment, Georges noticed, but the walls were lined with books.

Having interviewed many witnesses throughout my career, I could imagine that Svatikov, as well as other witnesses in the Berne trial, were faced with a dilemma. How would a young lawyer, born and raised in another world, understand and present to a Swiss court a set of facts that must sound completely incredible to one not familiar with the whole scene?

I was sure that these witnesses were not eager to relive those days, but having made a commitment to testify at the trial, they made every effort to make first the lawyers, and then the judge, understand how things had been in Russia. Much has been written about the Berne trial, but I have often thought that the witnesses, especially the Russian ones, have never received enough credit for their courage in bringing to light, in public, information about events that must have caused them much pain.

With Georges Brunschvig seated in front of him, Svatikov turned his gaze to the window and spoke in a quiet voice, as if talking to himself.

He remembered vividly those turbulent times of 1916–17, in which he had played his own small part. He had written about them, but testifying in a court of law was another matter. In order to make a Swiss judge understand the dramatic events of those days, he said, in order to describe the people involved and their mode of operation, Georges would have to create in the courtroom the atmosphere that prevailed in Russia in those last days of the great empire. Georges must insist that he be given the opportunity to do so.

It was with profound sadness, but also with a sense of longing, that he recalled those last days of the Romanov Empire, and the hope that arose in the hearts of men at the creation of the provisional government, hope that was completely shattered within six months. It was during those six months that fate brought him into contact with the facts to which he would now have to testify under oath.

At the end of 1916 Russia was nearing its inevitable destiny. Ten million Russians were fighting in the great world war, the hospitals were packed with wounded, terror reigned in the streets, the Revolution was almost at the door, the royal couple, Nikolai II and Alexandra, were nearing their day of doom, but in the capital life went on as usual. There were feasts every evening, the elite invited each other for dinner or tea, social life was at its peak. Concerts of the famous Russian composers, ballet and theater performances were held to packed halls. The ladies still traveled to Moscow to order clothes from the famous dressmaker Lomanova. Meetings with the tsar were held in full regalia and ceremony.

The famous Grigorii Rasputin was still the power behind the throne, although his end was near. He walked the streets of St Petersburg, a tall man, dressed in top boots and the long black caftan that well-to-do *moujiks* wore on holidays. He was easily recognized by his dark, long and ill-kempt hair, his stiff black beard, his high forehead, his aquiline nose. But most of all he was famous for his light blue eyes with their curious sparkle, their depth and fascination. His gaze was at once penetrating and caressing, naive and cunning, direct and yet remote. People called him 'the old man', the *staretz*; he called himself 'the emperor's minister of the soul'; those who were aware of his evil power referred to him as the incarnation of the Devil, some called him the Antichrist.

It was again the two Montenegrin princesses, Anastasia and Militza, who had manipulated the empress into admitting this new magician into the court. Exactly as they had, seven years earlier, introduced the former butcher-boy-turned-magician, Philippe, to the tsarina, they introduced her in 1907 to Rasputin, the son of a simple *moujik*, a drunken, thieving horse dealer from western Siberia. Rasputin was not his real name. It was a term of peasant slang, derived from the word *rasputnic*, which means 'debauchee', 'rake' 'woman-chaser', a surname well deserved by this so called 'holy *staretz*', which Grigorii had received from his comrades. Yet from the moment of his entrance into the palace Rasputin obtained an extraordinary ascendancy over the tsar and the tsarina. He wheedled them, dazzled them, dominated them. It was almost like sorcery. He soon became the friend of Madam Vyrubova, the tsarina's inseparable companion, and by her was initiated into all the secrets of the imperial couple and the empire. The empress made him her spiritual guide and he soon became privy to all the intrigues in the court, exerting great influence on state decisions and on royal appointments. He called the royal couple 'Papka' and 'Mamka'.

Svatikov still remembered how, in spite of growing criticism, the empress had ordered that Rasputin should take the sacrament with her when receiving holy communion at Easter in 1916. Russia had been shocked at the spectacle of their empress exchanging the kiss of peace with Rasputin. He publicly kissed her on the forehead and she returned a kiss on his hand.

The writing was on the wall, Svatikov recalled, but the dramatic events in Russia had to be played out to their bitter end.

On 2 December 1916, the matter of Rasputin was raised for the first time in the Duma. The leader of the opposition Purishkevich cried out against 'the occult forces that are dishonoring and ruining Russia'. 'It only requires the recommendation of Rasputin', he said, 'to raise the most abject creatures to the highest office.' He dared, for the first time, cry openly 'Revolution threatens! An obscure *moujik* shall govern Russia no longer.'

The royal palace did not heed his warning, but time was running out. On 30 December 1916, Rasputin was murdered by Prince Felix

Iusupov, Grand Prince Dmitrii and Purishkevich, leader of the extreme right in the Duma, the champion of Orthodox absolutism. When the corpse was discovered three days later in the ice of the little Nevka, there was great rejoicing. People kissed each other on the street and went to light candles in the churches.

Ignoring the feelings of the people, a letter signed by the empress was placed in Rasputin's dead hands. 'My dear martyr,' wrote the tsarina, 'give me thy blessing, that it may follow me always on the sad and dreary path I have yet to traverse here below. And remember us from on high in your holy prayers!' The emperor and the empress and their four daughters were present at the secret interment on the edge of the imperial park in Tsarskoe Selo. The empress asked to keep the bloodstained shirt of the martyr.

A little more than two months later, on 15 March 1917, the tsar was compelled to abdicate. The leader of the Kadet Party and of the progressive block, Paul Miliukov, was appointed foreign minister of the provisional government.

Georges Brunschvig noted that Miliukov was also on his list of prospective witnesses. 'You will not be disappointed,' Svatikov remarked.

One of the first decisions of the new government was to dissolve the organs of the secret police abroad. In the beginning of May 1917, the then 37-year-old Sergei Svatikov, a member of the Social Democratic Party, was chosen for this delicate project. He had served during the February revolutionary uprising as deputy and special civil adviser to the prefect of police in Petrograd and was highly recommended after only three months in that position.

He was dispatched to Europe with the title of 'Police Commissioner of the provisionary Russian government', entrusted with the job of liquidating the Secret Police of tsarist Russia, and inspecting all its former activities in various countries. He was also instructed to verify the involvement of some of Russia's representatives in counter-espionage. The minister of justice appointed him special investigating judge of the highest available rank, with full judicial authority.

He knew that his story would sound incredible in a Swiss courtroom, Svatikov repeated again and again to Georges, unless he succeeded in recreating the bizarre events and the demonic atmosphere prevailing in his homeland in those days. How would he explain to a Swiss judge the state of the Jews in Russia and the insane manipulations of fanatical magicians, manipulative politicians and crooked police agents who succeeded in placing on the shoulders of those poor devils the blame for everything that was wrong in their lives and in their country?

Like any intelligent Russian, he had been well aware of the existence of the 'Jewish Question', which they had started calling in jest the 'Jewish Answer'. He had hoped naively that the new regime would end the unequal treatment of Russian citizens, including the Jews.

He now recalled vividly an incident that happened on the first day of May at the Petrograd police station. The functionaries of the old regime had fled, and he was suddenly in charge. He decided to inspect all documents that would normally arrive at the desk of the chief of police. The first document he inspected on that particular morning was a telegram from the chief of police of the Poltawa region asking whether the 'category 2 merchant', Ziperovich, could be allowed to come to Petrograd for one week. Needless to say, Ziperovich was a Jew and thus needed a special permit to travel to the capital.

When his assistant offered to deposit the telegram in the 'Jewish file', Svatikov had to remind him that things had changed. 'Please', he said, 'write immediately to the chief of police in Poltawa, if he is still there, that the 'category 2 merchant' Ziperovich can come to Petrograd whenever he pleases, and can stay there indefinitely. Mr Ziperovich now has the right to free travel anywhere in Russia.

'And please,' he added, 'I shall sign this telegram myself.' He then immediately ordered the 'Jewish Bureau' disbanded, its functionaries relocated in other departments, and its files sealed to be later examined by a special commission.

Preparing for his mission abroad, Svatikov was positive that he had no Jewish item on his agenda until he sat at the Russian Consulate in Paris, which had also served as the headquarters of the Okhrana in Europe, and interrogated Henri Bint.

The Consulate had received prior notice of his function, and Svatikov was well received. He had feared that the Russian functionaries abroad, whose help he must solicit, would resent this young lawyer who was coming to investigate and report. But he had ignored the fact that in the Russian autocratic regime officials were used to obeying authority. The provisional government was now in power and he was its official emissary. He soon realized the importance of his new rank. On his arrival a spacious office was put at his disposal, and he wondered whether the same room had served the famous, or rather infamous, Piotr Rachkovskii, head of the Okhrana in Europe.

He was now facing, across a big desk, the oldest surviving Russian agent in Europe. Henri Bint had served many masters in his 37 years of service in the Okhrana, but the greatest master of them all had been Rachkovskii, in whom Svatikov was particularly interested.

To his surprise Bint was not only willing but eager to talk. It seemed as if the man who had kept so many secrets shut away in his memory was seeking a way to unburden himself. Formerly he could have paid with his head for breaking a confidence; more than one agent had lost his life in a fake accident when he was even suspected of divulging a secret. Now, suddenly, he was not only permitted but actually asked to speak up. Svatikov realized that he had found his best source. The job would not be as difficult as he had feared, he thought.

Bint had met Rachkovskii in 1883 in Moscow. He had been called to Moscow in May of that year for the coronation of Alexander III, as he was familiar with most Russian emigrants who were considered a security risk. At that time Rachkovskii had the appearance of a respectable functionary, in the uniform of the Ministry of Internal Affairs, but his functions were far from respectable. He was assigned to create tension among the various revolutionary groups, to spread false information in order to implicate their members in trumped-up charges, causing their arrest and incarceration for espionage and other crimes. He was considered an expert in provocation, Bint said with a smile. When his immediate boss and protector, Georgii Sudeikin, was murdered by one Degajeff, Rachkovskii was dispatched to Paris in the beginning of 1884 to try to apprehend the murderer. This turned out to be the beginning of his French career. He installed himself in a small hotel at the rue Pierre-Nicole, on the outskirts of the Latin Quarter, and established contacts with the French police. But his main efforts were aimed at discrediting the head of the foreign branch of the Okhrana. It took him no more than four months to be appointed, in the beginning of May, head of the foreign agency of the Russian police.

At this stage much of his work entailed the investigation of Russian revolutionaries living abroad. His agents bribed concierges, the keepers of most French buildings, and postmen, thus gaining access not only to the lodgings but also to the mail of Russian emigrants. In a short time Rachkovskii developed an elaborate filing system containing the name of every Russian arriving in Paris. Information arrived constantly from the French police, where foreigners were requested to report. Their photographs, received from Russia, were copied and distributed to all agents. Those whose photographs were not on file were surreptitiously photographed on the street.

A campaign of discreditation was soon instigated. Anonymous letters went out to employers of Russian emigrants, warning them that they had dangerous terrorists in their employ. The emigrants, who were thus brought to a state of complete destitution, were then approached and offered remuneration for betraying their friends.

Bint spoke at length of Rachkovskii's forgeries. Forgeries, he explained, were a routine way by which Rachkovskii and his agents implicated revolutionaries. Usually Rachkovskii would write the original fabricated text in his own hand and then give it to one of his trusted agents, Bint or Milevskii. They would print it on hectograph and deliver the carefully counted copies to Rachkovskii. But, unknown to his boss, Bint had always kept a few copies for his private archive as insurance. They made an effort to ensure that the printed material resembled that distributed by the revolutionaries. Rachkovskii himself, or the secretary of the agency, would write the addresses on the envelopes. The same secretary would also distribute the material to the designated mailboxes. They were all sworn to secrecy as to Rachkovskii's part in the affair.

The forgeries were not Rachkovskii's invention, Bint stated. They were part of the program and in line with the overall tactical plan initiated by the head of the Secret Police, Sudeikin, when the so-called 'Special Branch' was created in 1882. On 15 July of that same year an article appeared in issue 417 of the Russian foreign publication *Free Speech*, informing its readers of the establishment of the Special Branch. The functions of this department, according to Sudeikin, would be 'discreditation of active workers in revolutionary parties by distribution of forged records, forged manifests, etc'.

Rachkovskii, a former secretary of Sudeikin, had learned well and immediately on his appointment abroad he started putting into practice the teachings of his former boss. His most bizarre invention was the fictitious pair of agents 'Kun' and 'Gruen', whose non-existent names he signed to fabricated circulars and letters. It was these two imaginary 'agents' who openly implicated first one Elpidin and then the leader of the Russian Social Democratic Party abroad, Plekhanov, in the destruction of the publishing house in Geneva, an affair Bint promised to describe later. When this information met with total disbelief in the Russian community, he did not hesitate to have his two 'agents' confess to the act in an open letter. Evidently, the name of the collaborator who furnished them with inside information was withheld.

By 1892 the forgeries were becoming more devious and more intricate. Plekhanov was a popular target. Rachkovskii even went so far as to imitate Plekhanov's handwriting in what he pretended to be an authentic letter, in which Plekhanov complained that his party had been accused of printing false money. In the forged letter Plekhanov allegedly stated that he was tired of living with all the lies, and would now stay only within the law, urging all young people to follow his advice.

Plekhanov's signature was so well imitated that he found it difficult to convince his friends that it was a forgery. The hectograph was in constant use. Daily provocations were freely composed, implicating and incriminating large numbers of people at Rachkovskii's will. There was nobody to stop him, and he was constantly praised by his superiors for a system that was running so smoothly. The forgeries were so effective that French journalists complained that they no longer knew what they should believe and what was worth publishing.

Bint was so convincing that in his official report Svatikov stated that the forgeries, which were perpetrated by Rachkovskii in the span of many years, were now an undisputed fact. Their aim was the creation of confusion in the socialist camp, the degradation of socialist leaders in the public mind and the de-legitimization of the socialist movement. Sometimes the direct aim was the arrest and incarceration of socialist activists on their arrival in Russia. Rachkovskii had no need for finesse; he was not interested in the different political views and the agendas of the various revolutionary groups. To him they were all socialists and he treated them all as enemies to be destroyed. The forgeries were by no means his only weapon. He systematically supplied the French police with information, both true and false, about subversive elements in France, using for this purpose a journalist called Hansen, who doubled as an agent.

It would be almost impossible for someone living in a different time, educated in a different culture, to understand the political atmosphere and the international intrigues employed by Russians in those days, both in Russia and abroad, Svatikov mused even then as he listened to Bint. Thousands of agents and spies were spread everywhere, and you could never tell who was who. Revolutionaries arrested by the police were manipulated into turning against their comrades and becoming Okhrana agents. Some acted as mere informers, turning in friends and relatives; others, more daring, were actually involved in terrorist activities against the regime, while serving their police masters. Such methods, sometimes encouraged by police chiefs, included even murders of prominent persons. The master of deceit, the famous spy Azef, became a legend in Russia. He was said to have a hand in the murders of the minister of the interior, Pleve, and of Prince Sergei Alexandrovich, but also in the failure of the 1905 Revolution and in the prevention of the murder of the tsar.

It was Rachkovskii who headed these subversive activities abroad and refined the most successful and intricate methods of intrigue and sabotage, Bint stated. Forging and faking documents was a way of life for him and for his agents. Some forged documents purported to be written and signed by existing persons, while others were published under non-existent names and included totally false information. It was not only fictitious names such as 'Kun' and 'Gruen' that were often used in these forgeries; Rachkovskii himself used to write pamphlets under a pseudonym that did not even seriously attempt to hide the origin of the writer. Thus when he wrote and published, in 1888, a pamphlet pretending to be 'the confession of a nihilist', he signed it Philip Ivanov, easily detectable as signed by himself, whose name was Piotr Ivanovich. In a letter to Chief of Police Durnovo concerning this brochure, Rachkovskii explained the necessity to expose the dark sides of the life of the Russian nihilists, 'mostly of Jewish character', who populated the Latin Quarter in Paris. They were described as possessing bestial instincts, substandard habits, extreme intolerance even of each other, inclined to spy on everybody. Their leader, Tikhomirov, was said to possess 'the ferocity of a tiger and the cowardice of a rabbit'.

Another fabricated pamphlet, written by Rachkovskii under a pseudonym, was published in Paris in 1892, entitled *The English and the Nihilists are Collaborating*. The writer described all kinds of crimes, including bombings and murders, perpetrated by Russian nihilists in Europe, and maintained that the funds raised by the English group to help hungry people in Russia, were actually being used by the nihilists for acts of violence and subversion. The pamphlet was mostly intended to discredit two revolutionary groups acting in England, the Friends of Russian Freedom and a Russian group promoting the Free Russian Press in London.

In a letter to his chief in 1892, Rachkovskii explained that 1,000 exemplars of this brochure were intended for distribution among ministers, diplomats, MPs and top officials in London, while the other 1,000 would go to government officials in France, Switzerland, Denmark, Germany, Austria and other European countries, as well as to American newspapers. In the prevailing atmosphere, Rachkovskii wrote, after he had succeeded in his provocation of tying the Russian emigrants in Paris to the preparation of bombs and explosives, he foresaw that his brochure would create a big uproar. This would be the beginning of a big campaign of agitation against the Russian revolutionaries abroad, he stated.

The composition of the brochures, unlike that of other documents, was not entrusted to other agents. They were written by Rachkovskii himself, with his agent Hansen correcting Rachkovskii's French. Another one of Hansen's tasks was to find cheap printing houses, as Rachkovskii was requested to report costs to his bosses in Russia.

Even as a totally disillusioned Bint was pouring out all this information to Svatikov, the latter could still detect in Bint's recital a vestige of admiration for his former chief, Rachkovskii.

One of Rachkovskii's most ambitious projects was the destruction of the publishing house that served the revolutionaries, on the first floor of 30 rue Monbrillant, in Geneva, Switzerland. Rachkovskii knew that very important and irreplaceable literature was about to be published.

The most trustworthy agents, Bint and Milevskii, were dispatched to Geneva for day and night surveillance of the premises. They soon learned that the house was usually unoccupied from Saturday night until Monday morning. To make doubly sure, the agent Salomon Kogan, who lived in Geneva, visited the house to observe the work going on inside. Kogan, of Jewish origin, a former revolutionary, had been arrested in Odessa and, like his boss Rachkovskii, had turned agent. It was Kogan who supplied his co-conspirators with the apartment plan, marking the rooms where the most important material was kept.

The agents Milevskii and Bint were told that they were participating in an act of great political importance, and they were also promised fair remuneration. They were ordered to evacuate the rooms they had rented in Geneva and to send all their documents and belongings to Paris.

On 20 November 1886 at 9 p.m. the agents entered the premises and poured chemicals on hundreds of kilos of printed material, which turned into a sticky compact mass. Other documents were torn to pieces. At 4.30 a.m. they were through.

Bint reported to Svatikov that he himself had received 1,500 francs for this piece of work, as had his collaborator, Milevskii, who was also awarded a complimentary title. Rachkovskii received from the grateful Russian authorities the sum of 5,000 francs and the title of 'government secretary' (*gouvernement sekretaire*).

But Rachkovskii, who received a detailed report, was unhappy. He realized that some important documents had not been destroyed, and insisted that Kogan visit the place again, at great risk, and report on the exact location of these surviving documents. On the night of 1 February 1887, Bint was again dispatched to Geneva and succeeded in finishing the work. He received a gold medal and an extra payment of 500 francs.

In his full report, written in Paris on 19 November 1886, Rachkovskii boasted of his devious, well-prepared plan: not only did they succeed in demolishing the publishing house and in destroying a mass of material ready for distribution, but they also succeeded in throwing suspicion on the revolutionary leader Georgi Plekhanov, thus causing much confusion in the ranks of the revolutionaries. They avoided any diplomatic complications, and even prepared the ground for their government to lodge a formal complaint with the Swiss authorities for not properly protecting the rights of asylum of Russian emigrants under Swiss law.

Describing his years under Rachkovskii, and particularly Rachkovskii's provocations and forgeries, Bint added: 'I would like to draw your attention to the most outstanding forgery prepared by Rachkovskii's agents at the end of the last century, the so called *Protocols of the Elders of Zion.*'

Svatikov had heard of the *Protocols* but had never read them. He remembered vaguely leafing through some chapters in a book published in 1905, but in those days there were more exciting items on his agenda. He now asked Bint what these *Protocols* were all about. 'They describe how the Jews conspire to rule the whole world and how they actually succeed in doing so,' answered Bint. 'But, of course,' he exclaimed, 'it is all utter nonsense, these are fantasies in the style of Edouard Drumont.'

Having just arrived in France, Svatikov had to admit his ignorance.

He had never heard of Drumont. 'You will never understand the full story of these *Protocols*', Bint stated, 'unless you familiarize yourself with the full extent of the activity and influence of Drumont, the most outstanding champion of anti-Semitism in France in the second half of the last century. The book written by this man, *La France Juive*, was a household item in most French homes. It was published in more than two hundred editions.'

Surprised and a little embarrassed by his ignorance, Svatikov made a note to study the subject. His notebook was becoming quite crowded, he had so much to learn, he thought.

'Were the *Protocols* fabricated to initiate pogroms in Russia?' Svatikov asked.

'This I do not know,' Bint replied, 'but their purpose was definitely to incite Russians against Jews.' He then added thoughtfully, 'I am not even sure that the headquarters in Fontanka 16 in St Petersburg had a hand in the forgery. To my mind it was the personal decision of my old master. If you knew him as well as I did, you would easily detect his hand. It is as detectable as are fingerprints.'

Intrigued, Svatikov inquired whether Rachkovskii had composed the forgery himself.

'Oh no,' Bint exclaimed, 'he had special agents to do his dirty work. The actual work was done in this instance by the agent Golovinskii.' Seeing the blank look on Svatikov's face Bint added: 'Golovinskii served under Rachkovskii since 1892, if I am not mistaken. You must understand that I was familiar with all the agents and with their particular assignments, as I was Rachkovskii's paymaster. I paid their salaries and their expenses, all on the orders of our chief, and mind you, all payments were in private and in cash.'

'Are you sure that it was Golovinskii who forged the *Protocols*?' Svatikov persisted.

'Absolutely sure,' Bint immediately replied. 'Rachkovskii had two expert forgers, Kogan and Golovinskii. The latter was working on the *Protocols* in the National Library, and used to present Rachkovskii with each chapter as it was composed. I should know, because I was there and I knew exactly what was going on.'

'Could you let me have a copy of these so called *Protocols*?' Svatikov demanded.

'Unfortunately this is impossible,' apologized Bint. 'This was a strictly confidential job. We in the inner circle were aware of the work being done, but there were no copies to go around. It was to be presented as a document discovered from Jewish sources, there were to be no copies, or the whole project might be jeopardized.'

The information that Bint poured out during his interrogation, which lasted many days, was meticulously written down by Svatikov and included in his full report.

He was convinced that Bint's testimony was completely correct. He was never caught in even one incorrect detail. He was the oldest member of the foreign agency of the Secret Police, and he was reviewing all those years of his life, which were passing before his eyes. Bint had no reason to lie. He was assured that Svatikov's mission was to disband and liquidate the foreign agency in the most tactful and delicate manner, avoiding any accusations or legal proceedings against former agents. Bint and his colleagues were in no danger of reprisals of any kind and they had nothing to fear from Svatikov's investigation. Bint expressed his readiness to serve the provisional government and the new regime. He showed no vindictiveness and made no attempt to slander his colleagues.

Svatikov had not come unarmed. The information he brought with him tallied in all details with that received from Bint concerning names of double agents and their pseudonyms.

Svatikov had studied carefully Bint's biography, and knew that he had been fully trusted by his superiors. He had even been assigned to protect members of the royal family, including Alexander III and Nikolai II.

It was after the October Revolution that Svatikov was again reminded of the *Protocols of the Elders of Zion*. He had thought they had vanished for ever when he suddenly realized that the Jews were being blamed for the Revolution. At that time he was staying in the south of Russia, the provisional government having failed, and civil war was raging throughout the country. The White Army had organized an information agency called OSWAG, which was soon infiltrated by embittered Black Hundred supporters who blamed the Jews for all their woes: the February and October Revolutions, Bolshevism, the farmers who had taken over the lands of the gentry – in a word: everything.

It was at this time that he became aware of the fact that primitive reprints of the *Protocols of the Elders of Zion* were being circulated *en masse* in army units and actual new editions of the *Protocols* were appearing in various districts. Yet, until he fled from Russia, Svatikov was not aware of the fact that the *Protocols* had crossed the Russian border and were being published and distributed in other countries.

He arrived in Paris in 1920, one of many Russian refugees seeking asylum in France. In 1921 his friend, the well-known journalist Vladimir Burtsev, suggested that he re-establish contact with Bint, but that he first must read the Graves articles in *The Times* of London and the interviews with Princess Radziwill and Henriette Hurblut in *The American Hebrew*. He spent hours reading and re-reading the articles, pleased to note that his instincts had been right in believing the story of Bint. Indeed, the information in these articles fully supported the facts that Bint had relayed in his interrogation four years earlier.

It was also Burtsev's idea that he write a series of articles concerning the information he had received from Bint during the official inquiry he had conducted back in 1917. He had heard that Bint was in trouble. He had lost all the savings that he had foolishly invested in Russian securities, and with the downfall of the old regime he had also lost all his pension rights, after close to 40 years of service. He badly needed an income and was temporarily working as a minor official in a French ministry outside Paris.

Emigrés from the Russian community kept close contact with each other, and it was not difficult to obtain Bint's address and his consent to meet for tea on Sunday afternoon.

Bint was indeed a sorry sight, Svatikov thought – sad, discouraged, and badly in need of financial resources. He was eager to supply any additional information and even suggested selling the documents in his private archive.

When the conversation touched on the *Protocols of the Elders of Zion*, Bint became cynical. 'Would you believe it,' he exclaimed, 'this proven forgery is now being published in many languages. Rachkovskii must be laughing in his grave.' Nobody was interested in the truth, he said, although here was a living witness who had personally remunerated the forgers.

When Svatikov remarked that he might be interested in purchasing his archive, if there was any document relating to the *Protocols* story, Bint became thoughtful. There might be one document not directly related to the forgery, but it could prove Rachkovskii's obsession with implicating the Jews, he remarked. Seeing a glimmer of interest in Svatikov's eyes, he offered more details.

Rachkovskii had been obsessed with the Jews, Bint said. He was personally involved in promoting the *Protocols* in Russia in 1905. By that time Rachkovskii was back in St Petersburg, having spent some years in exile in Warsaw and in Brussels, until the death of his great enemy Pleve, who threatened to send him to Siberia if he dared set foot in the Russian capital. Rachkovskii was now in charge of the Okhrana at the headquarters of the police department on the Fontanka, and in close contact with the agent Ivan Manasevich-Manuilov. In this capacity he summoned the head of the Okhrana office in Paris and ordered him to go immediately to Frankfurt, in Germany, and visit bookstores specializing in Judaica. He was to seek out old Jewish books dealing with ancient Jewish practices. He mentioned special editions from the seventh and sixteenth centuries, naming titles, authors and editions. Bint was to personally mail these books in Paris for special delivery to St Petersburg. 'Here I might be able to supply you with a document,' Bint said. He thought he still had in his possession the handwritten instructions, in French, pointing out the addresses of the stores noted on the back of the document, in his own handwriting. Smiling, he remarked that there had been some difficulty in finding the books, as their Hebrew names were written in Latin in an incorrect manner. They were mostly books on Kabala, a general term used for esoteric and mystic teachings of Judaism, mostly in the *sepher*, being the Hebrew word for 'book', and *jetsiera* was the misspelled word *jetsira*, which means in Hebrew 'composition'. True, there was no mention of the *Protocols*, Bint remarked, but there was verification of the fact that even in 1905 Rachkovskii was busy preparing anti-Jewish material, attempting to prove his theories from Jewish sources. It was Bint himself who was dispatched to Frankfurt and as the books were rare, he ordered them and returned to Germany a second time to finalize the deal. He was told to spare no expense and he paid more than 3,000 gold francs for the books. Unfortunately he could not read them, as they were in Latin and in Hebrew. In Paris he was immediately sent to the post office. Trying to save money, he first attempted to send the books in big envelopes as regular mail, but on the advice of the postmaster he sent them as parcels, special delivery, to Rachkovskii's office in Fontanka 16, St Petersburg. It was remarkable what things one retains in one's memory, Bint said. Every detail was as fresh in his mind as if it happened yesterday.

It was the deputy minister of internal affairs and the St Petersburg governor-general Trepov who had appointed Rachkovskii, on 27 July 1905, to the post of deputy director of the Police Department, with full directorial power, even though officially one Garin held that post. And it was in this capacity that Rachkovskii established, in the autumn of 1905, with the help of a gendarmerie officer called Komissarov, behind the backs of his superiors, a printing press that turned out masses of pogrom leaflets distributed in all the big cities. Later Komissarov boasted to some leaders in the Duma that he could instigate, on demand, any kind of pogrom, whether its aim was to murder 10 or 10,000 Jews.

A good friend and co-agent told Bint about the close cooperation of Rachkovskii with Manuilov, who assisted him in every way in promoting the *Protocols* in Russia, and translated various Jewish books for him.

Svatikov had heard of Manasevich-Manuilov, and made a note to gather more information about him.

Bint promised to find what he called 'The Zionist Document' in his archive, which was kept at his home in the province.

On the advice of his friend Burtsev, Svatikov paid a visit to the Bibliothèque Nationale in Paris, where Golovinskii used to work on the fabrication of the *Protocols*. After reading the recent articles of Philip Graves he looked for copies of Maurice Joly's book, and was surprised to discover that one particular copy was unavailable to the public, under orders of the library management. Convinced that the book was hidden away by an old order of Napoleon III, who had banned it, he asked to see it and was astounded at the unequivocal refusal of the library authorities. He was told that the director would have to consult a committee that had formerly decided to forbid the public from seeing this particular book.

Georges Brunschvig had thought that he had in his possession all the dramatic publications of 1921. It now appeared that he had missed the article that Svatikov now showed him. It had been published in Paris in the Russian newspaper *Obtchee Delo* on 20 September 1921, entitled 'The End of the Zion Protocols'. Like Graves, Svatikov too had been convinced in 1921 that this fabrication, now dramatically exposed, was on its way to the scrap-heap.

In the first part of the article Svatikov described the history of the forgery, comparing the tactics of the former regime with those of the new communist rulers. To those who might wonder why they should be interested in the *Protocols*, he explained that they should read carefully the book by Maurice Joly. A minority, he wrote, can rule and oppress the majority only with the help of terror, lies and bribery. The weapons of tyrants are always the same. This was why it was not surprising, he wrote, that communists were adopting the policies of Napoleon III, as described in Joly's book in 1864, which in 1901 the Russian Okhrana tried to ascribe to the Jews as 'The Zion Syndrome', in order to frighten the weak Tsar Nikolai II.

In an optimistic mood Svatikov wrote in September 1921 'Everything will pass, only the truth will survive.'

Now he knew better, Svatikov remarked to Georges as they were having tea in his apartment. This was their fourth and last meeting. They would soon meet again in the courtroom, Georges said. What a pity that Bint had not come through with the promised document, he remarked.

'But he did,' Svatikov exclaimed. He had seen Bint again in 1926 and reminded him of his promise, but Bint said he could not find the document. It was only a few years later, after Bint's death, that his widow handed Svatikov a package of documents, saying that she did so at her husband's request before he died. What they referred to as 'The Zionist Document' was finally in Svatikov's hands. He would not let it out of his hands, but he showed it to Georges and promised to present it to the judge as part of his testimony.

What a witness, Georges said to himself. He could not wait to recount to his colleagues Svatikov's story. He only wished the other witnesses were as good.

'Why don't you plan your next interview with Vladimir Burtsev?' Svatikov remarked in parting. 'Not only will he verify my story, but he might furnish you with additional information.' He intimated that Burtsev had compelling reasons for not having made this information public until that time, reasons which might well have lost their validity.

Georges immediately fished out of his pocket his list of witnesses, and put Burtsev's name at the top of the list.

VLADIMIR BURTSEV

When Lifschitz had submitted his list of witnesses, Georges had been skeptical. All Russians were anti-Semitically inclined, he thought. How could they depend on witnesses who had been part of the old order, the old Russian regime, which promoted pogroms and suppressed five million Jews? He had been convinced that they would be compelled to rely mostly on Jewish witnesses.

That is why he was so completely surprised when he realized that prominent Russians, men of intelligence and integrity, some of whom had held important positions in tsarist Russia, had been bothered by the publication of the *Protocols of the Elders of Zion*, had investig-ated the subject, and were not only ready, but actually eager, to reveal the truth.

Vladimir Burtsev was as frank and as forthcoming in his long con-versations with Georges Brunschvig as had been Sergei Svatikov. For the sake of accuracy he would not rely on Georges' painstaking notes in preparation of his testimony, and presented him with a written document composed on 5 July 1934.

On a cold winter day in 1906 Vladimir Burtsev had been sitting at his desk in St Petersburg, proofreading the editorial he had completed the previous evening. He was then editor of the historical journal *Byloe* – 'The Past' – a popular publication dealing with relevant political mat-ters. Usually he had no difficulty in concentrating on the task at hand, but today his mind kept wandering. In an hour he would chair the edi-torial board and he would have to make a recommendation on the mat-ter that he himself had placed on the agenda. He had practically made up his mind, but was curious to hear what his colleagues would say.

Only a week ago one of his assistants had handed him a booklet, suggesting that he read it and consider mentioning it in the next issue of the journal. He took it home and spent a whole evening reading the *Protocols of the Elders of Zion*. Wishing to be completely accu-rate, he now told Georges that he could not recall whether it had been a reprint of the Nilus edition or of a new edition by Butmi issued at the beginning of that year.

He had been well aware of the wave of anti-Semitism that was sweeping Russia and of the constant process of brainwashing aimed at growing circles of the Russian public. He had addressed the matter repeatedly in his journal, convinced that it was harmful to Russia. He had heard some rumors about the so-called *Protocols of the Elders of Zion*, but, as the document had not caught the attention of the daily press, he had never bothered to read it. Sitting at his desk that morn-ing he felt that he should consult the editorial board, although he him-self was sure that it was nothing but a crude and absurd fabrication.

Years later Georges detected a note of satisfaction in Burtsev's voice as he recounted that the entire board had been unanimous in supporting his evaluation of the booklet. Even denying such a docu-ment would lend it undeserved recognition, they all maintained.

After spending some time in Paris, Burtsev was back in Russia in time to be arrested by the Bolsheviks on 25 October 1917, confined to a prison cell until May 1918.

Even more than his physical incarceration, he regretted the fact that he was denied the opportunity to report and comment on the great historical events taking place in Russia. Journalism was in his blood. Fortunately he was allowed to keep his notebook, and he could still think and make notes. He could also interview his fellow prisoners. One day he was transferred to another cell and found that he was sharing it with the former chief of the Police Department, Beletskii. To his surprise the man felt no loyalty to the regime he had served and was ready to speak freely. In the long hours they spent together Burtsev filled his notebook with enough background material to use in many of the articles he planned to publish abroad after his release.

Inevitably they discussed the Jewish question and the role of the police in the persecution of Jews. He now learned that back in 1911 his cellmate had taken an active part in preparing the prosecution of Beilis, who had been falsely accused of murdering a Christian child for ritual purposes. He himself had been in Paris at that time and had closely covered this scandalous trial. He remembered now how relieved he had been when Beilis had been acquitted.

To his surprise, Beletskii spoke freely, describing how the Beilis trial had been prepared and conducted. He made no secret of the fact that the charges against Beilis had been completely fabricated. Asked whether they had considered using the *Protocols of the Elders of Zion* in the trial, Beletskii exclaimed: 'No! We were advised by some people to use the *Protocols* but we were sure that this would definitely kill our case, as everybody knew it was a crude forgery!' Beletskii explained that in his discussions with promoters of the *Protocols* they had all admitted that the document was false, but maintained that the behavior of the Jews in the Revolution justified the use of any means to discredit them, including the use of a forged document.

Again in 1919, in the Crimea, in Sevastopol, as a volunteer in the White Army, fighting the Bolsheviks, Burtsev had noticed that the *Protocols* were massively used in anti-Bolshevik agitation against Jews.

He was very popular as the editor of an anti-Bolshevik publication in Paris, he explained, which was why General Salivanov, the editor of an army publication, had received him with great respect and thanked him profoundly for his contribution to the common cause. 'He suddenly pressed into my hand a pamphlet asking me to review it in my publication,' he now told Georges. 'It was a completely new edition of the *Protocols* issued in Sevastopol.' Although the general was aware of Burtsev's writings against anti-Semitism, he maintained that his opposition to Bolshevism should prevail, as the *Protocols* were proof that the Bolshevik Revolution was part of the Jewish plan.

'I explained that the *Protocols* were a scandalous and absurd forgery of the worst reactionaries,' Burtsev now said, 'and that were I ever to mention this document I would say that it is a criminal forgery.' After a heated argument the general broke off their meeting and they never discussed the *Protocols* again.

Back in Paris he became aware, in 1921, of the revelations of Philip Graves. Maurice Joly, Rachkovskii and Golovinskii were now often mentioned and discussed in Russian emigrant circles, and some of his memories suddenly took on fresh meaning.

The name Golovinskii was not new to him. He had made this man's acquaintance back in 1902 and had met him on numerous occasions over a period of two years. 'In our conversations he never mentioned the *Protocols*,' Burtsev now recalled, 'but he did talk of the Jewish world conspiracy, maintaining that the Jews were supporting revolutionary parties everywhere only to use them for their own purposes of world domination.'

Golovinskii had impressed him as a quite gifted man, but a very superficial writer, with good French and a good acquaintance with French journalism. 'After a while I recognized that he was a man without principles,' Burtsev told Georges, 'and I severed my ties with him. I remember that he spoke freely, in our emigrants' circles, of his connection with Rachkovskii. He had tried very hard to become part of our circle, but we were apprehensive of his connection with the Secret Police and his involvement in intrigues.' Now that he thought back of him, Burtsev said, he was convinced that Golovinskii was the perfect choice for Rachkovskii to fabricate the *Protocols of the Elders of Zion*, using Maurice Joly's book about Napoleon III, in order to give vent to his anti-Jewish convictions.

Asked about Manasevich-Manuilov, Burtsev recalled that his name had often been mentioned in connection with the *Protocols*, although he was not sure what actual part he had played. Indeed, Burtsev said, he had met him in 1915, during the war, when he was serving as official war correspondent. He had even established a relationship of trust with him. Manuilov, as he referred to him, was close to the Police Department. For all practical purposes he was then acting as secretary to Shturmer, and furnishing him with information about government activity. He also entrusted Burtsev with secret information concerning agents of the Police Department, including their involvement in the investigation of political murders. Both of them revealed this information much later, when they testified, after the Revolution, before the investigating committee appointed by the provisional government. Indeed, the committee attached importance to the information and included it in its published report.

In his conversations with Manuilov they often spoke of the Jewish question and of the *Protocols of the Elders of Zion*. 'He never mentioned, and I had never suspected, his personal involvement in the matter,' Burtsev said, 'but whenever we discussed the *Protocols* he stated his conviction of their falsity, and with a grin he used to say, "Only idiots would believe in the authenticity of such a document, but no politician would dare use this forgery." He mentioned again and again the fact that the government had never recognized the *Protocols* officially.'

Burtsev had been so convinced that the episode of the *Protocols* was a passing and an unimportant one that he never questioned Manuilov closely about his information on this matter. 'But I now remember', he said, 'that when I mentioned my meetings with Golovinskii, Manuilov retorted that he shared my negative impression and that the man was a criminal type and an agent of the Secret Police.'

Later Georges learned that others who knew Manasevich-Manuilov quite well spoke of him in the same terms as he had spoken about his collaborator, Golovinskii.

Since then, Burtsev now said, and particularly after the Philip Graves revelations in *The Times*, he had never encountered any person in political circles who maintained that the *Protocols* were authentic, but unfortunately there were those who would use them knowing they were false.

Georges thought he had enough material about Burtsev's encounters with the *Protocols*. He was now interested, he said, in substantiating the testimony of Svatikov. How had Burtsev come to make the acquaintance of Bint, he now asked.

He had met this man in Paris, after his release from the Russian prison. Bint had freely admitted that he had been Rachkovskii's French agent. Indeed, after the Revolution there was no sense anymore in hiding the secrets of the foreign Okhrana agency, and so Bint talked to him freely, even describing details of the surveillance of suspects, including himself. He was surprised to learn that Bint had watched him closely for 25 years and knew him quite well.

In 1918–19 they had met often, and he had received from Bint a wealth of information for publication in his journals. Bint spoke freely of Rachkovskii and of his own part in the fabrication of the *Protocols*. He also described his trips to Germany to purchase Jewish books for Rachkovskii.

'I was completely convinced of the truth of these revelations, and I shared them with my close colleague, Svatikov, with whom I maintained a relationship for 15 years,' Burtsev said. 'He told me that Bint had already mentioned the fabrication of the *Protocols* in his interrogation, and I encouraged Bint to reveal to Svatikov all the details, as he was more competent to deal with the matter, having been previously involved in his official capacity. Both Bint and Svatikov kept me informed of their conversations on the matter, so that I, myself, did not deem it necessary to follow it up. Again, I considered the matter closed, after Svatikov would publish the information he now had in his possession.' Unfortunately, I now learned that the matter of the *Protocols* was being raised again, particularly in Germany, and I decided to deal with it again.' Svatikov had mentioned to Georges that Burtsev was in possession of unique information, hitherto unrevealed. He felt that Burtsev was now approaching this delicate part of his story, so he kept his silence when Burtsev paused in his recital, seeming to hesitate.

'I was well acquainted, for 12–13 years, with General Globychev, the former director of the Okhrana, who later held a very responsible position in the army,' Burtsev resumed his story. 'Lately, he spent much time in Paris, where I met him again. In spite of our differences, we held each other in mutual respect. I have always considered him a real patriot, an honest man, and a conscientious servant of his country. We spoke often discussing our different opinions, realizing that we both meant well and wanted to serve the interests of Russia according to our convictions.'

They had first met in Constantinople, in 1920, and then many times in Paris, where he used to visit the general in his apartment. He recalled now how he used to complain to the general about the activities of his agents, warning that he would reveal the information in his journal. Unavoidably, they often discussed the Jewish question as it concerned the revolutionary movement and the relations of Russia abroad. Burtsev had also mentioned the *Protocols of the Elders of Zion*, but he understood that Globychev could not speak of these matters freely, although he was privy to a wealth of undisclosed informa-

17. Georges Brunschvig, president of the Swiss Jewish community (SIG)

18. Henry Ford, distributor of the *Protocols* in 17 languages

19. Princess Katerina Radziwill, who helped reveal the truth about the *Protocols*

20. Sergei Nilus, the Russian fanatic who first published the *Protocols*

22. Cover of a Brazilian edition of the *Protocols*, 1937

21. Cover of a French edition, 1934, later distributed through a shop selling Muslim books in London

23. Lawyers for the plaintiffs in Berne

24. Historian Boris Nikolaevskii, witness for the plaintiffs

25. Paul Miljukov, witness for the plaintiffs in Berne, one of the founders of the liberal Kadet movement in tsarist Russia and minister for foreign affairs in the temporary government

26. Cover page of the book by Maurice Joly from which more than half the text of the *Protocols* was copied

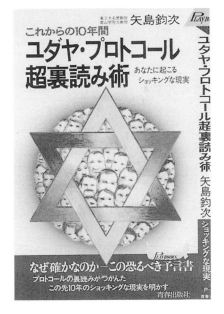

27. *The Jewish Protocols: Efficient Techniques for Reading Between the Lines*, by the Japanese author Professor Kingi Yaham, 1987. Subtitles: The shocking reality you will encounter in the next ten years. Why the scary prophecy in this book is so accurate

28. *Warning from Satan: Expected Fall of Japan in 1999*, by the Japanese author Eiesuka Saragawa, 1995. Subtitle: For the Japanese who don't know the Jews

29. Georges Brunschvig, lawyer for the plaintiffs in Berne

30. Judge Walter Meyer in the City Court of Berne

tion. 'I noted every remark he made in this connection,' Burtsev said, and then surprisingly he confessed to having used devious means to obtain the undisclosed facts. This is the privilege of journalists, he said in his defense. He had asked one of the general's agents, whom he called X, to question the general about the *Protocols*, pretending that he himself planned to write on the subject. He was fully confident, he said, that this particular agent would report to him truthfully, which he did. He framed the questions himself instructing the agent to make careful notes containing the general's answers.

After a few days X had returned with good news. General Globychev had confided in him that he was writing his memoirs for future use as a historical document, not for publication as long as they had any relevancy to actual current matters. He had written a special chapter on the *Protocols of the Elders of Zion* and on the Beilis trial, and he read it out loud to the agent.

'I was familiar with the writings of the general which contained reports on various subjects,' Burtsev told Georges, 'unlike others of the same milieu, his facts were always meticulously truthful and objective, and his remarks testified to a profound understanding of the political process.' He was sure that the same was true concerning his writings about the *Protocols of the Elders of Zion*, which were not for immediate publication. 'When you write for history,' he said, 'you tend to write the truth as you know it.'

From the careful notes prepared by X Burtsev learned that Globychev was familiar with the matter of the *Protocols*, both in his official capacity as director of the Okhrana, and in his close relationship with General Martynov, the director of the Okhrana in Moscow, who had been given the task of researching the matter of the *Protocols*.

For the sake of accuracy Burtsev read aloud the notes of X, from which he reported almost verbatim the information he had received from the general. He would not submit the original document even to the court, he said, for fear that the handwriting would disclose the agent's identity.

Georges sat transfixed as he listened to the information relayed by General Globychev to X and read aloud by Burtsev.

'The *Protocols* were created in the years 1896–1900, in Paris, by an agent of the Russian Political Police, who was eager to promote himself by undertaking this project. Apart from submitting the document to his immediate superior in Paris, the agent had also submitted it to "Hauptman" Piramidov, who was then director of the Okhrana in Petersburg. He lost his life in a military accident in 1901. Piramidov had given the manuscript of the *Protocols* to Baron Grotguss.'

Here Burtsev interrupted his reading and remarked that this baron later lived in Germany and participated in the Nazi movement. His two sons belonged in France to the anti-Semitic group Action Française. Grotguss, Burtsev said, returning to the document, had made great efforts to bring the *Protocols* to the consciousness of political and royal circles, in the years 1901–02, but had failed. Even the assistance of Manasevich-Manuilov, who did not believe in the authenticity of the *Protocols*, but wished to promote them for personal reasons, brought no results.

Leaders of the Association of the Russian People reported to the minister of the interior that they were planning to use the *Protocols* in their fight against the 'militant' Jews. By order of Lopuchin, Stolypin assigned two gendarmerie officers – Martynov and Vasiliev – to investigate the authenticity of the *Protocols*. The investigation was conducted both in Russia and abroad.

One of the most respected representatives of the Secret Police, Rataev, immediately expressed his opinion that the *Protocols* were a forgery. At the same time he loyally repeated his anti-Jewish sentiments and his belief that the Jews were to blame for the Revolution. Another representative of the Okhrana abroad, Harting, maintained the same position. Rachkovskii was also approached and although he avoided vouching for the authenticity of the *Protocols*, he stated unequivocally that they should be used in the anti-Jewish campaign.

In this manner, stated the general, the falsity of the *Protocols* was definitely proved. Stolypin had faithfully reported all details to the tsar, who was greatly shocked and ordered the removal of the *Protocols* from circulation.

The Revolution of 1905 gave new life to the *Protocols* and saved them from vanishing into obscurity.

It had previously been difficult to quote General Globychev publicly, for he was staying in Paris and holding an important post in the General Military Association (Obshchevoiskovoi Soiuz), Burtsev told Georges. Now the general was on his way to America, having severed his ties with this association. But he had preserved his intimate relationship with agent X, and he promised to send him the chapter of the *Protocols* from his memoirs as well as the report of the foreign agents to the Russian government, on the same matter.

X was convinced that the general would now be willing to allow him to use the material in his article. The general had told him, before departing for America, that he would help as much as it was in his power.

The agent promised to write to the general that he needed the material for his article, as soon as he had his address in America.

'I told the agent that his article on the matter would be published in the foreign press and I have offered him a substantive honorarium,' Burtsev told Georges. 'We shall see if the general makes good his promise. We are still waiting for the material.'

Burtsev was willing to reveal to the court the information received from General Globychev, which he fully believed to be correct, but regretfully he could never disclose the identity of X or the role he had played in obtaining this information from the general.

Georges Brunschvig loved Paris. He seized every opportunity to walk on the banks of the Seine, cross one of the magnificent bridges, and lose himself in the narrow streets of the Left Bank. He did not know how many hours he walked, when he realized that it was dark, and time to return to his hotel and pack the few belongings he had brought with him, having planned a short visit. He had stayed longer than he had anticipated and he was needed in Berne. He would have to return to Paris to interview the other witnesses, but he needed a respite after the excitement caused by the interviews with Svatikov and with Burtsev. He must digest all the information that now filled his notebook, and discuss it with his colleagues. Things were beginning to look better, but they still had much planning ahead of them.

8 French Fingerprints on a Russian Production

Georges took pleasure in the comfort of the Swiss train and let himself enjoy the beauty of the landscape. After an excellent dinner in the dining car, and a glass of superb French wine, he relaxed in his seat and spent the remaining hours planning his next steps.

The Russian picture was beginning to emerge, but there were still some gaps. He had more names on his witness list. He also needed more information about some of the people who might have been involved, directly or indirectly, in the fabrication or in the distribution of the *Protocols*. He had called Lifschitz from Paris and suggested that Tager might be able to supply information concerning Manasevich-Manuilov, whose name had cropped up in various conversations and documents. He was also beginning to realize that they had been mistaken in minimizing the French connection. It now seemed that the Russian agents had been fully assisted by their French collaborators, and that there was a French side to the story that must be studied. He was also curious about Maurice Joly, whose book he had not yet read.

They had scheduled a meeting of the committee immediately on his arrival. He had been warned not to relay important information over the telephone, and his colleagues were anxiously awaiting his report. Prior to the meeting he had sent to each of them, by messenger, the articles of Svatikov and the written report of Burtsev. He knew they would all spend a sleepless night reading the material, but he could not convey the full impact of the information he had gathered in a single meeting.

He spent a quiet evening with Odette, after having consulted with Emil Raas in their office. There was not much to report, Emil had said. Clients had not yet lined up in front of their door, he remarked with dry humor. Odette felt his excitement and was eager to hear about his trip. He was too tired to pour it all out, but she could tell that he was pleased. He did not look as worried as he had when she saw him off at the railway station, on his way to Paris. He mentioned that Emil thought the trial was hurting their fledgling practice, but, as always, she was in full support of what he was doing. This was important, she said, he had a whole lifetime to take on other clients.

They all arrived on time, Saly Mayer, Lifschitz, Dr Wiener, and Georges, and they sank into the comfortable chairs in the book-lined library of Professor Matti. They had read the documents, but the older men felt Georges' need to share his impressions of the two witnesses he had interviewed in Paris.

They must realize, Lifschitz said, after Georges finished his recital, that the judge would probably not allow the witnesses to tell the whole story in detail. This was the busy Berne City Court, he warned; they must not stretch the judge's patience. Noticing that Georges looked somewhat deflated, he promised to work with him in coaching the witnesses.

They must stick to essentials, Professor Matti agreed. This was the lawyer's craft, to create a plausible comprehensive story without drowning the judge in a multitude of unrelated facts. Witnesses must be meticulously coached to tell their story in a way acceptable in a court of law.

But this was not a routine case, Georges protested, this was a historical trial; history was part of it.

Yes, Lifschitz retorted, they must find a way to supply the historical background without turning the court into a classroom. They must seek a dramatic approach, as their opponents would surely do. Many good cases were mishandled because a meticulous and over-prepared lawyer bored the judge and lost his attention somewhere along the way.

Then it was time for Lifschitz to report. His news was no less encouraging. He had been in constant contact with Tager in Moscow, and was in possession of his report. Here, too, they had had some luck. On 14 March 1934 Loosli, the court-appointed expert, had written to the Soviet government requesting access to any material concerning the *Protocols of the Elders of Zion*. Surprisingly, the authorities were willing to cooperate and had authorized Tager to find the documents requested by Loosli. Thus Tager now had direct access to documents released by the Soviet government for use in the Berne trial, and he corresponded directly with Loosli. To answer Loosli's questions, Tager was combing Russian archives, supplying him with important information and documents.

In his latest letter Tager had reported that he had found in the department of rare books in the Lenin library in Moscow an undated anonymous manuscript entitled *Ancient and Contemporary Protocols of the Meetings* of *the Elders of Zion*. The manuscript had been copied on wax paper on a special printing press, and had arrived at the archive in 1919 from the private library of *Vikentii Vikent'evich Pashukanis*. According to the notes he had found in the library, the document had been created before the publication of the Nilus book in 1905. The notes also revealed that the document had been composed in the Police Department with the participation of Rachkovskii. Tager wrote that he had examined the document himself, and that it was clearly written in two different handwritings.

This supported the testimony of du Chayla and of Princess Radziwill and Madam Hurblut, Georges exclaimed: they had all mentioned that the text of the *Protocols* had been written in more than one hand.

Loosli was particularly interested in Rachkovskii's provocations and forgeries, Lifschitz told his friends, and indeed Tager had supplied some additional examples. One such example concerned the so-called Patrioticheskaia Liga (Patriotic League). 'So-called,' Lifschitz said with a smile, because it had never existed. It was one more of Rachkovskii's cynical inventions.

In 1902 Rachkovskii was intent on informing public opinion abroad, mainly French government circles, with which he was familiar, that there were popular forces in Russia opposing the revolutionary movement. He literally invented a non-existing organization called The Patriotic League, and published in its name public appeals and posters composed by him and printed at his secret printing shop. His tactics were so cynical and so devious, Tager wrote, that the concocted 'appeal' of the non-existent league, prepared by Rachkovskii, contained attacks against himself, to lend it authenticity.

As this was a common practice at the Police Department, he did not even make an effort to hide the truth. Tager had enclosed copies of reports sent by the minister of the interior, Pleve, to Tsar Nikolai II, which made it clear that the league and its posters were a figment of Rachkovskii's imagination. At the time there was no response from the palace.

Much later this activity was stopped at the request of the Ministry of Foreign Affairs. It might be embarrassing, they argued, if it were revealed abroad that the material distributed by official circles was signed by a non-existent organization.

This information was exactly in line with what the witnesses had told him in Paris about Rachkovskii, Georges exclaimed.

They spent the rest of the meeting discussing their assignments. True, they were accumulating important information, but they needed much more. 'Some names keep cropping up,' Georges remarked, 'but we still have no complete picture.' It was Professor Matti who suggested that they prepare a profile of each one of the key figures. 'You can start with Rachkovskii,' Matti suggested, 'but don't ignore characters like Manasevich-Manuilov.'

Georges offered to study the full report of Tager and bring it up for discussion at their next meeting. He would start preparing the personal profiles. He had promised Odette to take the weekend off and go up to the mountains. They deserved some time for themselves, but he was too eager to study the files accumulated on his desk. He would suggest a compromise.

He would take some work with him to the mountains, but would leave enough free time to spend with his fiancée. They would, of course, be accompanied by her parents, so she would not be lonely while he worked.

One of them would have to return to Paris, Lifschitz said, not only to interview Russian refugees but also to study the French connection. They might start with Henri Rollin, Dr Wiener suggested. Georges was once again surprised. Why would a former agent of the French Secret Service, as Wiener described him, be interested in the *Protocols*? He must have been privy, in his time, to so many secrets, to so many dramatic events. What could he add to what they already knew?

It was not a superficial interest, Wiener explained. Having had access to secret information, Rollin was convinced that the *Protocols* had been fabricated for political aims, and had indeed played, and were still playing, an important role in the politics of Europe. Not only had Rollin published articles about the *Protocols*, but he was actually involved in extensive research, preparing a book on the subject. They could find no better source for the French background of the *Protocols*.

Georges wondered how many more names would crop up as they were proceeding with their preparations. And so many of them non-Jews, he remarked. To his surprise, so many were not even Russians.

They were all disappointed when Henri Rollin refused to testify at the trial. As a former agent, he was still bound by an oath of secrecy, he said. He would not be able to reveal his sources to the court. Writing was different, he explained, but in his position he should not be exposed to a public interrogation in an open court. He was ready to help them and discuss his findings.

Wiener insisted that Rollin was important and must be interviewed. So far they had concentrated on witnesses of Russian origin, but they should not ignore the fact that the *Protocols* had been created in France, in the French language, a plagiarism from a French book, which dealt with French politics. There were many who maintained that in a way the *Protocols* were the result of French–Russian collaboration.

Saly Mayer wondered whether they should spend money and energy on more historical research. They would probably not be allowed to use all this in court. Historical background was indeed necessary, but they were not writing an academic thesis, he said. Did they believe the judge would allow them to hold a seminar in his courtroom? Were they supposed to go back all the way to the politics of Napoleon III, just because the forgers used as their model the book of Maurice Joly? It would not even be effective, he said; their opponents would use dramatic effects, and speak to the public and to the press. Who wanted an exposé on French politics, he exclaimed impatiently. They should stick to facts, he urged.

But Saly Mayer was overruled. Wiener was right, Professor Matti said. It was wrong for a lawyer to limit his research to the facts he would present in court. He told them how he used to explain to his students that they must study their case to its very depth, the how, and the when, and the why. They must have a plausible theory that explained not only all the facts but the motives behind them, even the inconsistencies, before they decided how to present their case to a judge. They must believe, to be believed. This was an important historical case, he said, they were not dealing with the forgery of a commercial document. If they wanted to expose this forgery, they must go to its roots.

There was another reason why they must contact Rollin, Wiener added quietly. This was 1934, he reminded them, the Nazis ruled Germany and they were gaining influence in other countries. Rollin had made a special study of the use made by the Nazis of the *Protocols of the Elders of Zion*. Had they not noticed how Hitler had used the text of the *Protocols* in his book *Mein Kampf*?

They had not read *Mein Kampf*, they confessed. Oh, they had read excerpts, they knew about Hitler's scandalous race theories, but they would not defile themselves by actually reading this trash.

It may be trash, Wiener said, but the man who had written it was now the elected ruler of Germany, and his book was very relevant to their trial. Hitler had actually adopted the theory of the Jewish conspir-acy, and whole passages of his book read as if they had been copied from the *Protocols of the Elders of Zion.*

He then surprised them by extracting a document from his briefcase. He had copied some passages, he said, offering to read them aloud. The Jews were not only described as a subhuman race, he said, in Hitler's words they were the mightiest counterpart to the Aryan.

Then, without comment, he started reading the passages he had carefully selected:

> As long as the Jew has not become the master of the other peoples, he must speak their languages whether he likes it or not, but as soon as they became his slaves, they would all have to learn a universal language (Esperanto, for instance!) so that by this additional means the Jews could more easily dominate them!

*   *   *

> To what an extent the whole existence of this people is based on a continuous lie is shown incomparably by the *Protocols of the Wise Men of Zion,* so infinitely hated by the Jews. They are based on a forgery, the *Frankfurter Zeitung* moans and screams once every week: the best proof that they are authentic. What many Jews may do unconsciously is here consciously exposed. And that is what matters. It is completely indifferent from what Jewish brain these disclosures originate; the important thing is that with positively terrifying certainty they reveal the nature and activity of the Jewish people and expose their inner contexts as well as their ultimate final aims. The best criticism applied to them, however, is reality.

*   *   *

> The higher he climbs [Hitler said of the Jew], the more alluring his old goal that was once promised him rises from the veil of the past, and with feverish avidity his keenest minds see the dream of world domination tangibly approaching.
>
> First, he used the bourgeoisie as a battering ram against the feudal world, then the worker against the bourgeois world. If formerly he knew how to swindle his way to civil rights in the

shadow of the bourgeoisie, now he hopes to find the road to his own domination in the worker's struggle for existence. From now on the worker has no other task but to fight for the future of the Jewish people. Unconsciously he is harnessed to the service of the power which he thinks he is combating. He is seemingly allowed to attack capital, and this is the easiest way of making him fight for it. In this the Jew keeps up an outcry against international capital and in truth he means the national economy which must be demolished in order that the international stock exchange can triumph over its dead body.

*   *   *

For under this cloak of purely social ideas truly diabolic purposes are hidden, yes, they are publicly proclaimed with the most insolent frankness. This theory represents an inseparable mixture of reason and human madness, but always in such a way that only the lunacy can become reality and never the reason.

*   *   *

With the shattering of the personality and the race, the essential obstacle is removed to the domination of the inferior being – and this is the Jew. Precisely in political and economic madness lies the sense of this doctrine.

*   *   *

For this prevents all truly intelligent people from entering its service, while those who are intellectually less active and poorly educated in economics hasten to it with flying colors. The intellectuals for this movement – for even this movement needs intellectuals for its existence – are sacrificed by the Jew from his own ranks. Thus there arises a pure movement entirely of manual workers under Jewish leadership, apparently aiming to improve the situation of the worker, but in truth planning the enslavement and with it the destruction of all non-Jewish peoples.

*   *   *

The general pacifistic paralysis of the national instinct of self-preservation begun by Freemasonry in the circles of the so-called intelligentsia is transmitted to the broad masses and above all to the bourgeoisie by the activity of the big papers which today are always Jewish. Added to these two weapons of disintegration comes a third and by far the most terrible, the organization of brute force. As a shock and storm troop, Marxism is intended to finish off what the preparatory softening up with the first two weapons has made ripe for collapse. Here we have teamwork that is positively brilliant – and we need really not be surprised if in confronting it those very institutions which always like to represent themselves as the pillars of a more or less legendary state authority hold up least. It is in our high and highest state officialdom that the Jew has at all times (aside from a few exceptions) found the most compliant abettor of his work of disintegration. Cringing submissiveness to superiors and high-handed arrogance to inferiors distinguish this class to the same degree as a narrow-mindedness that often cries to high Heaven and is only exceeded by a self-conceit that is sometimes positively amazing.

* * *

In keeping with the ultimate aims of the Jewish struggle, which are not exhausted in the mere economic conquest of the world, but also demand its political subjugation, the Jew divides the organization of his Marxist world doctrine into two halves which, apparently separate from one another, in truth form an inseparable whole: the political and the trade-union movement. The trade-union movement does the recruiting. In the hard struggle for existence which the worker must carry on, thanks to the greed and shortsightedness of many employers, it offers him aid and protection, and thus the possibility of winning better living conditions. If, at a time when the organized national community, the state, concerns itself with him little or not at all, the worker does not want to hand over the defense of his vital human rights to the blind caprice of people who in part have little sense of responsibility and are often heartless to boot, he must take their defense into his own hands. In exact proportion as the so-called national bourgeoisie, blinded by financial interests, sets the heaviest obstacles in the path of this struggle for existence and not only resists all attempts at shortening the inhumanly long working day, abolishing child labor, safeguarding and protecting the woman, improving sanitary conditions in the workshops and homes, but often actually sabotages them, the shrewder Jew takes the oppressed people under his wing. Gradually he becomes the leader of the trade-union movement all the more easily as he is not interested in really eliminating social evils in an honest sense, but only in training an economic storm troop, blindly devoted to him, with which to destroy the national economic independence.

He desires not the preservation of an independent national economy, but its destruction. Consequently, no pangs of conscience can prevent him as a leader of the trade-union movement from raising demands which not only overshoot the goal, but whose fulfillment is either impossible for practical purposes or means the ruin of the national economy. Moreover, he does not want to have a healthy, sturdy race before him, but a rickety herd capable of being subjugated. This desire again permits him to raise demands of the most senseless kind whose practical fulfillment he himself knows to be impossible and which, therefore, could not lead to any change in things, but at most to a wild incitement of the masses. And that is what he is interested in and not a true and honest improvement of social conditions.

As long as the insight of the masses remains as slight as now and the state as indifferent as today, these masses will always be first to follow the man who in economic matters offers the most shameless promises. And in this the Jew is a master. For in his entire activity he is restrained by no moral scruples!

Actually the Jew by means of the trade union, which could be a blessing for the nation, shatters the foundations of the national economy. Parallel with this, the political organization advances. It plays hand in glove with the trade-union movement, for the latter prepares the masses for political organization, in fact, lashes them into it with violence and coercion. Furthermore, it is the permanent financial source from which the political organization feeds its enormous apparatus. It is the organ controlling the political activity of the individual and does the pandering in all big demonstrations of a political nature. In the end it no longer comes out for political interests at all, but places its chief instrument of struggle, the cessation of work in the form of a mass and general strike, in the service of the political idea.

By the creation of a press whose content is adapted to the intellectual horizon of the least educated people, the political and trade union organization finally obtains the agitational institution by which the lowest strata of the nation are made ripe for the most reckless acts. Its function is not to lead people out of the swamp of a base mentality to a higher stage, but to cater to their lowest instincts. Since the masses are as mentally lazy as they are sometimes presumptuous, this is a business as speculative as it is profitable.

For while the Zionists try to make the rest of the world believe that the national consciousness of the Jew finds its satisfaction in the creation of a Palestinian state, the Jews again slyly dupe the dumb Goyim. It doesn't even enter their heads to build up a Jewish state in Palestine for the purpose of living there; all they want is a central organization for their international world swindle, endowed with its own sovereign rights and removed from the intervention of other states: a haven for convicted scoundrels and a university for budding crooks.

And in politics he begins to replace the idea of democracy by the dictatorship of the proletariat.

*   *   *

In the organized mass of Marxism he has found the weapon which lets him dispense with democracy and in its stead allows him to subjugate and govern the peoples with a dictatorial and brutal fist. He works systematically for revolutionization in a twofold sense: economic and political.

Around peoples who offer too violent a resistance to attack from within he weaves a net of enemies, thanks to his international influence, incites them to war, and finally, if necessary, plants the flag of revolution on the very battlefields.

In economics he undermines the states until the social enterprises which have become unprofitable are taken from the state and subjected to his financial control.

In the political field he refuses the state the means for its self preservation, destroys the foundations of all national self-maintenance and defense, destroys faith in the leadership, scoffs at its history and past, and drags everything that is truly great into the gutter.

Culturally he contaminates art, literature, the theater, makes a mockery of natural feeling, overthrows all concepts of beauty and sublimity, of the noble and the good, and instead drags men down into the sphere of his own base nature.

* * *

Religion is ridiculed, ethics and morality represented as outmoded, until the last props of a nation in its struggle for existence in this world have fallen.

* * *

Now begins the great last revolution. In gaining political power the Jew casts off the few cloaks that he still wears. The democratic people's Jew becomes the blood-Jew and tyrant over peoples. In a few years he tries to exterminate the national intelligentsia and by robbing the peoples of their natural intellectual leadership makes them ripe for the slave's lot of permanent subjugation.

* * *

The most frightful example of this kind is offered by Russia, where he killed or starved about thirty million people with positively fanatical savagery, in part amid inhuman tortures, in order to give a gang of Jewish journalists and stock-exchange bandits domination over a great people.

* * *

The defeats on the battlefield in August 1918 would have been child's play to bear. They stood in no proportion to the victories of our people. It was not they that caused our downfall; no, it was brought about by that power which prepared these defeats by systematically over many decades robbing our people of the political and moral instincts and forces which alone make nations capable and hence worthy of existence.

They were dumbfounded. Nobody spoke, while Wiener wiped his glasses and nervously pushed the offensive pages back into his briefcase.

There was no doubt, Professor Matti exclaimed, that Hitler had used the text of the *Protocols*, which had been very popular in Europe when he was writing his book in the early 1920s.

But this time Jews were not threatened by a mere pogrom, Lifschitz muttered. They had been prepared to deal with a forgery, whose authors were all probably dead. They had not planned to confront Hitler in a Swiss courtroom.

It was not their choice, Lifschitz said. Sadly, it took a non-Jew such as Henri Rollin to open their eyes to what they were actually facing.

They decided that Wiener would contact Rollin at his address in the seventeenth *arrondissement* in Paris, on 2 rue Gervex, and obtain as much information as possible.

Odette could not tell me whether Georges had followed the events concerning Henri Rollin after the trial. When I told her what I had found out, she remarked sadly that in 1939 Georges had other worries. She did not even remember the name Rollin – he was not one of the witnesses, was he, she asked. No, I said, he did not testify at the trial, but his extensive research and his close familiarity with the political and historical events played out on the European arena at the relevant period made him a witness in my own private investigation into the matter of the Protocols.

PERSPECTIVE OF A FRENCH SECRET AGENT

On 28 June 1939, Henri Rollin signed the final draft of the introduction to his book *L'Apocalypse de notre temps*. It represented years of research, and was the last of a series of books and articles he had published since 1913, dealing with military, historical and political subjects such as maritime battles, the Russian Revolution, the Nazi threat and the dangers of the emerging racist theories.

Rollin was almost 50 at the time of the Berne trial, and he had already distinguished himself as a highly placed and much decorated officer in the French navy, a valuable agent in the French Secret Service, and a respected writer on historical and political subjects. He had spent time in Russia and had developed an intense interest in the Russian Revolution, publishing, in 1931, two volumes on its origins and its results.

He had become interested in the Masonic movement when he had studied its role in the French Revolution. Later, preparing his book on Russia, he had become aware of the alleged existence of a Judeo-Masonic conspiracy, and the exaggerated role assigned to Jews in the Russian Revolution. A friend had given him a copy of the *Protocols of the Elders of Zion*, and, being thorough in nature, he had read it to the end. As he extended his studies of current events, Rollin seemed to notice the imprint of the *Protocols* on every major event in the last few decades, and he became intrigued by the fact that this strange document played such a prominent role in European politics. He seemed to encounter the *Protocols* everywhere: in his study of French politics at the end of the century, in his research on the Russian Revolution, and in his examination of the rapidly spreading racial theories and the Nazi movement, which was gaining dangerous momentum. How could it be, he wondered, that the same theory of a Jewish conspiracy could effectively serve all of them: the Russian monarchists as well as the Nazi racists.

Neither a Freemason, nor a Jew, but a good Catholic, as he stated in the opening sentence of his book, Rollin was convinced that the alleged conspiracy, presented in the *Protocols of the Elders of Zion*, constituted the fundamental argument in German Nazi propaganda around the world. He became truly appalled when the president of France, Mr. Doumer, was assassinated by the Russian refugee Gorgulov on 6 May 1932. From documents in the possession of the assassin and reports submitted to the court by psychologists appointed to examine him, it became apparent that he was an ardent anti-Semite, who believed that both France and England were instruments in the service of the Judeo-Masonic conspirators, and constituted a threat to European civilization. It was they who had provoked the Great War in 1914, as well as the downfall of the Russian, the German and the Austro-Hungarian monarchies, Gorgulov believed. Like Hitler and his disciples, this assassin was convinced that the free democracies, mainly England and France, were responsible for all the misery that had be-fallen Europe, and like the German murderers of Rathenau, in 1922, he too maintained that he was serving humanity by assassinating the president of France, who was manipulated by the Jews.

Signing the introduction to his book *L'Apocalypse de notre temps*, Rollin probably mused that he had not planned to write a 700-page book on the *Protocols of the Elders of Zion*, but one thing led to another and now he was looking at the bulky manuscript, hoping that his book would serve as a warning. But when the first copies of Rollin's book were finally delivered to the bookstores three months later, on 23 September 1939, it was too late. On the first day of September the German army had invaded Poland and the Second World War was upon them. In later years Rollin must have thought how right he had been when he wrote that the theory of the Jewish conspiracy, blaming the Jews for everything, was indeed the central theme of German propaganda.

Very few copies of Rollin's book had been sold when the German army invaded France, and not many Frenchmen were even aware of it. But the Germans had read it. They were great believers in the written word, and books that constituted a danger to the Nazi theory were systematically banned and removed from circulation. Between 1940 and 1942 the Nazi invaders issued in France three lists of banned books written by, or about, Jews, political refugees and others who might 'poison public opinion'. Rollin's book *L'Apocalypse de notre temps* appeared on every one of the three lists. It was consequently removed from all bookstores and even from the publisher's warehouse, and not counting rare copies, which survived, the book practically vanished and was not available for 50 years.

In May 1992 I was in Paris for a short conference. As had been my custom these last years, since I became interested in the *Protocols*, I was constantly on the look out for new material. Some time ago my friend Paul Levy, a retired judge, had sent me a cutting from the popular French newspaper, *Le Monde*, which mentioned a book on the *Protocols of the Elders of Zion*, recently published in Paris. After the conclusion of the conference, I went with Paul in search of the book, presenting the newspaper cutting in one bookstore after another, until finally, from a bookstore on boulevard St Michelle, a clerk called the publisher, Editions Allia, and two days later the newly issued reprint of Henri Rollin's book was hand-delivered to my hotel.

Indeed, I thought reading the book, Dr Wiener had been right to insist on interviewing Henri Rollin. What a pity that this man did not testify at the trial. Had he presented to the court his ideas about the *Protocols*, even in 1934, they might have reached a larger public. As it happened, his 700-page book, which contained a wealth of information and insight, had been absent from the market for over fifty years, although its title appeared on almost all bibliographical lists dealing with the *Protocols*.

Sixty years later, on 26 November 1998, another non-Jew, this time a German, presented his doctoral thesis at the Technical University in Berlin. Wolfram Mayer zu Uptrup had spent years researching how the *Protocols of the Elders of Zion* had influenced the anti-Jewish policy of the National Socialists in Germany, and how the Nazis had used the content of this document in rationalizing the 'final solution' – the extermination of 6 million Jews. His thesis was published in 2003 by Metropol, in Germany, under the title: *Kampf gegen die 'Jüdische Welverschwoerung'* (The Fight Against the 'Jewish International Conspiracy').

After reading Rollin's book I told Odette that I now understood why Dr

Wiener had been so eager to contact Henri Rollin. Thinking back, Odette said, she had a vague recollection of the name. Georges had told her at the time that at the insistence of Wiener, who had just returned from Paris, he must study the French part of the story. She remembered that one whole weekend he could not stop talking about Maurice Joly.

MAURICE JOLY: PROFILE OF A REBEL

What would Maurice Joly have thought, I wondered, had he known that he would be best remembered in future years not as the political rebel that he was, but as the man who inadvertently contributed to the creation of the most famous forgery in history? What would he have said had he known of the attempts to invent for him a Jewish origin, even a Jewish name? How he would have laughed if he had been present in the Berne courtroom, where it was seriously alleged that his true name was Moishe Joel. How he would have gasped had he realized that in 1937, in Italy, a priest by the name of Giovani Preziosi would write that Maurice Joly was half-Jewish, a Freemason and a revolutionary. All lies, he would have exclaimed. How he would have raged at the wicked implication that it was he who had plagiarized his book, using the *Protocols of the Elders of Zion*, three decades before the *Protocols* had even been created. Could he have dreamed that his name would go down in history in a context completely foreign to him, long after the name of Napoleon III, who had been the real subject of his book, had vanished from memory, relegated to history books?

Looking at his photograph I seemed to detect the fire in his eyes. His head was high, his shoulders held back in a stance of defiance. Here was a man of extreme courage, a lone fighter, I thought, who had so readily risked and even sacrificed his personal freedom to open the eyes of his fellow men. Here was a single man who declared war on a mighty monarch, and paid for it.

Familiar with the procedure in French courtrooms, which has not changed much since Napoleonic times, I could almost envision the scene that had taken place in the Cour Correctionel de la Seine on 28 April 1865. The Cour Correctionel is a lower court, where criminal cases are tried by a panel of three judges, without juries. I imagined how this proud and angry man had stood before his judges in their black robes when they convicted him of incitement against the state, and pronounced the sentence of imprisonment for 15 months and a fine of 200 francs.

On 14 February 1866, Maurice Joly was sent back to the same cell in the Sainte-Pélagie prison, in which he had previously waited, first for his trial, and later for his appeals in the Cour d'appel and in the Cour de Cassation. Now that his conviction and his sentence had been confirmed by the highest court in the land, he had a quiet year in which to ponder and to write. Counting the period of pre-trial custody, he had been imprisoned altogether for a period of two years when he was released on 14 May 1867. He was 36 years old.

It seems that his convictions remained unchanged. Prison had not intimidated him. He had been considered a rebel and a troublemaker since childhood, and he had never changed, as was apparent in the autobiography which he published in 1870, composed during another period of incarceration, which, this time, ended with an acquittal.

His bourgeois family in Lons-le-Saunierin did not know how to handle this difficult and rebellious child. They all held well-respected and prestigious posts. His father was an assemblyman in Jura. His grand-father had been paymaster of Corsica before becoming secretary-general of the Admiralty Ministry in Naples. Yet since his birth in 1829 Maurice had not conformed to any standards of behavior set down by his family. By the time he finally completed his studies in Paris, he had been compelled to change five colleges. Immediately after his admission to the Paris bar in 1859, at the age of 30, he started his writing career, which would continue until his last day. It soon became apparent that he would not settle for a routine practice of law. As was popular in those days, he adopted a satirical style, drawing critical literary portraits of famous lawyers and judges, exposing any trait or behavior that seemed to him dishonest or hypocritical. His booklet *The Paris Bar: Political and Literary Studies* was funny and well written, and became the talk of his colleagues in the corridors of the Palais de Justice, but it obviously did not endear him to his friends in the legal profession. His continuous involvement in politics marked him for constant surveillance by the authorities after his release from prison, a fact that did not make his books attractive to publishers. Joly, always on the warpath, sued ten newspapers that refused to print his critical articles, obtaining judgment against eight of them.

On this beautiful spring day of 14 May 1867, on his way to Paris, he must have remembered how it had all begun on that fateful evening on the banks of the Seine.

It had been a cold and rainy autumn evening in Paris. He was walking along the river in a need to clear his head and bring some order into his turbulent thoughts.

His friends were worried about him. Even those who shared his political views did not think he could make a difference. They warned him that he would get into trouble. This regime did not tolerate troublemakers, they argued. Napoleon III was a dangerous despot, he was ruining France, they agreed, but exposing him in a book was sheer lunacy. It would change nothing, they said: the public was too dumb to realize what was happening and too meek to react. Not only would his book be banned, they warned, he himself could end up behind bars. But he was convinced that one had to do something to turn the tide, and he had no other tools, he knew only how to write.

He had meditated for a whole year on a book that would show the terrible inroads that the imperial legislation had made on all branches of the administration and the gaps which it had opened by completely wiping out all public liberties. But he knew his French public. A serious severe analytical book would have no readers. They had a sarcastic temper, his French fellow citizens, he told himself – he must find a literary form that would appeal to their imagination. He must also disguise his real meaning, but this was nothing new. Since the time of the empire the French had been forced to make attacks on the establishment behind a disguise.

He was passing the Pont Royal when he suddenly recalled a book he had read lately, entitled *Dialogue sur les blés* (A Dialogue on Wheat), by Abbé Galiani. This was a dialogue between the dead and the living on current politics. The more he thought of it, the more convinced he became that his book should be in the form of an allegorical dialogue. He would have living or dead people converse on contemporary politics. He would have to invent the participants in his dialogue, for he could not use real people, but what kind of people would he create? Who would represent his own ideas, his thoughts? Who was the ultimate opponent to everything that Napoleon III represented? The name Montesqieu came to mind. So sure was he that this was the right participant that he would look no further. He was in such complete agreement with the views of this man that he could easily slip into his form. In his book he would merge with Montesqieu until they became one.

But who would be his opponent? Who was the proponent of everything that was wrong and evil in the policies of Napoleon III? Who was it who advocated that politics had nothing to do with morality, that legality need only be used by rulers as a thin disguise for the exercise of unlimited power; who was it that disdained democracy, had no respect for the rights of the individual, set forth a theory that served despots and convinced them that they could dupe their citizens with immunity? In short, who was it whose theory was built on the cynical premise that might is right?

He concentrated on the imaginary scene in heaven (or perhaps in hell), with Montesqieu speaking quietly and wisely. But try as he may, he could not attach to the other figure any face but that of the hated monarch. With a great effort he tried to concentrate on the theory rather than on the face. He repeated words that he would have put in the mouth of the ruler of France, if he only could. He would deal with any opposition easily, the ruler was saying. He would even make the people support him. To enjoy absolute power he must control the press, the police, the working place. He would impress people with a few easy victories, he would set them against each other by well-planted lies. They would come to believe that he was their savior, not their oppressor. 'Your fault is that you respect the people,' he would say to Montesqieu. 'You do not realize how stupid they are.' Who but Napoleon III would say this? As suddenly as he had thought of Montesqieu, another name pushed itself to the front of his consciousness. The other character in his imaginary scene now had a new face, that of Machiavelli. Who else was better to represent the abominable policies of Napoleon III?

When the book was ready Joly went to a small hotel in Geneva where he re-read the manuscript and wrote a short introduction, entitled 'Simple Avertisement'. His book could apply to all governments, he wrote, but in fact it personified one particular political system. 'We are too terrified to regard in their true light some of the things which we see with our eyes,' he wrote.

At the bottom of the page he wrote with a flourish 'Genève, le 15 Octobre 1864'. He almost signed his name, then remembered that he was committed to anonymity. This was why the book was later called *The Geneva Document.*

On his return to France Joly found a printer in Bourdier and told him the book was a translation from an English author named McPherson. But he had written too well, and his real meaning was too transparent. After reading the first three dialogues the printer refused to continue, having recognized Napoleon III. He needed the business, but he was afraid for his life. This was good news and bad news, a friend told him. The book had a chance of being understood by the public, his friend said, but wouldn't the authorities be as smart as the printer? The book must be published anonymously, his friend advised, preferably in another country. So he waited for his vacation and went to Belgium in search of a printer.

Maurice Joly hoped that even if his book was noticed by the French authorities they would have no proof of his complicity, as this was an anonymous unsigned foreign publication. Sadly, the man who was so aware of the brutal tactics of his government, was too naive to feel insecure. To his utter surprise he was arrested on arrival in France, incarcerated and charged with inciting hatred and contempt of the French government.

In their judgment the judges wrote that 'this work is neither an abstract and speculative criticism nor a political argument inspired by a sincere spirit; that the author charges the French government with having, through shameful means, hypocritical ways and perfidious contrivances, led the public astray, degraded the character of the nation and corrupted its morals ... finally, for having, as the writer himself describes it in his last page but one of his book, composed "this gathering of monstrous things before which the mind recoils in fright, this work that only hell itself could accomplish."'

'For these reasons,' the judges wrote, 'Maurice Joly, having committed the crime of inciting hatred and contempt for the government, is sentenced to 15 months' imprisonment, a fine of 300 francs, and to confiscation of the copies of the *Dialogues in Hell*.'

It was the porter of his building, 5 quai Voltaire, who called the police, on 15 July 1887, having missed Maurice Joly for two consecutive days. He was found sitting in his armchair, head lowered, arms hanging at his sides, a revolver at his feet. On his desk the police found an unpublished manuscript of a book and suicide letters to his mother, sister, brother, a friend, and two members of the bar.

Holding one of the rare surviving copies of Joly's book, I feel sad that this work of art remains unknown to the public at large. After 130 years its political message is still relevant, the wisdom of its ideas still appealing to the mind, and its elegant language still pleasing to the reader. Although it contains nothing but the dialogue between the two participants, one can actually envision the spirits of the two men, the author of *The Prince* and the author of *L'Esprit des lois*, amicably greeting each other on a desolate beach in hell, which Joly had chosen for this bizarre encounter, and which is mentioned in the opening words of Machiavelli.

There are 25 dialogues, in which each man argues his theory, but Machiavelli has the main role. His arguments take up most of the 324 pages of the small book, while Montesqieu's voice becomes weaker and weaker and he limits himself to short questions and remarks, with some expressions of surprise. But his is the last line in the book, when he cries in anguish: 'Oh God, what have you permitted?'

It is a tragic fact that Joly's book was not only used to create what turned out to serve as the Bible of anti-Semites, but was also fated to serve, in a most diabolical manner, as a manual for dictators. He wanted to show the world how dangerous absolute rulers can be; he meant to warn his people by proving how vulnerable democracy was and how easy it would be for a dictator to exploit its weaknesses. All you need, he tried to prove, was an economic crisis, a handy enemy against whom the public can be easily incited, and a fascist posing as the people's savior. Joly did not realize that, more than a weapon against dictatorship, he had inadvertently created a blueprint for the most dangerous theories and tactics, which would actually contribute to the most heinous crimes against humanity to be perpetrated in the next century. It was not Montesqieu who was the hero of his book, but Machiavelli. It was his voice that rang out loud and clear. It was his message that sounded convincing. The people for whom the book was intended mostly ignored its message, but those of evil intent did not. The forgers used it to create the *Protocols*, and Hitler used the Machiavellian recipe so well detailed by Joly to crystallize his own plan for world domination, and for justification of the biggest, best-planned and most systematic mass extermination of men, women and children in human history.

It remained a mystery, Wiener told his colleagues, how the forgers got hold of Maurice Joly's book and how they decided to combine the imaginary scene in the Prague cemetery, described by Herman Goedsche, with the beautiful text of Joly's *Dialogue*. But one thing was clear, he insisted: the Russians could not have done it without the active support and collaboration of their French counterparts.

After studying the information obtained from France, Georges was convinced that the *Protocols* should not be presented in court as the sole creation of the Russian forgers. The judge might consider the book to be the legacy of an extinct regime, adopted by European anti-Semites for their own purposes, but not really rooted in European culture. They must convince him that even though the actual forgery had been executed by Russian agents of the old regime, the so-called 'Jewish Conspiracy' was first and foremost the invention of anti-Semitic Western intellectuals. The idea that Jews were bound by their religion to ruin Christian society was not new, but they must impose upon the court that these anti-Semitic allegations, harmful as they were, had been forged into a much more lethal weapon endangering society at large. They must explain in court how this international libel, now being exploited by the emerging Nazi parties, was a political bombshell, created by a combination of French intellectual anti-Semitism and Russian Jew hatred.

He now agreed with Wiener that the theory of a political Jewish conspiracy to dominate the world had been mostly propagated by Frenchmen, publicized by Russians, and adopted by the rest of the world.

THE FRENCH CONNECTION

The more he read about French anti-Semitism, the more Georges strove to understand why it was that Paris, of all capitals, had served as a fertile ground for the fabrication of the *Protocols of the Elders of Zion*. In his discussions with Wiener late into the night, two factors seemed to materialize.

First, the sudden expansion of the Jewish population in Paris. Survivors of Russian pogroms had fled to France, where Jews had been granted full emancipation in 1791, and the Jewish presence was suddenly much more evident in the French capital.

But there were also the economic and political changes that French society was undergoing. Farmers and small businessmen lost their property as a result of industrialization and technological development, which threatened the old order. People felt threatened by the principle of equality, by parliamentarianism. Secularity seemed to undermine the foundations of the Church. Liberalism and democracy were viewed as dangers to the existing way of life, enemies of Christianity, undermining the established code of morals. Fear and apprehension, which gripped large parts of society, awoke and strengthened dormant prejudices, and people searched for a scapegoat. The Jews, who populated the big cities, who mostly supported the social and economic changes, who were traditionally viewed as enemies of Christianity, were the most available candidates. Anti-Semitism became a political doctrine. A big international conspiracy seemed to supply ready answers, logical explanations for all the evils.

The banks were viewed as 'the enemy', and Jews were said to be holding the purse strings. Many middle-class families were ruined in the collapse of the Catholic bank Union General in 1882, and it was easy to funnel the frustration of the public into well-used channels of

Jew hatred. The Jewish banks were flourishing, while the poor French Catholics lost their savings and were facing virtual poverty, cried the French press. The loudest and the most prominent in its anti-Jewish tirade, was the newspaper *La libre parole*, which made its first appearance that same year. Its publisher, Edouard Drumont, was already well on his way to becoming the most prominent figure in the anti-Semitic campaign that raged in France during the last two decades of the century. The idea that the Jew actually meant to dominate the world by usurping political power through economic means, was beginning to gain popularity in the minds of the French public. There had to be an reason why Jews, with no country of their own, no land they could call theirs, a persecuted minority in most countries, were doing so well both in the free professions and in the world of finance. The myth of an international Jewish conspiracy was emerging and gaining credibility.

There was no real proof for Henri Rollin's speculation that Edouard Drumont had actually been involved in the fabrication of the *Protocols of the Elders of Zion*, Dr Wiener told Georges, but he had definitely been instrumental in propagating the theory of the so-called 'Jewish Conspiracy', and he could decidedly boast of assuming a leadership role in the Dreyfus Affair.

It was no coincidence, Wiener insisted, that the *Protocols* had been fabricated in France at that particular point in time. There was surely a link between the two most outstanding anti-Jewish events that occurred in the same city at the same time.

Both events were based on a forgery, he reminded them. On 1 November 1896, a French major called Henri forged at his house two documents implicating Alfred Dreyfus, the only Jewish officer on the General Staff of the army, in acts of espionage. The famous forged *bordereau*, which purported to be in the handwriting of Dreyfus, had been inserted into the secret file delivered to the judges during the trial and served as the basis for the conviction of an innocent man. Years later, after Dreyfus had spent miserable years on Devil's Island in inhuman conditions, it was definitely proved that another officer, Esterhazi, had been the real traitor who had sold French secrets to the German Embassy. He was employed as a secret adviser to Drumont on *La libre parole*.

The ground had been well prepared for the emergence of Edouard Drumont. In 1847 Toussenel had published his book *Le Juifs, rois de l'époque* (The Jews, Kings of our Time), describing the Jewish economic domination of France. In 1869 Gougenot des Mousseaux had published *Les Juifs et la judaïsation des peuples chrétiens* (The Jews and the Judaisation of the Christian Peoples), accusing the Jews of converting the Christians whom they could not dominate. But these and other anti-Semitic books had but a limited audience until the last two decades of the nineteenth century, when Drumont discovered the right formula to foment and expand the popular anti-Semitic sentiment in France. His book *La France juive*, published on 14 April 1886, became an instant bestseller. One hundred thousand copies were immediately sold, and ultimately the book was published in no fewer than 200 editions.

Drumont's cryptic formula was: 'All comes from the Jew, all returns to the Jew.' He described the Jew as the essence of ugliness, a badly smelling creature, with a bloodless face, greenish skin, claw-like hands, the sign of Cain on his forehead. The Jew does not talk, Drumont wrote, he screams, he bites, he licks, he barks and he scratches.

In May 1892 Drumont initiated in his newspaper a vigorous campaign to free the French army of the hated and treacherous Jewish officers. *La libre parole* became the most effective vehicle in the anti-Dreyfus movement.

Drumont must have cheered with the crowd on the morning of Saturday 5 January 1895, Wiener remarked dryly, when Alfred Dreyfus stood at attention in the yard of the Military College at Fontnoi Square in Paris, while his military decorations were ripped from his uniform and his sword was broken in two. He must have sneered with the crowd when Dreyfus cried: 'Soldiers, they are ripping off the decorations of an innocent man, long live France, long live the army.' He must have cried with the crowd 'Death to the Jews.' He must have read with gratification what Maurice Barres said in his book *La Parade de Judas* about the ceremony: 'It was a show more exciting than the guillotine.'

When Dreyfus was sentenced on 22 December 1894, to spend the rest of his days on Devil's Island, *La libre parole* explained that the traitor had been motivated by the desire of his race for the ruin of France.

Edouard Drumont's fingerprints could be detected on any anti-Semitic activity in France in those days, Dr Wiener said. He had also been instrumental in forging the link with the Russians, whom he regularly met at the salon of Juliette Adam.

Juliette had been a prominent figure in social and political circles in Paris, a writer and a journalist in her own right and editor of her own journal named *La nouvelle revue,* which hosted many well-known figures and was as supportive of anti-Semitism as was *La libre parole.* She was well informed on matters of state and politics and an expert on Russia. Prominent Russians who stayed in Paris were frequent and welcome guests in her salon, on boulevard Poissonnière 23, among them agents of the Okhrana who had been introduced by her late husband, Edmond Adam, chief of police in Paris. This was most probably where Rachkovskii had met his French counterparts, and where he may have first seen the book of Maurice Joly.

Juliette and her friends had vehemently opposed the Franco-Russian alliance initiated by the Russian minister of finance, Witte, and the loans Witte obtained from French banks to finance his ambitious economic reforms in Russia. The ties between the two countries were strengthening. In 1896 the young Tsar Nikolai II visited France with Empress Alexandra and they were received with great pomp. A million Frenchmen from the provinces lined the streets of Paris to cheer them. Russian shares and securities went up and the whole of France celebrated.

At the same time the socialists became stronger and there were strikes all over France.

Juliette and her friends constantly used their contacts and their newspapers to warn the French public that Witte – who, they said, was married to a Jew – was in the hands of the Jewish bankers who were robbing the French masses. The Rothschilds, according to them, were the ultimate enemies.

Reading about Juliette Adam, Georges Brunschvig was surprised at the number of women involved, directly and indirectly, in the story of the *Protocols.* In Switzerland the world of politics, as well as that of journalism, was solely populated by men. He could not think of any woman of his acquaintance who was personally involved in public life, excepting charities. He had read about the nineteenth-century salons where ladies of society used to entertain the famous and the mighty in a cultured, elegant and sophisticated atmosphere. Although the conversation in these salons had not been devoid of gossip, they had also provided a forum for serious, sometimes heated, discussions on current events, and a golden opportunity for the discreet passing of information and even clinching of deals.

The compilation of the guest list was a task fit for a diplomat, and some ladies turned it into an art. The time was not yet ripe for women to play a direct part in matters of state or even in the world of culture and diplomacy, so some women had created their own center of power, a unique forum, recognized and respected by pillars of society. Being invited to one of these salons was a privilege and a status symbol.

To his surprise Georges learned that Juliette's salon had been frequented by a number of people whose names had cropped up in his research on the *Protocols of the Elders of Zion*. Among them were Lesley Fry, Ilona Glinka and Eli de Cyon, who replaced Juliette at a certain period as editor of her newspaper *La nouvelle revue*, which had its offices in the same building as her Paris apartment.

She herself bought in 1885 the site of a destroyed abbey in the town of Gif-sur-Yvette, some 30 kilometers from Paris, and built an annex to which she moved her salon. She has left her mark on that town, which to this day has a street named after her, and where her bust decorates the wedding hall of the municipality, which also carries her name. Documents and portraits of Juliette Adam fill a special archive in the town hall.

Her property, now privately owned, contains the ruins of the old abbey, beautiful gardens and her living quarters, including the original salon where she entertained her guests. The present owner proudly shows visitors around, pointing out her large portrait.

The Jewish lawyer Sliosberg, who was scheduled to testify at the trial, had told Georges that Witte had actually suspected Eli de Cyon of complicity in the fabrication of the *Protocols*. It might have been a well-founded suspicion, Lifschitz said, pointing out to Georges passages from Cyon's popular articles, accusing the Jews of conspiring with the Masons to dominate the world.

In Russian his name was spelled Eli de Tsion. He was of Jewish extraction, a former professor of physiology who had abandoned his scientific career when he settled in France and became involved in politics. He took up writing and journalism, and from 1887 he collaborated with Juliette Adam in the management of *La nouvelle revue*. By that time he had already converted to Christianity, in a ceremony that took place on 17 December 1886.

In the early 1880s Cyon abandoned Juliette's paper and became the Paris representative of the Russian minister of finance, Vyshnegradskii. He was involved with all the officials in the Russian

embassy who negotiated the treaty with France, but the Embassy officials soon learned that he was a troublemaker, constantly involved in
various intrigues. He became an unrelenting anti-Semite, and his
favorite accusation against Russians he opposed was that they were
Jews.

When Vyshnegradskii discovered that Cyon had received from the
French syndicate, with whom he was negotiating, a commission
amounting to some 200,000 francs, he demanded and forced his resignation. When Witte, who followed as the next minister of finance,
refused to reinstate him, barring his entry into Russia, Cyon became
his arch-enemy, dedicating a large portion of his writing to undermining the new minister and his financial reforms. The most powerful
weapon against Witte, both in Russia and in France, was the accusation that the Russian minister was being manipulated by the Jews and
was working in their service.

De Cyon was a formidable enemy, and his false accusations, which
incriminated Witte in traitorous involvement with Germans, were
not treated lightly. When he publicly stated, at the end of 1897, that
he possessed documents that proved Witte's treachery, Rachkovskii's
agents burgled his villa in Territet in canton Vaud, on Witte's instructions. Witte was familiar with the routine use made of forged documents in those days, and he was not willing to take chances.

Juliette Adam and Edouard Drumont were important, Lifschitz
said. They were figures of the first category in French political life.
Eli de Cyon was a well-known and respected scientist, writer and
journalist. His articles carried weight in French intellectual circles.
Both he and Juliette Adam were recognized experts on Russian
affairs. De Cyon was often quoted by Edouard Drumont and Juliette
Adam, threatening that the Franco-Russian alliance would end with
the Jews dominating the world. These allegations, invented for
French ears, were equally suitable for the Russian public. It would be
Eli de Cyon's ultimate triumph if he could undermine the Jewish
banks in Paris, and at the same time thwart Witte's plans of modern-
izing the Russian economy.

Another frequent visitor to Juliette's salon was her close friend
Ilona Glinka. Like many others whose names are inextricably linked
to the story of the *Protocols*, Glinka, a former lady-in-waiting to
Empress Maria Alexandrovna in St Petersburg, was given to mysterious supernatural beliefs. But it was the French chapter in her life that
was most significant. Fluent in French, she had spent long periods in

Paris, calling herself Justine and establishing firm ties with the elite of French society. General Orzhevskii, assistant minister of internal affairs and former high-ranking officer of the Okhrana, was her patron. Her mission was to supply information on the activities of Russian terrorists in the French capital. Exposed by the French press as a Russian agent, she was compelled to leave Paris. She established herself as a popular hostess in an elegant apartment in St Petersburg, filled with French works of art, but she soon incurred royal disfavor. It was her close friendship with Juliette Adam that brought down on her head the wrath of the tsar and caused her exile to her estate in the government of Oral. She was suspected of being the main source of information for Juliette's book, published under the pseudonym 'Count Vasilii', which described the royal court in Russia in most unflattering terms.

It was no other than the now familiar Lesley Fry, another friend of Juliette Adam, who supplied the link between Glinka and the *Protocols of the Elders of Zion.*

In her book *Waters Flowing Eastward* Fry described how Ilona Glinka, using the French name Justine, had served in 1884 as an agent in the service of General Orzhevskii, collecting what she called 'political information'. At that time General Orzhevskii served as secretary to the minister of the interior, Cherevin. Fry mentioned a manuscript in French, accompanied by a Russian translation, which Justine Glinka had forwarded to General Orzhevskii, who in turn handed it to his chief, General Cherevin, for transmission to the tsar. She also stated that Cherevin refused to transmit the document to the tsar, but instead filed it in the archives.

Here was confirmation of Princess Radziwill's testimony concerning a former version of the *Protocols*, Georges remarked.

Reading Fry's book Georges wondered at the amount of fiction presented as fact. This was the same Lesley Fry, he remembered, who had accused Ahad Ha'am of having composed the *Protocols*. Yet the book contained some valuable facts. Georges was intrigued to find confirmation that Glinka had been the mysterious lady who had delivered to her neighbor, retired Major Aleksei Sukhotin, the final version of the *Protocols of the Elders of Zion*. She maintained that she had found the document at the house of an unnamed Jewish friend in Paris, and had secretly translated it into Russian and brought it with her.

Georges remembered that Sukhotin had given the document to

Stepanov, who had printed it in hectograph jelly, and brought it to the house of Sergei and Elizaveta Fedorovna in Moscow in 1897. This fact was now fully corroborated by a reproduction of a facsimile of a handwritten affidavit made in 1927 by Philip Stepanov, included in Fry's book. Not only was he looking at what seemed as an authentic, handwritten, official document, which explained how the *Protocols* had arrived in Russia, but one fact immediately stood out: Stepanov testified, under oath, that he had received the manuscript from Sukhotin in 1895, two years before he had approached Grand Prince Sergei Alexandrovich and had the document properly printed. Georges knew that the date was crucial. The distributors of the *Protocols* maintained that they were authentic minutes of clandestine meetings held behind the scenes of the first Zionist Congress in Basle at the end of 1897. Here was definite proof that the manuscript had been brought from France to Russia two years before the Zionist Congress.

He read Stepanov's affidavit again and again, and had his secretary copy it for the benefit of his colleagues. It read as follows:

> In 1895 my neighboring estate owner in the province Tula, retired Major Aleksei Nikolaevich Sukhotin, gave me a handwritten copy of the *Protocols of the Wise Men of Zion*. He told me that a lady of his acquaintance (he did not mention her name), residing in Paris, had found them at the home of a friend of hers (probably of Jewish origin), and before leaving Paris, had translated them secretly, without his knowledge, and had brought one copy to him, Sukhotin.
>
> At first I mimeographed one hundred copies of the *Protocols*, but that edition was difficult to read, and I resolved to have it printed somewhere, without mentioning the time, the city and the printer; I was helped in this by Arcadii Ippolitovich Kelepkovskii, who at that time was privy councillor with Grand Prince Sergey Alexandrovich; he had these documents printed at the Provincial Printing Press; that was in 1897. S. A. Nilus reprinted these *Protocols* in full in his book, with his own commentaries.
>
> Signed,
> Philip Petrovich Stepanov, former Procurator of the Moscow Synod Office; Chamberlain, Privy Councillor, and at the time of the publication of that edition, Chief of the district railway service in the Moscow–Kursk railway (in Orel).

This is the signature of a member of the colony of Russian refugees at Stary and Novy Futog.

Witnessed by me, Stary Futog, 17 April 1927.
Chairman of the Administration of the Colony,
Prince Vladimir Galitsin.

They were all satisfied that Ilona Glinka had definitely been one of the links between the forgers of the *Protocols*, their French advisers, and their publishers in Russia. Another link in the chain of testimony had been confirmed.

Georges Brunschvig was astounded by the fact that his research into a book that he had thought had been fabricated by anti-Semitic forgers, to embarrass the Jews and to incite the mob against them, compelled him to delve into such a wide spectrum of political events. He was learning that one of the outstanding phenomena in the history of anti-Semitism was the cynical use made of the traditional – whether inborn, inherited or acquired – feelings of hatred against Jews to achieve political aims. He was becoming acquainted with the calculated manipulation and systematical diversion of real grievances towards the Jews; the scapegoating of Jews, refined through the ages, had become one more weapon in the arsenal of politicians. They used it at will, knowing that in the marketplaces of the world it was always good legal tender.

Lifschitz had just presented him with a book by the American clergyman Elias Newman, recently published in Minneapolis, in which the author declared unequivocally that the *Protocols* were a coarse fabrication. Leafing through the book he discovered that Lifschitz had marked one passage that he might want to use in his address to the court:

The Jews are as good as a foreign war in averting attention from the financial scandals caused by the unethical and unscrupulous manipulations of leading financiers, and infinitely more economical. Is it profiteering that agitates the public? It is the Jews who are the profiteers. Is it the menace of Bolshevism? They are the Bolshevists. Is it the hidden hand? That hand wears heavy Jewish rings. Is it a shortage of houses? It is the Jews who have monopolized all accommodation. Is it a dearth of bacon? It is the Jews who have eaten it up. Is it the awful consequences of imperialistic ambition? The Kaiser has Jewish blood. Is it the country suffering from a too ambitious form of clericalism? The

Pope is a successor of Peter and he was a Jew. If there were no Jews they would have to be invented for the use of politicians and a certain class of theological speculators both modernist and so-called fundamentalists – they are indispensable – the antithesis of panacea; guaranteed to cause all evils.

As the trial date approached, Georges found himself more and more in the habit of discussing the case with Lifschitz.

How bizarre, Lifschitz said in one of their conversations, pacing the room in a cloud of smoke, that it was easier to disprove a false conviction of aperson than the falsity of a book. Once the forgery of the Dreyfus documents was proved in a court of law, he was freed, although a few years were needed for the full process of his final vindication. Today nobody in his right mind would make allegations accusing Dreyfus of treason. Were it possible, France would gladly have deleted this black page from its history.

Not so with the *Protocols of the Elders of Zion*, he exclaimed. A book could be more dangerous than any man. Even Hitler would one day be dead, but a book may live on forever.

How right he had been, I mused. According to the rules we live by, it is permissible to incarcerate for life, or even execute, a man who has committed certain crimes and is dangerous to society; it is even permissible to bomb cities and cause the death of innocent people, as a measure of defense. But God forbid you should advocate the banning of a forgery that has caused the death of many and is still doing so. There would immediately be an outcry about the freedom of expression, the free exchange of views in the marketplace of ideas. It is permissible to limit the right of an individual to freedom, even to life, but not to prevent the publication of such a dangerous forgery. Even after the Holocaust.

Anti-Semites had found out, even before Goebbels, that printed lies were their best weapons. A lie in the form of a document, a book, takes on a life of its own. It has a presence. It is sold to innocent people in a bookstore, it is placed in prestigious libraries, it is quoted, and thus gains legitimacy. It is an evil presence not to be ignored.

A forgery, to gain immortality, must gain entrance to, and recognition by, a legitimate forum. It must don a convincing disguise. It may be then criticized, denied, refuted, slandered – all this makes no dent in the fact of its very existence. There will always be those who will believe the lie, those who will use it for their own means, even though they are aware of its falsity or, at best, don't care. The very fact of its existence is often used to prove its authenticity. For example, the fact that a copy of the *Protocols* is to be found in the British Museum is often offered as proof of its truth.

Learned argument has not succeeded in demolishing the forgery. Once the liar gains a platform, once he becomes party to legitimate discussion, he is safe. He has gained recognition. It is then up to a large, mostly ignorant, public to judge the lie. If the forgery is done in a manner that corresponds to existing prejudice, if it feeds on existing hatreds, and supplies answers to existing problems, if the liar is also highly motivated, his success is secure. The public does not possess the tools to judge the lie; it is almost impossible to disprove a positive statement. Denying it is an exercise in futility.

9 The Forgers

As they did on the completion of each chapter in their research, the group gathered for a long night meeting, to report and to discuss strategy. Their informers had reported that the defense was still looking for an expert. Who, in his right mind, would risk his reputation by testifying to the authenticity of a forged document, Lifschitz remarked. All the possible experts whose names had been submitted to the court had politely refused, and the court had been very patient with the defense, postponing the trial again and again. Some of them were upset by the judge's attitude, but Professor Matti was pleased. If they won, the public must be absolutely convinced, he said, that the defense had been given every opportunity to prove their case, otherwise the Nazis would say that the judge was in the pocket of the Jews.

'They will say so anyway,' Dr Wiener muttered. What was more, there would always be those who believed them.

Saly Mayer was skeptical. It was too early to speculate, he warned. They would produce an expert at the last minute. They would always find a Nazi who would pose as an expert. When Georges protested that they would not dare do so in a Swiss court, Saly exploded. How many times did they need to be reminded that the defense would not try the case to the judge? They would aim for the public.

This started the ongoing argument that was present in one way or another in all their discussions. Saly Mayer was impatient with their extensive scholastic research – it was good for a doctoral thesis, he snapped, but they should spend less time reviewing historical data and interviewing numerous witnesses. They should concentrate on strategy. In the final analysis the *Protocols* would be judged by the public, not by a court. They must use more press, more public relations. They would be pleading their case in a small courtroom, in the presence of a limited audience, but the defense would be speaking to world opinion. They would use the courtroom only as a convenient forum: the real drama would be played out outside. They must expect Nazi demonstrations in front of the court, he warned. Could they imagine Jews demonstrating? They would hardly dare appear in the courtroom. Jews always kept a low profile, he said, when they were being discussed. That is one of the reasons one could lie about them with impunity. They never fought back. Going to court was not enough, he summed up. This was not about history or truth, this was about prejudice, it was a battle in which the opponent did not obey the rules of warfare.

The lawyers resented his attitude. If their clients did not wish to conduct a proper trial, they should have represented themselves, they said. Lawyers of repute could not be expected to stoop to the level of Nazi propaganda. Not only did such tactics not befit the Jewish community, but the lawyers had their personal reputation to consider. How could he expect Professor Matti, a well-respected jurist, to be part of a populist approach, they asked Saly.

As always it was Lifschitz who settled the matter. They were not only trying a case in a Berne courtroom, he reminded them. They had a unique opportunity to prove in a public forum the facts concerning the *Protocols*. In another generation all the available witnesses would be dead. They did not need to worry about public relations – the press would be there, he assured them, the Nazis would see to it. They were performing a duty in the service of Jewish people everywhere. True, he said, the Jewish people did not empower them to speak in their name, but once they took upon themselves to do so, they must live up to their self-imposed commitment. They were involved in a historical project, they dare not adopt the contemptible tactics of their opponents. He had discussed the matter with Loosli, he reported, and he was of the same opinion. They must be at least as well informed as the court-appointed expert, and Loosli was indeed doing a very thorough job. Loosli was corresponding with Tager and, knowing Loosli, he was convinced that every little detail was being checked and rechecked. If they won, their real task would be to publish the proceedings and give them worldwide exposure. The research they were doing would also be published, even if most of it would not be presented in court. At this point they must continue their research and prepare their witnesses. Very soon they would convene to discuss tactics and strategy.

Georges should complete his research as soon as possible, Lifschitz urged. They were approaching the trial and it was time to comb the files for any additional information.

Consulting his notes Georges explained that he was planning to fill in gaps in the biography of Rachkovskii, concentrating on his activity in Paris and his ties with the French. He was intrigued by this man. What he had learned so far had aroused his curiosity. He was now confident that Rachkovskii had been involved in the fabrication of the *Protocols* in Paris in the nineties of the last century, as well as in their promotion in Russia, after his return from exile. Both Svatikov and Burtsev would testify to these facts, but he suspected that the defense would try to impeach them. When the day came he must be ready to describe to the court this complex personality, his motives, his aims and his tactics. The information supplied by Tager made his task easier.

Discussing the forgery with his mentor, Professor Matti, Georges often expressed his frustration. They would never learn the full details, he said. 'But one never does, does one,' the professor said. When one had participated in a hundred trials, he said, one realized that the full facts never came out. That was why judges were never required to base their conclusions on a proven certainty, and why each system of law had invented a formula instructing courts how to reach their decisions. The English required 'a preponderance of evidence' in civil trials, and 'beyond reasonable doubt', in criminal cases. The French instructed their courts to decide according to their *conviction intime*. The full undiluted truth never came out in a trial, Matti said, yet he was convinced that they had enough unbiased proof to 'convict' the *Protocols of the Elders of Zion*, and to prove that they were a vicious forgery. 'Men have been sentenced to death on less evidence,' he added.

Rachkovskii was the key, Matti agreed, and Georges had been right to insist on studying his whole career, even the parts that seemed irrelevant. They would be asking the court to accuse a man posthumously, and Judge Meyer might be reluctant to do so. After all, Matti mused, a man had a right to his reputation even after death. Any facts were relevant if they supported their thesis, even in an indirect manner, but even more important, they must not allow the opposition to surprise them with any facts unknown to them.

Georges needed no encouragement in that direction. He was fascinated by the documents supplied by Tager, and thought nothing of spending one more sleepless night with Rachkovskii's file.

But he had one more name on his list before that of Rachkovskii, a name that had often come up in conversations concerning the forgery.

If indeed this man had had anything to do with the forgery, he could not afford to ignore him. He knew that time was running out, so he decided to take home the file labeled 'Manasevich-Manuilov'. He would study it in the evening. Next morning he would start with Rachkovskii.

MANASEVICH-MANUILOV

On 21 May 1916, Ivan Fedorovich Manasevich-Manuilov paid a visit to the French ambassador in St Petersburg, Maurice Paleologue. Although he detested the man, the ambassador had his reasons for receiving him on very short notice. A few months earlier, on 3 February 1916, Paleologue had written in his diary 'Goremykin, president of the Council, has retired, and Khvostov, minister of the interior, has been dismissed. Shturmer succeeds to the places of both. He and the director of the Police Department are intimate friends of Rasputin. As director of his secretariat he appointed Manasevich-Manuilov, a choice regarded scandalous.'

It was generally known that Manuilov had gained this high position through Rasputin, a fact that immediately made him suspect in the eyes of the elite in St Petersburg, but his own reputation would have been enough for his appointment to be regarded as scandalous.

Paleologue fully shared the views of the St Petersburg elite concerning Manasevich-Manuilov. Recording their meeting in his diary, he wrote later in the day: 'The unspeakable Manuilov, Shturmer's "Chef de Cabinet" and the fit instrument of his low designs, came to see me.'

Paleologue, who served as the last French ambassador to tsarist Russia, faithfully recorded in his diary not only the events of the turbulent war years of 1914–17 in the Russian capital, but also his observations of the people who played a part in Russian politics and in St Petersburg society. His popularity in the capital opened all doors and made him a welcome guest not only at public functions but also at small intimate dinners and tea parties. He was the confidant of many people and an intimate friend of many ladies, who often confided in him and invited him to their salons. His own elegant dinner parties, in his well-appointed apartment on the banks of the Neva, attended by the *crème de la crème* of St Petersburg society, were the envy of many diplomats, famous not only for their French cuisine but also for the carefully selected guest list. Men of power used to visit him for an intimate chat, confident of his discretion and his good advice.

As he already planned to turn his diary into published memoirs, Paleologue recorced not only current events, but also information about various people, which might fade from his memory at a later date.

Manasevich-Manuilov was a good source of information and gossip and the ambassador did not hesitate to receive him, in spite of his low opinion of the man.

On the evening of 21 May 1916, he wrote in his diary:

> I met Manasevich-Manuilov in Paris about 1900, when he was working as an agent of the Okhrana under the orders of Rachkovskii, the famous head of the Russian police in France. He is an extremely curious person. A Jew by origin, with a quick and crooked mind and a strong taste for high life, pleasure and 'objets d'art', but without scruples of any sort, he is 'agent provocateur', spy, sharper, swindler, cheat, forger and rake in one ... During recent years he has contributed to several fine exploits of the Okhrana, as this moral outlaw dearly loves adventure and is not destitute of courage ... his hand can be traced in the preparation of the pogroms that devastated the Jewish quarters of Kiev, Alexandrovsk and Odessa ... of late, he has succeeded in getting into the good graces of the empress – a reward for his many services to Rasputin.

At their meeting Manasevich-Manuilov had described the situation in Russia in very dark colors; the war was not going well and revolutionary feelings were spreading in the army. After talking of the terrible hardships suffered by the soldiers, he added: 'The army behind the lines is rotten. You must not forget that they include men of all races of the empire, all nationalities, religions and sects, even Jews! I can tell you it's a wonderful forcing-house for revolutionary ideas.'

He had never kept secret his anti-Jewish feelings and his conviction that the Jews were to blame for the Revolution. Why was it, Georges wondered, that converted Jews so often became the worst Jew-haters? Was it out of a sense of guilt for having abandoned a persecuted minority?

There was no real proof that Manasevich-Manuilov had actually been one of the forgers. Not the kind of proof one could present in court, Georges thought. But the rumors and the speculation from various sources were convincing. After studying the file he was satisfied that Manasevitch Manuilov had, at the very least, participated in the plot in some way. He had admitted in a number of private conversations that the *Protocols* were forged. This was no mere speculation, Georges thought: it was a statement of fact.

This man would not have left any traces, and, unlike Golovinskii, he would not have boasted at tea parties of his role in a forgery. Manasevich-Manuilov was too devious to expose himself, but the man had been an important part of Rachkovskii's operation in Paris, and it was inconceivable that he would not be included in this kind of operation. Forgery and cheating were part of his life, and he had been familiar with them from his early youth.

He was born in Kovno in 1869 to a Russian Orthodox father and a Jewish mother. For reasons unknown he was adopted at the age of 5 by a wealthy merchant by the name of F. S. Manasevich-Manuilov, who was exiled to Siberia for forging financial documents. On return from his place of exile he became very rich through dealing in gold.

Manasevich-Manuilov senior was himself of Jewish origin, but had embraced the Christian faith. As his adopted son was considered a Jew, due to his mother's origin, he had him properly baptized.

In 1888 Manasevich-Manuilov got acquainted with his biological stepbrother, and there were whispered rumors that they had become lovers. He had never bothered to deny that he was indeed a homosexual. The brother was well connected and in future years he often used his influence to save the young Ivan from difficult situations. It was also he who recommended Ivan to the St Petersburg Police Department, where the young man was assigned to collecting information for the Okhrana, mostly about the activity of literary circles.

Ivan Manasevich-Manuilov was to keep up his contacts with the Ministry of the Interior and the Okhrana for most of his life and in time he became a most valued agent, but apart from his clandestine activities he also made a name for himself as a journalist, a writer and a critic, publishing articles, theater reviews and even some books on a variety of subjects dealing with the economy, the theater and life in St Petersburg. He was fluent in French and from the early 1890s acted as an agent in Paris, where he also published articles in a French newspaper using various pen-names.

One journal that published his articles characterized him as 'an expert in women, cigars, horses and foreign policy', and in the circles in which he moved he was labeled 'a journalist by profession and an adventurer by calling'.

With no firm convictions of his own, Manuilov was open to any suggestions, ready to sell his services to the highest bidder. Rachkovskii, who used him for special assignments but never trusted him completely, called him in public 'a dirty Jew'.

In 1905 he was sent back to Russia and was involved in various intrigues. His close relationship with the famous Gregorii Rasputin gained him, at, the beginning of 1916, the appointment of director of the secretariat of the minister of the interior, Shturmer, a position that carried much power in the Russian capital in those days. But it was short-lived.

On 2 September Paleologue wrote in his diary:

> Manuilov, the policeman convict, whom Shturmer had made the director of his secretariat, has just been arrested; he is said to be guilty of blackmailing a bank, a fact that is proved 'a priori', as swindling is his normal method of money-making and the most ordinary and venial of his crimes.

Although the investigation was repeatedly stalled by orders from above, Manasevich-Manuilov was sentenced in the end to 18 months in prison, but he had not learned his lesson and on his release he made his last mistake: he again used for blackmail a false document he had created for the Okhrana. When they came for him he tried to escape, but was caught and sentenced to death. This time there was no one to rescue him from the firing squad.

So much for Rachkovskii's assistants, Georges decided. The time had come to deal with the boss, the one figure who always emerged whenever one studied the stories of intrigue and sabotage, spies, secret agents and false documents, betrayal and false arrests, burglaries and even murder. Rachkovskii's name came up in every conversation concerning the *Protocols of the Elders of Zion*. Nilus had mentioned him to du Chayla as the man who had sent him the manuscript of the *Protocols*. According to the testimonies of Princess Radziwill and Mrs Hurblut, Golovinskii had boasted that he was executing the forgery at the command of Rachkovskii. Bint had told Svatikov that Rachkovskii had been behind the forgery, and this was first-hand testimony. Bint's detailed testimony, alone would be enough to convince any impartial judge. True, it was not direct testimony, but surely the court would realize how totally impartial and trustworthy Svatikov was. How lucky, Georges thought, that this man was ready to testify.

From Svatikov he already knew much about Rachkovskii's activities in Paris, but this man seemed to be the central figure in the drama and he must study his whole biography. When they went to trial he must know all there was to know about him.

He would catch a much-needed few hours of sleep and start with Rachkovskii's file in the morning.

PIOTR IVANOVICH RACHKOVSKII: SUPER-SPY AND MASTER FORGER

Letting his mind wander for a few moments, Georges speculated what would have happened if Piotr Ivanovich Rachkovskii had not suddenly died in October 1910, at the age of 59, at the railway station at Rezhitsa on his way to the estate he had lately purchased in the province of Vitebsk.

He had just returned to Russia and, surprisingly, it seemed that he was finally ready to retire. During the period preceding his sudden death, he had definitely acted like a man conscious of his own mortality who was considering his legacy. There were persistent rumors that Rachkovskii had completed his memoirs, rumors that in some circles caused much interest, in others fear and consternation. For a period that spanned close to three decades this man had played a central role in spectacular events and in clandestine intrigues in both the Russian and the French capitals. He held secrets that might embarrass many prominent figures, and he was in possession of documents that might cause diplomatic incidents of considerable magnitude. Some were interested in acquiring the memoirs in order to publish them, others were hoping to suppress them.

The long obituaries published by all the newspapers were followed by much speculation. Some reported that Rachkovskii had started to write his memoirs only several months before his death, and that they were not complete. Others said that he had been planning to leave the manuscript with friends, instructing them to withhold publication for a period of ten years after his death. One paper speculated that Rachkovskii's documents and memoirs were to be delivered to the Police Department, which had full discretion to use them as it saw fit. There were even rumors that several years prior to his death members of the revolutionary organizations had started negotiations with Rachkovskii suggesting that he pass to them some documents that had, by that time, only historical value. Rachkovskii, according to these rumors, had refused that very profitable proposal, saying that he did not wish his documents and memoirs to disappear in the revolutionary underground. They must be available in the future to historians, Rachkovskii had said according to these rumors, so that certain historical events not be perverted or incorrectly interpreted.

The previous evening Georges had discussed with Lifschitz the possibility of uncovering Rachkovskii's documents. 'We don't even know that they exist,' Georges had remarked skeptically. 'We can't rely on rumors.'

But these were no idle rumors, Lifschitz had said, asking whether Georges remembered the name Gottfried zur Beek. The name rang a bell, but he was becoming confused with all the names now stored in his mind. He could not immediately place him. Lifschitz reminded him that zur Beek had been named as one of the defendants in the trial initiated in Germany against the Nazi group calling itself the Iron Broom. Wasn't he the first one to have published the *Protocols* in Germany, Georges asked.

This was true, Lifschitz agreed, but Gottfried zur Beek was not his real name. It was Ludwig Müller, and he was also known as Captain Müller von Hausen. His was absolutely the first German edition of the *Protocols*, based on the Nilus edition of 1911, although the name of Nilus was conspicuously absent. Zur Beek, who had received a copy of the *Protocols* not long after the end of the war, in 1918, had immediately realized its potential. Blaming the Jews for the war, for its catastrophic aftermath, and for the Russian Revolution would not only be good for German morale: it could also serve as a common link between the winning and the losing sides. What better than a common enemy to serve as a bridge for the future between the vanquisher and the vanquished?

The first German translation of the *Protocols*, edited and published by zur Beek in December 1919, was entitled *Die Geheimnisse der Weisen von Zion* ('The Secrets of the Elders of Zion').

To serve its purpose, zur Beek knew, it must be heavily edited to attract the German reader, and mystic elements must be eliminated. That is why it was imperative to omit the name of Nilus, who might be considered an unreliable and suspect source. Instead, he quoted the rabbi's speech of 1901 and another rabbinical address that was supposed to have been delivered at a Zionist Congress held in Lemberg in 1912.

Having written his foreword, linking the Jewish conspiracy to current events, zur Beek was confident that funds would be forthcoming.

Indeed, Lifschitz told Georges, both the regular and the deluxe editions were sponsored by Prince Otto Salm and Count Behr, former president of the Conservative Party of the Prussian Upper House. A well-orchestrated propaganda campaign had been mounted, especially in the rural districts, but it had also been embraced by the royal court and by the elite circles. It became a popular gift, handed out in elegantly wrapped packages at various private and public functions. Chapters were quoted in the press, and even read out loud to entertain guests both in private homes and at small public gatherings.

By the end of 1920, 120,000 copies of zur Beek's edition of the *Protocols* had been sold in Germany.

Suddenly Georges realized that they were diverting from their subject. They had been speaking of Rachkovskii, he reminded Lifschitz. Zur Beek belonged to another chapter. Not so, Lifschitz insisted, they had been speculating about the rumors that Rachkovskii had hidden documents concerning the *Protocols*. How did that concern zur Beek, Georges asked. Lifschitz reminded him that the only German edition they were using was that of Alfred Rosenberg, the edition distributed at the Berne rally, which was why he had never had the opportunity to read zur Beek's edition. It was in his foreword that zur Beek had mentioned an interesting fact, unknown to others. He maintained that General Kourlov, who had been head of the Okhrana and had died in Berlin in 1923, had told him in secret his version of Rachkovskii's death. One day, according to Kurlov, he had summoned Rachkovskii and demanded a report about the origin of the *Protocols* and the relevant documents that he was keeping in a hiding place. Rachkovskii had promised to comply, but three days later he had died, suddenly and mysteriously, in a railway station, his promise unfulfilled. General Kourlov had been convinced, zur Beek wrote, that Rachkovskii's sudden death was a direct result of his promise to disclose all the facts about the creation of the *Protocols of the Elders of Zion*.

They must remember, Lifschitz said, that General Kurlov had told this story to zur Beek less than ten years after Rachkovskii's death.

But they had no time for idle speculations, Georges reminded his friend. In fact Rachkovskii had never revealed the truth to General Kurlov, his memoirs had never been published and his documents had never surfaced. Georges wondered whether they were still resting in some obscure and safe hiding place or whether they had been intentionally suppressed, or even destroyed.

Examining Rachkovskii's photograph, which had been sent by Tager, Georges found it hard to believe that this bald, potbellied, jovial, sympathetic man, with the well-trimmed mustache and small pointed beard, who looked like somebody's grandfather, had been the sinister and skillful super-spy, the much feared *agent provocateur*, who had orchestrated international intrigues in many European countries, implicated public figures in crimes they had never committed, and saved the reputation of others by suppressing their innermost secrets. His reputed jovial manner and his charming demeanor had revealed nothing of his iron will, his devious mind and his complete lack of morals.

One would expect, the newspapers wrote in their obituaries, official representatives of the administration to show up for the funeral of this man whom they had entrusted with their secrets and whom they had employed to carry out their most delicate missions. Yet official Russia had been conspicuously absent from the graveside, as were also Rachkovskii's close friends and associates. He was buried in the presence of only his wife, his son and his son's two friends. The reaction of official France was surprisingly different. The president of France had sent a representative to place a silver wreath on the grave.

Nothing in Rachkovskii's spectacular career conformed to conventional standards, I thought, when I realized that it had all started with his arrest by the Russian secret police.

Now that Russian archives were open and accessible, my Russian assistant, Boris, had obtained and delivered to my house a photocopy of file number 2586, from the State Archive of the Russian Federation (Gosudarstvennyi Arkhiv Rossiiskoi Federatsii), labeled in bold letters 'The Police Department. Special Union. 1905. Official for special assignments of the 4th Class, Deistvitel'nyi Statskii Sovetnik Petr Ivanovich Rachkovskii.'

Translating from the Russian, Boris remarked that the words preceding the name were a rank used in Russia prior to the Revolution. They wrote slowly in those days, he added, using a quill, which was why the handwriting was so beautiful.

The first page, dated 13.08.1879, was entitled: 'Special Police Card No. 2739.'

Boris, a historian and an expert in archives, explained that the contents of the file carried the original date of the recorded events, while the date on the cover was that on which the material reached the archive from the Police Department, in 1905.

On my visit to St Petersburg Boris had pointed out the police building where suspects had been interrogated in those days. It was a gray three-story building, with rows of windows, old-style wooden shutters, a narrow entrance and a chimney, standing out in its ugliness in the midst of all the splendor that still marks this magnificent city. When Rachkovskii was arrested on 13 August 1879, he was probably interrogated in this building, Boris said. Examining the printed card in the file, the blanks filled in black ink, I tried to imagine the young man sitting in front of his interrogator, dryly answering the routine questions:

> Name: Rachkovskii Petr Ivanovich
> Age: 28
> Rank: Nobleman
> Origin: Son of the mayor of the city of Dubossary
> Nationality: Russian
> Religion: Greek Orthodox
> Place of birth: The city of Dubossary (Kherson gubernia)
> Place of residence: St Petersburg
> Occupation: Attached to the Ministry of Justice

Sources of income: Earnings from writing, 'because I don't receive anything for my service'.

Financial status of parents: Father is working as mayor of the city of Dubossary and lives with his wife on his salary

> Family status: Married, but separated.

Schooling, financed by whom: Secondary school in the city of Kishinev, financed by parents

> If not graduated, state reason: graduated
> Was he abroad and where: Have never been abroad
> Had he been interrogated before: Never

> At the bottom of the same card the interrogator had written:
> Nature of accusation: Political unreliability
> Preventive punishment: Keep under arrest

Rachkovskii had been working for three years in the Ministry of Justice, as a court investigator, living on his earnings from writing in various magazines. In April 1879 he was appointed chief editor of the new magazine *Russian Jew*. Barely three months later, on 25 July, the police searched his apartment, having learned from one of its informers that Rachkovskii was very influential in student circles, that he was an outstanding propagandist, and that he was well acquainted with suspected revolutionists. One of them, Matrosov, was prominent on the police wanted list. The informer also revealed that Rachkovskii was in possession of a long list of addresses, printed in the same print as the title of one of the articles published in the underground publication *Zemlia i Volia*.

In Russia in those days this information was reason enough for a search and an arrest.

The police file contained a detailed report of the items found in Rachkovskii's apartment. It included various articles about Jews and Jewish customs, some poetry about Jerusalem, and manuscripts of articles intended for the magazine *Russian Jew*.

Even as a young man Piotr Rachkovskii had been very interested in Jews, Boris remarked, examining with me the list in the file. His hatred of Jews and his manipulations against them were to become a prominent issue in his life.

How had a suspect of political unreliability become a trusted agent of the Secret Police? I wondered.

From the report of the interrogation it seemed that Rachkovskii had been ready with all the answers: he was contacting students only because he was preparing to put on an amateur play; he had never held any socialist or revolutionary views; he had never met the people with whom he was said to be in contact, except the wanted man, Matrosov, whom he had met by accident in the house of Iasnivitskii ...

The police took their time, but could not substantiate their suspicion with any real proof. On 10 September, after having spent one month in custody, Rachkovskii was released, but the police were not ready to clear him completely. His contacts with some suspects still needed to be investigated. The decision noted at the bottom of the file read: 'Release Rachkovskii – continue surveillance.'

But Rachkovskii had had enough. He walked out of prison with a firm resolve never to risk arrest again. Looking back at the ugly gray building he promised himself that the next time he passed its portals he would be sitting on the other side of the table in the interrogating room. It was well known that the police were eager to recruit agents from the ranks of the revolutionists, a tactic that made it dangerous to trust even your closest friends, and Rachkovskii had no moral qualms about changing sides. Lies, pretense and betrayal were to become his stock in trade.

His superiors would have been surprised had they realized that this young man, still under a certain cloud of suspicion, who was starting out as an anonymous agent, would be appointed, after only five years, as chief of all operations of the Secret Police in Europe.

Of the five years between his release from prison and his appointment to the post in Paris, very little was known. It was only on 24 May 1912, almost two years after his death, that the newspaper *Birzhevye Vedomosti* (Stock Exchange News) investigated and published hitherto unknown details, in an article entitled 'Generals Novitskii and Rachkovskii' (Generals N. and R.)'. The article reminded the readers that they probably remembered the well-known Rachkovskii in connection with such dark pages of the Okhrana's activity as the establishment of a publishing house to print material promoting pogroms against Jews, and his involvement in the famous case of the spy Azef. But it was only after his death that they were learning new facts. The man Rachkovskii, they wrote, who had been registered 'on paper' as a second-rate official in the Ministry of Home Affairs, had been in reality one of the key figures in both the internal and the foreign policy of Russia. Only now, after his death, could it be told that Rachkovskii had served, for a long period, as head of the Secret Police not only in France but all over Europe.

The article relied on a document received from General of Gendarmerie Novitskii on the activities of the Okhrana, in which he had paid special attention to Rachkovskii's doings. Only after Rachkovskii's assignment to Paris did the Police Department in Kiev discover that a man calling himself Piotr Ivanovich had been the main organizer of an anti-government group in Kiev. Workers arrested and sentenced for having in their possession aggressive revolutionary proclamations had received the material from this man, who had actually been an *agent provocateur* in the service of the Okhrana. An investigator reported that this Piotr Ivanovich had established a secret publishing house, published criminal publications, distributed false passports and initiated active revolutionary propaganda. The report revealed that the man was Piotr Rachkovskii, and that he had been working under the direct command of the chief of the Okhrana, Moscow Department.

By then Rachkovskii had been posted to France, and any attempt to contact him, or even to obtain his photograph for identification, was blocked by the Secret Police. Rachkovskii was working under cover and any investigation involving him must be abandoned, they announced.

The Russian ambassador in Paris, Baron Morengeim, had not extended a warm welcome to the new agent, having been warned by his contacts in St Petersburg that Rachkovskii was an ambitious upstart, completely unscrupulous, not to be trusted. But Rachkovskii knew how to win friends when he needed them. He kept a low profile for a few weeks, humbly requesting advice from members of the Embassy, inviting them to lunch and proposing that his agents run errands for them when they were in town. His charm and his geniality gained him friends, whom he did not hesitate to use for his own purposes. Little by little the initial suspicion was replaced by a camaraderie, which Rachkovskii needed in order to secure for himself a base of operations without having to constantly watch his back. He knew that he had succeeded in winning the sympathy of the ambassador, when he was called into his chancellery one morning and told that two rooms had been allocated to him, next to the office of the consul-general. He immediately installed himself in the bigger of the two rooms, assigning the adjoining room to his closest assistant, Milevskii, whom he wanted close by as he himself spoke almost no French.

Milevskii was described in Embassy reports as 'an energetic Jew'. Rachkovskii hated Jews but saw nothing wrong in employing and using an agent of Jewish origin, as long as he was prepared to do his bidding.

The Embassy was alive with rumors about the activities of the new team, but they all respected the fact that these men were dealing in clandestine police matters and had to work under a cloak of secrecy.

From his headquarters in Paris Rachkovskii organized an impressive network of agents, covering all European capitals. They were all hand-picked by him, ready to perform any role assigned to them. They were all as devoid of moral compunction as was their boss, ready to participate in intrigues, even in crimes, planned by him. They were all adventurers by nature, enjoying life in the European capitals, well paid for the risks they were taking, and basking in the glory of the chief, who was a favorite of the authorities in the Russian capital. They knew that Rachkovskii could, if necessary, reach all the way into the royal palace.

Rachkovskii's function, as defined by his superiors, was to investigate and report the activities of Russian revolutionaries and terrorists. In consultation with his agents he decided to concentrate on the Latin Quarter, on the left bank of the Seine, where most of the revolutionaries were living. Renting a suitable locale in a small street in the quarter, he had one of his assistants open a restaurant, where he and his wife served favorite Russian dishes at reasonable prices.

The place became an immediate success, the most popular meeting place for Russian emigrants. They dropped in at all hours, enjoyed food that reminded them of home, read Russian journals and met friends. As expected, there was nothing like a drink or two, at a low price, to loosen the tongues of patrons. The genial atmosphere made them feel they were among friends, not suspecting that Rachkovskii's spies were everywhere.

The best spies were, of course, former revolutionaries. Such a spy would use his underground code-name, and if he had extensive revolutionary activity in his past he would immediately be accepted by Russian terrorists as one of them. Selected spies infiltrated underground revolutionary groups both in Paris and in other countries.

Rachkovskii now felt at home at the Embassy, and was therefore not surprised when the ambassador summoned him to his office on a sunny spring morning in 1885 for one of their routine meetings. But he was astounded when the baron suggested that the weather was too nice to stay indoors and that they should take a stroll. He understood immediately that he was to be let into a secret that was too dangerous to be discussed within the four walls of the Embassy.

As a rule, all Russian officials, both at home and abroad, spied on each other. Correct information was absolutely essential for self-preservation, sometimes even for survival. And, as the popular saying went, the walls had ears. He also knew that the ambassador was constantly being informed of his own actions, although he himself and his agents kept strict rules of secrecy. Operating from the Embassy was convenient, but he had reconciled himself to the fact that it was inevitable that Ambassador Morengeim would keep abreast of their activities. Taking a stroll to discuss matters of the utmost secrecy was a procedure he himself had established.

The initial wariness and suspicion towards Rachkovskii that Ambassador Morengeim had harbored in the beginning were slowly replaced by a respect for the man's ability. He would be a dangerous enemy, the ambassador realized, but he could be a valuable ally. He would still watch him carefully, the baron had decided, but if he ever needed his services he would not hesitate to use him. And now the time had come.

Rachkovskii had been aware of the new respect in the eyes of the ambassador during these last weeks. As soon as their relationship became more personal, he had found an opportunity to hint discreetly that he would be pleased to assist the Embassy if his assistance were ever needed. The ambassador, he knew, was not held in the highest esteem back in St Petersburg, but he needed him on his side. He was on his way to establishing himself as a major player in the world of intrigue and manipulation that was so dominant in Russian politics, but he aimed much higher. The ties between France and Russia were becoming a major feature in Russian politics, and if he played his cards right he might become much more than a super-agent.

So it was with a sense of excitement that he ventured out with the baron to take a stroll in the sunbathed streets of Paris. He felt that he was to be taken into the ambassador's confidence on an important issue, and his instincts had never failed him before. The energy he had invested in establishing a good relationship with the Embassy was about to pay off.

Listening to the ambassador, Rachkovskii realized that he was being entrusted with an extremely delicate mission. He had received an anonymous report, the baron said, that Princess Iurevskaia was involved in revolutionary activity. Anonymous reports were not rare in those days. Even reliable informants were not eager to reveal their names, unless they were expecting some kind of remuneration. This report, the ambassador revealed, was signed by 'a friendly diplomat'. There was no need to explain to Rachkovskii who was the subject of the report.

For 12 years Princess Ekaterina Iurevskaia had been the morganatic wife of Tsar Alexander II, openly living in the Winter Palace with her three children, who were recognized by the tsar as his own. When his wife died shortly before he was murdered, he married the princess in a secret religious ceremony in Tsarskoe Selo.

She was allowed to follow her husband's coffin in the funeral procession, but the new tsar, Alexander III, told her in no uncertain terms that she was an embarrassment to the royal family, and not welcome in Russia. Since then she had made her home in Paris, nurturing her resentment and hoping that one day her son Grigorii might be given the recognition he deserved as the son of the tsar.

Fortunately, before he had been murdered, her husband had issued a royal decree bestowing on her and on her children titles that nobody could take away. But more importantly, he had provided for them in his will. She could live comfortably to the end of her days and raise her children in the proper style.

It was imperative, the ambassador said, that this information be immediately checked. It had to be done discreetly, but thoroughly. The involvement of the tsar's widow would lend the revolutionaries much prestige. They might even be planning to use the young prince. He knew of no better man to undertake such an assignment, he told Rachkovskii.

This was a golden opportunity to ingratiate himself with the tsar,

Rachkovskii decided, accepting the assignment. He insisted on official confirmation by his superiors in St Petersburg, and he immediately wrote to them that this would advance his relations with the Embassy. He also required adequate remuneration for this additional effort, which was not part of his regular duties. He never missed an opportunity to line his pockets.

It took his spies 18 months of constant surveillance to furnish Rachkovskii with all the facts. He now had a full dossier on the princess, his agents having infiltrated her home and fully reported on her personal life. One never knew when such information might come in handy, he thought, as he was preparing his report. It contained full details concerning the princess and her children, her friends, her lifestyle and her indiscretions. There was no real proof of any revolutionary involvement, he stated, but one must take into consideration that if the revolutionaries did approach her, she might respond positively, owing to her unstable character, her naive pretensions to the role of the 'Widow Empress', and her anger against the royal family. 'The young prince may also be an easy target,' he wrote, 'and if he is approached I fear that no good will come of it.' He signed and transmitted his detailed report on 1 September 1886.

It seemed that his status in the halls of power in St Petersburg was now secure. His dedication to the Russian monarch was complete. Not only would he do his utmost to undermine all revolutionist activity in Europe, he decided, but he would also use his contacts in the French capital to facilitate financial and military ties between the two countries.

Georges had learned much from Svatikov and from Burtsev, but there were still many questions in his mind. Why, for example, had the president of France sent an emissary to place a wreath on Rachkovskii's grave? How had the head of the Russian secret service gained the gratitude of the president of the French Republic?

Leafing through Tager's report, he discovered an astonishing fact. One day, Tager reported, Rachkovskii had a surprise visit from an agent acting on behalf of President Loubet. The president was preparing to go to Lyons, he was told, and had been warned that there might be an attempt on his life. The president was convinced that Rachkovskii and his agents were better equipped to protect him than the French police, and had full confidence in him. He was asked, discreetly, to organize proper protection for the president.

Accepting the delicate assignment, Rachkovskii knew that his tactic was paying off. It was no secret that he was collaborating with the French police, and that he had established an impressive and efficient network of spies, whose function was to infiltrate revolutionary groups. The French were firmly opposed to revolutionary activity in their midst, even if its aim was to undermine the Russian regime. They did not relish the fact that France had become a center for Russian anarchists and were only too eager to cooperate with Rachkovskii, whose fame preceded him everywhere. He was the super-agent. His inventive methods soon led him to plan unbelievable intrigues and perform acts of sabotage in which he proved to be a master. His agents forged documents, planted false evidence, spread lies, implicated innocent people, broke into houses, stole documents, and even engaged in planting bombs and committing murder, tactics that gained him the admiration of police circles. Assisting the French police in investigating crimes he himself had manipulated, and arresting innocent culprits whom he had falsely implicated, he soon succeeded in establishing a close relationship with the French authorities, based on a mutual exchange of information. In 1890 Rachkovskii was instrumental in eliminating a whole terrorist group, on the basis of information supplied by the French police that its members were preparing in France bombs to be sent to Russia.

He could not have foreseen his future fall from grace, ironically caused by his attempt to protect the royal couple from the machinations of a swindler. But that was years away, and in the meantime he was cementing his ties with the French police, which gained him entrance into the salon of Juliette Adam, the widow of the former chief of police, Edmond Adam.

It was 4 o'clock in the morning, Georges noticed with surprise. He had spent most of the night reading the file on Rachkovskii, but it had been worth it. The name, which had been mentioned so many times in the past, had now become a living person. He let his imagination wander, trying to visualize Rachkovskii conniving with his agents, planning his campaigns, stepping out of a carriage in front of the elegant mansion of Juliette Adam. He was sure that it was there that Rachkovskii had met Edouard Drumont and Eli de Cyon, it was in this salon that they had probably discussed the Franco-Russian alliance, the policies of Witte and the French loans that Witte was seeking to finance his reforms. The incitement against Jews in the French army had been discussed in this circle and the anti-Dreyfus campaign had its staunch supporters among the guests of Juliette Adam.

Georges learned from the file that some of the ideas in the text of the *Protocols* could actually be traced to the writings of Eli de Cyon. In some quarters it was even believed that the *Protocols* had been created by him. Yet Georges was convinced that the actual forgery had been done by Rachkovskii's agents. There was enough evidence pointing in that direction. But the French were as much to blame as the Russians, he thought bitterly. It was men such as Edouard Drumont and Eli de Cyon who had probably planted in Rachkovskii's mind the idea of accusing the Jews of conspiring to dominate the world. Before he came to Paris Rachkovskii had not been aware of the extent of anti-Jewish feelings in some circles in the French capital. He knew that public opinion in France, as in other countries in the West, blamed Russia for its persistent persecution of Jews. Witte had explained to him how this was damaging Russia's reputation abroad and harming its diplomatic and economic relations with other countries. However, unlike Witte, he was in full agreement with the tsarist anti-Semitic policies. He supported them wholeheartedly. Yet France was not Russia. He feared that the French government would be reluctant to form an alliance with Russia, in the face of strong public opposition. But, if he could convince the French that the Jews were dangerous, that they constituted a threat, that they were a subversive element undermining society and planning its destruction, then he would be doing a great service to the Russian cause.

His introduction to the salon of Juliette Adam and, through her, to the champions of the anti-Semitic tirade in Paris were a stroke of luck. Listening to them Rachkovskii soon realized that they were acting at cross-purposes. His hostess was very critical of the Russian tsar and had even offended him in her writings. Eli de Cyon, whose aim in life was to discredit Witte, was doing his utmost to prevent the French loans requested by Russia to finance Witte's reforms. He, on the other hand, was assisting Witte in promoting an alliance between the two countries.

Yet, Rachkovskii realized, he had one thing in common with Juliette Adam and her circle. They were all trying to achieve their respective aims by blaming the Jews, whom they hated. The French group was agitating against the Jewish influence in the army and the Jewish bankers who, they maintained, were under German influence. De Cyon targeted his most vitriolic arrows at the Rothschilds. It was bizarre, Rachkovskii thought, that he was agitating against the Jews in order to facilitate the alliance that his French friends were trying to prevent.

Georges suddenly remembered the warning of Professor Matti in one of their discussions, realizing how right the professor had been. They should never for one moment forget that they were preparing for a trial in a court of law. They were lawyers, not historians. They were out to prove that a certain document was a forgery. They would try to prove how, when and by whom the document had been fabricated. This was the essence of their assignment, Matti had insisted.

Of course it was not that simple, Georges had said. It never was, Matti had retorted. They had no witness to the actual act of forgery, so they were compelled to rely on circumstantial evidence. This was sometimes the best evidence, Matti explained patiently. An eyewitness may lie, but circumstances never lie. It all depends on how you interpret them, and to what inevitable conclusion they lead. This is the art of the lawyer and the burden of the judge. It is in the presentation of the circumstantial evidence that a lawyer is tested. This is what separates the professionals from the artists. Law could be an art, Matti said dreamily. Georges had the potential of becoming an artist among lawyers, he added quietly, and this was his test case. He would have the opportunity to recreate in court the unique atmosphere that had prevailed in a society utterly foreign to Judge Meyer. He must use magic to convince the court that people such as Rachkovskii had really existed. He would have to make this Swiss judge believe that European politics had actually been influenced by bizarre magicians and by superstitious princesses, manipulated by devious provocateurs. He would have to convince a balanced, rational, middle-class Swiss jurist that cheating and forgery, in certain periods and in some societies, had been routine tools in the hands of officials, accepted and even blessed by their superiors.

But he must always remember, Professor Matti had warned, that this was all circumstantial evidence, admitted to prove background, opportunity and, possibly, motive. It was not their duty, the professor insisted, to prove the actual motive behind any act. A possible motive was enough. The rest must be left to the historians.

How right his teacher had been, Georges now mused. How could he ever decide what the exact motive for the fabrication of the *Protocols* had been? Different people involved in the forgery might have acted from different motives. Eli de Cyon wished to discredit Witte; Juliette Adam wished to prevent the French loans to Russia; Edouard Drumont was fanatical in his hatred of Jews. The French public was looking for a scapegoat to blame for their economic and financial difficulties. Blaming the Jews would serve all their interests. A Jewish conspiracy to dominate the world would explain both the hegemony of Jewish banks on the financial scene and the growing and dangerous influence of Jewish officers in the French army. Rachkovskii, on the other hand, had his own agenda. A Jewish conspiracy would serve to justify the pogroms in Russia, both there and in the eyes of foreigners. It may convince the tsar that the Jews had been behind the political murders in Russia and, perversely, if it was presented as a conspiracy between Jews and Freemasons, it might help remove Philippe from the royal court, as he had some connections with Masonic lodges. He, Rachkovskii, would gain favor with his superiors in the Okhrana by supplying them with a powerful tool to support their anti-Jewish campaign.

They may all have acted from different motives, he thought, but they had one thing in common: not only did they all hate Jews, but they all realized that Jews were an easy target in the society in which they lived, the most believable and the most available scapegoat.

On 6 June 1891 Rachkovskii wrote to his superiors describing the indignation of the French public at the tsarist anti-Jewish policies. Anti-Russian agitation, he wrote, was caused in great measure by West European Jews. This process, he warned, was contributing large sums of money to support revolutionary groups throughout Europe. The press in London and in Paris was strongly influenced by the Jews, he reported, and they might expect strong support from those quarters. In order to turn the tide, he argued, he would have to collaborate with French anti-Jewish circles to devise ways to show the French public 'what the Jews were really like'.

Reading Rachkovskii's letter, a copy of which Tager had uncovered, Georges suspected that this was when the idea of forging a document to implicate the Jews took form in Rachkovskii's mind. When Professor Matti argued that they had no proof to support such an allegation, Georges responded by describing how forgeries had been Rachkovskii's favored weapon. He had made a practice of implicating others with the help of forged documents, he argued, why not use the same method to implicate a whole people? It was an audacious plan, Georges admitted, but the more he learned about Rachkovskii, the more convinced he became that this was the right conclusion. There were other signs, Georges maintained, that even before the first publication of the *Protocols* in Russia, Rachkovskii had promoted in France the allegation that a dangerous Jewish coalition, planning to gain domination of the world, was controlling European politics and manipulating the peoples of the continent. It was generally accepted that Rachkovskii and his forgers were behind the publication, in 1902, of a book entitled *Anarchie et nihilisme*, under the pseudonym Jehan-Preval. Georges suggested to Matti that he read the book. The theories contained in it reminded one of the *Protocols*, he said.

In Paris Rachkovskii was exposed, for the first time, to a more sophisticated form of anti-Semitism than the one he had known in Russia. Okhrana tactics would be considered crude in the French capital. The French would never adopt a slogan like 'Kill the Jews and save Russia'. Jew-hatred in Russia was promoted by politicians and pogroms were orchestrated by secret agents. Not so in France. Here were intellectuals, writers and journalists, who had refined different weapons to use against the Jews, weapons that were proving to be very effective and could be adapted for use in the Russian homeland.

The *Protocols* would never have been fabricated, Georges thought, were it not for a combination of French ideas and Russian tactics. He was reminded of the Hebrew proverb: 'The voice is that of Jacob, but the hands belong to Esau.' Indeed, he thought, the voice was that of Drumont and of Eli de Cyon, who had furnished the diabolical ideas, but the hands that had committed the voice to the false document were Rachkovskii's. The French might even have come up with the suggestion of using Maurice Joly's book to create the forgery. They must surely have supplied him with a copy of Joly's dialogues, but it was Rachkovskii's agents who did the actual work. Not only did he have the testimony of Golovinskii and of Bint, but there was also the indisputable fact that the rewritten parts of the book, which were not directly copied from Joly's dialogues, were written in very bad French. This was proof indeed, Georges decided. French forgers would have done a better job.

Georges could find no direct link between Rachkovskii and Glinka, but he must have met her at the home of Juliette Adam, whose close friend she had been. Whose idea had it been to entrust her with the delicate mission of carrying the final manuscript of the *Protocols* to Russia? What had her instructions been? How much did she know? He wished he knew what part every one of them had played in the conspiracy to fabricate the *Protocols* using the book of Maurice Joly, but he was firmly convinced that most of them had a hand in the plot.

In his conversations with Odette Georges told her that he often imagined he could hear the horses trotting on the cobbled street, the welcoming voice of the concierge at Juliette Adam's elegant mansion, and the voices of the guests pouring out into the street through an open window. He could imagine the elegant splendor of the salon, the thick carpets and the brocade chairs, the small serving tables and the servants, in black and white uniforms, discreetly passing around dainty sandwiches and petitfours. The women were probably chatting in a corner, he imagined, the men surrounding the hostess, engaged in hot debate. How he wished he could recreate the exact moment when the idea had taken form. Who was it that first suggested the use of Joly's book? Who was it that introduced to them the book of Herman Goedsche? He was convinced that the scene in the Prague cemetery had played a major part in the creation of the fictional group labeled *The Elders of Zion*. Sadly, he reconciled himself to the fact that he would never have an answer to these questions.

Rachkovskii was a man to be reckoned with, and on his way to even more fame, when he suddenly fell from grace. Not surprisingly, he too fell victim to the eccentricity of the tsarina and her female entourage.

It began with the royal visit of the Russian monarchs to France in 1901. In later years Rachkovskii remembered with a bitter smile how he had dispatched Manesevich-Manuilov to present Philippe to the royal couple. He had no idea that this was the first step on his road to disaster.

It was one of the Montenegrin princesses who had approached Rachkovskii requesting his help in obtaining for Philippe a permit to practice medicine. They were trying to invite their favorite healer to the royal court in Russia, and he wanted the respectability of a licensed doctor. Rachkovskii's fame preceded him, the princess said, and she was confident that the French authorities would not refuse him such a small favor. He had not realized that by refusing the request he had gained a powerful enemy in the palace.

In later years Rachkovskii often wondered how he could have miscalculated so badly. He had been away from the Russian capital too long, he decided. He had not been aware of the total confidence the tsarina had placed in the Montenegrin princesses. He had no idea that these two women were holding the empress under their spell. For once he had no ulterior motive. When General Gesse wrote from St Petersburg seeking information about Philippe, he decided to conduct a thorough inquiry. He meant to present their majesties with the true facts about this charlatan, Philippe, who had wormed his way into the Russian palace under false pretenses. Using his most dependable sources he soon compiled a fully incriminating report, hoping to be commended for his efforts. He did not suspect that his career in Paris was about to be terminated.

He was so proud of his report that he took it with him on one of his business trips to the homeland, in April 1902, in order to present it in person. He was even hoping to present it to the tsarina herself. As was his custom, he showed the report to Sipiagin, the minister of the interior, before presenting it to General Gesse. Later he would often reconstruct in his mind this scene, wondering how he could have been so naive. It was his arrogance, he admitted to himself, which led him to ignore the advise of the experienced minister, who had been his true friend and protector. He remembered clearly how Sipiagin had blanched, how he had read the report twice before folding it carefully and returning it, how he had hesitated long moments before speaking, and how he had carefully chosen his words. As minister of the interior, Sipiagin finally said, he knew nothing of this affair and he wanted no involvement in it. But, he added, as a man and a friend, he would advice Rachkovskii to burn the report. This document would only lead to trouble, he warned, not even wishing to elaborate. Rachkovskii had never understood how he could have been so stubborn. He was proud of his sources of information and of his ability to compile in a short time such a full and comprehensive report. You didn't just throw such a document into the fireplace, he said. Did he not have a duty to try and save their majesties from a cheat and a fake? The sad fact was, Sipiagin said, that their majesties did not wish to be saved. They resented any information that tended to undermine Philippe's status in the palace. This magician had them completely under his influence. Rachkovskii would be risking his neck, he said.

Even though Rachkovskii had ignored his advice, Sipiagin had no intention of losing his super-agent in Paris, but he could protect him only as long as he was in office. When he was replaced by Pleve, Rachkovskii's time was up. An opportunity presented itself when it was publicly revealed that Rachkovskii had invented an imaginary Russian Patriotic League, aiming to combat 'the mysterious, occult, irresponsible power' of the Jews. As this was a document soliciting French popular support against the Jews, it came close to causing a diplomatic incident. Rachkovskii had become an embarrassment, and the palace was no longer prepared to protect him.

He was not only dismissed from his job. He was forbidden to live and act in France, or even to return to Russia. As was his custom, the tsar scribbled his decision on the margin of Pleve's report about Rachkovskii. It said in short: 'Rachkovskii's contacts with the French police must be stopped. These instructions must be fully implemented without delay.'

There had never been any definite proof that certain people had been murdered by Rachkovskii's agents, on his orders. But rumors, which were a major source of information in those days, persisted in the allegation that Pleve had paid with his life for his banishment of Rachkovskii from Paris.

But that was not the end of Rachkovskii, Georges realized. In a very few years he had been reinstated in Russia in a seat of power. General Trepov had recalled him in August 1905, and put him in charge of the Political Department of the Secret Police.

It did not take him long to become again involved in the project of implicating the Jews. He had been quite disappointed by the fact that the *Protocols of the Elders of Zion* had not made the desired impact in Russia. It was no accident, Georges mused, that the date of the publication of the *Protocols* by Nilus coincided with Rachkovskii's return to Russia. This was not idle speculation, Georges assured his colleagues. Had not Tager delivered proof of Rachkovskii's part in the printing of the *Protocols* at the Pachoukanis printing press?

10 A South African Saga

On 22 October a week before the opening of the trial in Berne, an excited Lifschitz burst into the office of Georges Brunschvig waving a thick sheaf of papers. He was constantly delivering new documents, Georges thought, but this time he would tell him, as tactfully as possible, that he must stop. If he kept reading more documents, he told Lifschitz, he would not have the necessary time to prepare for trial. There comes a time, before a trial, Professor Matti had taught him, when a lawyer needs to stop reading documents and interviewing witnesses, and dedicate all his time to marshaling his thoughts and plan his trial strategy. 'Stop working nights,' he had told him, 'and get enough sleep. Don't come into the courtroom bleary-eyed and distraught. You need to be on your toes in that courtroom. I don't want a tired colleague at my side.' He always warned his clients, he had said, not to interrupt him during trial by pushing documents and notes in front of him. 'Unless it was a revelation that could change the fate of the trial,' he had added with a wink.

This was important enough, Lifschitz said. He had just received a copy of the judgment in which the court in South Africa had ruled against the local Nazi defendants and condemned the *Protocols of the Elders of Zion*. The judgment, announced two months before, on 21 August, had made a big impression, he told Georges. Politicians praised it in public speeches, and newspapers published strongly worded editorials, causing a wave of public condemnation of the Nazi-oriented groups and parties that had been gaining power and popularity all over South Africa. They must study the judgment, he advised, and decide whether it should be presented to the court. His colleagues in South Africa had also furnished him with excerpts from the proceedings, that was why it took them so long to send the material. They thought the lawyers in Berne should be prepared for the kind of defense they might expect.

He wished he had time to read the whole material, Georges said, but it might only confuse him. He knew enough of the South African trial to realize that, from a lawyer's point of view, they were dealing with a different kind of approach.

In our conversations Emil Raas told me how curious Georges had been about the South African trial. He needed all his self-discipline to avoid studying the documents that had arrived from South Africa, but he had carefully planned his work for the week before the trial, and would not interrupt his preparations. Even in later years, Emil told me, when Georges had gained a reputation as an outstanding lawyer, he had never gone to trial without meticulous preparation.

In my private investigation I tried to follow in the footsteps of Georges, eager to follow him, step by step, into the Berne courtroom. But at this point, bowing to the sequence of events, I was tempted to take a look at the transcript of the South African trial, which Dr Jankelevich had sent me from Port Elizabeth. I would just glance at it, I told myself, and go back to the Berne trial. After all, I was not actually trying the case, so I could afford a small diversion.

But once I started, I could not stop. I soon abandoned in my mind the beautiful and familiar city of Berne, trying to imagine what it must have been like in Grahamstown, where I had never set foot.

I was soon completely immersed in the drama that had played itself out in that faraway city over fifty years before.

FORGERY SOUTH AFRICAN STYLE

As in Berne, it started with a public meeting, or rather two meetings, one on 27 March 1934, in Aberdeen, and another, on 4 April 1934, removed to the Feather Market Square of Port Elizabeth, after the town hall denied the organizers the use of the Feather Market Hall.

The meetings were advertised, and it was stated that only Christians would be allowed to attend. It was at these meetings that the speaker, one Johannes Strauss von Moltke, read aloud in the Afrikaans language the contents of a document, originally written in English, alleging that it had been stolen from the Western Road Synagogue in Port Elizabeth. The document had been delivered to him, von Moltke revealed, by Harry Victor Inch, who had himself committed the theft. *Die Rapport*, a news sheet published weekly in Aberdeen in both Afrikaans and English, printed the same document, in an Afrikaans version on 6 April, and in the original English version on 13 April, stating both times, in print, that the document had been procured by theft from the Western Road Synagogue. On the front page the paper carried the following statement, in bold letters:

FOR THE FIRST TIME IN THE HISTORY OF SOUTH
AFRICA A DOCUMENT HAS COME INTO THE HANDS OF
GENTILE SOUTH-AFRICANS WHICH THROWS LIGHT ON
THE PERSECUTION OF THE GENTILES BY ORGANIZED
JEWRY THROUGHOUT THE WORLD.

Von Moltke was the leader in the Eastern Province of an organization called the South African Gentile National Socialist Movement,
whose admitted object was 'to combat and destroy the perversive
influence of the Jews in economics, culture, religion, ethics and state-
craft and to re-establish European Aryan control in South Africa for
the welfare of the Christian peoples of South Africa'.

Die Rapport, the organ of the organization, was owned, edited
and published by David Hermanus Olivier.

Inch was the leader in the Eastern Province of a subsidiary of the
organization, the South African Grey Shirts Movement, which was
said to be the 'body guard' of the other movement. Its aim was 'to
combat the pernicious influence of the Jewish race'.

Like other countries, South Africa also had its share of newly
formed Nazi-oriented organizations that had surfaced boldly since
Hitler's rise to power in Germany. As early as 1 November 1933, the
minister of justice, General J. C. Smutts, had issued a statement warning against attempts to work up anti-Jewish feeling among the public
by the dissemination of leaflets and in public meetings, where 'wild
charges are made against the Jews as a community which are calculated to create ill feeling and racial prejudice'. There were indica-
tions, General Smutts said, that these charges represented an organized movement that, lamentably, had its origins abroad and was an
attempt to import into South Africa 'the alien hatreds and rancors of
the old world'. The minister of justice warned that if his appeal to the
people of South Africa went unheeded, those who were spreading the
anti-Jewish poison would find themselves in trouble.

But the Nazis were on the move and nothing would stop them,
not even the Smutts warning. The *Protocols of the Elders of Zion*,
which came to be known as 'The Bible of the Anti-Semites', strongly
promoted by Hitler and his disciples, were widely distributed. It was
for good reason that the Jewish community kept ordering from
London hundreds of copies of the Philip Graves articles published in
the *Times* pamphlet, in an attempt to prove the falsity of the
Protocols. Little did they dream that a four-page local document

would soon prove to be much more dangerous to the Jewish community of South Africa than the widely distributed *Protocols*. It was therefore with profound horror that the shocked leaders of the Jewish community in Port Elizabeth learned of the document that was allegedly signed by the rabbi of a large and respected synagogue. The word *Rabbi* appeared at the end of the document and was read by von Moltke and published by Olivier as part of the text. No name was mentioned, but it was public knowledge that Abraham Levy was the rabbi of the Western Road Synagogue in Port Elizabeth.

The first report came from some Jews who had attended the Nazi rallies out of curiosity. Aileen Pearson, a local Jewish housewife, supplied a copy of the document that had been distributed at the April rally. She had also made notes of the inflammatory statements and the derogatory terms used by the speaker, aimed at the Jews. Jacob Cohen, who had a farm near Aberdeen, reported that he had attended the Aberdeen meeting, but as he thought he was the only Jew present he had restrained himself. He reported that the speaker at the meeting had appealed to his race, the Nordic people of South Africa, to form a Racial Patriotic Organization as a defense against this occult alien organization harbored in the Jewish synagogue.

Cecil Neethling McDermot, a non-Jewish clerk, who had also been present at one of the meetings, was so shocked that he immediately wrote a letter to the editor of the *Eastern Province Herald* stating his firm belief that the document read at the rally was a forgery, and expressing his shame as a British citizen. He was not taking up the fight for the Jew, he wrote, but his love of honesty, freedom and British fair play compelled him to cry halt. He felt shame for the Christian race of South Africa, he wrote. The Jews had been instrumental in the development of this country; trade and commerce had progressed through the Jews, who had built up their great cities. Instead of running the Jew down they should respect him and raise themselves to his level.

Abraham Levy studied the document in utter disbelief. Surely somebody was playing a joke on him, he thought. It was no joke, the leaders of the Jewish community told him. But who would believe such utter nonsense; who would take seriously such a crude forgery, he cried. At the time Jews had ignored the *Protocols of the Elders of Zion*, they reminded him, also believing that people of common sense would realize immediately that it was a false document. This new document was more dangerous to the Jews in South Africa than the *Protocols*, they feared. Even those who had ignored the alleged existence of a world conspiracy aiming to undermine all Christian governments would hardly dare ignore 'proof' of a local conspiracy aiming to attain Jewish domination of South Africa. This document, they said, was an ingenious libel, based on the *Protocols*. It purported to be proof of the local application of the international plot. Using the tactics of the forgers of the *Protocols*, this document was not what others said about the Jews, this was the so-called 'Jewish Secret Plan' itself, stolen from the synagogue and published, in the nick of time, by a patriot who had put himself in danger in order to save his country. This was how it would be presented, they warned.

It looked like a carbon copy of an original document, typewritten on four pages of foolscap. At the top, in the right-hand corner of the first page, appeared the words 'copy of Mr M. Lazarus'. (But Mark Lazarus was a printer, who did not even belong to the congregation, somebody remarked.) Immediately below these words were badly formed Hebraic characters handwritten in real ink, signifying 'Fit for Passover' (*Kosher Lepesach*). Then came words written in similar characters making up the words 'The Book of Memorial or Remembrance' or 'The Book of Chronicles'. On the left side, similarly written, were Hebrew words meaning 'Holy Congregation'. After the words 'copy of Mr M. Lazarus' came the heading 'Lecture No. 2' and the title: 'Subject: Our Plan of Attack'.

They had thought they had heard the worst libels, but these had always been imported repetitions of old ones. This was new, and it was so close to home. It threatened to disrupt the very fabric of their lives in South Africa.

It was hard to believe that even a Nazi anti-Semite could concoct such nonsense. Only an ignorant and careless forger would use the words 'Fit for Passover' in a document that had nothing to do with food. They could just as well have written 'Buy Nestlé milk', somebody remarked. But Jews knew that non-Jews would hardly notice such a detail.

The alleged Jewish 'Plan of Attack' listed the following subjects: Our Attitude to the Christian Faith: The Unholy Christ; We are the Chosen of God; Division of the Churches; The Rebirth of Catholicism; The Greyshirt Menace and how it will be Combated; Gentile Decay; 'Live and Let Live' – Our Greatest Asset; Our Imperial Plan in Comparison to other Empires; Our Attitude to World Socialism; The Next Attack and Riot; How we shall Achieve our Wish; How the Gentile Dogs shall Crave Mercy and our Refusals; Our Bolshevik Propaganda Scheme.

This general plan was followed by a detailed one, appearing to be a record of an address delivered by the rabbi to the members of the Council. It read as follows:

A. OUR ATTITUDE TO THE CHRISTIAN FAITH

As I have explained to you in previous meetings, our attitude to Christianity is one of great interest to the High Circle of the Jewish citizens of Port Elizabeth. As you all know the divisions in the Christian Church were of our construction. It was our ancestors that urged Luther and the other reformers to break from the Mother Church, i.e., the Roman Catholic Church, for our own private purposes, which would hasten the fulfillment of our World Imperialism. The Roman Catholic Church was severely wounded in the head (that is, literally), and the Protestant Churches are as dead as mutton. But, my beloved Council, the R.C.C. has been unconscious for countless centuries, but it is beginning to stir to life again. It has awakened after a long and great sleep and its influence is beginning to be felt throughout the Earth. (Did not the Fascist, Mussolini, make treaties with the Pope, and is not Hitler a Catholic?) We must destroy it. It is interfering with our world socialism.

I mentioned to you before several times at our council meetings of the select that we are the pure people. The Nordics in our eyes are in no way different to the Chinese Dogs or the Turks. They are all our destroyers, our enemies. The Christian religion is wrong. Christ, in the Jewish sense, was a false prophet born of the womb of a foul bitch who was in our eyes never married to Joseph. In our *Talmud Torah* and other holy books it does say that the Gentiles will be made to drink the piss and eat the dung of the Jews.

'PHARAOH'

2. 'LECTURES ON JUDAISM V. CHRISTIANITY'

Anti-Semitism and the South African Greyshirts
Pharaoh, the King of Egypt, was the first Anti-Semite, and I can assure you that Hitler will be the last. As far as the Greyshirts are concerned, we shall cripple them as follows:

We have received information through A.4 that the Greys are to have a meeting in the Feather Market Hall after the Christian holidays. All preparations are being made, disguising a crowd of our most trusted servants as Greyshirts. We shall see that they are supplied with Swastikas and gray ribbon. Their duty is to hackle the speakers, kick up a row, and sing so-called patriotic songs, that to us, internationals as we are, have no meaning whatever, in preparation for the greatest riot ever witnessed from Cairo to the Cape. We are prepared for homicide, murder and manslaughter. Hit right and left, wherever you see a Gentile face. The equipment that must be brought are to be pepper-pots, blackjacks, knuckle-dusters, revolvers, lead piping, sticks, stones and boxing gloves. We have arranged that if there are no police around, for a contingent of our fellows, to be near the parapets ready to fling rocks and boulders through the opposite windows. We are confident in our success. We always get through unscathed. We who boast of our survival over all empires. We the Chosen of the Almighty, who guides and approves of our every action. Our cult is gold. These Greydogs are to us as the sowing of the wind on a wintry day – we who control, financially and even politically behind the scenes, yea, the chosen, who were promised all these things. Earthly pomp, splendor, imperialism, and ever lasting sovereignty over the animals of the earth.

Christianity, I repeat, is Satan's religion, the religion fit only for the dogs that they are, who go to their churches to see whether their neighbor has on a Paris model or print dress. What foolishness. What utter foolhardiness.

The 'live and let live' motto of the churches is our greatest asset I can assure you. The British Imperialism was one of help to Christian Civilization, but ours is the direct opposite.

We stand for World Communism, for dictatorship of the pro-letariat. Our Imperialism of *Pax Judaica* is one for the downfall of western civilization and its replacement by the eastern or Japanese system. We have seen the progress of the U.S.S.R. since 1917 when our agents, Lenin, Stalin, etc. murdered the Tsar. The Pope is a religious Imperialist, and that interferes with our world plan. As we have got control over Russia, so we will also control the Union, and so achieve our object in the destruction of the British Empire by making propaganda for wars that as a result it will fall to bits as did mighty Rome. Yet we survive and our object has been fulfilled. Such is the mission of Judah. It is our plan to give South Africa to the natives. 'South Africa and Africa for the Black Man' said Abdurahman and our several loyal agents. However, we have the prospect in view that if South Africa is given to the Sons of Ham, we shall not be in any way molested.

Of the British we may say that they are innocent of our plan to deprive them of the countless possessions she has herself developed, and of the Dutch we may say that they are the most lovely of our specimen of Gentile decay, and are of as much account as the unclean meat, pigs flesh that they consume in such large quantities. The natives are of no account. They are as brainless as their Teutonic cousins – rapists, blackguards, thieves and spies.

The following papers which financed us are the Empress (Mr Barlow editing with our approval The Socialist Review, The Anti-Nazi, and Mr Lazarus' Propaganda Scheme).

We will fool the public, so that their belief in 'Live and Let Live' will be intensified a thousand fold. We will make them digest as much silly rot as their decayed and filthy minds are capable of understanding. Hitler, Lunatic Goering, Von Papen and their co-lunatics, with the Asylum Contingent (namely the Brown Shirts) are guilty of devastation, and crimes against civilization, which we have built up. They raped our women, murdered our old men, bombarded and dynamited our synagogues, threw our children to our hunting dogs, made our little ones to dance on hot coals until they fried, made our husbands run the gauntlet in the passage ways in our clubs while they themselves struck them as they passed. These low common sons of a filthy womb know not the Japanese menace that is upon the face of Europe and Africa.

Brethren, although for countless centuries you have been despised and hated, in the near future the races of the Earth will kiss your feet and worship you, they shall bow down before thee and exult and praise thee. They shall beg mercy of thee and thou shalt refuse. They shall acknowledge that thou art the chosen, the infallible. Our elected leader will be the first sovereign over all the earth. The Communist World, and at last the *Talmud Torah* and prophecies will be fulfilled. I may say that we are on the threshold.

On our very life take care of these instructions, do not mention a word to not even your own what is contained in these pages. You know our law. You know the result. The propaganda that would shortly arrive from Moscow, that will be in our safe-keeping in the *Syn. West. Rd.* will be handed to trusted members of the local and Cape Trade Unions and F.S.U. as soon as the appointed time arrives. We shall instill into the warped minds of Goya then that we are the proverbial 'now know-alls'.

Issued by the select high circle of the anti-Nazi propaganda vigilance committee c.x.v.o. 3838 and authorized for use by the trustee and the six council members only.

RABBI

There were those who suggested that the incident be ignored. It would blow over, they said; nobody in his right mind would believe it, they argued; only a limited number of bigots attended the rallies, they maintained; legal action would only publicize the document; the Nazis would not dare print it in a newspaper, they assured each other. But a few days later the full document was published in *Die Rapport* and they learned by word of mouth that the document was beginning to have an impact. Stephen John Moore, a contractor from Aberdeen, a former policeman who belonged to the Apostolic Church, was overheard telling a neighbor how impressed he was with von Moltke's message. 'We were told that it was John Bull [meaning the English] who persecuted us and stole our diamond fields, but it has always been the Jew under the mantle of John Bull,' he said bitterly. He was also upset by the fact that the Jews were calling them *Goy* – he took it to heart, he said, for 'Goy' means animal. (What a joke, they said!) A mechanic who had attended the rally, Ellis Charles Simpson, confided to a co-worker how upset he was that there should be such a low thing floating about the world reflecting on Christians about the undermining of British justice, which had been protecting them for many years. 'I told my Jewish neighbors', he told his friend, 'that if that was proved as such I would not say good morning or good afternoon to them. I was inflamed against the Jewish people. I understood it to be a world plan with South African conditions superimposed.' Ebenhaezer Fourie, a pupil studying for matriculation, had also attended one of the meetings. He described to his friends in school how they all wore swastikas. He had read the document carefully, he explained, and understood that the Jews were filled with

hatred toward the Christians. Only after the meeting did he realize
that the Jews owned all the possessions worth having in South Africa.
Jacobus Petrus Johannes Kruger, a bachelor farmer, read about
the document in the paper. Now he was finally convinced, he told
his friends over a beer, that all the Jews were part of this terrible
conspiracy. 'I believed in the document seeing what happened in our
place,' he said. 'The Jews are progressing and getting possession of
our farms.'

It took the community leaders only a few days to come to a decision. They had been educated in the British system and had great
confidence in the legal process. They knew about the Berne trial, but
the South African legal system was different. They knew that this was
not a personal attack on the rabbi and that the real target was the
whole Jewish community, but since the document appeared to be a
record of his address to the council, signed by his title, although not
by name, the complaint would have to be filed by him.

Before long Abraham Levy filed in the local division of the
Supreme Court, sitting in Grahamstown, Eastern Province, civil
actions for damages, naming as defendants Johannes Strauss von
Moltke, David Hermanes Olivier (Junior) and Henry Victor Inch.
The rabbi was represented by Mr Reynolds KC (King's Counsel) and
Mr E. Stuart.

The trial date was set for Tuesday 10 July 1934, before His Honor
T. L. Graham and His Honor Mr Justice C. Gutsche. The claims
against all three defendants were consolidated.

As it was not a private matter of the rabbi, a committee was
appointed to instruct the lawyers and make decisions concerning trial
tactics. The pleadings of both sides had been filed, defining the conflict and the issues. The trial would begin in a few weeks, and it
looked as though the judges intended to dispose of the case as
quickly as possible. The issues seemed to be clear-cut: had the document, admittedly published by the defendants, originated from the
synagogue, and had it been stolen from there by Inch on Saturday
afternoon, 24 March as Inch maintained, or was it a false document,
forged and fabricated as a means of inciting against the Jews, as the
rabbi asserted? In the regular course of the disposition of court business the case should take up no more than a couple of days.

Hot arguments divided the Jewish community. Some argued that
they should keep a low profile. This was a simple case, the court
would not allow it to become a Dreyfus trial, they argued; it was not

the function of the court to combat anti-Semitism, the judges would admit only facts relevant to the issues set out in the pleadings; the defendants did not mention in their pleadings the *Protocols of the Elders of Zion* or the existence of a Jewish World Conspiracy. This was a local issue, and the court would not appreciate it if they dragged the problems of world Jewry into this court.

Others insisted that they would be missing the whole point of the trial if they allowed it to be limited to the stealing of a document. The document was the talk of the town and was causing harm to all of them; the fabricated facts did not concern the rabbi in his private capacity, they were horrible lies about all Jews; it was their duty to confront not only the technical issue of the theft, but the false allegations that would stick in the minds of people; they were not equipped to confront the Nazis in the public square, this was a unique opportunity to confront them in a court of law, open to the public; the forgers would soon realize that here the rules of the game were different, and they could not get away with crude lies; they must use this arena to confront the rising tide of Nazi anti-Semitism, as they might not have another such opportunity.

In the end it would be up to the court, the lawyers said – the decision might not be theirs. So they decided to be prepared. They would line up witnesses to testify on the bigger issues, if the court would allow it.

Studying the transcript of the trial, I was greatly impressed. Lawyers usually drag out trials, arguing that they need long periods of time to prepare their case and line up witnesses. Yet this unusual trial, which lasted from 10 July to 24 July, with a record exceeding 700 pages, was prepared by the litigants in less than two months. And it took the court less than a month to deliver, on 21 August, a detailed, well-reasoned, 31-page-long judgment.

Had the defendants been represented, their lawyers would probably have advised them to limit themselves to the technical facts. But when the day arrived they marched into court, Inch and von Moltke in uniform.

They had no money to engage lawyers, they announced – it was the Jews who had all the money. They raised all kinds of technical points, including the argument that there was no proof that they meant that particular rabbi.

The lawyers realized that it was the defendants who would define the scope of the trial, as it soon became apparent that they viewed the court as a proper arena for their propaganda. As the evidence un-folded, the issue was no longer limited to the authenticity of the document or the identity of the rabbi. It became clear that the court would have to address itself to the alleged existence of an interna-tional plot, to a Jewish conspiracy to gain domination of the world. The defendants maintained that the said document was only the local application of this international plot. It became clear that the court would have to rule not only on the authenticity of a local document, but on that of the *Protocols of the Elders of Zion*.

When it was their turn to present their defense, von Moltke, speaking for all the defendants, officially requested the court to allow them to amend their plea. They now pleaded justification, he said. They would prove and argue that they had been justified in what-ever they had done, for it had been for patriotic aims. They now officially pleaded the existence of a dangerous international 'Jewish Plot'.

Was it a coincidence, a friend asked me, that the two most important trials of the *Protocols* took place in the same year, independently of each other, in two countries, on two continents?

It was no coincidence, I assured him. Hitler had caused a revival of the *Protocols*. There was ample proof that the Nazi propaganda machine had identified the *Protocols* as the strongest argument in their attempt to convince the world that the Jews constituted a grave danger not only to world peace, but to the very existence of legitimate Christian governments. 'Here is what they will do to you', the Nazis cried, if they are not dealt with. The Weltdienst in Erfurt, headed by Ulrich Fleischhauer, was given the task of promoting the *Protocols* around the world as part of its anti-Semitic drive to de-legitimize the Jews and place them beyond the pale of legitimate human society. The unsus-pecting world, and even the naive Jewish communities, perceived this phenomenon as yet another routine outburst of anti-Semitism. Blaming the Jews was not a newly invented tactic; Jews had been persecuted and even massacred before; this wave would pass, like all its predecessors, they tried to convince themselves. Not only was there no premonition about the coming Holocaust, but there was no suspicion that the *Protocols* were more than just another tool in the hands of anti-Semites. The idea that Hitler was not only using the *Protocols* as a tool against the Jews, but had actually adopted the so-called 'Jewish Plan' of world domination, would have sounded preposterous had anybody voiced it in those first years of the Nazi regime. Nobody in his right mind would have dared announce that Hitler was using the *Protocols* not only as a common denominator that would serve as a basis for the organiza-tion of Nazi parties in other countries, based on the logic that both Jews and anti-Semitism existed everywhere, but to mask his own plan to attain world domination. They could not have known of the conversation with Hitler reported by Hermann Rauschning in his book *Hitler Speaks*. 'I have read the Protocols of the Elders of Zion,' Hitler told him, 'it simply appalled me. The stealthiness of the enemy, and his ubiquity! I saw at once that we must copy it – in our own way, of course.'

In 1934 Jews were not aware of the approaching disaster. Like the law-abiding citizens that they were, they thought that they could combat the Nazis in courts of law. Reading the record of the orderly conduct of the trials, the polite questions put to Nazi bigots, who were openly uttering the most unspeakable libels against Jews, and the learned and well-reasoned judgments, I suddenly thought of a man carefully plugging up a small hole in his boat, not realizing that in no time at all a huge wave would sweep it on to the rocks.

A TRIAL IN GRAHAMSTOWN

On 10 July it was cool and cloudy. It was the middle of winter in South Africa. The courtroom was packed from an early hour. Members of the Grey Shirts were in uniform, some in the courtroom and others outside, making loud derogatory remarks at passing Jews. A hostile and tense atmosphere prevailed. Reporters swarmed over the place, accompanied by photographers. The two robed judges took their seats and the court came to order.

On the witness stand, Abraham Levy carried himself with quiet dignity. The court attendant administered the oath, and his lawyer quickly led the rabbi through the technical facts. He described his functions at the synagogue. He had never seen the document published by the defendants – he never used notes in his sermons, and the only documents the synagogue sent out were notices of monthly meetings of committee, and annual reports. These were all printed, not typewritten. They did not even have a typewriter. The Hebrew words used in the document could not have been written by a Jew, even if he was illiterate.

Then came the first surprise. The rabbi placed a folded newspaper on the judges' bench, pointing out to the court that all the phrases in the document, purporting to have a Jewish meaning, were copied from one issue of the *Jewish Chronicle* dated 9 March 1934, some of them misspelled even in English. The *Jewish Chronicle* was published in London in the English language.

It was time to introduce the *Protocols*, Reynolds decided.

'Do you see any resemblance between this document and the *Protocols of the Elders of Zion*?' he asked the rabbi. 'Yes,' the rabbi answered, adding in an excited voice that there was no 'High Circle of the Jewish Citizens of Port Elizabeth', there were no 'Council Meetings of the Select', there was no 'Trustee and six members of the Council'. They had originally appointed two trustees who had no power to authorize anything, and, anyway, both trustees had been away in England for eight or nine years. They had never been replaced.

Getting down to specifics, Rabbi Levy stated that he had never heard that the Jews conspired with Luther and the Reformation. 'This is a new doctrine,' he said with a smile, noticing that the judges were also smiling.

The Jews had no 'World Socialistic Movement', the witness continued, and he had never heard that the Jews were behind the Revolution in Russia. Jews who were communists, he said heatedly, were those who had abandoned their faith. The Bolsheviks had no regard for religion of any kind, he stated.

They had no book called 'The Talmud Tora' – these words meant an elementary school for children, not a book. No Jew would make such a mistake. The judges could not help but notice the amused looks of the Jews in the audience.

Examining the Inch document once again the rabbi continued, saying that he had never organized anybody to go to a Grey Shirt meeting and they never instructed anybody to 'smash everything they could, carry pepper-pots, blackjacks, knuckle-dusters, revolvers, lead piping, sticks, stones and boxing gloves'. He had never heard such nonsense.

With his next question Reynolds knew he might be exercising the patience of the judges, but he decided to try and educate the court on some Jewish terms. How else would these Gentile judges be made to realize the extent of absurdity in the allegations presented in the forged document?

Reynolds knew that one cannot turn a courtroom into a seminar. His colleague argued that he might either alienate the judges or, what is worse, bore them. But he was an experienced lawyer. To win a trial, he used to say, it is not enough to prepare your witnesses well. This is not a solo game: you have an opponent, and you must be as familiar with his arguments as you are with your own. You cannot ignore even those that seem worthless. A judge might see them in a different light. Ignoring or underestimating an argument of your opponent is the most common way of losing a case.

He had spent the last weeks studying the matter of the *Protocols of the Elders of Zion*. He had collected various versions of the book concentrating on the introductions, which varied from one edition to another. He soon realized that the *Protocols* were presented as a modern version of the so-called 'Jewish Plot', which was supposed to be as old as the history of the Jews. As proof they often quoted the Talmud, sometimes using fake quotations, which their audience was not equipped to check, and other times using accurate quotes, completely out of their original context. This tactic, he soon learned, was very effective, as it lent to the promoters of the *Protocols* an image of learned academics. Suspecting that the defendants would use the same technique, he decided to be prepared.

Impressed by Rabbi Levy's vast knowledge on the subject, he was sure the judges would not be bored. But he also realized that they must find another expert witness, preferably non-Jewish. Unfortunately, the rabbi had remarked at one of their meetings, a Jewish scholar, even the most prominent one, would automatically be suspected of bias. If the court ruled in favor of the plaintiff, the judges would immediately be accused of being in the pocket of the Jews. 'Believe me,' the rabbi had said with a sad smile, 'this is no Jewish paranoia, this is the result of age-old experience.'

Keeping his fingers crossed and praying for the indulgence of the court, Reynolds now asked the rabbi with obvious distaste: 'They say in the document that the Gentiles will be forced to drink the piss and eat the dung of the Jews. And that there has been a conspiracy through the ages taught and founded on the Jewish books against Christianity.'

'It is a lie,' the Rabbi cried. Then, in a calmer voice, he patiently explained that the Talmud was comprised of discussions of rabbis on the text called the Mishna or Oral Law, extending over a period from 500 BC to AD 500. It was first transmitted from one generation to another orally and then written down. Various rabbis commented on the text and that was the Gemara, popularly known as the Talmud. There were all sorts of contradictory statements there representing the views of the rabbis in their debates. 'It is silly to maintain that there exists some sort of conspiracy,' he stated.

The judges listened attentively as the witness gave a short summary of Jewish history.

Surprising even his lawyers, the witness stated that the texts from the Talmud used by the defendants had already been the subject of litigation in a German court. The courtroom was now very quiet as the rabbi continued. Most modern anti-Semitic feeling is based on the perversion of Jewish texts, he explained. The first one to try to use the Talmud texts against the Jews was one Isenberger in his book *Judaism Unmasked*, published in 1700. At the end of the nineteenth century Professor Rohle from Austria propagated these texts supposedly taken from the Talmud. A man called Block accused him of being a perjurer and sued him. By the court's request the Oriental Society of Berlin and a Catholic professor in Prague nominated two scholars, Noldke and Wuenche, who presented a report on 400 texts, vindicating the Talmud completely. Rohle had to withdraw his defense and admit he was a perjurer.

Some of these same texts were re-used by the defendants, the rabbi said, pointing at them. 'It is a malicious lie that the Talmud says we are human beings and the nations of the world are beasts,' he cried. 'Nowhere in the Talmud does it say that a Jew may rob a Goy!'

The audience was probably fidgeting as the witness went on to explain in detail Hebrew terms and Jewish customs, but not once did the judges interrupt.

Then it was time for cross-examination.

Cross-examination can be a traumatic experience in any court operating under the English adversary system. In the inquisitory system applied in all countries on the European continent, it was the judge who questioned witnesses, and he would never badger or insult them. Even defendants in criminal proceedings are questioned politely and courteously. Not so in the English system, where cross-examination often resembles a police third degree. A lawyer may raise his voice to witnesses, accuse them of lying, expose them to every kind of embarrassment with questions concerning their private lives. Skeletons in their closets are dragged out in an attempt to impeach them, sometimes harming their reputations irreparably. Yet this is considered the best tool in the arsenal of a lawyer to try and get at the truth, and although some judges do their utmost to protect a witness, they are not supposed to deny an attorney his right to pressure a witness in an attempt to reveal facts beneficial to his client.

Rabbi Levy had never been in a court of law, and Reynolds had done his best to prepare him for what was to come. Yet he must have been shocked when Inch rose arrogantly and shot at him his opening salvo:

Q: Can one be a Jew and an Englishman?

A: Certainly, if he is born in England.
Q: Can a Chinaman be a Britisher?
A: Certainly, if he is born in England.
Q: But that means that a goat can be a horse!

It took the witness a minute to control his anger and respond with dignity.

A: A Chinaman has a land of origin, he originates from China, but if he is born in England he is entitled to British protection, he is also an Englishman.

'I want to prove that in South Africa a Jew can no more be a South African than a horse can be a donkey,' Inch stated, turning to the audience with a smirk. The judges sat stone-faced, but did not interfere.

Asked why he had 'dragged them to court', the rabbi cried out: 'I have suffered in my feelings, I have suffered anguish that such a statement should be fastened on me by the person who forged this document. I have suffered very grievously by having such a filthy, blasphemous and scurrilous statement fastened upon me.'

Trying hard to regain his composure, the rabbi answered every specific question with as much restraint as he could muster: no, they had no occult movements; meetings of Jewish bodies in the synagogue were open, nothing secret, they had no Higher Council, the *Protocols of the Elders of Zion* were false, they never existed, there was no Jewish plot, either local or international.

Suddenly Inch raised his voice: 'Why should we believe you?' he asked. 'Did not Jacob use camouflage to get the birthright of Esau?'

The witness looked helplessly at the court, not trusting his voice.

Then it was the turn of von Moltke, who read his questions from a prepared document, sometimes not even waiting for an answer:

Are you a Son of the Covenant?
Have you been circumcised?
Are you an Ashkenazi Jew and are you aware of the fact that this is the worst type of Jew you can get in the world?
What is your religion; you know Jews have all sorts of religions as long as they can pervert Christianity?
To whom are you subordinate ecclesiastically?

When court was recessed the rabbi seemed on the verge of collapse. Why didn't judges protect a witness from insulting questions, he asked his lawyers on the way out. This was the system, they explained, the judges must look neutral. This was the English way of finding out the truth. The rabbi shrugged. He knew by heart all the rules of the Jewish Halakha concerning the conduct of a trial. This was insane, he thought: the Jewish rules made much more sense.

Next morning von Moltke started as soon as the rabbi took the stand: 'Do the Jews keep two sets of Talmud, one to present to a Gentile court, and another one in a secret court? Are you acquainted with all occult movements or societies in South Africa? Is there no such thing as 'Jews of the High Circle' in South Africa in Jewish religion? Could you give us an explanation why the Jews are always persecuted in every country, by every nation?

He kept answering in a tired voice, sometimes in monosyllables. He was ashamed to have to answer such questions. He had never felt more degraded. But he could not believe his ears when von Moltke approached the stand and asked 'Why do you go out of your way to drag a few poor old Grey Shirts into court?'

Not able to restrain himself, the rabbi raised his voice: 'You have been cutting the Jewish people for months, and there are young Jewish children born in this country who look upon themselves as good citizens, and they cannot hear these words of blasphemy used day after day.'

Inevitably the *Protocols* came up again:

> Q: You say that the *Protocols of the Elders of Zion* are a forgery?
> A: Let me say definitely that there is absolutely no connection between the contents of these *Protocols* with any of the Jewry in any part of the world.
> Q: Would you consider the man who forged, or compiled or wrote this book of *Protocols*, would you consider him a prophet?
> A: Certainly not!
> Q: Would you consider Mr Henry Ford a prominent Gentile?
> A: Yes.
> Q: Do you know what Ford said about the *Protocols*?
> A: Yes, and do you know what he said after he said what he had said about the *Protocols*?

Then it was the turn of Olivier, but his questions were mostly repetitious.

Suddenly it was over and the court stood in recess. Everybody in the courtroom was looking bored. Long hours, which ran into days, were wasted on boring testimony concerning the theft of the document. Inch had presented an affidavit describing the manner in which the document had come into his hands. Two young boys, one blond and one dark, had watched the synagogue and had brought to him two unsigned documents that included suspicious remarks about a Jewish anti-Christian plan. That is when he had decided to break into the synagogue, where he had found the document. The two boys remained anonymous to the end of the trial, but his description of the synagogue and the manner of his entry did not fit the physical facts. So the court was compelled to listen for long hours to testimonies of witnesses on technical matters. Even the journalists looked bored, but then an old man took the stand and the atmosphere suddenly changed.

Preparing for trial, the lawyers were in a dilemma. They had only a few short weeks to create their list of witnesses. As soon as they decided to center their argument on the *Protocols of the Elders of Zion*, rather than the locally forged document, they realized the tremendous responsibility they had undertaken. Unlike their colleagues in Berne, they did not have at their disposal witnesses who could testify directly to the forgery of the *Protocols*. They would therefore concentrate on testimony proving the absurdity of the allegations both in the *Protocols* and in the Inch document. They needed an outstanding witness, of international repute, but how do you get such a person to travel to South Africa on such short notice, they wondered.

But luck was with them. A few days before the trial they suddenly learned that Nahum Sokolov was expected on a short visit to South Africa.

Sokolov was at that time president of the World Zionist Organization, having been elected in 1931 to replace Chaim Weitzmann. He carried his 75 years well. Against the advice of his doctors he did not spare himself, and traveled to Jewish communities to raise the necessary funds to keep the Zionist enterprise going. Hitler had risen to power in Germany and funds were urgently needed to help Jewish refugees settle in Palestine.

They knew what a burden he was carrying and hesitated to ask him to interrupt his mission and testify at the trial, but he readily volunteered. He was familiar with the matter of the *Protocols of the Elders of Zion* and would do anything to reveal the truth to the public, he declared. What better forum than a court of law. They warned him, describing the humiliating cross-examination of the rabbi, but he said Jews were used to such ordeals.

He was one of the most important Jewish leaders of his generation. A kibbutz and streets in most towns in Israel carry his name. Few are aware of the fact that it was Sokolov who gave the title *Tel Aviv* to his Hebrew translation of Herzl's book *Altneuland*, a name later adopted by the largest city in Israel.

A journalist and a writer of world repute, in full command of many languages, his writings published in many countries, Sokolov was received by heads of state and by the Pope, and had their ear and their respect. He had headed the Jewish delegation to the Paris Peace Conference after the First World War, and the committee representing Jews at the League of Nations. He was recognized as one of the best-educated persons on Jewish as well as on general matters. They could not have hoped for a better witness.

Duly sworn by the court attendant, Sokolov described his credentials. As instructed by the lawyers, he then patiently waited for Reynolds' questions.

> Q: Is there any truth whatsoever in the suggestion that there is a Jewish plot to overcome the other nations of the world or anything of that kind?
>
> A: No, I don't believe that.

Pointing to a locally published copy of the *Protocols of the Elders of Zion* and to the forged Inch document, Reynolds continued:

> Q: Is there any suggestion of truth whatsoever in any of the statements in these documents, is there any truth in what they say about the objects of the Jewish race?
>
> A: No, every word is a lie.

They needed this witness not only to deny the existence of a Jewish conspiracy. They needed his first-hand information to confront the specific allegation that the *Protocols of the Elders of Zion* were an authentic record of secret meetings held behind the scenes at the first Zionist Congress in Basle in 1897.

Questioned about Zionism in general, Sokolov now explained that the Zionist movement had nothing to do with Jewish ecclesiastical law, but was an attempt to re-establish the Jews as a territorial nation.

'I attended personally the Basle Congress in 1897 and took

considerable part in its organization and the drawing up of its agen-da,' he stated. 'There is not one word of truth in the allegation that the *Protocols of the Elders of Zion* were promulgated by Dr Herzl at the Zionist Congress.'

'In 1920,' the witness continued, 'I heard for the first time the claim that a document like that existed. It was hearsay. In 1897 this slanderous document was never even heard of.' They had made a special effort for the proceedings of the Congress to be public, he said. Everything was conducted in the most open fashion.

Sokolov then explained how in 1920, on a visit to Paris, he had learned that such a slanderous pamphlet was being circulated in London, having been brought there by some adventurer who came from Russia. It worried him, so he traveled to London to see for him-self.

Turning to the judges he stated in his authoritative voice: 'I can tell you that every word in the *Protocols* was a mischievous lie, it was clear to me it was written in order to excite the Gentiles against the Jews, as they always do!'

He then went on to describe how he had later met Philip Graves, how he had read his articles published in *The Times*, how he had gone to the British Museum, which he frequented for his own read-ing and research, and how he had seen there the book by Maurice Joly. He had personally compared the Dialogue written by Joly with the *Protocols*, realizing how cleverly the forgers had substituted the Jews for Napoleon III.

Hearing this story for the first time, the judges were so intrigued that, uncharacteristically, they interfered: 'Did you actually see the original yourself?' they asked.

'I saw the original in London', Sokolov answered, and explained how the articles in *The Times* had been published in the form of a pamphlet that can be presented to the court.

'I compared the original by Maurice Joly with this document,' the witness repeated, 'and we were very much amused at that sort of rot that the man should have taken out the whole text with the only dif-ference that instead of Napoleon III there was Herzl, and instead of the French people of the Napoleon supporters there were substitut-ed the Jews.'

It was Reynolds' turn to be surprised, realizing how attentively the judges were listening to Sokolov's testimony. They now asked him: 'Were you also acquainted with this incident concerning the Austrian

Professor Rohle?'

'Yes,' came the ready answer. 'I know the controversy between Dr. Bloch and Rohle. I knew Dr Bloch personally, he was a friend of mine in Vienna, and he controverted with Rohle, who was a professor in Prague and who was known as a very aggressive anti-Semite. Rohle used to write against Jewish religion much more than against the Jewish people and he wrote a number of articles about the Talmud. Let me say that I consider this literature as no literature at all, it is rubbish, it is full of ignorance. Rohle was an ignorant man, he could not read the Talmud, not even the Bible, in the original. You have to devote years to understand the language of the Talmud. Rohle was disproved by a number of very great Christians of great repute like Noldke and Professor Wünsche, who was a Protestant who translated a considerable part of the Talmud into German. He was recognized as an authority by the whole world. Rohle got his texts not from the originals but from some pamphlets. These scholars mentioned some 500 quotations of Rohle to be false! He quoted from anti-Semitic writings of the seventeenth century which were disproved a hundred times!'

Seeing that the judges had finished, Reynolds resumed his questioning:

Q: Are you familiar with what is going on in Russia?
A: I have never been in Soviet Russia but I know what is going on there. The Soviet is against religion, against nationalities in every respect in any race, it does not matter, Jew or Christian, we suffer very much from their persecutions and we have quite a number of Zionists who have been thrown in prison and made to suffer violently; some of them have been deported to Siberia and they ask for our help.

The testimony in chief of the witness ended with his firm statement: 'I say most definitely that there is no politics in any synagogue in the world. A congregation is a religious unit and the synagogue is a place of worship and also used for benevolent purposes of the congregation.'

It was time for lunch, and the old man on the stand descended with dignity, not revealing his great fatigue.

'I am a Jew, of the Jewish race, born in Poland, a naturalized British citizen, my real native national language is Hebrew,' the witness stated after lunch in answer to Inch.

Q: Why have you asked to give evidence at this trial?

A: Mainly because of this foolish mention of the *Protocols of the Elders of Zion* that never existed. As the president of the Zionist organization I know this document has never existed and had never been mentioned at the Zionist Congress in Basle.

Q: Are you here to clear the name of world Jewry?

A: I am interested in disputing foolish inventions against Zionism and to refute the existence of the so-called Elders of Zion I am not defending the Jewish race, as you put it, I am contradicting a blatant lie! I did not come especially for the trial, I happened to be here and I heard of this foolishness about the *Protocols of the Elders of Zion* and I offered to testify. I volunteered to give evidence.

Q: You are considered to be a very important Jew in your race ...

A: My modesty does not allow me to accept that.

Q: You say that the *Protocols* are completely false?

A: Yes.

Q: But will you admit that nothing can be false that turns out to be right?

A: This will never turn out to be right.

Q: The counsel for the plaintiff said there was no world organization of Jewry. Do you agree?

A: Yes.

Q: Do you admit that practically all the film agencies, cinemas, and so on, are controlled by the Jews?

A: I am not prepared to answer this question, I don't know the film business. I have never made any statistics as to how many Jews are in films!

Q: Do you agree with the barrage of filth that is usually shown in our bioscopes, or to be more open on this point, do you agree that they should put half-naked females on the posters for our children to see when they advertise a film, our womenfolk half naked, in a suggestive manner?

A: I am not a great admirer of nakedness, I do not agree.

No, he answered to another question, the Jews definitely did not control all the big newspapers in the world. Asked for examples he mentioned *The Times* and the *Daily Herald* in London, *Le Temps* in Paris and others. He admitted he had not personally checked the ownership of every newspaper in the world.

When Inch asked whether the Jews practically monopolized

the white slave traffic, even the court was outraged. Judge Gutsche interfered saying that this was a most improper statement.

> Q: You say everything quoted against the Jewish race is entirely false. Why, through the thousands of years has Jewry been persecuted and no other race has ever been persecuted in a similar manner?
>
> A: Please ask the persecutors!

'It is unfortunate to be a permanent minority in the world,' the witness added.

There followed numerous questions to show that Jews control everything under the sun and the witness answered them all with one word: rubbish. It was not true that the Rothschilds controlled all the gold in the world: 'Your country does,' he responded to one of the questions.

He was becoming very angry. He was not here to defend Jews to this ignorant, rude man. He came to testify about the falsity of the *Protocols of the Elders of Zion*. So, not waiting for another question, he declared: 'My conception of this book is that the author maintains that there has been since 1897 at the Zionist Congress under the leadership of one of the noblest men who lived on God's earth, Dr Herzl, and with the cooperation of your humble servant, such Elders of Zion who decided to conquer the world. That is the point that interests me. I do not make any declaration about Oppenheimer's diamonds, or Samuels' silver or about Rothschild's gold. I declare to you that that book is slanderous!'

> Inch: The *Protocols* are true because what they say has come true!
>
> Sokolov: It is a lie.
>
> Inch: Do you agree that Bolshevism is essentially Jewish in origin and practice?
>
> Sokolov: No.

Von Moltke was much better prepared, and now it was his turn. 'Do you admit that Great Britain, which was the Premier World State at that time, succumbed and humbly bent the knee to a handful of international Jews?'

Sokolov: I deny that most emphatically!'

For hours on end the witness had to stand and deny that the Jews and the Zionists were manipulating every prominent leader in politics, in the economy, in finance and in-press.

Most of von Moltke's questions were more like statements – a scurrilous excursion into Jewish history. The witness, tired of what he considered to be beyond his dignity, answered in monosyllables.

Olivier returned to the Talmud, they realized, when he compelled the witness to explain yet again that this was an old book and it did not refer to Christians but to pagans.

Everybody in the courtroom was beginning to look bored when Olivier shocked them all with his next question. Would it not be advisable for all the governments in the world to act in conjunction with the Jews and burn the Talmud and start a new one, he suggested with a straight face.

Not believing his ears, Sokolov exclaimed: 'Would you like to return to the Middle Ages, when they burned books, and they even burned people?'

They were all mesmerized and listened in stunned silence to Olivier's next words. Looking straight at the witness, he declared, emphasizing every word: 'If it is necessary at the present moment I would not mind if the Jews were burned and their Bible burned!'

The questions did not end there but Sokolov answered as if in a haze, not remembering later what he had said. Is this what is going to happen, he asked himself, not even daring to share the terrible thought with his friends.

He never learned the horrible answer. He died two years later, at the age of 77.

Unfortunately, they all thought that these were the words of a lunatic. Who could foresee that they were actually materializing into a plan of action, I think, almost sixty years later, reading again and again the printed words of the court record.

It had not been necessary to bring from abroad a non-Jewish expert. There was one obvious choice, right there, in their neighborhood: George Frank Dingemans, a professor of Dutch at Rhodes University College in Grahamstown, a Hebrew scholar, a Christian philologist and historian.

After presenting his credentials to the court, the professor came right to the point. He had examined the Inch document and stated unequivocally that this was not a secret document drawn up by an educated Jew. He based his view on the defective Hebrew script and

the ludicrous incongruity between the Hebrew words and the purpose of the alleged 'lectures'.

He followed this statement with a detailed and learned explanation, which the judges never interrupted. The content of the document was utter nonsense, reflecting the lack of intelligence of the
writer, he stated.

After the witness had torn the document apart, limb by limb, both
in language and in content, Reynolds sat down, turning the professor
over for cross-examination. He hoped they would not abuse this
man, who had courageously offered to testify.

Inch came first:

> Q: What is your nationality?
> A: I am a Dutchman of British nationality, born in Holland.
> Q: Will you explain why you are so sympathetic towards Jewry?
> A: I am sympathetic to all nations. And I am sympathetic to
>   the Jews because my Lord and my Savior was a Jew and he
>   said 'Salvation is of the Jew' .... I am not prejudiced in favor
>   of the Jews.
> Q: Did the Jews crucify Jesus Christ?
> A: Yes!
> Q: Have you any Jewish blood in your family?
> A: No.
> Q: If Jesus was a Jew, why didn't he have a crooked nose?

There followed a long inquiry into communism and Marxism and
a very long argument about the meaning of Christianity. With real
anguish in his voice the witness whispered, as if speaking to himself:
'The history of the Christian Church shows that we who constitute
the Churches are very often but poor specimens of what we ought to
be. We show so little of the spirit of Christ, and that is true of individuals, and I am afraid it is also true of Churches. The factor which
has contributed to that fact is that the Bible has so often ceased to be
the real law book of the Churches. There are Churches in which the
Bible is almost an unknown book.'

Then came the *Protocols of the Elders of Zion*.

He was an expert on the subject and was particularly upset by the
use made of this document by vicious and ignorant men. 'I wish to
inform you and the court', he said, looking at Inch, 'that this book, the
Protocols of the Elders of Zion, has been exposed over and over again
as a forgery.' Turning to the judges, he continued: 'If I am an enemy of

any particular race I can easily write stuff to vilify that race and attempt to create the impression that the statement which I made emanated from the people whom I wish to vilify. That is an easy thing to do.'

Pointing to the Inch document, the witness added: 'This document also pretends to be what it is not. It pretends to be stolen from a synagogue, it pretends to be written by a learned Jew, and I maintain that if it ever came from the Synagogue it was put there by the person who wrote it, and he was not a learned Jew, nor was he a learned Gentile.' Turning his attention to Rabbi Levy in the audience, he continued: 'A rabbi is the highest intellectual title it is possible for a Jew to achieve. A rabbi or a college of rabbis are what you may call the Ecclesiastical Supreme Court of Jewry ... Such a man is always a scholar.'

> Q: Could an uneducated Communist Jew have compiled that document?
> A: No, because I do not think that a Jew would ever sink so far.'

But the longest answer was delivered by the witness when asked about the Talmud. Although his answer was turning into a speech, nobody interfered.

> The Talmud is a vast work covering a period of more than a thousand years, the professor explained, from before the birth of Jesus Christ until roughly AD 1000–1100. It contains the opinions of a vast number of men living in various countries, and the opinions expressed are often contradictory and conflicting. It is 'the ocean of Judaic learning'. It may be compared with, say, the whole of the medieval literature in England, Holland and France ... A well-known rabbi says that the first few years of a child's education should be spent on the study of the written law, and then afterwards he should devote himself to the talmudic law.
>
> It is said that there are remarks against the Christians or Christianity – well, is that peculiar to the Talmud? No. There is such a thing as historic sense. A famous writer of about 1800 once and for all formulated the principles that ought to underlie all attempts at historic appreciation, and that principle is that men should be judged by the standards of their age. Now, some of my ancestors, for all I know, may have taken pleasure in burning witches or in capturing slaves and selling them, but it would be somewhat strange if I, living in the twentieth century, were to be charged with being in sympathy with witchcraft or

with the measures that were in the past adopted against witches. Such a charge would be perfectly absurd, because it violates every principle of historic criticism. There was a time when religious dissent was regarded as a political crime punishable by death. Subsequently in many countries, for instance in Protestant countries, religious dissent from the national Church, though not punishable by death any more, attracts severe and grievous penalties. What would any reasonable man say today if he was charged with the beliefs and practices practiced by his ancestors two or three or even more centuries ago. In the Talmud you will occasionally find bitter expressions about Christians, but it should be borne in mind that in the earlier parts of the Talmud the world was largely pagan still, and that the Jewish sages of the time often refer to idolaters and heathens. Subsequently, when, at least in the West, Christianity spread, then you will find sometimes references to the Christians, and no doubt, I feel quite sure, one could find somewhere in the Talmud bitter expressions about Christianity, and when one thinks of the barbarous persecutions that are matters of common knowledge to all students of history, when one thinks of the persecution to which the Jews in the past ages were submitted, if one thinks of the constant ignominy to which they were exposed, then one can hardly blame here and there a certain rabbi for indulging in strong language about the Christians. If they had not done so I submit that they would have been more than human.

In medieval literature you will find reference in Christian literature full of hatred against the Jews, and I submit that the men who still take that attitude towards the Jews are responsible for the bitter feelings that Jews sometimes entertain for so-called Christians whose conduct towards Jews seems to me to violate every principle of Christianity.

Tolerance is of slow growth but unfortunately hatred is of rapid growth, and those knowing it make use of the fact. It takes a wise man to sow sympathy between men but it often only takes a fool, inspired by hatred and possessing the gift of the gab, to sow hatred.

You could have heard a pin drop in the courtroom when the witness stepped off the stand and Reynolds announced that he was through with him, apologizing that he had taken up so much of the court's time.

It was time for the defendants to present their witnesses.

From now on he would speak in the name of all three defendants, von Moltke declared. 'We all realize outside and inside this court', he announced, 'that this case is of a very serious character.' It was not just a defamation case, he declared. As the defendants were pleading justification, in order to expose the international Jewish Plot, it was a case unique in the history of the British Empire.

Turning to the judges he declared: 'I must say, your lordships have been so lenient with us, seeing we are not represented here, and you have given us all the latitude which has been very favorably commented upon by our sympathizers.'

This was outrageous, Reynolds thought. This case was not tried in front of the Nazi sympathizers, he whispered to his colleague. 'Don't be too sure,' Stuart whispered back.

Addressing the court von Moltke announced that they would prove and argue the following points:

1. That the Christian people in South Africa were a divided people.
2. That the international Jew divided them and will keep them divided as long as he can exploit them.
3. That within a few generations all the Christian people in South Africa will have been forced into an unconditional bondage by the international Jew, if they did not awake.
4. The Christian Church and the Christian faith was being disgracefully undermined by the immoral code of the Jew.
5. Within the Christian state of South Africa there was a hostile Jewish state. Similar Jewish hostile states existed in all the countries of the world.

Some of the defense witnesses appeared in Grey Shirt uniforms, decorated with swastikas. They had all attended the meetings, but nobody referred to Rabbi Levy.

The defendants' tactic was clear. Fearing that they might have to compensate the rabbi for defamation, they were trying to minimize the effect of the forged document, at the same time using the court as a public forum for advertising the Jewish 'International Plot'. There was no question now, the lawyers realized, that the court would have to rule on the *Protocols of the Elders of Zion*.

Reynolds had decided to spare the court and keep his cross-examination to a minimum. It would be futile, he explained to his client, to argue with witnesses whose bias was apparent. What do you ask a witness such as Joseph Jacobus van Heerden, a missionary who preaches to natives, who had assured the court he knew the Bible well and that according to the Bible the Jews were out to dominate all other nations? They crucified Christ, the witness declared, 'because Christ was against dirty morality, and they could not stand his attitude and preachings against them'.

Even the judges had looked disgusted, Reynolds reminded the rabbi. It was much more effective to ignore such testimony completely.

At long last they were done with the witnesses concerning Rabbi Levy. It was now time for the witnesses against the Jewish people.

With a triumphant gesture von Moltke invited to the stand and introduced the expert for the defense: Henry Hamilton Beamish, son of an English admiral. He had come to Canada at the age of 18, and had taken part in the Boer War and in the First World War. He had also grown tea in Ceylon and worked in the mines in Rhodesia. But his claim to fame lay in his 'expertise' on the 'Jewish Question', as he himself boasted to the court. He was one of the mentors of the Nazis, he declared; he had traveled around the world and had visited every continent and scores of countries to promote Nazi propaganda. For 30 years he had been concerned with the 'Jewish Question', he said, and one of his main goals was to combat Jewish world dominion. He was one of the leaders of what he called 'The Nazintern', and served as president of numerous national as well as international Nazi organizations. He also headed publishing establishments, such as 'The Britons' in London, and had published important anti-Jewish books, which had been translated into many languages.

He was personally involved in various publications of the *Protocols of the Elders of Zion*, and he knew Victor Marsden, who had translated the *Protocols* into English, as well as Theodor Fritsch in Leipzig. Theodor Fritsch was the publisher of the *Protocols of the Elders of Zion* in Germany, the editor at Hammer Verlag, the publishing house that published the Henry Ford book and refused to stop publication even after Ford's retraction.

To top it all, he was personally acquainted with all the important Nazi leaders, who had drawn many of their ideas from his writings and from personal instruction by him.

He also knew L. Fry, the author of *Waters Flowing Eastward*, he volunteered, but gave himself away when he used the masculine gender, speaking of Lesley Fry as if she was a man. He called himself a 'student of raceology'. A real honest-to-God admitted Nazi, Reynolds noted.

The witness was not through with his boasts. To von Moltke's question about his formal position in racial movements, he stated, unblinking: 'I belong to most of the racist movements in Great Britain. When the League of Gentiles was started some years ago I believe they made me president ... and I have been asked to attend the Pan-Aryan Congress to be held in Bavaria. I am also told that I have just been made president of the Bund Volkischer Europaer, which in English is for keeping the European races pure ... mainly to keep them free from Jew blood.'

Western civilization was in a sorry plight, he continued, and these various movements had been established for the avowed purpose of re-establishing European-Aryan control in government.

Reading the record I suddenly thought: was he describing Protocols of the Aryan Elders of Europe?

On the stand Beamish was warming up to his subject: 'I defy anyone to name any government in the whole of Europe today that is not absolutely controlled by Jews, with the exception of Germany, because she set an example.'

Then, with a voice of authority, he delivered his well-rehearsed 'Expert Opinion' on the *Protocols of the Elders of Zion*. Adopting the well-rehearsed 'Ford tactic', Beamish stated that the *Protocols* were true because he could prove how the whole Jewish plan was being implemented.

The plot had not started with the publication of the *Protocols*. It was a very old plot, he assured the court, and the Jews had been involved in manipulating world history for thousands of years. Both the court and Reynolds questioned him in detail, politely trying to expose the absurdity of his allegations, but he was undeterred: the Jews had engineered the Russian Revolution, the Hungarian Revolution, the Spanish Revolution. The list was endless. Also the Boer War, the Russo-Japanese War, the First World War.

The Jews had also financed William the Conqueror in 1066, they had used Cromwell, and the revolt against Charles I was arranged and financed by Jews. They had corrupted the Church and caused Luther to break away from it. There was not the slightest doubt that Ghandi was manipulated by the Jews, Beamish declared, although the population of India was 240 million, and only about 10,000 Jews.

He had seen documents that the Jews offered to buy St Paul's Cathedral and turn it into a synagogue, and he had seen a photograph of a monument to Judas Iscariot that the Jews had erected in Russia. The judges looked at each other in astonishment, but the witness, unabashed, continued. He had seen matchboxes issued by Jews, having as a trademark the crucified Christ.

When Reynolds remarked with sarcasm that he assumed the witness had not brought these documents and photographs with him, there were some sniggers from the audience, and Beamish turned on the lawyer, whispering audibly: 'I shall deal with you later.'

Then came the institutions: the Jews were in charge of all governments, all institutions, both political and financial, the press and what not. Name after name of all the famous world leaders was mentioned – they were all either Jewish or manipulated by the Jews.

When Reynolds asked with a smile: 'Is there any institution in England that you are prepared to acquit from Jewish influence?' the witness answered, unabashed: 'I candidly do not know of anything except possibly the Church, to a minor extent.'

> Q: Take the Archbishop of Canterbury, he said he does not believe in the *Protocols*.
> A: I have written to him and complained.

Jews definitely ruled South Africa, he volunteered, in spite of the fact that there were only two Jewish members in Parliament. It took only one mosquito to give you malaria, he explained.

Beamish occupied the witness stand for three consecutive days, six sessions, morning and afternoon, on 17, 18 and 19 July. His typed verbatim testimony takes up 119 pages of the court record.

I forced myself to read every page. I reminded myself that it was the year 1934. The world was beginning to realize that Hitler was indeed in power in Germany. Jews in other countries were beginning to be apprehensive. They read their morning papers with a worried expression, then went on with their lives as usual. They calmed their collective conscience by donating money to help Jews who were smart enough to leave Germany.

Most Jews never took the trouble to read Hitler's *Mein Kampf*, I mused, just as they never read the *Protocols of the Elders of Zion*. What garbage, they said. Had they taken the trouble, I thought, they might have seen the writing on the wall. Or maybe they wouldn't have believed even then.

Coming back to the courthouse in Grahamstown, I tried to imagine how it must have seemed then. This was a unique situation, I told myself. What other forum provided an opportunity for such a frank confrontation in July 1934? Here were prominent Nazis, under oath, describing in detail and with straight faces the essence of their theory. They were also stating in public what should be done to the Jews. Yet the procedural decorum was perfectly observed. No matter how insulting and threatening a witness sounded, he was treated by the lawyers with the utmost respect. The people in the audience were quiet and well behaved. The judges wore straight faces, allowing a witness like Beamish to make the most outrageous and revolting statements, carefully observing the rules of procedure.

Beamish was treated as if he was a real expert, his revolting statements taken at face value. When he boasted that he had taught Herr Hitler early in his career and instructed him on the Jewish question, the judges politely asked for details of their conversation.

Beamish was most forthcoming: 'We met in 1921,' he recalled. 'I said to him "How do you propose to deal with the Jews?" because naturally that was the subject, and he said "I have made up my mind." I said "What is that?" – I always get others' opinions first – and he said "We are going to send all our Jews to the allies", and I said "I think they thoroughly deserve it." "But", I said, 'that won't cure the disease: if you have a mad dog and you tie him up in your backyard, that does not get rid of the mad dog." And then Hitler became more reasonable.'

With a smirk on his face Beamish winked at his friends in the audience, who winked back. Nobody said anything. The court decorum was not disrupted.

At the end of the session they all went home to have dinner. The Jews shook their heads in disgust. 'What a lunatic,' they must have said to each other, dismissing Henry Hamilton Beamish from their thoughts.

'What utter rubbish,' the lawyers must have said to each other. They were sure they had succeeded in making him look ridiculous. The court would never believe such a witness.

Unfortunately, I thought, the Jews did not believe him, either.

In front of the courthouse Nazis in uniform were congratulating Beamish, shaking the hands of the defendants.

The judges would wipe that smug look off their faces, the Jews said to each other. 'Wait for the judgment,' they said, not realizing that Beamish was not trying to convince the judges with his lies. He was not talking to them, for the real battle was not being fought in the courtroom and it was not the judges who would deliver the final judgment on the Jews.

The same was happening today with the denial of the Holocaust, I suddenly thought. Not realizing the extent of the denial, the growing movements, the hundreds of publications, the massive use of the internet, all flying in the face of the most recorded event in history, learned judges were presiding over trials, hearing testimony of Holocaust survivors, arguing about rules of evidence, not raising their heads from their judicial benches to see what was really happening out there.

Certain facts are usually presumed by courts in all countries, not requiring proof. In the English system courts take 'judicial notice' of facts which are uncontested by all. Under this rule a litigant is not required to prove that the earth is round, that the sun shines during the day and the moon at night, that the week has seven days and that the Japanese bombed Pearl Harbor. A litigant who would deny these facts would probably be a candidate for a lunatic asylum. But survivors of the Holocaust are asked to relive their traumatic experiences in courts of law where the Holocaust is denied by growing numbers of Neo-Nazis.

With a start I returned to the Grahamstown courtroom.

Inch and Olivier testified first, interrogated by von Moltke.

Inch repeated his story of breaking into the synagogue. He presented an almost too easy target for the cross-examination by Reynolds. His testimony, which takes up 84 pages of the record, was basically worthless in the eyes of the lawyer. It was obvious that he was an uneducated man and a bad liar. He could not have composed the document himself, but he refused to divulge the names of his colleagues, even when ordered by the court to do so. They would be victimized by the Jews, he stated. 'Yet you will victimize the Jews?' Reynolds asked. 'This is a different matter,' Inch responded. 'This is for the Cause.'

Olivier was more intelligent. He had full confidence in the Inch document handed to him by von Moltke. He knew from his experience with Jews that these documents were true. There did exist a Jewish conspiracy. He admitted that the testimony of Inch about breaking into the synagogue 'sounded peculiar' but he could not doubt his word for he was a believer in Christ and if he were to lie under oath he would have to be 'worse than the worst Jew'.

Von Moltke was the last witness for the defense. It was immediately apparent that this witness was trying to address the intelligent public. He started his testimony with a monologue, as there was nobody to interrogate him.

When Hitler came to power, he opened in a conversational tone, he had started pondering how it was possible that an entire nation such as the Germans, one of the most highly cultured people in the world, a nation that had led the Western world, could become barbarians. He had ultimately come to the conclusion that if the Jews, who constituted such a small percentage of the German population, could have wielded that stupendous power in Germany, it was worthwhile studying the subject in his own country for the sake of his own race. He began wondering, he said, whether the 7 per cent of Jews in South Africa could possibly be behind all the havoc wrought in this country, especially during the last 30 or 40 years, and whether it could be their fault that 56 per cent of the European population in South Africa had become 'poor whites', living below the breadline

'It became clear to me', he said, 'that there must be an alien community, a race that would not assimilate with my race, who must be the key to the whole situation.

'My country,' he continued, 'for which my ancestors fought on father's and mother's side. Some bought under the Republic flag, others under the Union Jack, my country for which they spilled their blood, the birthright that they thought they were going to give me, was being rapidly taken away from me and snatched from the Gentile posterity of South Africa by a community of people, who are not interested in the tilling of the soil and were only interested in exploiting the labor of the Gentiles.'

The book that had convinced him of this truth and opened his eyes was the excellent book by Mr Beamish. He had become convinced that his dear homeland was being ruled and controlled by what he called 'octopuses'. Quoting from Beamish he then listed ten of these octopuses: the Diamond Octopus, the Gold Octopus, the Land Octopus, the Food Octopus, the Wholesale Octopus, the Retail Octopus, the Schlesinger Octopus, the International Finance Octopus, the News Octopus, and the Press Octopus. They were all ruled by the interests of these international Jews, and were organized to perfection. He then presented a historical lecture, explaining how the Jews ruled everything. The Jews had four rules, which he had found in documents, von Moltke declared:

1. Whatever we do must be done through others. Use officials such as prime ministers, and ministers not quite prime, first lords, war ministers, and Christian partners.
2. Spend money in improving parliaments, that is spend the people's money in bribing and blackmailing the so-called people's representatives.
3. We don't want to shell out ourselves, i.e. make Christians pay. Make gentiles pay.
4. 'Now he has gone, his widow has nothing, while we have made a large fortune out of him.'

He understood that last rule to mean that Jews should make fortunes out of Gentile ruin.

Then he went on to mention by name all the Jews in South Africa who were wealthy and prominent, and, as such, influenced government although they had only two members in Parliament.

Perfecting the 'Ford tactic' he explained: 'If you stand in front of a building with the plan in your hand, and you find the building coincides in detail with the plan you have in your hand, you have every right to believe that the building was put up by the persons responsible for drawing up the plan.'

In his cross-examination Reynolds established easily that von Moltke had joined 'the cause' only after he had become unemployed, and that he had left many bills unpaid, including his rent and telephone bills, although he owned a few farms and other assets, as the lawyer proved in detail. He answered that the money was more necessary for the movement than to pay the landlord.

Pretending that he had no income, he said that the movement had no bank account, and received small donations, and that he and his wife and children lived on 'a 'few shillings a week' received from Inch. He could not explain how he went around in a luxurious motorcar and kept a bodyguard.

His blatant racism soon became embarrassingly apparent when he stated that if he were leader of the country, he would know how to deal with the colored people. 'They are the sins of our fathers,' he announced. He stated that he was in favor of racial purity.

Judge Gutsche finally intervened, asking how it was possible that he himself had been living in this part of the world for 30 years and had never heard of the 'Jewish Conspiracy'. Von Moltke replied: 'My Lord, you should read the *Protocols*.'

When the judge persisted, putting to him further questions, von Moltke suddenly announced that their cause was being put to ridicule by the court, so he was withdrawing from the case. Having said this he walked out of the court.

The judges seemed unimpressed.

On 21 August 1934, in a somber atmosphere, the court delivered its judgment to a packed courtroom. Members of the community knew that they had won, but were in no mood to gloat.

In the judgment, His Lordship Judge Graham, stated that Inch had not stolen the document, but had concocted it himself or with the assistance of Grey Shirt members, and that von Moltke had deliberately refrained from investigating the truth of the story told by Inch. Olivier, too, should not have published it without proper investigation.

In its dry language the court also found that the existence of a so-called 'World Plot' organized by the Jews, with the object of destroying 'the Christian Church and religion generally and Judaizing the civilized world', had not been established, the defendants having failed to produce a vestige of proof in that direction.

The court stated that the Inch document could reasonably be construed as referring to Rabbi Levy, and that it was most defamatory. It was not necessary, the court ruled, that the whole world should recognize the libel. It was sufficient if those who knew the plaintiff could tell that he was the person meant. A group could not sue for libel under English law, the court explained, so where whole nations or classes or professions are defamed, and no particular person was directly or indirectly indicated, the defamatory statement was aimed too widely and therefore had no legal effect. But where the words referred to all the members of a particular number, group or class, such as 'all the officers of this regiment' or 'all the members of that jury', each one of that particular group or class could sue.

The rabbi noted that, looking for a legal precedent, the court had quoted a Canadian case of 1914, which also concerned the libeling of a Jew. 'Indeed,' he told the community, 'we Jews can claim to be heavy contributors to the laws of libel in every country.'

Members of the community were particularly interested in what the court said about the revolting testimony of Beamish: 'Beamish', the court said, 'impressed us as a man obsessed with the views he enunci-ated. Intolerant in his beliefs, with an exaggerated idea of his own importance ... he has greedily swallowed every anti-Jewish publication that he has discovered and accepted as facts every anti-Jewish statement they contained, and upon this question he is a fanatic. He has been unable to produce a vestige of relevant evidence in support of his charge.'

The damages that the court awarded the rabbi against all three defendants were of no importance, he told the assembled members of the community, but this judgment would convince the public that one could not libel Jews with impunity.

The defendants would not dream of paying the damages, they guessed, and, knowing the rabbi, they assumed that he would do nothing to enforce the judgment.

A few months later they learned with satisfaction that Inch, at least, was made to pay. In criminal proceedings that followed the judgment in the civil case, after a trial that lasted nine days, Inch was convicted by a jury of issuing a forged document and committing perjury at the first trial. The foreman of the jury asked the judge's permission to make a statement, in which he said that the jury considered the crimes committed by Inch to be racial and political.

To general surprise the court sentenced Harry Victor Inch to six years and three months imprisonment with hard labor. Looking straight at the defendant Judge Pittman, who presided over the criminal trial, announced the reasons for this surprisingly harsh sentence:

> I am bound to say that I regard your offenses in a very serious light. Your conduct in hatching this plot was one that was calculated, I think, to work disaster of the most serious character on the community. You launched your plot with extreme recklessness as to the consequences, and in your furtherance of it you have been guilty of what I can only regard as a most flagrant attempt in this court to pervert the course of justice ... I cannot shut my eyes to the harm you might have brought to a community, and which in some measure you actually did bring about. Other persons who may be disposed to follow in your footsteps ... must be warned by the sentence I impose upon you that any such indulgence on their part will meet with the severest retribution.

On 29 October all three Natal newspapers devoted a large amount of space to report on a statement issued by Minister of the Interior J. H. Hofmeyer:

> Unhappily, there is no lie so foolish but some witless folk will be found believing it, and no libel so cruel but eager zealots will give it wider currency once they hear it. People talk about the sacred rights of freedom being in peril, but the sacred right of freedom should not carry with it the license to propagate mass attacks upon communities or sections of a community, or any title to put into circulation statements that can only result in setting race against race, creed against creed or faith against faith. Unhappily it proves too often that those who talk loudest about civil freedom ... are those least fitted to enjoy the rights they speak about ... it is the business of the government to see at all times that negligible minorities are not permitted to go outside the bounds of legitimate propaganda and let loose such doctrines as are bound to breed counter-activities among people as earnest as they, with the inevitable result that the peace of the land is temporarily endangered.

11 Justice in Berne

On Monday morning, 29 October 1934, after it had rained for some days, the people of Berne woke to surprisingly mild weather. Shopkeepers and restaurateurs were looking forward to much business, as they realized that hotels in town were filled to capacity. Representatives of Jewish communities from all over Europe and journalists from around the world had swarmed into the city for the trial. They could not remember when an event had aroused so much interest.

From the early morning hours a queue formed in front of the courthouse, but when the doors opened it soon became clear that most spectators would remain outside, in spite of the fact that the trial had been moved to the largest courtroom in the building. Yet the ushers saw to it that people were admitted in an orderly manner. Nobody pushed. The Frontists, in uniform, were standing around in groups. Many of their sympathizers quietly mixed in the public. The police were there, but had orders to stay in the background as long as their interference was not absolutely necessary.

It was a well-dressed crowd, the men in three-piece suits, the women in tailored costumes. Some seats had been reserved for family members and Odette was there, accompanied by Georges' father. The lawyers sat in the first row, in the customary pinstriped trousers and black morning coats.

Judge Walter Meyer could feel the excitement in the air. He knew that both sides, as well as the representatives of the press, would watch him closely. He must have been awed by the list of witnesses, which he had received in advance. He had never had so many dignitaries in his courtroom, and he had never tried a case that aroused such intense feelings and so much public interest. He had always concentrated on events in his courtroom, with no regard to what was happening outside. He was a no-nonsense judge, and his trials were conducted with dignified decorum. If he was ever criticized by lawyers in their corridor talks, it was for the boredom in his court-room. There was no drama, they sometimes complained to each other, even when a case was a little out of the ordinary. But his instincts told him that this was going to be different. He could not remember any serious disturbance in his court, let alone outside its doors, but he was not surprised when the chief of police came to his chambers that morning and assured him that they had taken all nec-essary precautions to prevent any behavior that might disrupt the court proceedings. It was apparent from his conduct of the trial that he had made a conscious decision to keep to protocol and adopt an attitude of 'business as usual'.

Reading the verbatim record of the trial, it is easy to reconstruct the atmosphere in the courtroom as if one was actually present. To save public expense, the proceedings were recorded by a stenogra-pher hired by the plaintiffs, the record later ratified and adopted by the court. Unusually descriptive, the recorder faithfully noted the behavior of the participants, as well as their words: one witness raised his voice, another one waved his arms or banged the table.

The judge was always addressed as 'Herr President', a lawyer was called 'Fuersprecher'.

Announcing the opening of the trial, Judge Meyer first checked the presence of the parties. The plaintiffs: Herr Marcel Bloch, for the Swiss Jewish community, represented by Professor Dr Matti. Herr Emil Bernheim, for the Jewish community of Berne, represented by Herr Fuersprecher Brunschvig.

In spite of all the pre-trial publicity the public did not know who the actual defendants were. The judge now addressed them one by one: Herr Silvio Schnell, publisher of the *Protocols*, Herr Georg Haller, editor of the National Socialist newspaper *Eidgenossen*, flanked by the legal adviser of the paper Dr Juris Johann Konrad Meyer and the architect Walter Aebersold, a prominent member of the National Front. They rose one after another to confirm their presence.

The defendant Herr Theodor Fischer was absent. Also absent was Fuersprecher Ursprung, who was representing Schnell and Haller. Fuersprecher Ruef announced that he was standing in for him.

Judge Meyer opened by describing the preliminary proceedings, which had started on 16 November 1933. He reminded the parties that the trial had been delayed for almost a whole year, failing to mention the delay tactics in which the defendants had engaged. They had even petitioned the president of the court to disqualify the judge. He had decided to appoint experts, the judge said for the record, to answer four questions:

1. Are the *Protocols of the Elders of Zion* a forgery?
2. Are they a plagiarism?
3. If they are, what was their source?
4. Do the *Protocols* fall under the term *Schundliteratur*?

It had proved difficult to find experts, the judge reported. Pastor Münchmeyer, suggested by the defendants, had not responded to the letter of the court. The plaintiffs knew that Münchmeyer was a well-known German anti-Semite who lived in Oldenburg.

Professor Hause, the judge continued, suggested by defendant Fischer, had informed the court that his expertise was in oriental languages only.

The judge then presented the two experts who were present in court. Professor Arthur Baumgarten had been appointed by the plaintiffs. He was of German origin, but had given up his post as professor at the University of Frankfurt-am-Main after the National Socialists took over, and was at present teaching legal philosophy at the law faculty of the University of Basle.

Herr Carl Albert Loosli, whom the judge presented as a writer from Bumpliz, had been appointed by the court.

As the judge mentioned their names they both rose and bowed.

So far the defendants had not found an expert.

'The plaintiffs will call their first witness,' the judge announced.

Georges Brunschvig and Professor Matti had discussed at length the order in which they would call their witnesses. They must presume, they decided, that Judge Meyer was completely ignorant of the situation of the Jews in other countries, and particularly in Russia. In order to prepare the ground for their Russian witnesses they needed a very prestigious Jewish leader, who was also a man of the world, as their first witness. There was a consensus that they should open with the testimony of Professor Chaim Weizmann.

Born in 1874 in the village of Motol near Pinsk, in the Russian Pale of Settlement, Weizmann was 60 years old at the time of the trial. Educated in the Jewish tradition in the *shtetl* of his birth, he later turned to scientific studies and became a famous scientist. He was also one of the most outstanding Jews of his generation. Barred from Russian universities, where a *numerus clausus* was strictly applied, he had studied in Germany, where he first joined a Zionist group of students. Having completed his studies at the University of Geneva, he was fluent both in German and in French. Later he settled in England, adopting its language and culture, and made this country the center of his scientific career.

Active in the Zionist movement from its beginning, Weizmann was a firm supporter of Asher Ginsburg, known as Achad Ha'am, who visualized Palestine as a cultural and spiritual center for the Jews of the world, but he was also influenced by Herzl, and became an ardent supporter of Jewish political nationhood, believing the two could be combined. He pleaded the Zionist cause before presidents, kings and political leaders around the world, and was instrumental in convincing Lord Balfour to issue, on 2 November 1917, the famous Balfour Declaration, promising to create in Palestine a homeland for the Jewish people. Jews around the world considered this document as their Magna Carta, and rejoiced when the British Mandate for Palestine was ratified by the international community at the Peace Conference in Versailles in 1919. It was at this conference that crude copies of the *Protocols of the Elders of Zion* were anonymously placed in front of each delegate's seat.

In 1920, at the Zionist Congress in London, Weizmann was elected president of the Zionist Organization. When the State of Israel was established in 1948, Chaim Weizmann, universally recognized as the most eminent figure in Jewish life, became its first president. But Weizmann was not only a political figure. He was first and foremost a scientist and a man of culture, and his lasting contributions to the State of Israel were the two outstanding academic institutions founded by him: the Hebrew University in Jerusalem and the Weizmann Institute of Science in Rehovot, where he lived from 1937 and where he died in 1952.

His first witness, Georges Brunschvig informed the court in Berne, was Professor Chaim Weizmann, who introduced himself as a professor of chemistry. He had arrived the evening before and there had been no time to interview him, but this witness did not need to be coached, Georges had assured Matti. There would be no surprises here, he said with confidence.

The judge plays an active role in Swiss proceedings, and from his first question the lawyers realized that he had done his homework.

Q: Did you attend the first Zionist Congress in Basle?

A: No. I was spending a vacation in Russia with my parents, and I could not raise the fare and get the necessary papers to leave Russia in time for the Congress.

Q: You were introduced as one of the Zionist leaders. Do you know if there were any secret meetings at the Congress?

A: Definitely not. All meetings were open to the public, and this includes not only the plenary but also committees.

The next question put by the judge went directly to the heart of the matter.

Q: Were you familiar with the agenda of that Congress?

A: Yes, indeed.

Q: Can you confirm that part of the agenda dealt with establishing world domination by the Jews?

A: No, your honor, nothing like that was ever discussed.

Fischer, who had arrived by then, sniggered loudly and was admonished by the judge.

Q: Were all Jews in the world represented at the Congress?

A: No, your honor. It was mostly the poor Jews from Eastern Europe. Jews in Western Europe opposed Zionism and were not represented. The prominent Jews in finance and industry were not present, but many came who belonged to intellectual circles. Jews in Western Europe thought the Zionist movement would harm their standing in the various communities.

They had planned to hold the Congress in Munich, Weizmann added, but the Jews there opposed it so much that they rented all the big halls in the city so that the Congress could not be held there as planned! The organizers were lucky to find a suitable hall in Basle, the witness recalled, so they had moved the Congress to that city.

Weizmann had given much thought to the manner in which he would explain to a Swiss judge the essence of Zionism, so he was pleasantly surprised at the judge's next question.

Q: Is the essence of Zionism exactly what the League of Nations has resolved, a Homeland for the Jewish People under the British Mandate?

A: Exactly, your honor. No world domination!

Then, without further ado, the judge introduced the *Protocols of the*

Elders of Zion, asking the witness whether he was familiar with this document.

To everybody's surprise Weizmann admitted that he had never read the *Protocols* in full, but he described how he had first heard of them. In 1918 he had been sent to Palestine by the British authorities as head of a commission attached to the headquarters of General Allenby. One day General Deeds (known as Sir William Deeds), the representative of the Department of Intelligence, had shown him four or five typewritten pages and asked his opinion. 'I read the text and retorted that it was utter rubbish,' the witness recalled. The general had claimed that it was an important document that should not be ignored – it was in the handpack of every Russian officer, junior and senior alike. It had been given to him, the general said, by British officers who had served at the headquarters in Kawkaz, who had translated it for his benefit.

This was the first time, the witness said, that he had seen some pages of the *Protocols of the Elders of Zion*. Shaking his head in disgust, Weizmann looked at the judge, stating in a clear voice: 'These *Protocols* surely stem from a sick fantasy – something from a different planet.'

To Georges Brunschvig's question Weizmann stated: 'I am no expert on religion, just a chemist, but I am familiar with our prayers, there is nothing in them to even remotely remind one of the *Protocols*. We Zionists have no world-domination appetite or tendencies ... it is all false, maliciously false ... aimed at making things even tougher for the Jews, who have a tough life anyway.

'Unity of the Jews is yet another legend,' he added with a sad smile, and went on to explain how Jewish texts were often misquoted, or quoted out of context. The defendants laughed loudly, inviting another stern admonishment from the judge.

'Why are they upsetting the judge?' Georges asked Matti.

'They are playing to the audience,' the professor whispered. 'You had better get used to it. This is how they are going to conduct the whole trial, for want of a proper defense.'

To forestall the defense, Georges Brunschvig faced the witness and held up the Alfred Rosenberg edition of the *Protocols*.

> Q: In his introduction Alfred Rosenberg quotes something you said in one of your lectures, which to him sounds like an admission of the existence of a Jewish conspiracy. You are quoted as saying: 'We shall be in Palestine, whether you want us here or not. You can delay our arrival or hinder it,

but you would be better off helping us, otherwise our growing power will turn into a destructive force, which will cause a crisis in the whole world.'

A: I am not sure that the journalist quoted me correctly, because in Palestine I made it a practice to speak Hebrew. But the idea expressed there was one I repeatedly used in my lectures and in my conversations with world leaders. In countries like Russia, where millions of Jews were persecuted and discriminated against, it is only natural that young people, out of despair, would join revolutionary movements. This is the Jewish tragedy. Treated in an inhumane manner, our young people have nothing to lose. We are fighting these tendencies. We wish our young people to use their energy in a positive constructive manner, and indeed, in free democratic countries, like England, France, Switzerland and Holland the bulk of the Jewish population belong to conservative circles. We in the Zionist movement have given the youth a new hope, and there are no Zionists in the revolutionary circles. We do not wish to harm others, but we warn that people who are driven to despair should not be pushed in the wrong direction. As history shows, this is not a tendency unique to Jews.

The experts were allowed to intervene at any stage, with the permission of the judge. Professor Baumgarten now stood and, with a nod from the judge, he explained at length the well-known tactic used in anti-Semitic propaganda to quote Jewish texts out of context.

When Weizmann explained to the court that there was division even in the Zionist movement, Fischer, who had been making vocal remarks all along, rose ceremoniously and declared that he himself was a Zionist because he wished all the Jews to go to Palestine.

Weizmann responded in a sarcastic tone: 'Your support of Zionism leaves me cold. Friends like you I don't need.'

The judge was about to release the witness, when he noticed that Loosli was standing. Bowing to the bench he explained that a basic premise of the *Protocols* was that Jews were united, acting under one leadership. In his research he had examined this premise and had come to the conclusion that in actuality Jews were as divided as could be. Permitted to question the witness on this issue, he asked him to describe to the court the differences between Sephardim and Ashkenazim.

Sephardim were the descendants of Jews who lived in Spain or Portugal before the Jews were expelled from those countries in 1492, Weizmann explained. They were now scattered in many countries. Ashkenazim, in the broad sense, were Jews originating from Western and Eastern Europe.

The two didn't easily mix, Weizmann explained: they differed in their traditions, in their customs, in their culinary tastes, in their styles of prayer. They actually worshipped at different synagogues. Each group had their own rabbis, and there was very little intermarriage and even social contact between them, he added.

But this was not all, Loosli stated, having made a study of Jewish modern life. Could the witness now describe to the court the difference between Chasidim and Misnagdim.

Chasidim, the witness replied, were members of a popular religious movement started in the latter part of the eighteenth century. It was marked by ecstasy, mass enthusiasm and charismatic leadership, with particular stress on prayer rather than learning. Misnagdim, on the other hand were Jews who advocated study of the Torah and the Talmud, and held intellectual endeavor in the highest esteem. Not only was there bitter disagreement between the two groups, but the Chasidim were also divided into various groups, led by their own charismatic leaders with recognized lines of succession.

There was also much strife among the Zionists, but the court may rest assured, he added with a smile, that not one Zionist was a Bolshevik.

Later in the trial they would call witnesses who had attended the Basle Congress to testify to the fact that there had been no secret meetings, and that all meetings had been public and open to the press. They even called stenotypists who had recorded the proceedings for the record and swore that no secret meetings could have taken place. But Professor Matti had insisted that the most effective witnesses be called as early as possible in the trial. If they allow the judge to become bored by technical details, they would lose his interest, he maintained. They must keep him alert, intrigued by the story unfolding in his court. This was also true for the media.

It had been agreed that Georges, who had interviewed the witnesses, would be the one to interrogate them.

Their next witness, Georges Brunschvig announced, was Graf Armand Alexander du Chayla.

He had been born in 1885, the witness said, in answer to the judge, after stating his full name for the record. He had no defined profession. He lived in Paris on avenue Conférence. He was a practicing Russian Orthodox Christian, of French citizenship.

This witness had a long story to tell, and the lawyers knew that the judge might get impatient listening to all the details. Having interrogated him in Paris, Georges refused to skip any part of the story. To facilitate matters they decided to introduce the articles published by du Chayla, and give the judge an opportunity to read them at his leisure. The articles had been translated from the French for the benefit of the court.

Glancing at the articles presented to him, du Chayla verified their content. Indeed, these five articles published in the newspaper *Dernières Nouvelles* on 12 and 13 May and on 1, 2 and 3 July in 1921 had been written by him.

At Brunschvig's suggestion the court allowed the witness to tell his story in his own words.

In the year 1909, du Chayla started, he had been in Russia to study the Russian Orthodox Church. He had then met Sergei Nilus, who lived in the province of Kaluga in the state of Kassiew. Nilus had a brother who was president of the Moscow court. He was married to Madame Ozerova, the daughter of a former Russian ambassador to Athens, but had previously lived for a long time with Nataliia Komarovskaia. When his former lover became sick and completely ruined, as the witness described it, Nilus took her in to live in his house. He had a son born out of matrimony, who had been legitimized by the tsar.

Du Chayla had been told by the lawyers to stick to the most important facts, as the judge would have an opportunity to read all the details for himself.

Nilus had been a religious writer, he continued, and had a place in the province of Ural. Then he joined the government, served for a while as investigating judge in Kawkaz, left his job and lived mostly in France, in Biarritz. He returned to Russia after facing financial ruin, and lived as a religious writer in a monastery. His property was mostly in real estate, but it was heavily mortgaged and in the end he had nothing.

Du Chayla still felt uncomfortable testifying about Nilus, whose hospitality he had enjoyed, he had confessed to Georges. But he must convey the right impression, Georges insisted. So, choosing his words carefully, the witness now looked directly at the judge: 'I had the impression that the man was a paranoid. He was of good cheer, well educated and talented but in the grip of an *idée fixe*: his thoughts concentrated solely on the coming of the Antichrist.'

Nilus had insisted that he read *the Protocols of the Elders of Zion*, and watched over him while he sat in his house and read the whole French version of the *Protocols*.

'It was handwritten', du Chayla recalled, 'in various handwritings. It was obvious that more than one person had worked on the same text. It was entitled in French *Le Protocoles des Sages de Sion*. I cannot remember the length, although I held the manuscript in my hand, and sitting at the table in Nilus's apartment I read it from beginning to end. It was an exercise book. I clearly remember that there was a light blue stain on the first page and some of it was not written in literary French. I seem to remember that there were some expressions that were not in good French. Nilus told me he had received the manuscript from General Rachkovskii indirectly. He told me that he had received the French text through the intervention of Madame Komarovskaia. This was the original, he stated.'

Everybody was holding his breath. For the first time a live witness was testifying under oath that he had held in his hands and read the original text of the *Protocols of the Elders of Zion*. You could hear the pens scratching as the journalists busily made notes.

Discussing with the witness his testimony Georges had insisted that he mention the story of Balaam's donkey. He explained that whenever the veracity of the *Protocols* was challenged, its promoters usually evaded confrontation with facts that proved the forgery, by invoking 'the Ford tactic'. Even if the document was false, they said, its content illustrated actual reality. The *Protocols* only described and explained what was happening before their very eyes, they told the public. This was the reason, Georges explained, why every published version of the *Protocols* was preceded by a long introduction that compared current events with parts of the 'Jewish Plan' set forth in the *Protocols*.

It was generally believed that this tactic had been invented by the editor of the *Dearborn Independent* to evade a libel suit. It now appeared that it had been invented by Nilus, who was the source of all the publications of the *Protocols*. 'Please, do not forget to repeat in court the story of the donkey,' Georges had urged. The judge might not be familiar with the story of Balaam's donkey, Professor

Matti had said, he himself remembered it only vaguely. Lifschitz had immediately removed the Bible from a bookshelf and read aloud Chapter 22 of the fourth book of the Torah, Numbers.

In the bible the donkey is called an 'ass' and the ass is a she.

Moab was preparing for their confrontation with the children of Israel, who had come out of Egypt, and Balak, king of Moab, had sent messengers to Balaam, asking him to curse the children of Israel because 'He whom thou blessest is blessed, and he whom thou cursest is cursed.' But God came unto Balaam and said: 'Thou shalt not curse the people, for they are blessed.'

After much hesitation and repeated offerings of honors and gifts from Balak, Balaam finally succumbed and saddled his ass and went with the princes of Moab, accompanied by two servants, ignoring God's warning.

God's anger was kindled and he sent his angel to block the way, but the only one who was permitted to see him was the ass. There followed a series of attempts made by the ass to circumvent the angel, and each time Balaam smote the ass with his staff. Finally the ass fell down under Balaam, who smote her again.

Now they were coming to the relevant passage, Lifschitz said, for at this point the Lord opened the mouth of the ass, and she said unto Balaam, 'What have I done unto thee, that thou hast smitten me these three times ... am not I thine ass, upon which thou hast ridden ever since I was thine unto this day?' Then the Lord opened the eyes of Balaam, and he saw the angel of the Lord, who explained to him that the ass had actually saved his life, for had she not turned from him, he would have slain Balaam and saved the life of the ass.

The story is used in literature, Lifschitz pointed out, as an example of the many ways in which the Lord may deliver his message, even 'from the mouth of an ass'.

It was the judge who provided the witness with the perfect opening, when he asked if Nilus himself had believed that the *Protocols* were genuine.

'I had the impression that Nilus himself doubted the authenticity of the *Protocols*,' du Chayla recalled with a smile. 'When I said that it must be a forgery, a provocation, he replied: 'Yes, but God has used a donkey for his purposes in the story of Balaam, he can therefore use a forgery to expose the truth.'

There was open laughter in the courtroom, and even the judge could not suppress a smile. The story sounded funny in a Swiss courtroom, du Chayla thought, but it had been far from funny when he had listened to Nilus in Optina Pustyn. The ravings of a fanatic were never funny, he thought.

Nilus may have been just one eccentric man, the judge wondered, but what about the others who had distributed the *Protocols* in Russia? Why was it done, and how effective had it been?

'Right to the point,' Matti whispered to Georges.

The *Protocols* were distributed in Russia with the purpose of influencing the tsar to take a reactionary and anti-Jewish stand, du Chayla stated. Their intention was to blame the Jews for everything. And, yes, indeed, the *Protocols* had a direct influence on the 'armies' of Denikins, Wrangels and Petlura, who were responsible for the big pogroms. The *Protocols* served as an important means of incitement in the promotion of the pogroms.

The judge wondered whether Nilus might have forged the *Protocols* himself. That was impossible, the witness retorted: Nilus was an honest man but he would not vouch for his sanity, he was in the grip of this *idée fixe*, he believed that the Jews and the Freemasons were in cohorts to destroy Russia and the Christian world.

What stand did the Church take concerning the *Protocols*, the judge asked. In the Church the opinions were divided, du Chayla answered, and in the end, in 1910, a bishop was dispatched to Optina Pustyn to conduct an inquiry. As a result Nilus was asked to leave the monastery.

Did the witness ask Nilus if he had conducted any inquiry as to the origin of this handwritten notebook, the judge wanted to know. Nilus insisted that he had received the *Protocols*, indirectly, from Rachkovskii, whom he knew to be high in the official hierarchy, and he had therefore no reason to doubt his word.

The lawyers were confident that the judge was impressed by du Chayla. Even a poker-faced judge cannot completely hide his feelings and his attitude to a witness, especially when he poses the questions himself. They were sure that Judge Meyer would read the articles and not insist that the witness repeat all the details. 'Never bore a judge,' Matti had insisted. 'Confine yourself to the most important facts.' He had been pleased to notice how quickly Georges learned.

The defense tactic soon became apparent: if you cannot confront the testimony, try to impeach the witness.

What kind of paper was *Dernières Nouvelles*, in which the witness had published his articles, Fuersprecher Ruef opened.

This newspaper represented and supported the military, the monarchy and anti-Bolshevik ideas, du Chayla explained. It was a National Democratic paper that supported all spiritual movements. Its editor was Miljukoff, a supporter of the monarchy, a well-known historian, professor at various foreign universities.

Asked by the defense whether the paper was pro-or anti-Jewish, the witness could not contain his anger: it was exactly like all papers in France. This question did not exist in France. 'Jew' was a religious term, like 'Catholic' or 'Protestant'. He then went on to explain that he had previously acted as a freelance journalist, mostly in religious matters, and that he had written the articles on the *Protocols* at Miljukov's suggestion.

To another question du Chayla answered that he had last seen Nilus in 1910, when he had enrolled in the Petrograd Faculty of Theology, where he had stayed until he was drafted in 1914 with the outbreak of the war.

The defense had no more questions and the witness was excused.

The lawyers had wisely decided to present at this time documents that supported du Chayla's testimony: first, the affidavit of Princess Radziwill, while the description of the document was still fresh in the judge's memory. He could not help but be impressed by the mention of the copybook, the various handwritings and the blue stain on the cover of the original manuscript of the *Protocols*.

Next came an impressive document they had received from the famous historian, Boris Nikolaevskii, who would testify later in the trial. It was a statement made by a neighbor of Nilus, and confirmed in the presence of the witness on 1 June 1934. Her name was Maria Dmitrievna Kashkina, *née* Countess Buturlin, and since her marriage in 1905 she had lived with her husband on an estate near the monastery Optina Pustyn. Actually her husband's ancestors had donated the land on which the monastery had been built.

She and her husband had known Nilus well, she said in her sworn statement, but her husband considered him 'a very tricky and shady character, who ought to be very carefully watched'.

Describing the household of Nilus, Kashkina revealed that apart from his wife and Madame Komarovskaia, whom she called 'his former wife', there was another woman who lived with her daughter in an adjoining little house. The daughter served as a medium in spiritual seances conducted in the circle in which Nilus moved. According to village gossip she was his daughter.

In those years, Kashkina said in her statement, Optina Pustyn was a center for all sorts of 'holy idiots', such as one Mitya Kozelsky, a butcher by trade, a big strong fellow who could hardly utter recognizable words. Mitya had the reputation of being able to cast out devils by hitting patients with his fists and submitting them to all kinds of indignities. He actually married a rich widow from whose body he was supposed to have driven seven devils.

It was Nilus, Kashkina said, who introduced Mitya to the higher spheres of society in St Petersburg, where he himself was admitted as Ozerova's husband.

Mitya's success was complete when Nilus accompanied him for an audience with the royal couple. The tsar had been impressed by a painting in which their ailing son was being rescued by Mitya from a host of devils with horns, tails and hoofs, who were trying to get at the young tsarevich.

The local population was extremely angry, blaming Nilus for embarrassing the tsar by presenting an idiot in court. Not only were the local peasants aware of the true character of Mitya, they were also familiar with the unholy doings of the monks of the monastery. It was an open secret, Kashkina said, that not far from the monastery there was a whole hamlet populated by 'the monks' sins'. They had no high esteem for those 'fools of God' as they called them.

Kashkina's detailed description of the Nilus household was very similar to that in du Chayla's articles.

The judge might wonder whether all this was relevant, the lawyers thought, but decided that Nilus, whose 'masterpiece' was being presented all around the world as the work of a great writer and philosopher, must be presented in his true light. The judge must be made to realize that the man had been a fanatic, immersed in Satanic studies, a firm believer in supernatural powers, a friend of idiots. Sergei Alexandrovich Nilus was a key figure in the story of the *Protocols*. They hoped to impress the judge with reliable evidence of his true character.

Judge Meyer glanced at the documents and promised to read them at his leisure. The defendants looked completely uninterested.

'Please call your next witness,' the judge said to Georges Brunschvig and Professor Matti.

Their next witness, Georges announced, was Sergei Svatikov.

Svatikov mounted the witness stand with confident steps and announced that he was a professor, born in 1880, living in Paris.

His doctorate from the University of Heidelberg was in philosophy, and he therefore spoke German. In St Petersburg he had been on the faculty of law.

He had first heard about the *Protocols of the Elders of Zion* in St Petersburg in 1905 and read them at the Academy of Science, in Russian. This was the Nilus edition, he explained to the judge.

Without waiting for further questions he exclaimed:

'The so-called *Protocols* are a forgery! I have dealt with the matter in two capacities: first, as a high-placed official of the Provisional Government, between February and October 1917; and second, as a journalist and political emigrant in Paris in 1921.'

Repeating the full story he had told Georges Brunschvig, he described how he had been dispatched to Europe as a police commissioner of the provisional government around April 1917, to liquidate the Secret Police of tsarist Russia, having been appointed by the minister of justice as special investigating judge for important affairs. It was in Paris that he again heard of the *Protocols of the Elders of Zion*.

> In 1905 I myself, as well as the Russian intelligentsia and the media, did not take the *Protocols* seriously. We all saw that it was a forgery, or, at best, a figment of somebody's fantasy. I was not aware that the Russian government was at all interested in this document in 1905. Graf Popov, who had served as cabinet minister in the years 1903–1916, told me he had never heard of the *Protocols*. There may have been individuals in the government who were familiar with the *Protocols*, but not the government as such. The same is true of the Church – individuals may have been involved but not the Church as such.

Asked about Jewish influence, he stated categorically that there was no such thing. Equality of rights was proclaimed for all citizens and there might have been a bigger number of Jews in office. 'We thought we had done away with the "Jewish Question" once and for all.

'May I tell a little story, to illustrate the atmosphere in Russia?' he asked haltingly, and continued at a nod from the judge.

> There was only one time that I heard of the oncoming Jewish 'takeover' of Russia. I served at the time as deputy governor of Petersburg. One day a man suddenly entered my office in a state of great excitement and cried: 'Arrest me, beat me, tie me up!' I said: 'What do you want, dear sir?' He answered: 'I cannot

wait any longer, for a whole week I have been waiting for the Jewish police to come, for now the Jewish government is coming and I wish to drink the goblet (*phiole*) of the Jewish revenge!' I inquired who he was and he told me he was a very reactionary journalist who had always written against the Jews and he believed he was immediately going to be murdered or something similar. He was convinced that it was the end of God's kingdom on earth and from now on the Jews would reign in Russia. I told him: 'My dear sir, you are free to think what you like, I can't even say that I liked your articles very much, so now you may indeed have your *phiole*.' I had somebody bring in a glass of cold water, handed it to him and said: 'Drink your *phiole* then go home and calm your wife.'

This time the whole courtroom burst out laughing, relieving the tenseness in the air. Even the judge smiled.

'I must say that we in the provisional government did not see or feel anything to make us aware of any Jewish influence,' the witness concluded.

After a small pause he resumed, without waiting for another question.

It was true, he said, that many Jews got posted to government positions that had previously been closed to them. Many Jewish young people got into the local administration. 'I can speculate that the bureaucracy of old did not change its ideas and many were sent to Siberia. The Jews, on the other hand, responded to the search for new officials, joined the Bolsheviks and got posted. This was a fact and I am not judging anybody.'

Asked by Professor Matti about anti-Semitism in government he answered that neither the provisional government nor the Bolshevik one were anti-Semitic. As to the tsarist government, it was the most anti-Semitic in the world, except the Rumanian government. 'Today again the Jewish masses suffer terribly under the present Bolshevik regime,' he added sadly. 'These people have lost everything, the money they had earned in their small businesses and craftsmanship. They are also enslaved like all other 130 national groups of the old regime. Nevertheless there are now more Jewish functionaries than under the old regime, when this road was officially closed to them.'

The Russian Orthodox Church had never forgotten its Jewish origin and was never officially anti-Semitic, although individual priests might have been.

The judge thought the testimony of this witness was drawing to an end, but Georges Brunschvig asked for his indulgence, explaining that the witness had much more to say. They had now come to the story of the agent Bint.

Speaking in German, Svatikov referred to him as Heinrich Bint. He then repeated to the court everything Bint had told him about the activities and the forgeries of Piotr Rachkovskii, and how he had personally taken some part in what the witness called 'the last and biggest forgery, the *Protocols of the Elders of Zion*'.

Bint had been in the service of the Secret Police even before Rachkovskii, Svatikov explained. In the nineteenth century the Russians had secret agents in Paris and Geneva. After the death of Alexander II, a Secret Police was established in Paris with the purpose of protecting the life of the tsar, and Bint became part of this organization in 1880. Four years later, in 1884, Rachkovskii was appointed director of this foreign agency. Since then Bint had been asked again and again to prepare all kinds of forged documents without telling the other agents.

Svatikov then repeated in detail what Bint had told him of all Rachkovskii's forgeries, of his numerous provocations and of the agents who had been assigned to these duties – everything he had told Georges Brunschvig at their meeting in Paris.

Rummaging in a bag he had brought with him, he presented to the court a forged book printed in Paris, but purporting to be printed in Switzerland. He now had everybody's attention, but Georges directed him back to the *Protocols*.

Bint had told him, the witness said with a firm voice, that the biggest forgery was a document called the *Protocols of the Elders of Zion*. These were the alleged protocols of a high council or something like that, where the members, the Elders of Zion, sat and discussed how to organize the Jewish kingdom on earth. Bint could not furnish him with a copy because he said that it was too secret.

The courtroom was completely silent as Svatikov described how Golovinskii had worked on the forgery in the Bibliothèque Nationale in Paris, under the guidance of Rachkovskii. The excitement mounted as he related Bint's admission that he had personally remunerated the forgers for their work, paying them in cash, with no receipts and no witnesses.

Georges kept still for a few seconds, not wishing to spoil the moment. This important testimony needed to sink in. He knew that the witness had another surprise for the court.

The judge then asked whether the witness knew the source used for the forgery of the *Protocols*.

Oh, Svatikov replied, there could be no doubt that the forgers had used the famous book by the French lawyer Maurice Joly, *Dialogue aux Enfers entre Machiavelli et Montesquieu*. As far back as 1921, he added, on the advice of the famous journalist Burtsev, he had gone to the Bibliothèque Nationale in Paris and found the four copies of Maurice Joly's book. In one of them he had discovered marked passages corresponding to the passages used in the *Protocols*.

'I do not know whether they had been marked by Golovinskii,' he added, wishing to be completely accurate, 'but it was Bint who told me that Golovinskii had worked on the *Protocols* in the National Library.' Georges had advised him to let the judge draw his own conclusions. This was the province of judges, not witnesses, he had said with a smile.

Brunschvig chose this moment to approach the bench and place before the judge the copy of Maurice Joly's book. It was a dramatic moment and Georges made the best of it. 'This, Herr President, is the book from which the *Protocols of the Elders of Zion* were plagiarized.' Alongside it he placed a document where passages of the Joly's book were printed alongside identical passages of the *Protocols*. The judge took a few minutes to examine both the book and the document, and they were all aware of his total absorption. They noticed his reluctance to put the book aside when he finally turned back to the witness.

Svatikov then described how the *Protocols* had been reproduced in many languages, adding: 'I myself, as bibliophile and bibliograph, have held many editions in my hands. People like Professor Sokolov and General Dragomirov, who were part of the information department of the so called "White Army" in south Russia, had distributed many copies of this document in cities like Kiev, Kharkow and Odessa. The aim was to convince the people that everything, the Civil War, the October Revolution, the February Revolution, they were all the work of Jews. As proof they were told: please read the *Protocols of the Elders of Zion* and see who is now king of the Russians, the Jews!' The witness spat out this last sentence with obvious disgust.

Some people had feelings about things to come, he said, and Nilus had actually foreseen much of the coming Revolution, but had dressed it up as the coming of Satan and the Jews. That is why he published the *Protocols* in three or four editions.

Matti had some more questions about the *Protocols*.

He had seen the *Protocols* in many languages, Svatikov said, but never in Hebrew.

The man who had executed the forgery, using Joly's book, did not know French very well. He translated the passages from Joly into Russian very badly and then sewed the parts together with crude white yarn! Like all other forgeries of Rachkovskii, this work had no literary merit. It was apparent that it was done in a hurry, for immediate use.

All the forgeries of Rachkovskii prepared between 1884 and 1902 were produced in the same way.

'Watch now', Matti wrote to Georges, 'how they will use their routine tactic of ignoring the facts and trying to impeach the witness.'

Georges bowed to him in agreement when Fischer asked his first question: 'I would like to ask the witness whether he is a member of the Jewish Nation.'

> A: Of course not, we have been authentic Russians (*echte Russen*) since many centuries. We never had a Jew in our family!
>
> Q: Is it not logical that the Jews initiated the revolution as the Tsarist regime was against them.
>
> A: The Jews were victims of official Russia so it was only natural that they should oppose the regime. But in the beginning their part corresponded to their percentage in the population – 4 per cent. Later, when many of them were compelled to emigrate in the wake of the pogroms, their numbers increased, but they were never anarchists like Bakunin. They were a thinking, state-oriented element. I myself wrote a book in 1914 about the Jews in the Russian Revolution, which was never published.

The experts also had some questions. The witness first responded to Baumgarten.

In 1904, after Rachkovskii had lost his Paris job, he was still active at home, and was indirectly involved in the murder of Minister of the Interior von Pleve. Later, in 1905, Rachkovskii became the favorite of Tsar Nikolai II. He was recalled from his obscure exile by General Trepow, the commander of the Palace Guard, who appointed him director of police, but actually he served as deputy director of political affairs. For a few months he almost ruled Russia and initiated

many provocations, such as the affair of Lapuchin, the former director of the Police Department.

Then Loosli rose, saying he had but one question, which Svatikov
answered in a loud voice: 'Kerenskii was not Jewish! Neither was
Lenin or his wife. Her mother was buried in Berne!'

Bowing to the court, Loosli explained that he was referring to
actual allegations that had been made.

Then the defendant Haller rose, and made the witness repeat at
length his relationship with Bint.

To one of the questions Svatikov responded: 'I was sure that the
Protocols would be buried after the revelation of *The Times* in 1921,
but I saw them again even in 1929. I offered proof to Russian newspapers that they were a forgery, but they advised me to save my proof
for my private archive! They were not interested,' he said with a
shrug.

Facing Haller he continued with sarcasm in his voice: 'I must say
to Herr Nationalsocialist that I am sorry that they have to use such
poor weapons like the *Protocols*. They could fight their enemies, or
their imaginary enemies, with real honest weapons. This is not the
Jewish language! These forgeries were done by Russian functionaries.'
Turning then to the court he cried out:

> As a Russian citizen and former member of the democratic pro-
> visional government, I must tell you that this concerns our
> national pride! We must defend our national honor! This is a lie,
> a legend, a forgery, arranged by the criminal Rachkovskii.
> Therefore it is in our interest to learn what this independent
> court of a free people, in the most free democratic country in
> the world, will have to say in the matter. I, as an honest and
> truth-speaking witness, who has held confidential posts in the
> Russian democratic government, I am telling you, most honor-
> able judge, this is no more than a legend!

Taken back by this sudden announcement, and without thinking,
Haller exclaimed that as the witness had never before made such a
declaration, how could they have known that this was a forgery?

Fuersprecher Ruef seemed shocked.

'Is this an admission?' Georges whispered to Matti. 'They will
soon recover,' Matti whispered back.

And indeed they did, as Georges realized when Fuersprecher Ruef
began his interrogation.

He started by trying to undermine the credibility of Bint, maintaining that Svatikov had paid him for the information.

'In 1917,' Svatikov replied in an offended voice, 'when I was an official, I paid nothing for Bint's information. This would have been illegal. Later, in 1921, Bint was a poor man and I was an independent journalist and I bought from him not information but documents. The information was the same as in 1917.'

The witness seemed very disturbed. 'I am a lawyer, and I know exactly where this line of questioning is leading!' he added after a pause, banging the table and then apologizing to the court. 'I have never paid for a certain kind of information, I paid for a mass of documents in Bint's possession, the content of which was even unfamiliar to him.'

In his excitement Svatikov suddenly reverted to French: 'Ce n'est pas pour le contenu dans un certain sens que j'ai payé, mais uniquement pour le matériel!'

Mercifully, they had no more questions, but before he could step down, the judge surprised them all with his last question. Had he ever witnessed a pogrom, Judge Meyer wanted to know.

Svatikov was apparently very agitated and it took him some moments to respond.

> This is difficult to answer. What is a pogrom? If you ask a reporter he would say that it is robbery and murder. Yes, I have seen a pogrom which raged in Russia for three days after the publication of the famous October Manifest of the tsar on 7 October. It was horrible, your honor! A mass of people moved in the streets and whenever they encountered a Jewish home they broke into it. In previous pogroms it was mostly robbery and looting. But in Rostov, for example, it was murder of whole families. I myself have urged policemen to interfere, to do their duty. They replied: 'Dear sir, indeed it is horrible, but we have no order to interfere.' Their real meaning was that they had been ordered not to interfere. I cried that an honorable Russian cannot remain calm, so I joined the Jewish self-defense groups. I held it to be my duty to protect these poor Jews with a weapon held in Russian hands. I was twice wounded in the big war, I lost my hearing and part of my eyesight. I broke my left arm and had a big wound in my head. I believe I have done my duty to my country. But, Mr President, in 1905 it was my duty as a Russian citizen to go out in the street and protect Jews, just as it is my

duty in 1934 to appear in this court to protect the truth and assist you in finding it.

The courtroom was mesmerized, and Georges noticed that even the reporters seemed paralyzed. They could not put pen to paper and were later compelled to copy the last statement of the witness from the record.

The court announced a recess and Georges Brunschvig quickly followed the witness from the courtroom, lending a supporting arm. His ordeal was over, he said, thanking him.

They decided to meet over lunch in a small restaurant, where they had reserved a table. Lifschitz arrived after the first course, reporting that he had stayed behind to talk to some journalists. He was impressed, he said, by their number. They could not have hoped for better coverage. They were most impressed by the witnesses, they had told him. He was now completely convinced that their gamble had been justified. Even if Judge Meyer would not adopt their interpretation of the legal paragraph, it was still worth it. How could they ever have succeeded in lining up such an impressive group of witnesses, and so many members of the press, unless it was in a courtroom? But the best was yet to come, he said. He was sure that the press would soon realize that the defendants did not have any real defense. They were going to make fools of themselves, he said, with the whole world watching.

Not wishing to spoil their appetite, Dr Wiener kept still, not sharing with them his certainty that the Nazi defendants were also going to have their day in court. They would not even try to prove the authenticity of the *Protocols*, he was sure, but they would also use the courtroom as a public forum, speaking to a different kind of audience. Their audience out there might be much larger than ours, and their voice was definitely going to be much louder. He was afraid it was also going to be much more effective.

He forced himself to keep his pessimistic thoughts to himself. They had a right to enjoy this first day of the trial. They had done good work, and the witnesses had all come through brilliantly. The judge was definitely impressed.

When the afternoon session commenced, the court was still packed.

The next witness was Wladimir Burtsev, Georges Brunschvig announced.

He had brought with him the meticulous notes Burtsev had given him, and he now spread them out on the table. He wanted to make sure that not one detail was omitted of this important testimony.

Professor Matti let Georges interrogate all the witnesses. He was content to lend his passive support. This was a rare opportunity to see a former student of his at work, and he was proud. There was a Jewish saying, Saly Mayer had told him during one of the court recesses: 'A father is not jealous of his son, and a teacher is not jealous of his pupil.' Like all sayings, Matti thought, it was not always true. He could think of some of his colleagues who would not be pleased to sit in the courtroom and let their pupils steal the show.

Burtsev announced that he was currently living in Paris, but chose to testify in Russian. An interpreter took his seat opposite him.

Judge Meyer was now quite familiar with the subject, and he knew who the witness was. That same morning Svatikov had mentioned that it was Burtsev who had insisted that he meet again with Bint when he arrived in Paris in 1921. Burtsev had also inspired him to write and publish the articles describing his initial meetings with Bint in 1917.

To save time, the judge came straight to the point: 'What do you know about the *Protocols*?'

'I learned of the existence of these *Protocols* 30 years ago and have never since stopped being interested in them.'

In a clear voice Burtsev now re-created in the courtroom that cold winter day of 1906 in St Petersburg, when he had first laid his eyes on the *Protocols of the Elders of Zion* in preparation for the meeting of the editorial board of the historical journal *Byloje*, which he edited at the time.

He explained to the court why the entire board had been unanimous in supporting his evaluation that the *Protocols* were not even worth mentioning. Repeating what he had told Georges in Paris, he said they had all felt that even denying such a document would lend it undeserved recognition.

'But I myself was intrigued by these Zionist *Protocols*,' he added, 'and decided to inquire further into the matter. I had spent 15 years abroad and had many friends and I was surprised that none of my friends had ever heard of the *Protocols*. This strengthened my suspicion that they were forged.'

The judge asked about Rachkovskii. He did not know him in person, Burtsev replied, but he knew much about him. He had good contacts as editor of a journal, and through these he had learned of

Rachkovskii's forgeries. He also knew well Rachkovskii's assistant
Bint. He had learned that one of Rachkovskii's agents, Golovinskii,
had been involved and active in the forgery of the *Protocols*. 'I had
this information from the former Chief of Police Beletzky.' He then
asked the court whether he might describe other sources from which
he had learnt that the *Protocols* were a forgery. At a nod from the
bench he continued: 'I had confirmation of the forgery from two
chiefs of police: Lopuchin, who supplied me with information about
the famous spy Azev, and Belevskii, with whom I had shared a prison
cell. They both named Rachkovskii and Golovinskii as the forgers of
the *Protocols*. A less dependable source also mentioned Manuilov.'

Asked by Georges Brunschvig why they had not exposed the forgery in their journal in Paris, the witness said that they had decided
it was no longer necessary after the publication of the articles of
Philip Graves in *The Times* of London.

As Belejewski had been behind the Beilis trial, he had asked him
why they had not used the *Protocols* as part of the fabricated evidence of the blood libel. He answered that they could not risk the
embarrassment of using such a well-recognized forgery, Burtsev
recalled.

'Golovinskii is apparently the man whose name was connected to
the issue of the *Protocols* that had a dark blue stain. Have you ever
seen this manuscript written in various handwritings?'

'In those days', the witness recalled, 'I did not yet know that
Golovinskii had been involved with the forgery of the *Protocols* and
I have never seen this manuscript. But later I did know of this document in the possession of Nilus and I discussed it with Lopuchin. He
asked me why I was interested in the matter and added: "This matter is finished!"'

Asked about Nilus, he claimed that the man had used the
Protocols even when he could no longer deny that they were fabri-
cated. This made him an accomplice to the forgery, he firmly stated.
Unlike other witnesses, Burtsev was not willing to make excuses for
Nilus.

As he continued, Georges was checking his notes, making sure that
nothing had been left out. Indeed, he thought, the witness repeated
the exact facts he had related to him in Paris. Matti nudged him with
his elbow, and he realized that the witness was still speaking.

> In 1916 a police agent called Globitschow had been assigned to
> watch me. Later, in 1920, he and I met in Konstantinopol and

discussed two issues: the war and *Bolschevismus*. A short time ago I met him again in Paris. This time the *Protocols* were mentioned and he told me that they had been forged abroad sometime between 1896 and 1900. The forgery was done to influence the tsar. This much he knew. They knew that the tsar sympathized with the anti-Semites. At first he was impressed and made marginal notes that everything that happened in the revolution since 1905 was caused by these *Protocols*. The Palace Party was opposed and Lapuchin was allowed by the tsar to conduct an independent inquiry. In the end it was accepted that the *Protocols* were a forgery. Even Rachkovskii did not deny this but maintained that it would still be useful to use the document. To this the tsar made his famous reply that a just cause should not be promoted by the wrong means.

Georges Brunschvig had never realized how strongly important Russians felt about the *Protocols*. Like Svatikov, Burtsev also let his temper rise, as he exclaimed: 'To my mind these *Protocols* were a catastrophe for Russia.'

For the defendants only Fuersprecher Ruef had some questions, to which the witness responded coldly:

I was never a member of a party, always a journalist, but I was a sympathizer of the left.

I met Bint in 1918 and he told me that his assignment had been to watch me. In 1919 I invited him to my house. As to his trustworthiness – at that time he had no more reason for fear and he told me things of his free will. In this spirit he talked about Rachkovskii. Whenever the *Protocols* were mentioned he always connected them with Rachkovskii. I knew that Bint also made the acquaintance of my friend Svatikov who was very interested in the matter. It was I who established contact between them.

They were now going to call one of their most important witnesses, a well-known and respected historian. They considered requesting a recess till next morning, fearing that the judge might be tired after listening to long testimony all day, but decided against it. It was Judge Meyer's court and it was up to him to call a recess. He had explained to them that he had a responsibility to other litigants who were waiting to be heard. He had not expected this trial to take up so much time.

They did not wish him to suspect that they had some undisclosed problem, so without interrupting their pace they called Professor Boris Nikolaevskii. He agreed to testify in German, but asked the court's indulgence if he sometimes used Russian expressions.

Nikolaevskii said that he now lived in Paris, and was a writer by profession.

'I have dealt with the *Protocols of the Elders of Zion* as a historian and I am familiar with everything that is known about them,' he opened in a matter-of-fact voice, 'but I prefer to respond to specific questions.'

'Do you know how these *Protocols* were composed? According to one version they were adopted more or less unanimously at a Zionist Congress in Basle in 1897.'

'Please, your honor, this is not to be considered seriously. This false version has first appeared in writing in the fourth edition of Nilus' book in 1917, and it was vigorously supported by German publishers after the war. Everybody knew that this document had nothing to do with Zionism.'

The first publishers of these *Protocols* maintained that they had first appeared in the early nineties of the previous century, the witness explained. According to them a Jew named Shapiro had stolen them from the archive of a Freemason's lodge called Misradim, at the behest of a Russian lady called Glinka.

'Just imagine,' he said in a mocking voice, 'in the beginning of the nineties a small Jew, who has later been exposed as a forger, steals the *Protocols*, and a few years later, in 1897, they are adopted by the Zionist Congress! Is this to be taken seriously?!'

Glinka had been part of the Private Secret Police, which had been established when the regular Secret Police was considered inefficient in carrying out its duties. She belonged to a prestigious family of landowners.

The lawyers were faced with a dilemma common to all litigators. How many witnesses should testify to the same facts? Was a judge liable to be more convinced by numerous repetitions, or should they run the risk of boring him and losing his attention? The judge already knew who Madame Glinka was – why did he have to hear it again and again, Saly Meyer asked at one of their meetings. Each of these witnesses carried much weight, Lifschitz insisted. Their testimony would be quoted outside the courtroom. They should all be on record to corroborate each other's story. Professor Matti concurred. 'Judges have ways of letting you know when you overdo it,' he added with a wink.

Judge Meyer showed no signs of boredom, even when Loosli asked the witness to describe the character of the newspaper *Znamia*. 'The *Znamia* (Banner) was a paper that appeared after the Kishinev pogrom and lived only six to eight months. Its editor was the famous Russian anti-Semite Krushevan who was supported by the government. I learned that he had received 25,000 roubles from Pleve. The chief aim of the paper was to defend Krushevan's anti-Semitic policies and to promote pogroms.

'Who was Butmi?' Loosli wanted to know, reminding the court that this was another publisher of the *Protocols* in the years before the Revolution.

'Butmi was a landowner from Bessarabia, in the same region where Krushevan acted, and they presumably knew each other. He was the publisher of another version of the *Protocols*, and you will notice that there appear in his version remarks by the translator who maintained and underlined that these Elders of Zion have nothing to do with the Zionist organization. The translator wished to correct Butmi, who argued in his foreword that there was much in common between the *Protocols* and the Zionist organization.

Butmi did not use the original of the *Protocols* for his edition, published in 1906. He used one of the versions that had been translated and had a wide circulation.

Asked about Princess Radziwill, Nikolaevskii explained that she came from an old aristocratic family and had been born Princess Roschewuski. Her father was general-adjutant of the tsar. In 1872 or 1873 she married Prince Radziwill, a brother of Anton Radziwill, the famous friend of Bismark, who took part in the German–French war. 'I have never met the lady,' he stated, 'but I have published her memoirs in French and in German.' There was not much he didn't know about her, he added.

This lady tried to meddle in high politics, the witness explained. Hers was the most famous political 'salon' in Germany. Her correspondence with various important persons had appeared recently in French in the *Revue Universelle*. From the letters it appeared that she had established similar salons in St Petersburg and in Paris.

This witness did not volunteer much, the judge noticed, but waited respectfully for each question, then presented a full and clear answer.

Asked about Sukhotin he said that he had come from an aristocratic family. Alexander Nikolaevich Sukhotin was Adelsmarschall
in the district of Tscherno. He had participated in a very rightist
publication in Moscow. An extreme conservative. He was chief of a
small farmer district. 'May I tell a little story?' he asked the judge,
adding that it would describe the man better than any words. One
day, he continued at a nod from the bench, one of Sukhotin's
horses contracted a contagious disease. He ordered some farmers to
empty his stable but they feared to go near the sick horse and
refused. Sukhotin retaliated by arresting the whole village for a
week. The story was later repeated in court and in the Senate and
caused a big scandal. 'This goes to show, your honor, who this man
was.'

In response to expert Baumgarten he answered that the Freemason
organization had been outlawed by the tsar in 1823 and again in
1826. It was virtually illegal. 'But we now know that some *loges* did
exist in Russia in the beginning of the twenties. I learned lately that
two such *loges* existed in the palace and there was a rumor that the
tsar even belonged to one of them. These were Martinist loges.
'Philippe was a Martinist,' he stated dryly, hoping they already knew
who Philippe was. They told him that they did.

Officially, he now recalled, the first version connecting the
Protocols of the Elders of Zion with the Zionist movement appeared
in 1917, but Butmi had maintained that some connection with the
Zionist movement had existed as far back as 1906, an allegation
firmly denied by the translator in the same edition. It was interesting,
the witness speculated, why this version was first denied and then
reinstated. This had to do with Russian politics or the policies of the
Russian police. The Jews took part in the great revolutionary movements which were afoot. Pleve was minister of the interior. He tried
to establish contact with Zionist leaders and to recruit the Zionist
organization in the fight against the revolutionary movements. This
was in 1902–03. He even invited Herzl to come to Russia. Herzl, the
founder and leader of the Zionist movement, actually visited St
Petersburg and conferred with Pleve in 1903. As a result the Zionist
movement was legalized in Russia. It is noteworthy, he remarked,
that a Zionist Congress was allowed in Russia even though a purely
Russian Congress was prohibited. The idea was, as he had already
mentioned, to harness the Zionist movement to the anti-revolutionary
campaign. As a result Jewish revolutionary circles argued hotly

against Herzl. In Wilna leaflets were distributed naming him an agent of the Russian Secret Police. As Krushevan enjoyed large financial contributions from Pleve, he had to support the alliance with the Zionists. That was why he wrote in those days expressly that the *Protocols* had nothing to do with the Zionist movement. A few years later, when it became clear that the alliance with the Zionist movement had failed, it was again allowed to link it to the *Protocols*.

'It is that simple,' Nikolaevskii said, spreading out his palms in a suggestive gesture, hoping the judge would realize how things had been in Russia in those days.

'There is much speculation in literature', he continued, 'about the possible link between Zionism and Bolshevism. The Stalinist circles and the Black Hundreds maintained that "All Jews were Bolsheviks and all Bolsheviks were Jews." It is well known that Russian Jews had their own revolutionary parties like the Bund. In the years 1917/18/19 this organization fought hard against the Bolsheviks. It is not true that all Bolshevik leaders were Jews. This is true of only a few leaders. All the rest were not Jewish, but as they acted under false names, some of these sounded Jewish.'

This was new information by an expert, and the judge was definitely interested. This trial was like an academic course in history, he thought.

In response to a question by Loosli concerning the sudden death of Rachkovskii, the witness recalled that this was in 1910 or 1911, after Rachkovskii had stopped all his official activity. 'I do not know much,' he said carefully, 'but some newspapers maintained that he had been involved with the spy Azev in an assassination attempt against Pleve.'

Rachkovskii's death had been announced after a thorough search of his apartment, although according to one version he had died several months later.

He was also familiar with the name Alfred Rosenberg, the German publisher of the *Protocols*. Rosenberg came from Esthland. In the first years of the Revolution he had lived in Moscow. It was known from literature that he had emigrated to Germany in 1919 where he became active in the National Socialist movement. He had close contacts with rightist Russian circles.

Fischer now rose, telling the witness in an arrogant tone that he demanded 'yes' or 'no' answers. Georges Brunschvig had prepared him for this tactic, telling him that he was not compelled to comply.

He could answer each question in his own words. No one had a right
to dictate the answers, he assured the witness.

Would they never change their pattern, Georges whispered, when
he heard the first question:

Q:	Are you Jewish?
A:	I am not Jewish. My father was a Russian priest and so was my grandfather. My father told me that priests go back in my family for seven or eight generations. My mother was the daughter of a Russian farmer, who later turned businessman.
Fischer:	There are many Jews who are priests!'
Q:	What is your *weltanschauung?*
A:	I am a social democrat.

Asked if he had ever seen the original *Protocols*, he readily replied:
'There is no "original". It is a forgery. But I believe I have read all the
editions of the *Protocols* beginning with the Nilus and Krushevan
ones. I have no interest in the German editions, only in the Russian
ones. These are the real sources. I may add that the translations are
also a kind of forgery because they include many changes from the
original forgery.'

Fischer:	I asked the witness if he had compared the *Protocols* with the original, I meant the original protocols of the Basle Congress. These are the true *Protocols!*'
Witness:	I have no interest in the protocols of the Zionist congress! They have nothing to do with this forgery with the *Protocols of the Elders of Zion!*
Judge:	'Tomorrow we shall have witnesses who attended the Basle Congress. They are the proper witnesses to answer this question.
Nikolaevskii:	I repeat, there are no 'original' German editions, every one of them is a translation from the Russian, which was also a forgery.
Fischer:	These are all speculations, not proof. I am waiting for something to be proved at this trial!

Ignoring him, the judge asked the witness: 'How about the English
editions?'

Witness:	They also were translated from the Russian.
Fischer:	My question is still unanswered! Have you compared this edition with the original one?
Judge:	If you don't know, who is to know? The witness maintains there is no original.
Fischer:	Then we must adjourn these proceedings!'
Judge [patiently]:	When you ask the witness about the 'original' *Protocols* you must tell him what you mean! In what language?
Fischer:	I am speaking of the *Protocols* that exist according to the testimony of the second president of the Zionist movement. The protocols of the Zionist Congress.
Judge:	These have nothing to do with what we are considering!'
Fischer [arrogantly]:	How about letting me continue?

They were all surprised at the patience of the judge. He was trying very hard not to be drawn into unpleasant exchanges with Fischer, sensing that this is what he was trying to provoke.

Georges Brunschvig also had some questions, to which the witness answered in detail.

I am familiar with all the Russian editions of the *Protocols* except the one mentioned in the book of Madame Lesley Fry, published in 1895 or 1896, which to my knowledge nobody has seen. In the early publications it was categorically stated that the *Protocols of the Elders of Zion* had nothing to do with Zionism! Neither the Zionist movement nor the Zionist Congress had been mentioned in the early Nilus editions. It was only in his fourth edition, in 1917, that the *Protocols* were tied in with the Zionist Congress. There is definitely no mention of this idea in the former editions. I wish to make clear: Butmi only published a translated edition of the *Protocols*, by an anonymous translator. The fact that the *Protocols* had nothing to do with the Zionists was included in the translation, it was not a statement made by Butmi. Butmi did maintain that there was a connection between Zionism and Freemasonry. As a historian I can state categorically, and it is a well-known fact, that the publication of the *Protocols* in Russia was an instrument of inciting to anti-Semitism and promoting pogroms. There can be no serious argument about that.

Fischer: Please note in the record that the witness has said there was a connection between Jewry and Freemasonry!

Witness: That is not what I said! I only described what Butmi said!

Fischer: This is not true!

Examination by Fuersprecher Ruef:

Ruef: Can you describe the connection between the *Protocols* of 1894 and the Zionist Congress?

Judge: No, the witness only expressed surprise at the fact that on one hand you maintain there was an edition in 1893 or 1894 and on the other hand you maintain that the *Protocols* were composed at the Congress in1897.

Witness: That is right.

Ruef: Do you know that Princess Radziwill was sentenced to prison for forging a cheque of Cecil Rhodes in 1902 or 1903, as reported by Lesley Fry?

Witness: I do not know. Everything is possible. But keep in mind that this is the same Mrs Fry who maintained that the *Protocols* had been composed by Achad Ha'am.

Now even the judge looked tired. They exchanged glances, hoping he would call it a day, but all they got was a short break. The witness also looked in need of some well-deserved rest, but he was not to get it. Instead he was asked by the judge to use the recess to examine the documents that had been obtained from Russian archives, and see if he could confirm their authenticity. The suggestion had been made by Georges Brunschvig, but he had not intended to burden the witness with this task during a short interval in the proceedings. No matter, Nikolaevskii assured him, he could do it easily.

When the session resumed the witness declared that all the documents were authentic. He mentioned as an example the document signed by Plekhanov on the activities of Rachkovskii. This was published in a Russian-German newspaper, which he was ready to present to the court on the next day, if requested to do so. 'I knew from Minister von Pleve that Rachkovskii had been fired from his job in 1902. I now see a document that verifies what I had been told, that he had received a very sizable pension. When I say that these documents are authentic, it is not only from a general examination but I have very specific proof. I am quite familiar with them.'

They all looked completely exhausted and were greatly surprised and relieved that there were no more questions to the witness. They would resume at 8 a.m. the following day, the judge announced. They could hardly believe that the trial had only begun that morning.

They were ready to rise when the judge announced that he was planning to hear all the remaining witnesses the next day. He would hear the experts on Wednesday, but he would be willing to give them some time if they needed to correct their expertise after they heard the witnesses. Both Baumgarten and Loosli declared that they were ready to work in the evenings. They would be ready at 8 o,clock on Wednesday morning.

The judge then informed Fischer that as their suggested expert, Pastor Münchheimer, had not been found, he would be willing to allow them time to find another expert. He had made every effort to find their expert, the judge stated for the record: 'I have made numerous telephone calls, I have asked the assistance of the police, I have invited defendant Silvio Schnell to my chambers to discuss the matter, but he did not show up.'

Turning to all the defendants Judge Meyer added: 'My experience with the Front and the National Socialists is not of a kind that would make it possible for me to find an expert who will be acceptable to you.'

Fischer demanded that the protocols of the Basle Zionist Congress be made available to him. Turning to the judge he complained: 'I understood that you have already decided that these records have nothing to do with the *Protocols* published by Fritsch. I could stop cooperating from now on but shall not do so.'

The judge, with a smile, replied: 'It would be a pity.'

At Loosli's request Svatikov would be called back next morning.

They were all impatient to leave, but Fischer had another request: he needed another 30 tickets for his people in the courtroom. They had a right to be present. The judge was surprised to hear that in view of the large crowd the court attendants had actually handed out tickets to the courtroom. There was not enough room, the judge explained, why didn't holders of tickets take turns.

He then quickly rose, fearing more delays.

Going back in his mind to those days Emil Raas later recalled that he had been assigned the task of buying all the available newspapers and reporting to the group on the extent of the press coverage. They were all to meet for breakfast in a small café near the courthouse at 7 o'clock the next morning. The owner had agreed to open at this early hour. He was doing good business these days.

Odette implored Georges to go home and get some sleep, but he was too nervous. He needed to share impressions of the first day in court. Lifschitz had invited the out of town witnesses for dinner. He would join them for a little while. He promised not to stay late.

In the morning they were pleased with the favorable and quite accurate coverage of the newspapers. Whole pages of all the important dailies were dedicated to a full report of the testimony in court. It was evident that the witnesses had left a good impression on the journalists. They were so eager to read every word that they did not notice the time. They were ten minutes late and the judge admonished them. The record showed that the first session on Tuesday 30 October opened at 8.10 in the morning.

The courtroom was as packed as it had been the previous day. A crowd was waiting outside in a tense atmosphere. The police were present, not taking chances.

All the litigants were present, as were their lawyers.

'The first witness this morning is Henri Sliosberg,' Georges announced.

The witness declared that he was 72 years old and was a former lawyer in St Petersburg, presently living in Paris. He was ready to testify in German.

Sliosberg had been an outstanding figure in the Jewish community in the Russian capital. An honors law student at the university of St Petersburg, he was denied a teaching position because of his Jewish origin, but was used by government authorities as an unofficial legal adviser. It was in this capacity that he had been requested by Witte to present an opinion on the *Protocols of the Elders of Zion*. Apart from his legal practice, Sliosberg had devoted himself to Jewish communal work representing Jewish interests in various capacities. He was particularly active in the 'defense bureau' set up by Jewish intellectuals in St Petersburg to defend the rights of the Jews through organized legal action. He had been imprisoned during the Revolution and his property confiscated. He had made his home in Paris, where he soon became head of the Russian Jewish community.

Without any preliminaries Judge Meyer now asked him whether he was familiar with the history of the *Protocols of the Elders of Zion*.

He spoke in correct German, with a Russian accent. He had first become aware of these *Protocols* at the end of the century, in 1899 or 1900. He was acting as a lawyer in St Petersburg and was very active in Jewish charities (*hilfswerke*). The minister of finance, Witte, who later became Graf Witte, commissioned him through one of his senior officials to submit an appraisal of a manuscript entitled the *Protocols of the Elders of Zion*. The manuscript was hand-typed, in Russian. He had prepared an opinion stating that the document was an absurd forgery. Unfortunately, he added, he had left his written opinion in his office when he fled from Russia in 1920. He had had no idea he would have any use for it, he added.

On what had he based this opinion, the judge asked.

'I was well aware of the relevant basic facts and relationships and could say with certainty that the document had been invented,' he replied. The booklet itself, in the form of a copybook, which was being circulated among senior officials, did not mention any sources, and its author remained anonymous. He remembered the content well because it later appeared in the *Znamia*, published by the well-known anti-Semite Kruschevan, an instigator of pogroms. He saw it in print in the paper of Kruschevan and in the book of Nilus.

At the time he was convinced, and he had said so in his appraisal, that the aim of this fabrication was to incite hatred not only of the Jews, but also of the Democratic Party, and especially against Witte and his finance policy. Witte's financial reform of 1899 had been much criticized by reactionary circles. It was plain to the eye that many points on which the financial, economic and agrarian policy of Witte was criticized were mentioned in the *Protocols* as part of the so-called 'Jewish Plan'. This could be no coincidence.

'I am as convinced now as I was then', he announced, 'that the Jews were used as a tool to attack the liberal movement and all revolutionary circles, but especially Witte, who was hated by the reactionaries. They left no stone unturned to undermine his authority in the eyes of the tsar.'

He knew at the time that the Secret Police were involved and that there were definite signs that pointed to Paris. Only people such as Drumont and his collaborators, who were involved in the Dreyfus trial, the 'grand priests' of anti-Semitism in France, who knew nothing of Russian Jews, could speak of the Jewish bankers! In Russia there were 7 million Jews. Only 20 or 30 of them were wealthy in a real sense. A small minority were medium rich, but the masses were very poor, on the verge of starvation. They could afford to eat meat only on the Sabbath. They could not make ends meet and had very little interest in world domination. They only wanted to know who was going to be chief of police in Kiev or in Riga, and whether he could be bribed with a small sum of money. This was more important to them than what son of David would rule the world.

The judge then asked him what he knew about Nilus.

'Everybody knew who Nilus was,' he said with a forgiving smile. He wrote mystic and apocalyptic books about the Antichrist. He knew something of the Jewish belief in the coming of the Messiah, and had created a whole 'mishmash' evoking from this innocent belief the idea that it concerns the coming of the Antichrist who will rule the world.

Was he familiar with the name Rachkovskii, the judge asked.

He was not only familiar with the name, but had met Rachkovskii in person. He was a well-known *agent provocateur*. He composed all kinds of provocative documents that purported to emanate from *émigré* circles in Switzerland and France. He pretended they were printed by a secret press, but those who knew anything about politics did not believe him. 'I myself had many contacts in those days in senior bureaucratic circles and I even acted as legal counsel to the Ministry of the Interior, by invitation of Stolypin. I was able to show positively that the pogroms had in part been instigated by these officials.' Yes, he added again, Rachkovskii was well known to everybody as a dangerous *agent provocateur*.

He did not know Golovinskii, he replied to another question, but he knew Manuilov. He had been a well-known agent of Rachkovskii. He had also acted as a secretary to Witte and his follower Stuermer.

Replying to Loosli, Sliosberg said that the *Protocols* had appeared in Germany in 1919 and a little later in France. In Russia they had no real influence, they were considered a bad joke. The most serious anti-Semitic paper, *Novoje Wremia*, never even mentioned them. Everybody knew they were an invention of the Secret Police and that their documents were not reliable. This was common knowledge.

They felt that the judge was already convinced that the Zionist Congress in Basle had no relevance to the matter of the *Protocols*, but

Lifschitz insisted that they present all the witnesses he had lined up to cover this matter. They had traveled far to be there, he argued: they might as well testify.

So they next called Dr Juris Mayer Ebner from Chernowitz, who had repeatedly served as member of the Parliament and the Senate in Rumania. He had been a member of the Aktionskomitee at the Basle Congress, which consisted of 23 persons.

He repeated that all the meetings at the Basle Congress, both in plenary and in committees, had been open to the public and to the press. There were no secret meetings.

The main subjects under consideration were the plight of Jewish communities around the world, and of course the Palestine question. This was supposed to be a turning point in Jewish history, he explained, with the new dimension Herzl had provided for the Zionist movement.

Were there no arguments? he was asked. Oh, yes, a very heated argument raged about the Hebrew language and literature, and the question how Jews could be settled in Palestine and turn it into a homeland, and whether it should be done in legal and political terms.

Was it not true that there were differences of opinion, as between Herzl and Achad Ha'am, the judge asked.

Yes, there were discussions, the witness recalled, but not a real clash.

Then came the mandatory question: was it true that a plan for world domination had been prepared in Basle?

The witness became very upset. 'Unfortunately, being a religious Jew I am not allowed to use the Lord's name in vain, because I would have liked to swear before the whole world that this is an evil invention. There is not one iota of truth in it! Were such a subject ever raised at the Congress, I, and to my knowledge all other participants, would have protested vigorously.

'Although I was only 25,' he continued, 'I played an important role in the Congress and was an active member in a central committee. It is definitely impossible that any secret meetings were held, or any subjects discussed, without me being aware of it.'

All morning they had been curious about the large package that rested on the bench in front of the judge. To the surprise of the whole courtroom the judge suddenly unwrapped it, announcing that on his own initiative he had required and received from the Swiss Landebibliothek in Berne the official record of the Basle Congress, printed in Vienna in 1898.

The witness was invited to identify it and did so, saying that he possessed an identical copy. There was no other record of the proceedings of the Congress, he assured the court.

Lifschitz had insisted that they let the witness describe the Zionist Congress in his own words. The record of this trial was going to be a historical document, he reminded them again and again. They would stop the witness if the judge became impatient. But Judge Meyer was learning all about Jews and Zionism, subjects of which he had known very little. As long as he seemed interested, they were content. So the witness was allowed to talk without interruption, although the defendants were visibly fidgeting in their seats.

This was by no means the representation of world Jewry, the witness continued, going back to the Congress: the Zionist movement was quite small and had to fight the rabbis. 'The leaders of Jewish communities in Germany were against us,' he said. 'So were also the big financiers like Baron Hirsch and Rothschild. It was mostly a movement of young people who had to fight the older generation. We were revolutionaries on the Jewish scene, fighting against the Jewish establishment.'

The big success of the first Congress was that they openly discussed their problems, for the first time, in the presence of the press and in the eyes of the world. Herzl had always maintained that the question of the Jews concerned not only Jews, and should therefore be discussed with the utmost publicity.

It was absurd to say that Achad Ha'am would be party to a plan for world domination. He was one of the spiritual leaders of his generation and was even against the idea of a political homeland. He wanted to establish in Palestine a spiritual center for the Jews of the world.

Georges Brunschvig presented the witness with an affidavit, signed on 30 August 1933 by 18 participants in the Basle Congress. It would save time if he could confirm its contents. After reading it he assured the court that it was completely accurate, and confirmed in essence his own testimony.

When Fischer arose they all expected some new obstacles. They were not disappointed. He suspected that the record of the Basle Congress might be forged, he said with a straight face. He wished to compare it with the original. In a resigned voice the judge told him that he may examine the witness on this subject.

The witness said that he had lost the first edition of the record printed in Vienna, during the Revolution. 'I own now the second edition, printed in Prague.'

Fischer: This may well be another forgery.

Witness: You will have to prove such an absurd allegation.

Fischer: We, the National Socialists, have a real interest in finding out the truth.

Witness: The second edition, exactly like the first, is a verbatim record of the proceedings at the Congress.

Before Fischer could proceed in the same vain, the judge raised his voice for the first time: 'This is enough!'

After a few stunned moments the witness resumed: he had heard before of the *Protocols of the Elders of Zion* but had only read them on this journey. It was totally impossible. The Jews had lived for 2,000 years in difficulties. Their economic situation, especially in the east European countries, had been bad, for they did not have full citizenship. It was completely inconceivable that such poor, lonely and tortured people should dream of world domination.

'When I first read the *Protocols* I was embittered, but at the last chapter I had to laugh. I have traveled in many countries and met many Jewish communities. I have never heard of one Jew who maintained he was a direct descendant of the House of David! Nobody can trace his origin to those times.'

Again, they expected a short recess but were told to call their next witness.

They were very proud that they could present such an outstanding witness as Paul Miljukov. He was 75 years old and traveling was quite an effort, but he had readily agreed to come. He had also studied the *Protocols of the Elders of Zion* and considered them a blemish on Russian history.

He presented himself modestly as a historian, an expert in Russian history. He had published scientific articles both in Paris and in Russia, and three volumes in French on Russian history.

Not one to boast, Miljukov did not volunteer the information that he had been one of the principal architects of the liberal policy in Russia, and one of the founders of the Kadet party, later appointed minister of foreign affairs in the provisional government. His party had advocated constitutional reform, and bitterly opposed the right-wing policies based on Jew-baiting. He refrained from telling the judge that they had sometimes been referred to as Kike-Freemasons.

Like most of his colleagues he had emigrated to Paris, where he now lived, publishing a newspaper for the Russian diaspora. He also served as president of the trade union of the foreign correspondents in Paris.

There were various reasons for the Revolution, Miljukov said, but they had nothing to do with Jews or Freemasons. Jews were involved in the Revolution like others, maybe in a little higher percentage, because of their persecution by the old regime and their better education.

'I am not a Jew,' he responded to a question by the judge. 'We stem from Prussia – an old aristocratic family.'

The judge felt he had to apologize: 'I have only asked in order to prevent others from posing the same question.'

The judge listened patiently as Miljukov described the inherent anti-Semitism of the Russian authorities, and the process that culminated in the Black Hundreds gaining representation in the third and fourth Dumas.

'The Revolution was not started by Jews,' he stated with conviction. 'It would be unworthy of the Russian people to transfer the burden of both failure and success to the shoulders of the Jews.'

Strangely, he said, the Bolsheviks now used anti-Semitic slogans exactly like those used by the regime of the tsar.

Asked about the Church, he declared that the Church was not known for its stand on doctrines. It was mostly neutral on matters of other denominations, including the Jews, but where the government was involved it always sided with the government. Unfortunately the Church had also remained neutral in its attitude toward mystics such as Philippe and Rasputin.

It was his newspaper, *Dernières Nouvelles*, that had published du Chayla's articles, and he was proud of it. He also knew and highly respected both Svatikov and Burtsev. Finally he was asked about the *Protocols of the Elders of Zion*.

They were a crude forgery, he assured the court. The forgers perverted the text of Maurice Joly, who was a fine writer. Not only was Joly's style too elaborate for them, but it would also have been beyond the understanding of their potential readers.

The myth of a secret Jewish society that aimed to dominate the world had been mentioned in Russia as far back as 1880, before the actual publication of the *Protocols*. As a historian who had researched the matter, he was sure that the *Protocols* had been forged to substantiate an existing libel.

'This is an interesting theory,' the judge remarked, as the witness continued: 'I was a member of the Duma for ten years, where the Black Hundreds were represented, and not once did they mention the *Protocols*. They feared that any mention in the Duma would be followed by an inquiry that would publicly expose the forgery. It was much safer to leave them in a fog. This was also why they were not specifically mentioned in the Beilis Trial. A forgery could not stand up if it is challenged in a court of law, he concluded, looking at the judge. They had been afraid to risk it even in a Russian court, he added pointedly.

> Baumgarten: Do you know of one historian who takes the *Protocols* seriously?
> Witness: No! Out of the question. The same is true of any educated man.

Surprisingly the defendants had no questions for this witness, limiting themselves to derogatory gestures.

The next day the newspapers would report that Rabbi Ehrenpreis was the most impressive witness in the trial. Indeed, the chief rabbi of Stockholm, who also held a doctorate in philosophy, was an outstanding figure. Judge Meyer recognized the stature of the witness from the moment he opened his mouth. Quiet, firm, dignified, never raising his voice, he commanded the attention of his audience.

He had been initially invited because of the absurd allegation that he was the composer of the *Protocols of the Elders of Zion*. It was one of many versions, but this one could easily be refuted.

His testimony should be short and to the point, Professor Matti suggested. But he was overruled. This was an opportunity not to be wasted, Lifschitz argued, as he was the only one who had met the rabbi in person. They all agreed with him when they were exposed to the rabbi's unique personality at the dinner the previous evening.

Surprisingly the judge did not show any signs of impatience, even when Rabbi Ehrenpreis repeated what others had already said.

Not only had he attended the Basle Congress, but he had been secretary of the committee, chaired by Herzl, which prepared its guidelines. He had issued the invitations to the delegates, in which Herzl specifically said that all proceedings of the Congress must be absolutely public. He remembered that Herzl insisted that the last two words be underlined. The invitation also assured the participants that nothing in the proceedings would be opposed to the laws of any country or to their duties as citizens.

He remembered very well his meeting with Herzl in Vienna in March 1897, when the text of the invitation had been composed, after much deliberation. Herzl believed that the nations would be interested in solving the 'Jewish problem', which had caused much distress, and would therefore be sympathetic to their movement. He wanted the emigration of Jews to Palestine to be arranged in a lawful public manner. It actually came true in the Balfour Declaration.

Standing very erect the witness declared: 'I consider it to be the highlight of my life and my good fortune to have been able to participate in this important project of my people and to collaborate intimately with this pure, idealistic and worldly man of stature, Herzl, to whom any form of national chauvinism had been absolutely foreign. He believed that he was not only helping alleviate the sufferings of his poor brethren, but was helping solve urgent European problems.'

His eyes were actually filled with tears when he said in an almost inaudible voice: 'I can still see him as if he was standing here today to confront the lies about these *Protocols*.'

After calming himself, he opened a fat portfolio, handing the bailiff a full stenographic record of the proceedings of the Basle Congress, and a new edition of the *Protocols* just published in Stockholm, entitled *The Secret Protocols of Israel's Elders*.

How many more copies of the Basle records did he need, the judge wondered.

The *Protocols* include 24 chapters, the judge reminded the witness. Could they possibly have composed them, or even read them, during the Congress, what with all the proceedings of the plenary and the committees?

> Witness: It would have been physically impossible. During those three days in Basle we worked very hard and spent half of each night in committee meetings, which were also public and open to the press. The day would need to have 88 hours to leave us time to even consider such *Protocols*. But physical impossibility aside, I must repeat that it was impossible in every other sense. These forged *Protocols* are opposed not only to the spirit of Herzl and Achad Ha'am, but also to the spirit of Judaism.

It was the next passage of his testimony that most newspapers quoted verbatim the next day:

> This trial is not about the forgery of the *Protocols of the Elders of Zion*, your honor, or about the Zionists. This is about the forgery of Judaism. This court would have to rule on Jewish history, the Jewish people and their character, their life for 3,000 years, everything we have ever stood for and given our life for.
>
> Here in this courtroom in Berne a chapter in world history is being written. This is the first time this question is being openly considered by an unbiased court of law in a civilized country. The eyes of many people in the world are glued today to this courtroom, with curiosity, expectation and excitement. It is not only the claim of the Jewish community in Switzerland against Mister Fischer and his collaborators. It is the claim of Judaism against those who spread libels against us, wherever they may be. Every one of us, 16 million Jews in the world [there were still 16 million] feel deeply insulted, their honor dragged through the mud, by this shameful lie, which never stops and is spreading like a contagious disease from land to land. In the future people will be surprised at the depth to which our era had sunk, that such a forgery, such crude idiotism, could make any kind of sense to thousands of people.

Odette recalled how they had all held their breath. Even the defendants hung their heads, momentarily unable to absorb this powerful message. The witness, standing proud and erect, had them all fascinated. They felt they were in the presence of a great man. Moments passed before Loosli broke the silence. They all needed some light relief, and he supplied it. Had the witness read the chapter about the Jewish cemetery in Prague, by Herman Goedsche.

> Witness: It was common knowledge that only two tribes survived the destruction of the Second Temple, Jehuda and Benjamin. All the other ten tribes had vanished. You can quote that as one reason why the novel of Goedsche is totally wrong when he speaks of a meeting in Prague of representatives of the twelve tribes. The only thing resembling the truth in that chapter is the fact that there indeed exists a Jewish cemetery in Prague!

There had been no sect in Judaism since the times of the Bible that believed that a descendant of David would rule the Jews. Genealogically there were no such descendants.

Loosli proposed to use the fact that they were privileged to have in court a man of such profound learning, and asked him to explain to the court what the Talmud was.

The witness hesitated. He did not believe the president would allow him to present a lecture on the subject.

The judge stated: 'It depends on the length of the lecture.'

He had just published a book in Swedish on the Talmud, the witness said. He would start by telling the court what the Talmud was *not*. It was definitely not what the anti-Semitic literature said. It was not what it appeared to be when quotations were used out of context. It was an anthology of literature composed over 1,000 years. The word 'Talmud' meant study or learning, but was most commonly used to denote the body of teaching that comprises the commentary and discussions of learned rabbis who interpreted the oral law called 'Mishna'. It was one of the most outstanding creations of human culture, reflecting daily life of the people of a certain era, their customs, beliefs, and even superstitions. It was a source of law, history, medicine, commerce and agriculture, as well as culture and science. It dealt with every aspect of human life and human behavior, on every possible level. The judge listened, fascinated, as the witness explained at length, with much erudition, the essence of the Talmud.

'This is the Talmud,' the rabbi concluded, 'a product of 1,000 years and of 2,500 learned men. It represents an era in our history.'

It seemed that all the defendants had delegated Fischer to interrogate the witnesses. Misquoting a phrase of the witness, he asked:

'You said the real *Protocols* are the holy writs of the Jews. Well, which is it, the holy writs or the stenographic protocols of the congress?'

> Witness: You must be joking, but I am not opposed to jokes. I only said that if you wish to study Judaism you should read our holy scriptures: these are our true *Protocols*.

When Fischer persisted in asking again the same question, the president excused the witness, saying that they must not bore him with such inconsequential questions.

Professor Matti was worried. 'They don't care if they antagonize the judge,' he whispered to Georges, 'for they have no real defense. They invite the judge to make these remarks, which they would later use to prove that he had been against them all along. Not only are they planning to discredit the witnesses, they are trying to lay the ground for the discreditation of the judge.' Georges agreed, but did not see how they could prevent it.

It seemed that the defendants had adopted the version that the *Protocols* had been composed at the Basle Congress. If that was so, some of the community leaders thought, why involve the Freemasons in the trial? But it was always Lifschitz who reminded them of the historical scope of the trial. One day they might revert to the old version of the Jewish–Masonic plot. This was an opportunity to expose that lie, he said: it must not be wasted.

So they called Swiss Freemasons, who vehemently denied that their movement had any plans to dominate the world, with or without the Jews. Among them was Herr Tobler, the chocolate magnate, who was later accused by Fleischhauer of perjuring himself in court. Tobler promptly sued him for libel, quoting from the court record and from Fleischhauer's expert opinion.

Before the court rose, Brunschvig reminded the judge that Maurice Joly had been presented as Moishe Joel, a circumsized Jew. Saying so, he placed on the bench a certificate of baptism in the name Maurice Joly. After a long search they had found it in the archive of the town Lans-le-Saunier in the district of Jura, and it certified that Maurice, son of Philippe Lambert Joly, advocate, and his wife Fortune Florentine Elizabeth Courtois, who resided in the same town, was born on 22 September 1829, and baptized on 17 December of the same year in the parish of Saint-Désire.

The judge could now retire to his chambers with a smile on his face, Matti remarked.

At this point, the defendants said, they did not wish to present witnesses.

Loosli and Baumgarten were tired and red-eyed. They had declared in court that they would be ready to testify on Wednesday morning, and had promised the lawyers that they would not be the cause of another delay. In some procedures an expert offers his written opinion and is immediately handed over to opposing counsel for cross-examination. But Judge Meyer had announced that he would hear oral testimony of the experts, and they needed to address some parts of the previous testimony. This was partly why the plaintiffs went to great efforts and expense to keep a stenographic record of the proceedings, compelling the stenographers to work day and night transcribing their notes.

For two consecutive nights Loosli and Baumgarten had studied the records and made notes, drinking gallons of black coffee. Matti and Brunschvig were keeping their fingers crossed, praying that the defendants would not dare ask for another postponement. They had not even discussed how they would react to such a request, which was why they had asked for a short recess when the defendants complained to the court that they had not had enough time to find an expert.

The defendants had been active these last two days. They had known that the plaintiffs were going to present impressive witnesses, but they had underestimated the impact of these witnesses on the court, and, more important, their impact on public opinion. The Swiss members of the defense team were worried about the Swiss press, which was definitely impressed and published extensive parts of the testimony. Their lawyers warned that they had no real defense and that the testimony of the experts would secure a verdict in favor of the plaintiffs. The defendants feared that, the way things were going, public opinion in Switzerland would make their future work difficult. This was not Germany, they warned.

But Fleischhauer was ready for them. He was surprised that they had not yet realized what this trial was about. It was not about the *Protocols of the Elders of Zion*, he thundered. It was not about Switzerland. This was the big confrontation between the Jews and the Aryans: it was not about a little booklet. He had been waiting for this opportunity a long time. While the naive Swiss lawyers were discussing points of law and procedure, he had been busy activating the anti-Semitic International through the Weltdienst. They now had branches in many countries and dedicated members to spread their gospel, and funds were beginning to pour in. Although the fundraising was mostly done for support of the defense in the Berne trial, he did not have to account to his Swiss counterparts where the money was going. Von Roll, who had dared question his leadership role, had been removed, and Toedli, who took his place, was very cooperative.

He had let them make futile attempts to find experts, he said, because they needed to impress the judge. Did they really think they would find an expert to convince the judge that the Jews had held secret meetings in Basle composing their world plan?

They had no idea, he said, what was happening around them. The Aryans were finally in a position to take over, and Hitler was their leader. But it was not enough to get rid of the Jews in Germany. They must convince public opinion in other countrie, and a whole department in the German government was working on effective ways to do so.

This trial was a godsend, he said. They now had the world press at their disposal. 'They ignore what we say at our meetings,' he said, 'but they could not afford to ignore what will be said in this courtroom, after having reported in detail the testimony of the witnesses for the plaintiffs. Whatever is said here will be reported worldwide.' Even if some journalists sounded unsympathetic, he could assure them there would be many who would listen and agree.

Did they want to waste this golden opportunity arguing about a Russian fanatic? They had the floor now and they would present the Jews in all their ugliness, as a threat to the peace and stability of the rest of the world.

That is why it was imperative that he himself appear as expert. He was not an expert on the *Protocols*, he agreed, but could they offer a better expert on the Jews?

They had known for a long time that the Weltdienst in Erfurt had taken over the Berne trial, and that Fleischhauer was calling the shots, but they had deluded themselves that he would realize in time that a Swiss judge would not tolerate the tactics used these days in German courts. They now felt like puppets on a string, manipulated by Fleischhauer, but they had no choice. They announced to the court that Fleischhauer was their expert and that he needed enough time to prepare his opinion.

Lifschitz and Saly Meyer were adamant. They had gone along with the maneuvers of the defendants long enough. It was time to impress upon the judge that another delay was totally unjustified.

And yet, Professor Matti quietly intervened, what would they gain? They would be playing into their hands, providing them with a ready argument that the defense was being treated unjustly. They knew how to spread misleading propaganda, he said. They would say that they had been deprived of their right to put on a proper defense, just because the Jews had more money to hire experts. 'We should not oppose any defense maneuver, but rather leave it to the decision of the judge.' Loosli and Baumgarten reluctantly agreed with him.

When the judge granted the required postponement they all wondered what kind of expert they could expect. They knew very little about Oberleutenant Ulrich Fleischhauer, but they soon had an opportunity to make the acquaintance of the Weltdienst in Erfurt.

The judge allowed the defense six months to prepare their expert opinion, and scheduled the next court session for 29 April 1935.

Georges Brunschvig had hoped to finish the trial and resume his life. He felt guilty toward Emil Raas, who was trying to keep their meager private practice alive. Now that he had six months he would go back to work. He would also marry Odette, who had waited so patiently. It was time they set up their own household.

But the defendants had other plans. The long recess in court must be well used, Fleischhauer insisted.

First they started an unprecedented campaign in the press against the appointed experts, particularly against Loosli. They aimed to disqualify him in advance in the eyes of the public, but they also hoped to unnerve him. Their press in various countries began calling him 'The Jewish Witness'.

Another tactic concentrated on filing criminal complaints against the witnesses, naming Weizmann, Sliosberg, Ehrenpreis, Mayer Abner, Bodenheimer, Farbstein, Miliukov, Svatikov and Nikolaevskii. The complainant was the National Socialist Ortsgruppenfuehrer Wuergler from Zurich, a man with previous convictions of fraud. He had also published a brochure about the *Protocols*, decorated with bloody cartoons. His unfounded complaint was accompanied by a request for the immediate arrest of the witnesses.

On 2 January 1935, two days before the court threw out the complaint against the witnesses, deciding it had no merit, a German newspaper in Berlin described the complaint in bold letters as the 'sensation' of the Berne trial.

But they were not through. On 17 March 1935 Fuersprecher Ruef filed another complaint against a number of witnesses. The Weltdienst in Erfurt proclaimed another sensational event in the Berne trial.

THE EXPERTS

They were getting ready for the last court sessions, scheduled for 29 April 1935. Lifschitz warned them that Fleischhauer's expertise would be the worst anti-Semitic document to be published in years, and whatever the outcome of the trial it would be distributed as a court document.

They might be over-confident, Brunschvig and Matti argued, but they did not believe even a Nazi agitator would dare present to a court of law a blatantly biased document and call it an 'expert opinion'. They knew Fleischhauer was no expert, but he would probably have some phony 'expert' prepare the document. Even though the lawyers for the defense had posed ridiculous questions, they would surely not allow the presentation of anti-Semitic propaganda under the title of 'expert opinion'.

Dr Wiener wondered how they could still be so naive. The Swiss litigants and their lawyers were not conducting this trial. It was not the Swiss Front they were facing in this courtroom, he insisted: this was a confrontation between the Jews and the German Reich, and he had known in his heart long ago what the Nazis were capable of. They played by different rules, he insisted repeatedly. Fleischhauer would surprise them all, he warned. Expect the worst, he told them again and again.

But even Lifschitz and Wiener were horrified when they saw the 600-page document delivered by the court. It looked like a book, but they did not need to read it all. Leafing through it was enough to convince them that Fleischhauer had not even made a feeble attempt to formulate his vitriolic attack on the Jewish people in scientific language. They had feared the worst, they thought, but this was even worse.

They had read the articles in the Weltdienst stating that the Jews were a mixture of dozens of races combining the worst characteristics of all these races. Their criminal inclinations could even be discerned in their physique, the Erfurt publication said. They were an immoral and an amoral race, members of a criminal gangster band, who would fight the Christians to the end.

After describing Jews in the most horrible terms they said that no half-measures should be engaged. 'The Jew must be excluded from our cultural environment. There is only one way to free our land of this horrible plague: total, untiring, one hundred percent exclusion of the Jew, which can be achieved only by physical extermination.'

Among the recommended methods of getting rid of the Jews were castration, or the denial not only of citizens' rights but of all human rights.

They were all shocked when they realized that Fleischhauer's so-called 'expert opinion' was written in the same vein.

Georges Brunschvig insisted that he would attempt to disqualify him as an expert at the opening of the court session. Matti wished him good luck, but assured him that he would fail. How would it look if the only expert ready to testify for the defense was disqualified? They would cry from the rooftops that they did not have their day in court. This was a prudent judge, Matti said. He would bite his lip and treat Herr Fleischhauer with courtesy.

The hall of assize in the Berne court was overfilled. Reporters from around the world manned the press table. Fleischhauer had reserved two rows of seats for his followers, who came in full uniform.

The judge read without comment a telegram received from the defendant Theodor Fischer: 'Bin verhindert an den Verhandlungen teilzunehmen.' (I am prevented from participating in the proceedings.) Not even a feeble excuse, Georges thought.

The judge informed the litigants in a dry voice that all criminal complaints filed against the witnesses had been found by the president of the court to be without basis, and there was no reason for further investigation in the matter, whereupon Ruef immediately rose to demand another postponement. They needed to examine this matter, he said.

This time Matti had enough, but before he could rise the judge refused Ruef's demand.

All eyes were on Fleischhauer, who was ready to present his written opinion formally to the court, but Brunschvig announced that he wished to interrogate him. His questions concerned Fleischhauer's role in the anti-Semitic Weltdienst, his close ties with the Nazi leaders in Germany and his leadership role in international anti-Semitic organizations. To all this Fleischhauer brazenly admitted.

But, as Matti had predicted, the judge decided that the defendants were free to choose their expert. Fleischhauer had found his forum, Georges dejectedly remarked to his colleague.

The opinions of Baumgarten and Loosli had been in his possession for months, the judge announced, and now that he also had the opinion of Fleischhauer they could move to the final stage of the trial. Each expert would make an oral presentation and would answer questions of the court and of the litigants. First, the expert for the plaintiffs, Professor Baumgarten, then the expert for the defendants, Herr Fleischhauer, and finally the court expert, Herr Loosli. He would read the opinions carefully, the judge announced, and the experts should therefore present their oral opinion in a concise manner. They could not have foreseen that while Baumgarten and Loosli would each take a few hours, Fleischhauer, totally oblivious of the judge's instructions, would be on his feet almost five days.

Baumgarten was well prepared. He opened by stating that the *Protocols* were a historical fabrication, and went on to describe how and by whom they had been forged – and plagiarized, he added after a slight pause, comparing the text with that of Maurice Joly.

To be perfectly accurate, one would have to say that in their present form the *Protocols* had been composed in the years 1890–1900. He personally would not commit himself to a particular date, although from the testimony the court may draw more specific conclusions.

Ever the pedantic scientist, Professor Matti noted with a smile.

He could not exclude the possibility, Baumgarten continued, that the forgers had used other sources, not confining themselves to the book of Maurice Joly. They most probably also used the book by Hermann Goedsche. But there was no indication that Goedsche himself had used that book.

Referring the judge to the abundant evidence presented in this case, he said he did not wish to exercise the court's patience by repeating all the testimony, but must address himself to some particular issues. Not only had there never been any proof of the authenticity of the *Protocols*, but he could definitely state that these so-called *Protocols of the Elders of Zion* were completely opposed to the spirit of Judaism, which was responsible for presenting to the world the concept of monotheism.

Describing the tactics of the anti-Semites, he allowed himself a smile: 'If a Jew joins a cosmopolitical organization, they immediately use it as proof of the Jewish conspiracy and of the *Protocols*. But if a non-Jew joins the same organization, he is immediately stamped as a Jew.'

The Jews had nothing to do with the Freemasons, and they did not rule the world, the professor declared in an authoritative tone. Not only were they not unified in one program and under one leadership, they were a spectacularly divided people.

The Zionist movement had but one aim, he stated: a homeland for the Jewish people. They proved this not only in words but also in deeds. The *Protocols* indeed foresaw modern dictatorships, he said, pointedly looking at Fleischhauer, but the kingdom of David was not one of them.

Asking for the court's indulgence, he proposed to point out the absurdity of the allegations. The Jews were identified by their religion, while Bolshevism was atheistic; the *Protocols* were reactionary, while Bolshevism was revolutionary; these were but examples, he said. He could go on and explain how each allegation made against the Jews in this document was devoid of simple logic, but it was all in his written opinion.

If the *Protocols* were authentic, he said, and there was a global Jewish conspiracy, then one must accept that all history was only an outward appearance, and historians were only fooled victims, because behind the scenes were the bearded sages of Zion, who pulled the strings of the emperors, the kings, the generals, the Popes, the poets and the philosophers. This theory was very dangerous: it distorted the social and political outlook; it diverted attention from the real causes of evil; it slandered the ideas of liberty, liberalism, social equity; it undermined all the values of the European culture.

Finally, he was firm in his belief that the *Protocols* were *Schundliteratur* in every sense of that expression. They had no great influence in Russia because too many people knew Rachkovskii and his forgeries, he said, but they had caused pogroms there and were liable to do so elsewhere, inciting one part of the population against another. This was a real threat to any society wishing to preserve its freedom and its democracy.

After exactly three hours Professor Baumgarten bowed to the judge and marched to his allocated seat.

Both Emil Raas and Odette Brunschvig could never forget the five days of Fleischhauer's testimony. Georges had suggested that she had better stay home, but this was one of the few times when she refused to take his advice. She was not a child to be protected, she had argued: she would be sitting in the courtroom throughout this ordeal, lending him her silent support.

It had indeed been an ordeal. Odette remembered how the judge had to admonish Fleischhauer time and again that he should address the court rather than the public in the courthouse. Fleischhauer had apologized, explaining that he was used to speaking at public meetings, and two minutes later turned again to the public.

She did not remember all his testimony, but of all the insulting allegations against the Jews one in particular stuck in her mind, although it had by far not been the worst. He had actually said in court that Jewish children were dirty because Jewish mothers used to wash them with spit, to save water and soap.

In a confident voice, without referring to any authority, Fleischhauer stood on his feet for five days making unfounded statements.

Maurice Joly was a Freemason and probably a Jew. He was a descendant of the Merano Jews from Spain, who had been compelled to convert. As proof he presented to the judge two pictures: of Maurice Joly and of Karl Marx, who had similar beards, which were common in those years.

The discovery of Philip Graves he named 'A Turkish Legend'. The testimony of du Chayla he called 'Jewish Camouflage Maneuvers'. He attacked every author who had written against the *Protocols*. Parts of the *Protocols* contained complimentary remarks about Jews, he argued, and therefore could not have been composed by an anti-Semite. As the police were described in the *Protocols* in negative terms, he said, how could the document have been composed by a member of the Russian police?

He shamelessly quoted Lesley Fry, who had maintained that Achad Ha'am had composed the *Protocols*, presenting him as the proponent of *Symbolzionismus*, which directly promoted the domination of the world by Jews, while Herzl, himself a Freemason, the proponent of *Realzionismus*, wished first to establish a Jewish state and then take over the world.

The *Protocols* did not include all the ideas of Maurice Joly's *Dialogues*, he seriously explained, because the Jews were in a hurry in Basle.

The *Protocols* were not based on the chapter of Goedsche's book. Like Maurice Joly, he said, Goedsche had also drawn his material from an ancient secret document that originated in Russia, quoted there as *The Rabbi's Speech*, which stemmed from a speech by a rabbi in the year 1859 in Simperofol. He completely ignored the fact that the chapter was Goedsche's fiction, and had only in 1880 been turned into the rabbi's speech.

The authenticity of the *Protocols* was confirmed by the history of the last decades, he said. In his view the Jews caused the world war, gave rise to Bolshevism, wrote the Versailles Treaty, which humiliated Germany, and created the League of Nations, which was to unify the world in accordance with the Jewish model. 'The struggle against the Jews in Germany', he said, 'will be fought to the end.'

The *Protocols* were true because they confirmed the well-known Jewish hatred of anything non-Jewish, he maintained. As proof he quoted Jesus Christ, Muhammad, Napoleon, the Jewish prayerbook, Voltaire, Kant, Wagner, Goethe, Theodor Momsen and others.

He quoted freely and indiscriminately from all kinds of Jewish writings: the Bible, the Talmud, documents from the Middle Ages, Jewish newspapers and almanacs, as well as from anti-Semitic writers such as Alfred Rosenberg.

The quotations were separately bound as an addendum to the expert opinion. The Freemason procedures were described as stemming from Jewish rituals. Further proof of how the Jews undermined the economy, was the boycott initiated by Jews against the German National Socialists. Prominent Jews were described as criminals. Sir Philippe Sassoon, the British minister of aviation, was described as a former private secretary of Lloyd George and a pusher of opium.

In the final part Fleischhauer addressed the legal arguments. The German Hammerverlag edition of the *Protocols* could not be considered a forgery, as it was a translation of a foreign book. The foreign book could not be considered false, as it only confirmed Jewish beliefs and behavior. The plagiarism, even if proved by literary standards, could not be considered as such in legal terms. The *Protocols* were in no way to be considered obscene literature.

As Fleischhauer had misquoted texts of Bible researchers, their organization immediately dispatched a letter of protest to the court, calling his testimony an outright forgery in itself, and stating that they were not taking any steps against him as he had testified in open court and they were leaving the verdict to the judge.

The press was full of Fleischhauer's testimony. As was to be expected, it was highly praised in Germany and in some Nazi-oriented newspapers abroad, but all other newspapers were extremely critical.

This would be the last witness, Georges told Odette on the evening before Loosli was going to take the stand. They were all exhausted, but sleep still did not come easily. Georges wondered if he could have done more or better. The circle had met in the late afternoon but there was nothing more to discuss. They had decided how he and Professor Matti would divide between them the final arguments, the '*plaidoirie*'. Until now Georges had done most of the work in the courtroom; Professor Matti was proud of his pupil and would gladly have left the podium to him, but he knew that they needed a prestigious non-Jewish lawyer to make a final statement.

They had both worked nights to polish their closing speeches but they knew they might have to revise them after Loosli's testimony. They had studied carefully his written opinion, but over these last few days they had noticed a change in Loosli's attitude. As he sat in the courtroom listening to Fleischhauer's testimony he could hardly contain his frustration and his growing anger. Non-Jews were sometimes less tolerant of anti-Semitic propaganda, Lifschitz said to Georges Brunschvig. Jews had been exposed to similar attacks for generations and learned to live with them. 'That is your trouble,' Loosli thundered, having overheard the remark. Nobody should have to live with this, he cried, nor tolerate it.

More than anger, Loosli felt great shame that a Swiss courtroom had been converted into a forum for such vile anti-Semitic propaganda. His level of tolerance was stretched to the utmost and he hoped he would be able to contain his feelings and deliver his testimony in the proper tone fit for a courtroom, but in the end his testimony was more personal and more emotional than he had planned.

Bowing to the court, he began by stating that each one of the three experts had written his opinion independently, and must therefore carry full personal responsibility for its contents.

He then surprised the court by a dramatic announcement. He had just received information that Hammerverlag in Germany was preparing a new edition of the *Protocols*, using Fleischhauer's opinion as an introduction. The same opinion was already being used for anti-Semitic purposes in many countries under the title *The True Protocols of the Elders of Zion*. And all this before the trial was over, he added with a meaningful tone.

The judge looked surprised, but said nothing.

In his opening remarks he suggested that they all remove themselves from the choking anti-Semitic fog that had permeated the courtroom for the last few days, and re-enter the clear atmosphere of sanity, wisdom and human understanding.

He was most outspoken in voicing his conviction that these court proceedings were being manipulated by Germans. That was why he allowed himself to speak in a Swiss courtroom of German imperialism, he said, having heard from childhood *Deutschland, Deutschland Über Alles*.

Even before he had listened to the evidence presented to the court, he had carefully studied all the available documents. He was most lucky, he informed the court, to have in his possession a large number of Russian documents, supplied by the archive in Moscow on condition that they not be published and that they be returned to Moscow after the trial.

He could vouch that not one document pointed to the authenticity of the *Protocols*. Indeed, it could be taken for granted that the Russians had not been above using false documents in their persecution of the Jews, but in their secret correspondence they did not need to pretend. Had they believed in the *Protocols* they would certainly have used them, or at least mentioned them in their secret documents. To give but one example, there was no mention of the *Protocols* in the memoirs of General Gerassimov, head of the Okhrana from 1905 to 1912, who was considered the best-informed person in Russia. He did mention that the tsar had asked him for information of possible ties between Freemasons and Bolsheviks. In his answer he assured the tsar that in Russia there did not exist any Jewish Freemason lodge. Not one word about the *Protocols*.

He had not meant to speak of the Basle Zionist Congress, Loosli said in an apologetic tone. He had assumed that this false theory would be abandoned in a court of law. But as the defendants and their expert held on to it, he too must address it.

For the last 15 years, he continued, the anti-Semites had maintained that the *Protocols* had been prepared during the Zionist Congress in 1897. Other than quoting each other, they had never presented even a shadow of proof to substantiate this allegation. They might as well maintain that the *Protocols* had been prepared at a meeting of the Swiss chimney cleaners, he exclaimed.

Then, in a calmer voice, he related an episode that, unlike the allegations of the defendants, was well documented.

On 5 August 1903, four months after the horrible Kishinev pogrom, the Zionist leader Theodor Herzl traveled to Russia in an attempt to alleviate the situation of the Jews there and to gain Russian support for the Zionist program. He had two meetings with the minister of the interior, Pleve, in the course of which he asked for Russian support in his negotiations with the sultan of Turkey concerning the settling of Jews in Palestine, which was then part of the Turkish Empire.

In preparation for Herzl's visit Pleve had asked the head of the Okhrana, Lopuchin, to prepare a report on Zionism. Extracting a document from his leather case, Loosli announced that he was holding in his hand a copy of this report and there was no mention of any

Protocols. On the contrary, four months after the Kishinev pogrom, after extensive use had been made of the rabbi's speech, after private copies of the *Protocols* had been circulated to government officials, there was no word in that report about a Jewish conspiracy. In fact, the report was so positive that Pleve promised to support Jewish settlements in Palestine. He could state with certainty, Loosli assured the court, that the Okhrana had never possessed any document confirming the truth of the *Protocols.* Not even a secret one. Any such document would have surfaced by now. Nor did they believe in the myth of the Jewish conspiracy, he declared.

Encouraged by the promises he had received from Pleve and by his warm reception by the Russian Jews, Herzl had traveled to Basle to attend the sixth Zionist Congress, which opened on 22 August.

This had been a traumatic Congress. Herzl's proposal to organize Jewish emigration to Uganda, as a temporary emergency measure to save Jews until they succeeded in obtaining permission for their return to Zion, was met with vehement opposition. This man of prophetic vision, the father of modern Zionism, the founder of the Zionist movement, had no inkling of the fact that while he and his colleagues were arguing about possible ways and means of saving Jews from persecution, a printer in St Petersburg was proofreading the first publication in print of a vile libel about the Jews. While the Zionist Congress was still in session, on 26 August 1903, the first installment of the *Protocols of the Elders of Zion* was published by Kruschevan in the newspaper *Znamia.* This was the general rehearsal, Loosli said: the premiere was to come in October 1905, with the publication of the book by Nilus.

In his written opinion he had spoken much of Maurice Joly, Loosli reminded the judge, and he did not wish to take up the court's time with unnecessary repetition. There had never been any proof, he added, to substantiate the ridiculous allegation that Joly had been Jewish. Maurice Joly's book was no more and no less than a literary declaration of war on the regime of Napoleon III. This was clear not only from the court verdict in the trial of Maurice Joly but also from other original documents in his possession. Asking the indulgence of the court, he proposed mentioning one document. In his investigation of Maurice Joly's background, he had visited the archives of French newspapers of that period, and to his surprise he had found in the mass of old material in the archives of the French newspaper *Le Figaro,* which had been marked for destruction, the manuscript of

Joly's book on the dialogues. The secretary of the editorial board had noted in the margin that the book had to be printed abroad, as it was a critique of the French government.

He assured the court that he had personally compared the texts and had found 176 passages that had been copied from the *Dialogues* into the *Protocols of the Elders of Zion*. Wherever the text described the government and politics of Napoleon, the forgers had substituted the Jews, without any serious attempt at disguise. He had dedicated a special chapter in his opinion to the publishers of the *Protocols*. There was little he could add.

Like Hitler in *Mein Kampf*, and like Fleischhauer in his testimony, they all used the old trick of inferring the truth of the *Protocols* from the very fact of their existence.

To protect themselves, publishers of the *Protocols* were sometimes careful and did not vouch for their authenticity. One example was the most important publisher of the French version, Lambellin. He had never asked his readers to believe in the truth of the *Protocols*. He would be ready to publish any material to the contrary, he announced.

Loosli looked at the judge, hoping he had made his point. How clever: in this fashion one could publicly say of any organization, without proof, that its members were criminals and sub-humans. When challenged, all the publisher had to do was say that he was willing to let the victim defend himself.

There had been no time, he informed the court, to obtain documents refuting erroneous allegations made by Fleischhauer, but surprisingly he had succeeded in obtaining a letter from former Russian Prime Minister Kerenski, whom Fleischhauer had accused of having suppressed the *Protocols*, being himself Jewish. Kerenski was no Jew, Loosli declared, pointing to the letter, he was the descendant of a family of priests. There had been no Jew in his government, and what is more, at that time he had never heard of the *Protocols of the Elders of Zion*.

Unfortunately he must address himself to Fleischhauer's testimony, distasteful as it might be. Even talking about it was painful to him, he said looking at the judge and finding understanding in his eyes.

'How does Fleischhauer prove his allegations? Your honor, he quotes the *Protocols* to prove that the Jews are bad, and uses the fact that they are bad to prove the authenticity of the *Protocols*.'

They had refined a system that they were repeatedly using. They even forged the forgery, for each publisher had taken liberties with the text. They wrote introductions and quoted each other as sources. They misquoted and quoted out of context Hebrew sources, and systematically ignored scientific proof refuting their theories.

It might be considered a bad joke, he said resignedly, that on the one hand they described the Jews as clever and devious, and on the other hand they alleged that these clever people had committed such a primitive, and easily exposable, plagiarism. Could they not have prepared a plan of their own, without adopting Joly's allegory?

Having got away with such a clear act of plagiarism, they continued spreading lies that were so easily disproved.

Not only did Fleischhauer maintain that Maurice Joly had been a Jew, but according to his so-called 'expert opinion', he had also belonged to the Paris Masonic lodge. Actually, Loosli said, consulting his notes, that particular lodge had been founded 48 years after Joly's death.

How could he confuse between Freemasonry and the Jewish organization of B'nai B'rith when the two had nothing in common?

This document, Loosli declared, pointing to Fleischhauer's opinion, was completely false, unacademic, polemical, groundless. Not one basic rule of objective research had been observed in its preparation.

'It is no more than an anti-Semitic propaganda pamphlet. It should never have gained admission to a court of law,' he cried with mounting rage.

His embarrassment was clearly evident when he recited the history of anti-Semitism in Switzerland, mentioning acts of murder and persecution committed years ago against Jews. 'We don't need a recurrence of such acts in our country,' he cried in an excited voice. 'Would we let Hitler dictate our policy towards our Jewish citizens?' he asked, quoting passages from *Mein Kampf.* 'Are we too blind to realize that Hitler has adopted the so-called Jewish plan and is in fact practicing that of which he accuses the Jews?

'If there is a world conspiracy, it is headed by the German National Socialists and it threatens all of us,' he warned.

How had the *Protocols* helped the Jews, he asked. Who were those Jews who have dominated the world so far? Were they Bernheim, Hirschl and Levy, with whom they had shared a classroom? With whom they had done military service? With whom they had fought and argued, lending each other assistance when necessary? What science was it that taught that each Sternickel, Haarman, Denke, Julius Streicher possessed purer nord-Aryan blood than Jews, Freemasons, Socialists, free thinkers, democrats? If this were true, he would have no wish to live in this world one moment longer, he cried, indicating that he had nothing more to add.

'I wish we could forgo our closing speeches,' Professor Matti whispered to Georges Brunschvig. 'Loosli has actually said it all.' But of course they were going to sum up. They were pleased that the judge adjourned till next morning. Nothing could follow immediately after Loosli's closing words.

THE LAWYERS SPEAK

Georges Brunschvig's summing up lasted six hours. He informed the court that he would address himself only to the *Protocols*. Matti would deal with the other publications and the legal points.

What other publications, the judge wondered. He had almost forgotten that the plaintiffs had mentioned in their complaint a libelous newspaper article.

Georges Brunschvig had the makings of a great lawyer. As every judge knows, it is not a matter of training or experience: it is a gift. Listening to Brunschvig the leaders of the Jewish community were satisfied that they had no reason to regret their gamble in entrusting such a historical case to a young, unknown and inexperienced attorney.

He had given much thought to the tone he would use in his address. The facts were so clear, and the allegations of the defense so silly and groundless, that he decided to treat them with a touch of ridicule. How else could one treat such a bundle of nonsense, he said to Professor Matti, who warned that one should not overdo it. He reminded Georges that the judge had been very careful throughout the trial to treat the defendants in a correct manner, to which Georges remarked that he had not always succeeded. Sometimes it had been clear from his behavior what he thought of them.

'But don't worry,' he calmed Matti, 'I have accumulated so much frustration and anger during these proceedings that I shall not confine myself to ridiculing their story of the *Protocols*. There is nothing ridiculous in what they are doing to the Jews, and even if I tried I could not hide my rage.'

The previous evening Georges had discussed his dilemma with Emil Raas. The judge seemed to be fully acquainted with the facts described by their witnesses, which had not been contradicted by any valid testimony. He was also in possession of the expert opinions of Baumgarten and Loosli, and their impressive testimony was fresh in his mind. Would he not be trying the judge's patience by unnecessary repetition?

He must play it by ear, Emil advised, but he should also remember that a closing argument is the high point of a trial, tying up all loose ends and presenting the whole story in its proper perspective. 'This speech you will deliver tomorrow', Emil told his friend, 'will be quoted for years to come. It must contain the full story. It will also be your calling card. Who knows if you will ever again be involved in a trial of such caliber. You cannot omit any relevant part just because Baumgarten or Loosli have dealt with it. What is said in this trial will be quoted for years to come. Give them a reason to quote you. You have worked hard enough.'

'This is not about my reputation,' Georges said quietly.

That had been the previous night, but when he rose to speak he was surprised at the confidence he felt. He knew he was as ready as he would ever be.

'I am here', he began, 'to speak of the Elders of Zion, these almighty fantasy characters who are supposed to have orchestrated, for hundreds of years, every discernible satanic event against the nations and the peoples of the world.'

In a dramatic gesture he raised the booklet in his right hand. 'Look closely at this unique brochure, which stands alone against all recorded history. Indeed, we might have to re-write all history books, for according to Herr Fleischhauer it was the Jews who were responsible for the French Revolution!'

He looked pointedly at the judge. 'You would think, Your Honor, that such a brochure would be published by a collegium of academics, but in fact it was composed by three Russian reactionary anti-Semites, two of whom were known instigators of pogroms against Jews. You would think that they would have made even a feeble effort to prove the authenticity of such a ridiculous fabrication, but they never did. You would think that they would at least have attempted to coordinate their stories, but I propose to show how they not only contradicted each other but they sometimes even contradicted themselves, inventing new versions as they went along.'

He would try to be as brief as possible in describing the facts, he said, asking the court's indulgence for repeating a story that by now everybody in the courtroom had had ample opportunity to memorize. Encouraged by a nod from the bench, he reviewed the evidence masterfully, picking out parts of testimony as if they were pieces of a puzzle, and joining them into an impressive coherent sequence. He described in lively detail the fabrication of the *Protocols* in France by Rachkovskii and his assistants, the plagiarism from Maurice Joly's book, the Nilus chapter, the involvement of Henry Ford, all the time referring to the historical and political background. He tried hard not to sound didactic, remembering that the experts could get away with a historical lecture, but the judge might not tolerate another one from a lawyer.

What was it that captured people's attention, that kept a whole courtroom mesmerized, sitting forward in fear of missing one word, Lifschitz wondered, looking around. Was it the physical stature of the man, the way he carried himself, the right tone of voice, the charm, or was it his ability to create the proper atmosphere, to bring alive the men and women who had all been part of this fantastic tale, to tell a simple credible story without getting lost in a multitude of facts? It was all these and more that made those present oblivious to the passing hours.

That was how it most probably happened, Georges Brunschvig concluded the first part of his address, spreading his arms in a disarming gesture.

People had been holding their breath, and he now paused, allowing them to move in their seats, cough, whisper to their neighbors. The only one who did not move was Judge Meyer, who nodded slightly in Georges Brunschvig's direction, inviting him to continue.

He had spent sleepless nights planning his approach. It was obvious that the document entitled *Protocols of the Elders of Zion* was a fake and a fabrication, but this was not the major issue. To prove that the document was 'obscene' he would have to confront the allegation of the existence of a 'Jewish conspiracy' and prove the real motives behind the publication and distribution of the *Protocols*.

For the first time he acknowledged his opponents, turning in their direction. The court was confronted with two opposing stories, he began in a conversational tone, and it must decide which one was true and which a vicious lie. Did the Jews constitute a danger to all humanity? Did their leaders meet in secret and conspire to undermine the existing order in all Christian lands? Were they actually in the process of realizing their horrible plan, and would the world wake up one day soon to find that it was ruled by a 'Prince of Juda'? He could not keep the sarcasm from his voice. If this were true, a judgment of this court of law may help save the world.

But if, on the other hand, it was all an impudent lie, a libel so grotesque, yet so dangerous, that innocent men, women and children might very soon be its victims, not only in Switzerland but in neighboring countries, and indeed around the world, then this court could virtually save not only the reputation of a whole people but who knows how many human lives.

That was the real issue, he said, facing the judge. Considering the stakes, he could not think of any court that had been faced with a similar task, and of a judge who was destined to take upon himself a bigger responsibility.

Called to decide between truth and falsehood, and not being endowed with divine powers, a judge was sometimes faced with an impossible task. But not so in this case, he said, allowing himself a smile, to relieve the tension. The presentation of the case by the defendants should be considered an insult to the court, and to basic human intelligence. What other litigant would dare, he asked, present to a court of law an unfounded allegation, without offering even a shred of evidence to support it?

But that was exactly what the defendants had done here, he said, raising his voice and pointing at his opponents. They had thrown mud, they had made arrogant speeches, they had used this court as a forum for the most vile propaganda, but they had never even pretended to present a scintilla of proof to support their fantastic story.

Had this been a regular trial about a forged document, the plaintiffs would probably have rested their case here, for the onus of proof was on the defendants. He who published a libelous document should be made to prove its authenticity. These plaintiffs, he said, pointing to the representatives of the Jewish community who were sitting behind him, should not be expected to disprove a lie. Yet they were offering to do so, as this lie had assumed monstrous proportions and was causing indescribable harm. Indeed, he stated, emphasizing each word, they would be on firm ground were they to ask the court to rule that the defendants had failed to prove their case. But to them such a verdict would be absolutely unsatisfactory. In fact they were asking the court to state positively, on the strength of the evidence presented at the trial, that the *Protocols* were a forgery and a plagiarism and that the allegations of the existence of a Jewish conspiracy to dominate the world were a vicious lie.

The closing address in a big complicated trial is the test of any lawyer. Struggling with hundreds, sometimes thousands, of pages of evidence, facing heaps of documents, needing to facilitate matters for the judge, who might miss an important point, tying up facts and law into a package that made sense – all this and much more went into the preparation of an effective closing argument in a trial. If you failed at this last stage, you might have wasted the energy invested in the preparation and conduct of the whole trial. Brunschvig was doing well, Professor Matti wrote in a note to Lifschitz, taking pride in his pupil. What a typical understatement, Lifschitz thought. Why wouldn't the professor use the term 'masterful'?

Realizing that he had the full attention of the court, Brunschvig now proceeded to describe how the plagiarism and the forgery had been revealed, quoting Radziwill, du Chayla and Philip Graves, tying their stories to the testimony of the impressive witnesses whom the plaintiffs had presented. Lawyers would give their right arm to be in a position to present such witnesses to a court, he thought.

He had talked without interruption for a long time, and now allowed himself a short pause, pouring water from a glass carafe.

Placing a small stack of notes in front of him, he turned to the judge and resumed his address in a calm tone. He had come now to a crucial part of his address and was confident that any judge would be impressed by it.

One should keep in mind, he began, that the trial was basically about a document. He now proposed to speak about this anonymous document, called the *Protocols of the Elders of Zion*, which had suddenly appeared from nowhere.

Looking into the eyes of the judge, talking to him as if they were alone in the courtroom, as if he was speaking a language the judge alone understood, Brunschvig continued slowly, spacing his words.

No original document had ever surfaced, yet the published document purported to be a true record of secret meetings of Jewish leaders. In examining the alleged authenticity of such an anonymous document, a number of questions immediately came to mind: If there had ever been an original, where and how had it vanished? Who had seen it? What did it look like? In what language was it written? Where and when had it been composed, and by whom? Who were those mysterious Elders of Zion and whom did they represent? When and where had the document surfaced and how had it made its way from the committee room or the archive of these Elders to the hands of the publishers?

Fortunately, the publishers themselves, all the publishers, in all languages, had offered answers to these questions. It only remained, he said with a smile, spreading his arms, to examine the answers.

Even if there was but one version, it could be false and would therefore need careful examination and corroboration. But what if there were numerous conflicting versions? Which one would the court be required to believe? He left the question echoing in the air, before taking up his recital. There was a murmur in the courtroom and he felt he had aroused everybody's curiosity.

The only point on which all publishers were agreed was the allegation that at some point the original *Protocols of the Elders of Zion* had come into the possession of a person who had obtained them by illegal means, and that they had then been transferred to certain other persons. Nobody had ever explained what happened to this so-called 'original' document from which copies and translations were supposed to have been made. So, he said thoughtfully after a moment's silence, they were dealing with alleged copies of a document the existence of which was only confirmed by word of mouth of persons who had not even pretended to have themselves laid eyes on the so-called original.

A copy of a document could never replace the original, unless there was firm independent proof that such an original had ever existed and that the proposed document was a faithful and accurate copy of said original. If the existence of a document was contested, it could not be proved by an unauthorized and unauthenticated copy.

When asked about the primary source of the *Protocols*, all publishers, in every possible language, consistently pointed to Nilus, and sometimes to Butmi. It was their editions of the *Protocols* that were translated into every possible language. They were both presented as honest and orthodox men, whose belief in the *Protocols* was universally accepted as guarantee of their authenticity. One must therefore start with these early Russian publications.

Not only had the court had no opportunity to hear the person or persons who had allegedly delivered the *Protocols* to Butmi or to Nilus, but they themselves were now deceased, and could not be called to testify. The judge would have no opportunity to listen to them and watch their demeanor. They could not be called to explain any inconsistencies in their versions. All the court could do, he said, was to examine their published stories, evaluate them, compare them to each other and to that of other witnesses, and test their logic. This court, therefore, should ask itself on what these two Russian publishers had founded their so-called 'guarantee' of the authenticity of the *Protocols*.

Comparing the introductions to the various editions of the *Protocols*, one is immediately struck by the fact that the stories contradict each other in most relevant facts. Surprisingly, these discrepancies are found not only between the versions of different publishers, but even between different editions of the same publisher.

Not wishing to tire the court with lengthy quotes, he had prepared a list of contradicting versions, which he presented to the court, handing a copy of the list to the defense lawyers.

He asked the defendants to tell the court which version they wished to support in this courtroom, and why that particular version had more merit than any of the others.

Had the alleged original *Protocols* been stolen by a Russian noblewoman, or by the lover of a high-ranking Freemason?

Had they been delivered by a Jewish traitor to a Russian spy, or had they been caught by the Russian police at the home of an unnamed Jew?

Had they been stolen or copied?

Had they been obtained from a Masonic lodge, from a Zionist iron vault, or from Theodor Herzl's apartment?

Had the original been discovered in France, in Switzerland or in Vienna?

Had they been discovered as a separate document, or had they been copied from a book of protocols?

Had they been delivered to Russia in 1895, 1897 or 1901?

Had the alleged original *Protocols* been in French, Russian or Hebrew?

Had they been translated by an anonymous translator who had delivered them to Butmi, or had they been delivered to Nilus in French and translated by him into Russian?

Had they been composed at the Zionist Congress in Basle in 1897, or had they definitely existed before that date?

Had they been composed by Theodor Herzl, by Asher Ginzburg, known as Achad Ha'am or by Rabbi Ehrenpreis, or were they verbatim records of meetings of the Jewish *Kahal*?

One last point, Georges Brunschvig said, facing the judge. Those who attempted to link the *Protocols* to the Zionist Congress had never offered any explanation why they had not been written in German, which had been the official language of the Congress.

Collecting his notes and pushing them into his briefcase, he let some minutes pass in order, to let it all sink in. By the looks on the faces of the defendants, he was confident that he had scored an important point.

Resuming his address, Brunschvig announced that he was through with Russia. It was time to speak of Europe, where the *Protocols* had first surfaced in 1919.

After the war Europe had been particularly ready for such a publication. It had probably been the despair of most people with the consequences of the war that had made them receptive even to such nonsense.

It began in Germany, where militant anti-Semites adopted this outrageous forgery, blaming the Jews for the atrocities committed in a war they themselves had started, and for its outcome.

It was very quiet when Georges Brunschvig read out in court three documents describing the loss of Jewish soldiers in the German army during the war. This was the same war, he cried, that Fleischhauer had described as 'A Jewish Slaughterhouse'.

Now again Germany was in the forefront of this atrocious use of the *Protocols*. How cynical could they get, he cried, holding up the German newspaper *Voelkischer Beobachter* of 31 March 1933. When the Jews in other countries boycotted German wares to protest against Nazi racist attacks on German Jews, the paper described the boycott as part of the Jewish plan, quoting the *Protocols*.

But it was not enough for the new German regime to exploit this forgery in their own land. They had now not only exported it to Switzerland, but had placed themselves squarely in the forefront of this trial, manipulating it from behind the scenes and dispatching a German agitator to pose as expert.

Not that this country was devoid of its own brand of anti-Semitism, Brunschvig said sadly, hanging his head. To the surprise of the audience he extricated from his file and read out a list of atrocities committed in Switzerland against Jews, including incidents of desecration of Jewish graveyards. They had enough of their own brand of anti-Semitism to deal with, and definitely did not need imported poison from across the border, he concluded.

The last part of his address was dedicated to the expert testimony of Fleischhauer.

'We have listened to him for five days and all this time we have kept quiet. We have appointed an important professor as expert, but to attack the honor and the reputation of the Swiss Jews they were compelled to import a German so-called expert, whose testimony was no less than a 'hate speech' (*Hetzrede*). It was noteworthy, he said, that they could not find one Swiss expert to support their allegations.

'This man', he said, pointing to him with distaste, 'has insulted and libeled the Jews in this courtroom for five consecutive days.' He had accused Jews of perjury, murder, poisoning of wells, kidnapping, spreading of pornography, concubinage, obscene acts with under-aged children, blood libels and polygamy. He had actually copied Chapters 6 and 7 of the Berne Criminal Code, accusing Jews of all offenses listed in those chapters. He was jubilant when he could prove that one Jew had actually committed a criminal act, as if there were no Christian criminals; as if Christians had never committed, and were not committing at that very moment in history, acts of which they would forever stand accused in the eyes of mankind.

Looking at his notes Brunschvig quoted Nazi songs that rejoiced at the murder of Jews. 'This is what Fleischhauer would have us import from across the border,' he cried.

Fleischhauer was completely undeterred by the fact that great leaders of the world, as well as the Catholic and Protestant Churches, had recognized the falsehood of the *Protocols*. Saying this, Brunschvig presented Church documents obtained from Germany. 'It took courage', he said quietly, 'to publish such documents in today's Germany, where the survival of the Church itself is threatened.'

He revealed to the judge that they had considered opposing the nomination of Fleischhauer as an expert, as he was a published, outright anti-Semite. But they were so sure of the evidence they had presented that they thought even the devil himself could not undermine the truth. Little did they know how devious Fleischhauer was. He could present white as black, green as red. In spite of the fact that he had behind him the Third Reich, he pretended to be the small David confronting the huge Goliath, the Jewish International. But they were sure the judge would see through his facade. This man had used a whole arsenal of rusty arms, starting with Pharaoh and ending with Chamberlain and Streicher, and everything in between, falsifying dates and historical events without batting an eyelid. When he was finished with 'facts' he resorted to insults, claiming Jews preached that Christians be treated as dogs.

Leaving the courtroom one day, he told the judge, he had overheard one of the spectators saying to his friend that Fleischhauer condemned God for creating the Jews, he condemned the sun for shining for the Jews, he condemned the air, which let the Jews breathe. This indeed was his motto and his pleasure.

He was getting carried away, but at a worried look from Professor Matti he continued in a calmer voice.

The German press did not just report the proceedings of this trial: they treated it as belonging to them. Fleischhauer had used this Swiss court to propagate the German National Socialist venom against the Jews. He should not be permitted to do so.

The plaintiffs, on the other hand, did not rely on Jews or those who were reputedly friendly to them. They had chosen Professor Baumgarten and they were perfectly in agreement with the court expert Loosli, both of whom were respectable, objective non-Jews.

In his arrogance Fleischhauer had used the Talmud as proof of the Jewish conspiracy. These allegations did not even deserve to be denied. The Talmud had been recognized by renowned scholars as an outstanding achievement of human wisdom, culture and learning, and it would be ridiculous to attempt to defend it in a court of law.

He would like, he said, to quote a famous talmudic scholar. 'The Talmud', he had written, 'does not exist so that any boor with unwashed feet may trample on it and boast that he has mastered it.'

It is an encyclopedia, not a holy book. Some things in it do not stand up to current morals, but this is true of any writings of that period. The Talmud stated that the whole world was held up by three columns: Truth, Justice and Peace. That is a passage from which Fleischhauer did not choose to quote!

Indeed, he had quoted not only from anti-Semitic literature, but also from non-existing and false documents. He had carefully ignored any proof that undermined his theory. He had even misquoted Goethe, he said with visible disgust, as if this should be considered the ultimate crime.

Georges had decided that his best tactic was to hold Fleischhauer up to ridicule, but at times he became serious, his anger getting the best of him.

The plagiarism was clear even to a blind man, but how did Fleischhauer treat it? If you could not refute it, then Maurice Joly was Jewish, as were also Philip Graves and Loosli.

A child could see that the rabbi's speech derived from the book of Goedsche and his famous, or should one say infamous, chapter on the Jewish cemetery in Prague. But Fleischhauer had no problem turning it around, pre-dating the rabbi's speech as if it were the source of Goedsche's book. Dates, like facts, had no meaning to him.

Like a magician, Fleischhauer drew out of a hat names of Jewish organizations: B'nai-B'rith, B'nai Moshe, Alliance Israélite respectable organizations with public agendas and well-known records of performance, and presented them, without a shred of supporting evidence, as organs of the diabolical international Jewish conspiracy, doing the bidding of the Elders of Zion.

Raising his voice Brunschvig cried, 'There is no international Jewish Conspiracy, but there does exist an international anti-Semitic conspiracy, aimed at the extermination of the Jewish nation, a conspiracy fully and shamelessly documented and published in books, articles, speeches, cartoons and manifests.

'These Aryan Elders are situated in Erfurt, headed by this man,' he said, pointing at Ulrich Fleischhauer. 'They are sworn to eliminate all freedoms, to fight liberalism, socialism, democracy. This international alliance uses persecution of the Jews to implement their unholy plans, and they are using this trial and this courtroom to further their aims.

'Thank God', he said with a trembling voice, 'that there still exist Aryans like Baumgarten and Loosli.'

He was nearing the end of his address and his voice was becoming more intense.

'He who incites and paints Jews as sub-humans, as beasts, is responsible for the spilled blood. When Jewish blood will paint the sidewalks they will most probably blame the Jews, not their murderers.'

He now looked at the Jews who filled the benches behind him.

'We are defending ourselves against the forces of evil, we must fight it to our last drop of blood, but at the same time we must teach our children what is taught today in all Jewish schools in Switzerland, that every human being is related to us, we are all created in the image of God, who is our father. Do to thy neighbor what thou wouldst have him do unto you. This is what Judaism teaches us.'

He now faced the judge. 'My clients have made my mandate here difficult, by instructing me not to react to provocations. I had to exercise strict discipline, and could only do so owing to my trust in the justice of this court. I therefore rest my case with full confidence in the democratic process of Berne. May the truth shine forward from this courtroom to secure for all of us a better future without hate or violence, filled with the spirit of love.'

What a pity, Lifschitz thought, that the trial did not end here. But it was not finished, and they all looked somber leaving the court-room. Even congratulating Georges Brunschvig would have to wait. It needed to be done in private, not in front of an audience.

As Emil Raas had predicted, the newspapers carried large parts of Georges Brunschvig's address. Editorials were most complimentary. But he was too tired to care and too anxious for the trial to end. He knew he could have done no more. Now it was in the hands of others. But he was still tense next morning listening to the address of Professor Matti.

Unfortunately, Matti said, there had always been some form of anti-Semitism in Switzerland, but since 1933 there had been a new kind of anti-Semitism, imported from across the border. The waves of the political upheaval in the neighboring country had sprayed Switzerland. There were new ideas across the border, and ideas are custom-free (*zollfrei*). 'The neighboring country had an interest in exporting its ideas, and unfortunately, these poisonous ideas some-times find fertile ground in our country.

'Among these imported ideas we find the revival of Jew-hatred. Switzerland had had its share of latent anti-Semitism. People may like or hate others, as long as they express their views in ways allowed by law and by accepted moral standards. But this imported form of anti-Semitism is new to our country, and is not to be suffered in a society that lives under the rule of law.'

The Jews had a long history of suffering, and were not known to react in extreme ways. They had tried to confront this new trend by going to the authorities, but those had pointed the way to the court-house. 'This is why my clients are here, Your Honor,' he declared with dignified simplicity.

He spoke quietly, as if he were addressing his students, but everybody strained to listen. He was a well-known professor, of high standing, and he was treated with deference. The Swiss legal system deserved great praise, he said, for the patience exercised by this court in listening to all that was said these last days. 'It is a very serious matter with which we are dealing here,' he stated.

He then surprised the court by announcing that the plaintiffs would not pursue their complaint against three defendants, whose complicity had not been proved to his own satisfaction. They had ini-tially been sued because the plaintiffs had not possessed enough infor-mation about the part each of the defendants had played.

Two defendants were left: Theodor Fischer, who had admitted his responsibility for the publication of material relevant to the trial, and Silvio Schnell, who had admitted to the distribution of the *Protocols*. But more important than the condemnation of these two defendants, Matti said, removing and wiping his spectacles, was the condemnation of the act itself.

As expected, he proposed to deal with the legal arguments first. In a dry voice he quoted paragraphs 14, 15 and 16 of the Berne law dealing with obscene literature. It was no accident, he argued, that the legislator had left the term 'obscene' to be interpreted by the court. An American judge had once said that he could not define pornography, but would have no difficulty in recognizing it on sight. The court was in a unique position, he said, to state, in the same vein, that obscenity might be difficult to define, but was easy to recognize. What could better fit the definition of these *Protocols of the Elders of Zion* than the term 'obscene', he asked.

He would point out, he said, that to be obscene a document must not necessarily be forged. Even true and authentic documents could be condemned under these paragraphs, but the falsity of the documents had much meaning. The judge could therefore not avoid the question: who was the author of the *Protocols*?

For many years it was stated that the *Protocols* had been created at the Basle Congress, where the authoritative leadership of the Jewish people were gathered to connive in the domination of the Christian world. It should be no surprise that, confronted with the impressive testimony presented in this trial, the defendants had apparently decided to ignore this thesis, and now seemed to base their theory on the allegation that the 'Jewish Conspiracy', as presented in the *Protocols*, was part and parcel of Jewish religion, tradition and philosophy, deriving from the spirit of Judaism, even if the document itself was not authentic. He was astounded, he said, that such a ridiculous argument could be presented in a legitimate court of law. Would anybody dare argue that a painting was done by Hodler just because it was as good as one painted by him, whether he had actually painted it or not?

The *Protocols* were false whether Joly was Aryan or non-Aryan. They were false whether they had been composed by a Jew or by a non-Jew. Suffice it to state that they were not the product of organized Jewry!

The defendants could have proved the authenticity of the *Protocols*, said to be part of the record of the Basle Congress, by using one of three methods. He raised three fingers, bending them as he counted each method:

- By quoting from the original record of the Basle Congress. This had not been done.
- By presenting witnesses who had actually participated in the alleged meetings. Not only had this not been done but numerous witnesses, including non-Jewish stenographers, had testified to the contrary.
- And finally, by presenting scientific evidence of authenticity, which was totally absent.

He spoke in a pedantic, matter-of-fact voice, but it was precisely this scientific tone that was so impressive, Georges Brunschvig thought.

Those who persisted in distributing this lie, Matti continued, were criminally responsible. A document that presented a whole nation as a band of criminals must be considered obscene. Such literature did not deserve the protection reserved for free speech or free press.

He hoped that the verdict of this court would help remove such literature once and for all from the Swiss scene, he said. 'It does not originate here and we don't need it. We don't need a newspaper like *Eidgenossen*, which imitates the German *Stürmer.*'

Leaving the *Protocols* for a moment, he now addressed himself to the article warning Swiss maidens to beware of Jews. This was the worst he had ever read. It labeled all Jews as sexual offenders. 'This was not written by a Swiss,' he exclaimed, allowing his outrage to show. 'This came straight from Berlin! He who dares dish out such filth must consider us Swiss to be dumb. The outcome of this trial does not concern Jews alone. It concerns all of Switzerland.

'When a neighboring country swamps Switzerland with such criminal material,' he continued with excitement, 'our very existence is endangered. It is an act of pure despotism, to try to deny their rights to Swiss Jews.'

Freedom, not oppression, was the hallmark of true human history, he said, resuming his scientific tone. 'The irresponsible citizens who seek to plant here foreign poisoned trees are doing a disservice to their fatherland. We don't presume to be the teachers of other countries, but neither are we their pupils. We are nationally ripe to decide how to run our country. If this court brings to their senses certain Swiss citizens and sends a clear message to the public that this is not the Swiss way, then the time, the effort and the expense of this trial will not have been wasted.'

How right they had been to engage a Gentile professor, Lifschitz whispered to Wiener. How right had they been to pick Professor Matti, Wiener replied.

This time the judge allowed a short recess, sensing that the defendants should not immediately follow the impressive address of Professor Matti. He was curious to learn what their arguments would be. Fleischhauer had had his days in court, but these were Swiss lawyers, arguing in a Swiss court. Would they align themselves with the German brand of anti-Semitism?

Dr Ursprung began by arguing that the burden of proof rested with the plaintiffs, and that they had not proved the falsity of the *Protocols*. It soon became apparent that the defendants were shifting responsibility from one to another. He quoted Fleischhauer, praising his opinion. He was sure the Jews would have thought twice before initiating this trial had they known what an important expert the defendants would present.

He could not add much about the *Protocols*, he stated, but he had much to say about the Jews. They were undoubtedly a different race, but somehow they were taking over Switzerland. Anti-Semitism was not a German product and was not imported from Germany. Their growing role in theater, films, literature, academia and press must be stopped.

The Aryans of the world had finally woken up to the fact that they had been suffering under the yoke of the Jews, who were unfortunately supported by some Gentile Talmudic scholars. Great men had warned the world of the Jews, among them Kant, Napoleon I, Goethe and Ambrunnen.

They all looked at each other, embarrassed that they had never heard this last name, until they learned that this was the pseudonym of Dr Zander, who had testified at the trial. He was a known anti-Semite, who was publishing anti-Semitic material under that pen-name and had himself been sued in another trial. He, Dr Ursprung, would be happy to see the Jews installed in their own isolated territory, like Madagascar, but the rest of the world should not be forced to be exposed to them.

The *Protocols* was an important academic book, and he hoped that after this trial Fleischhauer's opinion would be found in every Swiss home. The authenticity of the *Protocols* was not important as he had maintained at the beginning of the trial it was the plaintiffs who had insisted that experts be appointed because they wished to prove obscenity.

'The *Protocols* are here,' he exclaimed, 'and they are here to stay. This is proof enough of their existence. Whoever opposes them must undertake the burden of proving them false and this was not done.'

He made fun of the testimony of Baumgarten and Loosli and attacked the statement of Princess Radziwill, because she had mentioned the wrong date.

The press should be ignored, he said, as it was in the hands of the Jews.

He was a true democrat, he stated, and opposed pogroms. But these could not be blamed on the defendants, who were only expressing their opinion and were free to do so.

So what if the *Protocols* had not been composed at the Basle Congress, but at another congress of the B'nai B'rith, as Fleischhauer had stated. Was this reason enough to ignore them?

When he suddenly folded his notes and bowed to the court, they realized with surprise that he had finished.

Next came Fuersprecher Ruef. He was a Swiss democrat, he said, and he did not represent the Third Reich or the National Socialist movement. He had understanding for the wish of the Jews to protect their honor and try to prove the truth. He agreed that they may have taken one more step in the search for the truth about the *Protocols*, but the witnesses had only expressed their individual opinions and there was no way the judge could state what the objective truth was. These very days new material was arriving in his office that could throw light on the matter, but it would be too late for this trial.

After a short consultation, Georges Brunschvig and Matti announced that they were not going to use their right of reply, not wishing to tire the judge. They had said all they needed to say in this trial.

DAY OF JUDGMENT

The courtroom was packed not only with journalists but also with lawyers, judges and public officials. Surprises never ended in this trial, they realized, when the judge said he had an announcement. In a formal tone he declared that he had been summoned by the president of Switzerland, in connection with an official complaint lodged against him by Fleischhauer. The German expert had maintained in his complaint that in his testimony the expert Loosli had insulted his 'fatherland', the German Reich, and the judge had not admonished him and had not defended the honor of a foreign state.

He regretted that Herr Fleischhauer had not seen fit to address him on the matter before going to the president, but if he had in any way failed to protect the honor of Herr Fleischhauer's fatherland, he now formally apologized. He hoped, the judge added, that this was the end of the matter, to which Fleischhauer agreed, nodding his head.

The judge then got down to the business of announcing his judgment, speaking in clear and measured tones. He had come to his conclusions, he said, on the basis of the evidence, the conduct of the trial, his experience and his convictions as a jurist and as a human being.

The complaint dealt both with distribution of the *Protocols of the Elders of Zion* and with the publication of the article warning Swiss maidens of Jews, in *Der Eidgenossen.*

He then described the document called the *Protocols of the Elders of Zion*, which he had thoroughly studied. It was a brochure containing four parts: first the introduction; then a foreword; then the text of *Protokolle der Gelehrten Altesten von Zion*, as they were called by Fritsch in the edition presented in the trial; then the epilogue, which described the Jews in most horrible terms, urging that they must be dealt with and calling for their virtual extermination. The Jews were said to spread moral and spiritual sickness and to poison the air that they breathed. The Hebrew was said to be a born forger, a spy and a traitor.

Surprisingly, the judge stated that he could have considered the *Protocols* obscene even without the testimony of experts as to their authenticity. The epilogue alone would have sufficed. It incited individuals to acts of violence, creating a pogrom atmosphere. Nevertheless, expert opinions were necessary, otherwise they would probably continue distributing the *Protocols*, leaving out this epilogue, and another court would then have to deal with the question of authenticity.

Since 1921, when the articles of Philip Graves had been published in *The Times* of London, hundreds of thousands of copies in numerous editions had been published, yet there was not one word in the long introductions about the plagiarism from Maurice Joly. Could it be that Herr Rosenberg and Herr Fritsch had never heard of Maurice Joly, he asked with sarcasm. The first mention of Maurice Joly in anti-Semitic writings began only after the beginning of this trial. Now they maintained that Maurice Joly was of Jewish origin.

Even if this were so, how did it affect the problem of the authenticity of the *Protocols*? Was it not evident that his book dealt with Napoleon III and not with a later disguised version of a Jewish conspiracy to dominate the world? 'I shall not be surprised', the judge continued, 'if the future publishers of the *Protocols* confront the problem of the plagiarism from Joly's book by maintaining that Machiavelli was also of Jewish origin, and that his program of dominating the world corresponded with that of the Jews.'

His judgment would most probably not stop the publications of the *Protocols of the Elders of Zion*, but it might produce the first crack in the wall that could, in the future, assist in crumbling it. It might be the first dent in the armour of those who still insisted that the *Protocols* were true.

It was true that the witnesses presented by the plaintiffs had not always testified of things they had heard or seen. Some of them had testified to opinions and conclusions. Some had erred in dates or other details. But on other matters they were unanimous and their testimony trustworthy.

All parties had had equal opportunity to name their experts. Both Baumgarten and Loosli had stated that the *Protocols* were a forgery and a plagiarism, while Fleischhauer categorically denied it. The judge quoted the two experts on the matter of plagiarism, and placed the date of the final text of the forgery in the nineties of the last century, based on a document prepared in the eighties. He described the role of Rachkovskii and the impossibility of linking the *Protocols* to the Basle Congress.

On the basis of the evidence and the Russian documents, he decided to adopt on all points the opinion of the two experts, including the legal definition.

What a surprise, Matti and Georges Brunschvig said, looking at each other with obvious satisfaction.

The judge then listed his reasons for rejecting the opinion of Fleischhauer:

- His general attitude towards Jews.
- His method of treating the questions posed by the judge.
- The total lack of proof as basis for his opinion.

He was the owner of the U. Bodung Verlag in Erfurt, which published the anti-Semitic lexicon *Sigilla Veri* and the anti-Semitic journal *Welt-dienst*, distributing them in various countries.

Fleischhauer was a close friend of the publisher of the *Protocols*, the late Theodor Fritsch, whom the judge called 'a professional anti-Semite'.

He needed to explain, the judge said, why he had agreed to accept Fleischhauer as an expert: the defendants could not find a Swiss expert and he did not wish to deny them the right to present their own expert. But Fleischhauer had overreached himself. Describing Fleischhauer's methods, the judge explained that the so-called expert had collected from the whole world books, articles, speeches, brochures and statements, and examined them all carefully, seeking anything he could find against the Jews, and omitting anything which testified in their favor.

Judge Meyer then examined Fleischhauer's argument that the *Protocols* possessed an inner truth. This tactic was tantamount to a confession that the *Protocols* were not an authentic document. Also, he had completely failed to prove his argument that the content of the *Protocols* was in line with Jewish religion and philosophy.

Fleischhauer had misrepresented the Talmud, which was one of the greatest literary works ever published. How could one accept that this small brochure represented the Jewish spirit and philosophy contained in the 36 books of the Talmud?

He had used false and misleading quotations, and had often quoted phrases and passages out of their context. He had even invented some quotations. But be that as it may, could one quote the personal convictions of an individual to condemn a whole people?

He had maintained that somewhere, at some time, some Jews had connived to dominate the world, all this without a shred of real proof. On the other hand the plaintiffs had proved conclusively that the document was a plagiarism and a forgery.

These *Protocols* presented the Jewish citizens of Switzerland in a most negative light, and were therefore obscene literature.

Then came the final passage, which would be quoted in every language for years to come.

> I hope that a time will come when nobody will understand how in the year 1935 almost a dozen sane and reasonable men could for 14 days torment their brains before a Berne court over the authenticity of these so-called *Protocols*, these *Protocols* which,

despite the harm they have caused and may yet cause, are nothing more than ridiculous nonsense.

Jews around the world read the detailed press reports of the judgment and were jubilant. An observer in the Jewish information office remarked that in a political trial the echo was all, the judgment nothing. But this time, in Berne, both the echo and the judgment were everything they could have prayed for. Not only were the *Protocols* recognized as a forgery and an obscenity, but the judge wrote his judgment in a manner both learned and smart, with humane reasoning (*menchlich begruendet*).

They wondered how a non-Jew could have grasped and explained the Talmud so well. This was the first time a court of law had declared the *Protocols* false, after examining testimonies and listening to arguments on both sides. And this was a Swiss court, they told each other, respected everywhere as representing a neutral country. This was going to be a strong weapon against anti-Semitism. There had never been a moral judgment to equal this one! Some described it as a confrontation between Judaism and anti-Semitism, between human rights as formulated in 1789 in France, and Hitler's inhuman laws of 1933. In their eyes it was the first victory over the National Socialist party.

WHO WON IN BERNE?

Their joy was premature. The defendants appealed and on 1 November 1937 the Court of Appeal in Berne set aside Judge Meyer's judgment, deciding that the law had been misinterpreted. When the legislator said 'obscene', they maintained, he meant 'pornographic'. As wrong as the *Protocols* were, they could not be termed obscene by law. The court also found some technical errors in the conduct of the trial.

Unlike Judge Meyer, who had recognized the historical dimensions of this trial, the three appellate judges preferred to concentrate on the procedural and legalistic points. They even refused to allow the presentation of the Toedli letters, although newly discovered evidence is admissible in a Swiss court of appeal.

The appellants were jubilant. They presented the appeal court judgment as vindication of the *Protocols*, a death blow to the Jews.

But as usual they missed the real essence of the judgment, and even ignored specific statements of the court. Far from vindicating the *Protocols* or the appellants, the judges in the Court of Appeal essentially concurred in the opinion of Judge Meyer, and stated unequivocally that the authenticity of the *Protocols* had not been proven. The president of the panel, Judge Peters, recognized the difficulty in which the Jews found themselves. Had their religion been attacked, they could have argued in public, he said, but how could a group defend itself from an obscene document that said they were all sub-humans? Unfortunately, he added, the law did not provide a proper defense, and it was only to be hoped that the Swiss citizens would not be influenced by such libels.

But this was not the end of it. Judges have various ways of saying what they think, and in this case they did so by placing the burden of costs in both instances on the shoulders of the appellants. Ignoring the usual practice of imposing the costs of a trial on the losing party, the judges concluded their decision with these words: 'This scurrilous work contains unheard of and unjustified attacks against the Jews and must without reservation be judged to be immoral literature. It will be for other authorities to forbid, for reasons of state, the propagation of writings of this kind.' Refusing to award damages and costs demanded by the appellants, the court said: 'Whoever disseminates libelous and insulting writings of the greatest possible coarseness runs the risk of being summoned before the courts and must take the consequences.'

The Jews in Switzerland and the whole team – lawyers, experts and witnesses – were greatly disappointed. Even though the judges had said in no uncertain terms what they thought of the *Protocols*, they had inadvertently placed a dangerous weapon in the hands of anti-Semites, as was proved when, later that same year, the Weltdienst Congress passed a resolution reaffirming the authenticity of the *Protocols*. Fleischhauer had become a hero in Germany, and was much in demand as a speaker in many countries. His 'expert opinion' presented at the Berne trial became a manifesto and was used by Nazis and by anti-Semites everywhere. The Berne trial was presented as a great victory over the Jews.

But the effort had not been wasted, as court judgments sometimes have a surprising impact, and judges in independent courts in free democratic societies play a role that goes far beyond the formal outcome of the cases they try. In his judgment a judge often makes value statements on public issues, he defines acceptable norms of behavior, he sets moral standards. His words sometimes take on a life of their own and are quoted and referred to, even though his judgment may have been set aside by a court of appeal on some technical point, or even when his was a minority opinion. The words of a dissenting judge may sometimes be remembered far longer than those of his colleagues who constituted the majority in a particular case.

This is exactly what happened to the judgment of Judge Meyer. The legal interpretation of a phrase in an old law is of little interest to the public. What remains from the Berne trial is the impressive testimony of the witnesses and the final statement of the judge.

The Protocols of the Elders of Zion survived the Berne trial, but their survival stems from reasons that have nothing to do with the decision of the Court of Appeal in Berne.

12 The Lie Wouldn't Die

A JAPANESE GIFT

'If you are writing a book about the *Protocols of the Elders of Zion*, my Uncle Danny told me on one of his frequent visits to Israel, you should know that the *Protocols* actually saved my life.'

My uncle was a very colorful person, famous for his sense of humor, and he would often surprise us with a shocking statement, which was always followed by a story. As he was a born story-teller, I gladly settled down to listen. To my surprise I soon learned that his statement about the *Protocols* saving his life was far from the joke I had thought it to be. Danny was the only member of my family who survived the Holocaust. Actually, he had not been in the Holocaust, for he escaped in the nick of time. His father, my paternal grandfather, made him leave home early in the war, at the age of 19, and join a Yeshiva in Vilnus, which was in those days one of the most famous centers of Jewish learning. He was saved, together with a large group of Jews, by the consul-general of Japan to Lithuania, Chiune Sugihara, who, contrary to instructions from his government, issued Japanese visas to hundreds of Jews, who then traveled through Siberia to Japan, and later to China, where they stayed till the end of the war, when the United States let them in.

My father was the eldest of seven children, my Uncle Danny the youngest. Their five sisters perished in the Holocaust, with their parents, husbands and children.

Although the fascinating story of this group's survival had been told both in the media and in books, I am convinced to this day that it had never been told as my uncle told it to me that day in Jerusalem. It had taken me some time to realize that a humorous description of certain events was my uncle's way of coping with his memory of the tragic circumstances of his early years as a penniless refugee, and the loss of his family. I still weep with laughter remembering his vivid description of the encounter between the Japanese public and the group of Jewish orthodox Yeshiva students, in traditional attire, their side-locks flying as they walked.

We both became so immersed in his story that it was only when he had finished that we remembered the *Protocols of the Elders of Zion*.

Would you believe, he said, that when the Japanese Consul was approached by a group of Jews begging for Japanese visas, he knew nothing about Jews. In his search for information he came upon the *Protocols of the Elders of Zion*, and actually believed in them. Contrary to the reaction of Europeans, the Japanese admired the Jewish plan. The so-called Jewish Conspiracy, in Japanese eyes, was a model to be imitated.

My uncle believed, to his last day, that the *Protocols of the Elders of Zion* had been instrumental in saving his life.

I had completely ignored my uncle's story, until the day I met by accident Professor Ben-Ami Shillony, head of the department for East Asian Studies at the Hebrew University in Jerusalem. Since I had become involved in the story of the *Protocols* it became a constant subject of conversation in my presence, and people often recalled relevant stories.

One day, in 1978, Professor Shillony told me, he had hosted a delegation of some 15 businessmen and professionals from Japan, who were on their first visit to Israel. Apart from touring the country, they were also interested in exploring business opportunities as well as the possibility of professional and cultural cooperation with Israel. The fact that Professor Shillony was not only fluent in Japanese but also familiar with the history and culture of their country greatly facilitated their efforts to learn as much as possible about Israel and its people.

At a reception held by Professor Shillony at the end of their visit, the guests expressed their fascination with what they had seen and learned on their tour and as a token of appreciation the leader of the group presented the professor with an elegantly wrapped parcel.

There was a moment of stunned silence when Professor Shillony opened the parcel and did not immediately express his thanks, as etiquette demanded. He could hardly hide his surprise and embarrassment at what he saw. Had he not been very familiar with the Japanese, he would probably have thought that it was some kind of distasteful practical joke, but he discarded this possibility even before it formed in his mind. Why would anybody hand to a Jew a gift-wrapped elegantly bound copy of the *Protocols of the Elders of Zion*? The Japanese guests soon satisfied his curiosity. They had decided to educate themselves about Jews and about Israel and had therefore purchased copies of this book to read on the flight. Indeed, they were full of admiration for the Jews who were so successful in executing their ambitious plan, so clearly described in the book.

He was aware of existing anti-Semitism in Japan, and of the fact that not only the *Protocols of the Elders of Zion* but other similar books had been sold, and were still being sold, in millions of copies in this country, where there were practically no Jews. In some circles Jews were targeted as scapegoats, blamed for everything that was evil. In other circles Jews served as a role model, admired for their success in attaining positions and influence in many countries, well beyond what could be expected. In a country where few people had ever seen a live Jew, Jews were either hated or admired, seldom ignored. There actually existed a Jewish problem in this almost completely Jew-less society.

Yet he was shocked at the fact that a group of intelligent, well-meaning Japanese would actually present a copy of the *Protocols* as a gesture of good-will to an Israeli professor.

That evening he carefully examined the doubtful gift.

It was an impressive edition, in a red glossy cover, entitled *The Jewish Protocols*, presented as *The key for understanding of the Jewish Problem*.

Turning it in his hand the professor soon realized that it was written in two languages. From the left it was written in Russian, and contained the full text of the 1911 Nilus edition of the *Protocols*, including his introduction. The 64 pages of the Russian text were in small print.

The Japanese translation, in large bold type, printed Japanese-style, from top to bottom, in lines running from right to left, took up 226 pages. It included intro-ductions by the publisher and the translator, and photographs of famous Gentile kings who had been Masonic leaders, as well as very uncomplimentary photo-graphs of Jews and Jewish gatherings. Pictures of Columbus and of President Roosevelt were printed alongside photographs of Rothschild, Einstein, Trotsky, Mendelssohn and other famous and outstanding men who were considered to be either of Jewish origin or under the influence of Jews.

It was the seventh and newest edition of the well-known translation of the *Protocols* prepared in 1938 by Eikichi Kubota, and reproduced in 1959.

It was by no means the first version of the *Protocols* in Japanese.

The *Protocols* were first brought to Japan by Japanese officers who had been part of the expeditionary force of 75,000 men dispatched to Siberia to assist the White Army in its attempt to reinstate the tsar. Defeated by the Red Guards, the Japanese had been convinced by Russian army officers that the Jews had been the instigators of the Revolution, and they had carried back to Japan the *Protocols of the Elders of Zion*, which had been distributed to soldiers in the White Army by order of General Grigorii Semenov.

In 1924 Captain Yasue Norihiro, who had been attached to General Semenov's staff in Russia, and believed in the authenticity of the *Protocols*, translated the book into Japanese, publishing it under the title *The Jewish Peril*.

Since then the *Protocols* had appeared in Japan under various titles, although they had been denounced as forgeries by some Japanese writers. These dissenting voices were silenced during the Second World War, when the Japanese adopted the Nazi anti-Jewish ideology. German anti-Semitic books were translated and distributed in Japan, and the Jewish conspiracy became a popular theme. The end of the war did not stop the publication of the *Protocols*, or of other anti-Semitic books. Two paperbacks published in 1986 entitled *If You Know The Jews, You Will Understand The World*, and *If You Know The Jews, You Will Understand Japan*, sold one million copies. The author, Masami Uno, claimed that the trade disputes between Japan and the USA and the 'High Yen' crisis could be traced back to the Jewish conspiracy.

In the same year, 1986, Manji Yajima, a professor of international economics at Aoyama University, published his book *The Art of Reading Between the Lines of the Jewish Protocols*. The author claimed to give a new interpretation to the modern *Protocols*, asserting that the Jews were inciting quarrels between Japan and the USA. The book accused the Jews of having been behind the Russian Revolution, both world wars, the war in Vietnam, Watergate, the oil crisis, and Japan's trading troubles. The author also revealed to his readers that both President Nixon and the Japanese Prime Minister Tanaka Kakoei fell from power because they had both spoken out against the Jew Rockefeller. He warned that within ten years the Jews would totally ruin Japanese–US relations, and Japan would therefore reach a state of hunger, poverty and bankruptcy, while the Jews continue to flourish.

Israeli diplomats in Tokyo have long stopped being surprised by experiences similar to that of Professor Shillony. The *Protocols of the Elders of Zion*, often perceived in an anti-Semitic context, are at the same time held up by others as a model for admiration, a program to be imitated, a sure way to success.

THE UNITED STATES SENATE INVESTIGATES

In 1964 the Senate of the United States set up a special committee to study the *Protocols of the Elders of Zion*.

Concerned with the danger of communism, the Judiciary Committee of the Senate had become aware of the fact that the fight against communism was being subverted by those who claimed that the real danger to the USA did not come from international communism, and that it was the *International Plot of the Jews* that was endangering America. This absurd allegation made such an impact that it was decided to set up a special subcommittee to investigate the matter.

On 6 August 1964 the Committee on the Judiciary resolved that the report of the subcommittee, entitled *Protocols of the Elders of Zion – A Fabricated 'Historic' Document*, be approved as a report of the Internal Security Subcommittee to the Senate Committee on the

Judiciary. Acting on the recommendation of the subcommittee, the committee resolved that the report be printed and published.

The report, unanimously adopted by the nine members of the subcommittee, was signed by its chairman, Senator James O. Eastland from Mississippi, and by its vice-chairman, Senator Thomas J. Dodd from Connecticut.

In the introduction the senators stated: 'Every age and country has had its share of fabricated "historic" documents which have been foisted on an unsuspecting public for some malign purpose ... One of the most notorious and most durable of these is the *Protocols of the Elders of Zion*.

According to the *Protocols*, the committee stated, international communism was simply a manifestation of a world Jewish conspiracy that sought to subjugate all non-Jewish peoples of the world. The real enemy, therefore, according to the *Protocols*, was not international communism but international Jewry. On the other hand, books published in the Soviet Union, which bore a remarkable resemblance to the *Protocols*, tended to equate international Jewry with international capitalism.

Although the *Protocols* had been repeatedly and authoritatively exposed as a vicious hoax, the report said, 'they continue to be circulated by the unscrupulous and accepted by the unthinking. It is impossible not to be concerned over the cynical way in which some groups in the name of anti-communism continue to use the *Protocols*, to promote prejudice and hostility among Americans, and thus to weaken this country's efforts in the real fight against communism.'

Using surprisingly strong language, the subcommittee said that the *Protocols* were written 'in a rambling, incoherent and turgid style', that they were 'absurd, contradictory, childish', that they were 'obviously gibberish', that they dealt in psychological warfare, that they were 'the greatest forgery of the century ... one of the stupidest forgeries in all literary history ... one of the classics of anti-Semitism ... a fictional product of a warped mind'.

The peddlers of the *Protocols*, they said, 'use the Hitler technique of the *Big Lie*. They play upon the well-founded concern of the American people over communist advances to exploit groundless prejudices. They offer a key – their key – to understand the hodgepodge that is the *Protocols*. What the fabricators of the *Protocols* didn't say, the modern-day peddler does – in sensational style.' They concluded:

In the subcommittee's judgment, those who would mislead the American people by continuing to peddle this crude and vicious nonsense, impede and prejudice the Nation's fight against the Communist menace. The subcommittee believes that the peddlers of the *Protocols* are peddlers of un-American prejudice who spread hate and dissension among the American people. Falsely using the guise of fighting communism, they, like the communists who set class against class, would set religion against religion. Both would subvert the American system.

New editions of the *Protocols* have appeared since then all over the United States, more than thirty editions since 1990. In 1993 a new edition of *The International Jew* by Henry Ford was published. The theory of the Jewish Conspiracy was adopted by Christian Fundamentalists, right-wing militia groups, Holocaust deniers, and to a large extent, by African American activists. The *Protocols* are available in black nationalist bookstores, they are quoted by African American leaders, and they were distributed free of charge to participants at a New York rally held in October 1996 by the Nation of Islam and in the well-publicized *Million Men March* in Washington DC in October 1995.

The Common Law Courts movement, run by military members of the armed militias, plans to defy the legitimate institutions of government, especially their judicial and law enforcement arms, by replacing them with a parallel structure of their own creation. They often use the *Protocols* to prove Jewish complicity in the evil scheme of the federal government to strip Americans of their constitutional rights and impose a tiranical 'New World Order'.

An ad in a local newspaper, announcing the sale of the *Protocols of the Elders of Zion* for $1, explained that this was a translation by Victor E. Marsden, from the Russian of Professor Nilus, 'the most diabolical plot in world history, proof that communism is a Jewish world plot to enslave the Gentiles by creating wars and revolutions, and to seize power during the resulting chaos and to rule with their claimed superior intelligence as chosen people. Fulfillment steadily progresses while the Gentiles as predicted by the *Protocols*, sit supinely by from one event to another, unaware of the overall plan which is fast encircling them.'

In an article entitled 'Fakes that have Skewed History', published on 16 May 1983, *The Times* of London stated that 'In Europe and South America, wherever there are fringe resurgences of Nazism or

Fascism, the *Protocols* seem sure to follow. Given the tragedies they have abetted and their poisonous potential for more, the *Protocols* may be the most successful and insidious forgery in history.'

RETRIAL IN JOHANNESBURG

The telephone rang one day just as I returned from my morning swim. My friend Henry Shakanowski, a former judge in Johannesburg, who had recently made Alyia to Israel, was calling from South Africa, where he was visiting his children. The year was 1991 and South Africa was in the middle of the painful process of reform that would finally rid the country of the scourge of apartheid. For many years books considered to be 'undesirable', had been banned by the white regime, which was now un-banning and releasing for publication carefully selected lists of books. To the surprise and consternation of the Jewish community, Henry told me, the *Protocols of the Elders of Zion*, banned in South Africa since 1945, and declared 'undesirable' in 1979, were prominent on the list of books to be un-banned. On 12 July 1991, an *ad hoc* Committee of Publications', acting in its legal capacity, had now declared that the *Protocols of the Elders of Zion* was a book 'not to be considered undesirable'.

I had told Henry that in my presence a delegate of an African country had said on the floor of the UN Assembly: 'The Jews are to blame that our brethren are held in bondage in South Africa.' Now the Jews would be blamed for the abolition of apartheid, he said on the telephone.

A group of lawyers were discussing the possibility of initiating legal proceedings, he told me, asking for my opinion. While they were all concerned as to the possible repercussions which could follow the publication of the *Protocols* at this point in time, there were some who argued that the initiation of legal proceedings might be even more harmful to the Jewish community. Jewish leaders had been in the forefront of the struggle for the abolition of apartheid. The banning of books had been one of the tools used by the white racist regime of South Africa, and as such had been condemned by liberals who welcomed the process of un-banning, although they were advocating the adoption of total freedom of expression, as practiced in free and democratic countries. If the Jews tried to prevent the un-banning of a book, would they not be perceived as opposing the liberalization that was taking place? Would they not be presented in the press as hypocrites, who abandoned their principles and advocated freedom of expression only as long as it did not concern them? Would they not say that Jews were supporting the freedom to say anything about anybody, as long as you did not say anything derogatory about them?

What about a proven forgery, I asked, does the freedom of expression provide a license for spreading dangerous lies? Isn't it time we start seriously re-examining some of the sacred constitutionally based rules, which some of us accept unquestionably? Isn't it time to confront the danger of individuals and groups who openly preach hatred and fabricate lies which incite to violence, protected by constitutional rights and freedoms which they cynically abuse? How many more innocent people must be victimized, because we allow the villains of this world to set them up as targets?

Yes, Henry offered, surprised by the vehemence of my feelings, still playing the devil's advocate, but who decides what is a lie?

What about a recorded judgment of a South African court? I reminded him.

How bizarre, I thought, that of all places, the *Protocols* were again emerging in South Africa, where, 57 years before, they had been condemned in no uncertain terms as a lie and a forgery, by a court of law. Could they not argue that the matter had been finally decided by a competent South African court in a published judgment?

On 2 August 1991, an appeal was submitted to the Publication Appeal Board in Johannesburg by the Directorate of Publications against the Committee of Publications, in the matter of the *Protocols of the Elders of Zion*.

The South African Jewish Board of Deputies and the International Association of Jewish Lawyers and Jurists (South African Chapter) were named as 'Intervening Parties'.

They claimed that this publication fell within three categories of the definition of 'undesirable publications' in section 47(2) of the Publication Act, which stated:

> For the purposes of this Act any publication ... shall be deemed to be undesirable if it or any part of it –
> Is blasphemous or is offensive to the religious convictions or feelings of any section of the inhabitants of the Republic;
> or
> Brings any section of the inhabitants of the Republic into ridicule or contempt;
> or
> Is harmful to the relations between any section of the inhabitants of the Republic.

Clearly, they argued, the Jewish Community of the Republic of South Africa which constituted a 'section of the inhabitants of the Republic', had a right to protect its interests and to be represented by those who were well equipped to present its views to the board.

Unlike the trial in Grahamstown, they did not need a private plaintiff to prove personal harm. The law applicable in this case protected groups and sections, therefore a group of people whose interests were threatened had a right to be represented.

There was also no need to speculate about the possible danger from the *Protocols of the Elders of Zion*. This was the post-Holocaust era and there was ample proof of the use the Nazis had made of the *Protocols*. It was also evident that neo-Nazi groups were reviving the *Protocols* and new publications were appearing all over the world.

Their impressive legal brief held 137 pages. It included the history of the *Protocols*, the revelations of their origin, the description of the harm they had done, and the attitude of prestigious academic bodies as well as governments, parliaments and courts, in other countries, to this particular publication.

On 12 November 1991, the seven members of the Publications Appeal Board, chaired by Mr D. W. Morkel, delivered its unanimous judgment, setting aside the decision of the *ad hoc* 'Committee of Publications'. The *Protocols of the Elders of Zion* was declared an undesirable document, not only its publication but also its possession prohibited.

The lawyers, who had almost closed their offices to the public to prepare in record time the legal brief, convened with their clients to study the decision of the Board.

They had won an important legal battle and they had set a precedent. On the question of representation, the Board decided that the Jewish community of South Africa constituted an important section of the inhabitants of the Republic and as the publication in question purported to be an important Jewish policy document, the Jewish community had a vital interest to make representation. 'It would have been contrary to the principle of natural justice and the flexibility and fairness normally associated with the proceedings of administrative tribunals not to afford them the right,' the Appeal Board stated. Had the representations not been filed, he would probably have approached the Jewish Board of Deputies for expert advice, the chairman added.

They were particularly impressed by the Board's perception of the danger the *Protocols* created. They had succeeded in convincing the tribunal that South Africa should join other countries that had found it necessary to deal with the publication of the *Protocols* in the post-Holocaust era.

Now, the Jewish community noted with satisfaction, South Africa was making a clear statement that libelous lies against a group of citizens did not deserve the protection accorded to other forms of speech.

The Board had specifically addressed itself to the problem of anti-Semitism. Unlike other legal proceedings concerning the *Protocols*, the respondents in this appeal did not argue against the facts presented in the legal brief of the Jewish lawyers, which was highly praised by the board. They openly agreed that the *Protocols* were a fraudulent document and that they fell within the definition of 'undesirable publications'. But, the committee said, they had decided to 'un-ban' the *Protocols* as they had come to the conclusion that the document had been overtaken by history and that the relations between Jews and non-Jews in South Africa had been so good as to render the publication harmless. Rejecting this argument, the Board said it was convinced that in many countries of the world anti-Semitism was on the rise and that this publication served as the 'Bible of anti-Semitism':

> South Africa finds itself in a fragile and transitory period where attempts to promote racial and ethnic harmony are of the utmost importance ... the board is convinced that the publication is inundated with material which is likely to offend both Jews and non-Jews. It has great potential for fanning racial tension and in the hands of malicious individuals could be used as a tool to that end ... both Jews and non-Jews would be mortified by passages in the publication ... the fact that the publication has been proven to be fraudulent but can be applied to reality makes it exceedingly dangerous.

The *Protocols* were not only anti-Jewish, the Board declared, accepting the argument of the Directorate of Publications that the book brought the non-Jewish section of the population of the Republic into contempt and ridicule. The 'Goyim' were stated to be brainless dupes, beset by drunkenness and immorality. They were the real villains of the *Protocols*, the Directorate argued. The court agreed, stating that South Africa could do without a publication that apart, from being extremely anti-Semitic, also expressly advocated the killing of non-Jews.

BACK TO RUSSIA – A TRIAL IN MOSCOW

In 1993, exactly 90 years after chapters from the *Protocols* were first published in the newspaper *Znamia* in 1903, 88 years after the appearance of the book by Nilus, the *Protocols* were brought up for the first time in a Russian court.

One day, in June 1996, three years after this trial in Moscow, I was reading about the upcoming elections in Russia. Some communist supporters of Zyuganov were accusing Yeltsin of being 'in the pocket of the Jews'. They were calling the Jews 'Zhydki'. The ten years of economic and social reform in Russia were, in their propaganda, the materialization of the Judeo-Masonic conspiracy. In the mass rallies held in support of Zyuganov the *Protocols of the Elders of Zion* were sold to the public.

I wondered whether Judge Belikova would have made a difference had she been as courageous as Judge Meyer in Berne 60 years before, and declared unequivocally that the *Protocols of the Elders of Zion* were a false document. Had she realized that she was missing a historic opportunity to right a century-old wrong perpetrated by her compatriots? Or were her actions dictated from above?

The trial in Moscow was brought to my attention by a friend who had actually been present in the courtroom. I knew her as an educated, intelligent person, and was therefore surprised at her request: 'If you ever write about this trial, don't mention my name.' When I learned the facts, it did not seem to be a case of unfounded paranoia.

The Revolution in 1917 had been the beginning of the communist regime that had existed for more than 70 years. Russia had undergone the tremendous trauma of the Second World War and the Cold War that followed. It had now chosen to break down the barriers that separated it from the Western world, and was carefully and painfully undergoing a process of democratization, having given up its supremacy over all the countries which were part of the communist bloc. Yet, through all these changes, the *Protocols of the Elders of Zion* had never been abandoned. Having been created by tsarist Russia to blame the Jews as leaders of the revolutionary movement, they were later transformed by the communist regime as a tool in their traditional anti-Jewish policy, their persistent opposition to Israel, and their support of the Arabs in the Middle East. The so-called 'Jewish Conspiracy' had easily been transformed into a 'Zionist Plot'. The Jews were still accused of holding the purse strings through the bankers in Wall Street, manipulating presidents and governments and brainwashing the uninformed public through the media, which was completely in Jewish hands, but the image of the Jews as 'Bolshevik anarchists' was now replaced by the image of the 'omnipotent capitalist'.

The 'Jewish Conspiracy' that had been originally presented as a threat to Christendom was now presented as a plan to dominate the Arab countries, through the State of Israel, as a step on the way to world domination. In spite of their hatred of Nazi Germany, which had almost devastated their country and caused the death of millions of Russians, official Communist Russia used Hitler's theories based on the *Protocols* to explain all governmental shortcomings and failures. As in tsarist Russia, the Jews were still the most convenient target and the theory of conspiracy was still an effective tool to divert attention from national disasters. The traditional historical animosity of the Russian people towards Jews could still be gainfully exploited.

The Russian anti-Zionist propaganda became even more aggressive when the Soviet Union and all the countries in the Soviet block except Rumania, severed diplomatic relations with Israel after the Six Day War in June 1967. In August 1967 an article that appeared in various Russian publications, entitled 'What is Zionism?', stated that 'an extensive network of Zionist organizations with a common center, a common program, and funds much greater than those of the Mafia *Cosa Nostra*, is active behind the scenes of the international theater'. The global 'Zionist Corporation' was composed of 'smart dealers in politics, finance, religion, and trade, whose well camouflaged aim is the enrichment by any means of the international Zionist network'.

The theme of the *Protocols* was used by the Russian delegation to the United Nations in their aggressive support of the UN Resolution on 10 November 1975, equating Zionism with racism.

In its review of the play *Herzl* by the Israeli writer Amos Elon, the newspaper *Sovetskaia Kultura* (Soviet Culture) wrote:

> According to Herzl's assertion, he was moved in Paris to write the brochure *The Jewish State* – today proclaimed *The Bible of Zionism*. The idea of the book, he stated, was supposedly inspired from above, and during his writing of it, he had heard the rustling of eagle's wings ... In reality it all took place in a much more prosaic manner. One day, Herzl happened to take into his hands the book of the French Mason, Maurice Joly ... which had been published anonymously in Switzerland thirty years earlier. Herzl thought the content of the book was interesting and the half-forgotten brochure became the foundation of a shameless literary plagiarism. Herzl stole from Maurice Joly 18 basic provisions without changing a thing and presenting them as his own revelations; in addition, he slightly altered over thirty passages.

Now the communist regime was dead. The new regime had not only re-established diplomatic relations with Israel, but had changed its policy towards Jews, abolishing the restrictions on Jewish education and Jewish immigration. They had freed Jewish dissidents after years of imprisonment. Yet the *Protocols* were enjoying a new revival, circulated this time by opponents of the government, from both the communist left and the extreme right wing.

There was much opposition in Russia to the new regime, which had dissolved the Soviet Union, and the transition was causing great difficulties for the Russian government. Although a small elite had become tremendously rich, the masses suffered from economic difficulties, which made people wonder whether the new freedom they had acquired was worth it. It was time to blame the Jews again, and what better tool than the *Protocols of the Elders of Zion*. The dissidents had suddenly become great proponents of the freedom of speech.

One of the most prominent anti-Jewish organizations in Russia is Pamiat, an extreme right-wing organization that enthusiastically supports Russian nationalism. In 1991, Pamiat started a new publication, also called *Pamiat*, immediately using the first two issues to quote long excerpts from the *Protocols*, accompanied by cartoons resembling those published in old German Nazi publications. As a supplement to the excerpts of the *Protocols* the newspaper printed an article, published in Buenos Aires in 1955, under the title 'La Conspiracion Mundial Oculta' (The Occult World Conspiracy), in Russian translation, which claimed that the *Protocols* were a translation from the ancient Hebrew, and that there were testimonies of people who had lived in Odessa in 1890 who had seen the book.

On 7 May 1991, the *Jewish Newspaper* published a list of anti-Semitic newspapers, including major newspapers such as *Pravda*. There was no reaction for a year and a half, until 26 November 1992, when Pamiat initiated legal proceedings, suing the *Jewish Newspaper* and its editor, Mr. Golenpolskii, for libel. Their name had also been included in the list but they were not anti-Semites, they said, as could be proved by their friendship toward the Arabs, who were also Semites. Calling them anti-Semites harmed their reputation, as it created a false image spread by international media, controlled by the Jews. The sum of the claimed damages was 20 million roubles.

Mr Golenpolskii maintained that the publication of the *Protocols of the Elders of Zion*, in itself, was an act of anti-Semitism, and therefore justified the inclusion of *Pamiat* in the list.

On 26 January yet another chapter began in the never-ending tortuous saga of the *Protocols of the Elders of Zion*, in a drab Russian courtroom, on the second floor of an old building in a Moscow neighborhood called Cheremushki.

Judge Valentina Konstantinovna Belikova presided, flanked by two members of the public, as local procedure demanded.

There was a feeling of *déjà vu* among the Jews, who learned that the court was yet again appointing experts to testify whether the *Protocols* were true or false.

Like Judge Meyer in Berne, the court in Moscow also presented the experts with a list of questions:

1. Are the *Protocols of the Elders of Zion* a publication that purports to reveal a Jewish conspiracy to dominate the world and subjugate all nations to Jewish rule, a forged document?
2. Did Hitler use the *Protocols of the Elders of Zion* in his book *Mein Kampf,* and were the *Protocols* part of Nazi propaganda?
3. Are the *Protocols of the Elders of Zion* one of the main tools used in anti-Zionist propaganda, and had they served as an ideological vehicle in the performance of Genocide against the Jewish people, both in Russia (in pogroms) and in Germany?
4. Was the publication of the *Protocols of the Elders of Zion*, accompanied by certain drawings, in two issues of the newspaper *Pamiat*, an act of anti-Jewish propaganda, liable to incite nationalist hatred and to humiliate nationalist honor and self-respect?

The plaintiff, Vasil'ev Dmitrii Dmitrievich, editor and publisher of the newspaper *Pamiat*, had dressed for the occasion in a proper business suit, but a large and loud group of his followers appeared in black uniforms.

The lawyer, Mr David Akselband, announced that he was representing the defendants, the *Jewish Newspaper* and its editor, Mr Golenpolskii, who was also present. A tall handsome man, with a pointed goatee, rose and bowed to the court. The Jews of Moscow were absent from the courtroom, whether fearful for their safety or from lack of interest.

The judge was not pleased with the photographers engaged by *Pamiat*, but when she asked them to stop taking pictures (no order, just a polite request, Akselband whispered to his client) Vasil'ev retorted that they needed it for their record, promising that 'this would not go anywhere else'. The photographers kept on clicking their cameras. The judge looked embarrassed, but did nothing.

The first sessions were dedicated to a futile discussion of the meaning of the term 'anti-Semitism'. *Pamiat* argued that Jews constitute only 7 per cent of the Semites in the world, and *Pamiat* was definitely not anti-Arab. As a matter of fact, they said, they were not even anti-Jewish, they were only stating well-known facts.

Everybody looked bored and the judge found it hard to keep order in the courtroom. The *Pamiat* audience was loud, unruly, and utterly oblivious of the court's warnings. They often laughed and sneered at the witnesses.

On 29 October the court heard with close attention the testimony of three experts. A fourth expert, a certain Ms Malkova, from the research institute of the Ministry of the Interior, had resigned. The plaintiff and his lawyer had been informed by a private source that she was afraid for her life.

The three remaining experts, all non-Jews, were high-ranking scientists: Alexander Krylov, an expert in historical science from the University Institute of African and Asian studies, religious historian Leonel Dadiani, and Zoya Krakhmalnikova, a well-known writer on Russian orthodox subjects.

All three had studied the history of the *Protocols of the Elders of Zion* and were unanimous in their opinion that they were a blatant forgery and a highly anti-Semitic document, composed and used for the purpose of anti-Jewish incitement.

Their testimony came as a surprise to Vasil'ev, who knew that at least two of them, Krylov and Dadiani, were on record as ardent anti-Zionists. He even greeted Dadiani by stating that he had two shelves of his books at home, and frequently consulted them. But these were serious scientists and they were court-appointed experts, sworn to give their honest scientific opinion.

Krylov informed the court that he and his friends at the Institute, who had all confirmed his opinion, had been embarrassed by the court's request. They had thought that for the Russian people the question of the *Protocols of the Elders of Zion* had been long resolved. Even the Black Hundreds had avoided mention of the *Protocols* at the Beilis trial because the Russian intelligentsia was aware of the fact that this was a forged document with no basis in reality.

The witness revealed that he was also an expert in the Hebrew language and had studied Jewish documents. The *Protocols* used terms that a Jew would never use.

In answer to a specific question of the court he explained at length how the Nazis had used the *Protocols* in their propaganda, quoting from Alfred Rosenberg and from Hitler's *Mein Kampf*. This book was actually based on the *Protocols*, he said.

When the judge asked his opinion as a scientist as to whether this book should be forbidden, he was uncomfortable at the attempt to shift responsibility to his shoulders: 'This is the court's decision, not mine,' he answered. He then added: 'There is of course the moral responsibility of a scientist.' He then told the court that he had studied the history of Zionism at the university of Moscow with a teacher named Iurii Sergeevich Ivanov, the author of a book entitled *Beware, Zionism!* which was considered highly anti-Semitic. When the students had asked him why he had not included the *Protocols of the Elders of Zion* in his book, as they fitted its content, he replied by quoting the tsar's famous remark about not performing a good deed with dirty hands.

For a time, the witness said, the *Protocols* could be found only in archives. Now they were sold everywhere.

Dadiani announced that he fully agreed with Krylov's opinion. There was no end to the circulation of false information, he said, – one writer, a former drummer, even maintained that Nilus had been a Jew.

The lawyer Akselband asked if a man in the street who read the *Protocols* would develop anti-Jewish feelings.

That was a rhetorical question, Dadiani answered. A Russian man, particularly if he was a little drunk, facing all the present difficulties, would automatically be inclined to beat up any man who looked Jewish.

But the most moving testimony was that of Krakhmalnikova, a staunch supporter of the Orthodox Church. Gray-haired and simply dressed, she said with conviction: 'I have come to this court because of my conscience.' Pointing at Vasil'ev, she added: 'You personally and *Pamiat* have inflicted an insult not only on the Jews, but also on the Russian people, especially on Christianity and the Church ... The *Protocols* are a false document, they were the basis for the fascist theories of Hitler ... You have done an anti-Christian and an inhuman deed, and you must do an act of Christian repentance for it ... Christianity is about love and not about hatred towards any people, especially not towards the Jewish people, among whom God had his son, Jesus.'

On 26 November the court held its last session. There was much expectation in the air, and this time some Jews were present. At long last, they said among themselves, a Russian court would pronounce the falsity of the *Protocols*. They might even try to have the book banned by the authorities, as was the case in France, where the authorities banned the *Protocols of the Elders of Zion* on 25 May 1990 after the desecration of the Jewish cemetery in Carpantras.

Mr Golenpolski and his lawyer looked very pleased. When the representative of the state attorney rose and urged the court to rule that *Pamiat* was an anti-Semitic newspaper and that the *Protocols* were a forgery. Judge Belikova nodded in a definite gesture of consent and announced her decision in favor of the defendants, ordering *Pamiat* to pay the *Jewish Newspaper* and Mr Golenpolski their costs in the sum of 250,000 roubles. She promised to announce her full reasoned judgment at a later date.

When they received the full judgment some time later they were all shocked. They were convinced that something had happened to the judge since the last court session. All signs indicated that the judgment had been dictated from above.

The only reason for dismissing the claim of *Pamiat* was now 'freedom of speech', under paragraph 7 of the new Media Law, enacted in 1990. It now seemed that under this law *Pamiat* was allowed to publish the *Protocols*, and the *Jewish Newspaper* was allowed to include them in their list of anti-Semites.

The word anti-Semitism was not mentioned even once.

As to the *Protocols of the Elders of Zion*, the court said, both sides had presented their subjective views, as was their right, but such views did not constitute proper evidence on the matter. The court was not competent to rule on the authenticity of the *Protocols*.

But what about the experts, people in the audience asked each other. If their testimony was also considered to be 'a subjective view', why appoint them in the first place? And why conduct such a long trial? In the frame of the right to total free speech the claim of *Pamiat* could have been rejected in the first court session!

Both sides appealed to the Moscow City Court.

Pamiat wanted the judgment set aside. Golenpolski asked for a court decision on the issues raised at the trial. They quoted the relevant paragraph in the law, which empowered the judge to rule on the authenticity of a document, and to appoint experts to present their opinion on the matter. The court had indeed done so, they claimed, but had then completely ignored both the impressive testimony of the experts and the mass of documentary material presented by the defendants from foreign courts. The court had not even said that the *Protocols* were an anti-Semitic document. Rejecting the claim of *Pamiat* was not enough in this case, they argued.

But it was a foregone decision. This time a different lawyer represented the state attorney, and it was apparent that she had not even read the transcript of the trial. Neither had the judges, who listened politely to the arguments and retired to chambers to consider their decision. People in the audience joked that consultation in chambers was probably conducted on the telephone with higher authorities.

Sure enough, the court announced that it was rejecting both appeals.

The political system might have changed, Jews said to each other, but this was still Moscow, not Berne.

THE MUSLIM VERSION

In October 1976 Professor Bernard Lewis of Princeton University, one of the foremost experts on Islam, stated in an article published in the *Journal of Foreign Affairs* that the *Protocols of the Elders of Zion* were universally cited in Arabic literature on Jewish matters, and noted that to his knowledge, their authenticity had never been refuted, or even called into question, by an Arab writer.

In a letter to the editor of the same journal, published in April 1977, Dr Abdelwahab M. Elmessiri, assistant professor of English and American poetry at the Al-Shams University of Cairo, begged to differ. He wrote that the Research Center of the Palestine Liberation Organization in Beirut, which was 'among the leading institutions which publish literature on "Jewish matters", had never made reference to the *Protocols*, except perhaps in derogatory terms'. He added that: 'Dr Razzuk's study on Talmud and Zionism vigorously opposed the "conspiratorial view" of the Jews and Zionists.'

He then mentioned Arab writers who had questioned the authenticity of the *Protocols*, such ase Dr A. Al-Attiyeh, director of the Palestine Research Center in Baghdad (on Iraqi television in the spring of 1974), and Abdelwahab el-Kayyali, a leading figure in the PLO in Damascus. He himself had worked for four years as director of the Zionist Ideology Department of the Al-Ahram publishing house in Cairo, and had published an article in *Al-Ahram* in February 1974, entitled 'The Protocols of the Elders of Zion'.

'In it I traced the history of the pamphlet and specifically pointed out that it is believed to be a forgery,' he wrote. 'Furthermore, the article in question noted that the diversity of the historical experience of the Jewish communities in the world disproves the simplistic theory of a "grand conspiracy" or "a world government" by the Jews.

'All this is to underscore the fact that almost all the Arab institutes engaged in Palestinian, Jewish or Zionist studies hold a negative view of the *Protocols* and classify them as among the more objectionable anti-Semitic literature,' he concluded.

Why did Elmessiri use phrases such as 'of questionable authenticity' or 'believed to be a forgery', Professor Lewis asked. Why not say outright that the book was an anti-Jewish fake?

Eighteen years later, after Israel had made peace with Egypt, in June 1995, the same publishing house, Al-Ahram, published an Arabic translation of *A New Middle East*, by Shimon Peres 'as a service to the reader', part of a series entitled *Know Your Enemy*.

In his book Peres, who had won the Nobel Peace Prize for his part in initiating the peace process between Israel and the Palestinians, had described his vision of a Middle East that would flourish when peace was finally attained. He must have been very surprised to read in the preface to his book the following passage:

> When the *Protocols of the Elders of Zion* were discovered 200 years ago and translated into various languages, including Arabic, the International Zionist Organization tried to deny the existence of the conspiracy and maintained that it was a forgery. The Zionists even tried to purchase all the existing copies in order to prevent people from reading them. But now Shimon Peres supplies definite proof that the *Protocols* are indeed authentic and absolutely true. His book is another step in the realization of this dangerous plot.

The writer of the article had ignored some undisputed facts: the *Protocols* had not been 'discovered' 200 years ago, and 200 years ago there was no Zionist organization!

In fact, the Arab and Muslim countries had adopted the *Protocols of the Elders of Zion* as part of their anti-Zionist ideology, including its anti-Semitic connotations. The *Protocols*, originally fabricated as an alleged Jewish plot against Christendom, had long ago donned an anti-Arabic disguise. The Jews still meant to dominate the world, but the first stage on their agenda was the domination of Israel's neighboring countries in the Middle East. Had the conspiracy not been shaped at the first Zionist Congress in Basle? The establishment of the State of Israel and its victories over the Arab countries, supported by foreign states, whose leaders were always manipulated by the Jews, served as solid proof of the inner truth of the *Protocols* and of their authenticity. Unlike other countries, where new publications of the

Protocols were mostly published, quoted and distributed by racist and anti-Semitic groups, in major Arab countries they were part of the mainstream literary world, published by the most prestigious publishing houses and widely quoted by official and semi-official newspapers. They were also distributed in Muslim communities in Western countries, and among Muslim and Third World students in Western universities.

In his 1987 book *Semites and Anti-Semites*, Bernard Lewis noted that:

> The demonization of Jews in Arabic writings goes further than it had ever done in western literature, with the exception of Germany during the period of Nazi rule. In western countries anti-Semitic divagations on Jewish history, religion, and literature are more than offset by a great body of genuine scholarship ... in modern Arabic writing there are few such countervailing elements.

Abas Mahmud Al'arad, one of the most famous Egyptian writers, had written an introduction to the first Egyptian publication of the *Protocols*, in 1951. By that time ten Arabic editions had appeared in other countries.

It was strange, Al'arad wrote, that this wondrous book had only now appeared in Egypt in its full text, although the Arab countries should have been made aware of this document, as they had experienced the crimes of the Balfour Declaration and the establishment of the Jewish state in the land of Palestine.

He noted that all the publishers of the *Protocols*, in all languages, acted not for profit, but for ideological reasons, and every publication of the *Protocols* had been sold out in one week.

The translator had written a lengthy introduction, in which he revealed to his Arab readers that the Jews had decided on their secret plan to dominate the world and establish the Kingdom of David at the first Zionist Congress in Basle, in 1897. According to his information, the '300 Jewish Elders' had all participated in this fateful congress.

As to the argument that the *Protocols* were a forgery, the writer said, 'The truth is that the facts speak for themselves.'

Economic domination was persistently described by the Arab press as part of the Jewish plot. In November 1985 the Syrian paper *Al-Aktazad* published an article by Ali Hag' Bakhri, maintaining that the Jews and the Zionists had been attempting for hundreds of years to dominate the world's economy, as recorded in the *Protocols of the Elders of Zion*. These *Protocols* were considered by the Jews as a message from their prophets, as binding as any tenet of the Torah or the Talmud. The writer quoted passages from the *Protocols* to show how important gold was to Jews as a source of power. The 'Hidden Hand' of the Jews was at work, in their ongoing effort to take over banks, media and businesses. In time the importance of 'yellow gold' had diminished, and the 'black gold' had increased Arab influence. That was why the Zionists were now conspiring to dominate the oil fields of the world. Again they were using the well-tried plan of the *Protocols*, trying to create international crisis in both the economic and the political sense. Confronted with this Jewish cabal, the Arabs were helpless and inexperienced, he maintained.

To convince his readers, Bakhri drew heavily from well-tried 'historical data': Napoleon's minister of finance had been a Jew, and he had made the emperor attack the holy land; the Jewish Prime Minister Disraeli had been behind the acquisition by Britain of the Suez Canal shares; the Jews had brought about the downfall of the Ottoman Sultan Abd-el-Hamid through a group of Jews who had pretended to convert to Islam; in 1968 this 'Hidden Hand' had succeeded in creating a financial crisis in France, as punishment for de Gaulle's support of the Arabs. Again this was done by a group of Jews who had pretended to convert to Christianity. Even the Egyptian policy of making peace with Israel had been manipulated by the Jews. Between 1938 and 1948, the article said, 1,200 Jewish families had converted to Islam, as foreseen by President Benjamin Franklin in 1879, thus succeeding in seizing positions of power, disproportionate to their numbers in Egypt.

But it was not only countries such as Syria, still officially at war with Israel, that used the *Protocols* as a tool in their anti-Zionist propaganda. Surprisingly, the *Protocols* were sold in major bookstores in countries that had signed peace treaties with Israel, such as Egypt and Jordan, and they continued to be used in programs of education and constantly referred to in the official and semi-official press.

In the middle of the peace process between Israel and the Palestinians, officially supported by Egypt, an Egyptian edition of the *Protocols* appeared with an introduction arguing that the *Protocols* were true and the Jewish plot was alive.

On 8 September 1993, the semi-official Egyptian magazine

OCTOBER published lengthy extracts from the *Protocols*, stating that they were a true record of secret meetings held behind the scenes of the First Zionist Congress.

The Jews were quoted as saying: 'The Goyim are sheep and we are wolves'; 'War is a necessity to increase confusion, which creates blind submission'; 'We are Kings of the Universe and all the others are our slaves'; 'We are the only ones who were created in the image of God, the others are like beasts'.

Again, the '300 elders' were all present.

Nilus was described as a 'Russian scientist'. He had foreseen the establishment of the Jewish state in Palestine, the downfall of all the monarchies in Europe and both world wars, in which the Jews would triumph. It all happened as he had predicted. Herzl had announced that the *Protocols* had been stolen and the Jews said they had been forged. But the *Protocols* only repeat what was said in the Talmud and they were materializing 'before our very eyes'.

After quoting extensively from the *Protocols*, they quoted Hitler, who had realized that the Jews were defrauding the whole world. He had said that the Jews would not settle for one state: they were out to dominate the whole world.

They ended by crying: 'Will the world never learn?!'

There are also specific accusations, reminiscent of the blood libels. This time the Jews do not settle on murdering a single Christian child. The Zionists were actually distributing illicit drugs and narcotics and luring Egyptian youth into a Satanic cult; they were flooding Egypt with fruits and vegetables laced with poison they were even exporting to Egypt chewing gum intended to make Arab women promiscuous. Massacre, murder, and genocide were described by Mustafa Mahmud in *Al-Ahram* as 'central tenets of the Jewish religion'.

On 23 January 1997, the Egyptian *Al-Ahram* accused Israel of spreading HIV among 305 Palestinian youths in Gaza and the West Bank. In spite of the fact that the newspaper retracted the information on its front page four days later, in the face of loud protests, the same accusation was made on 11 March 1997 by Mr Ramlawi, the delegate of the Palestine authority, at a session of the UN Commission on Human Rights in Geneva. This was on 4 April 1983, addressed to the UN secretary general, accusing Israel of poisoning with genocidal intent 300 Palestinian children.

In January 1997 the *Egyptian Gazette* published an article quoting the *Protocols* in support of its thesis that the Zionists were taking over Egypt's economy, as part of their overall plan to dominate the world.

When the Anti-Defamation League complained that a government-owned newspaper was promoting so-called 'scientific studies' with blatant anti-Semitic motivations, the *Gazette* published a response quoting the *Zionist Wisemen* of the *Protocols of the Elders of Zion*, 'a book acknowledged by many world institutions to be telling the secret motivations of the Zionists' intentions and plots'.

In a public speech delivered on Friday, 10 October 1997, the prime minister of Malaysia, Dr Mahathir Mohammed, said that the Jews were spearheading a campaign to devalue the Malaysian currency and thus undermine its economy. The local newspaper *NATION* headlined its report in thick letters: 'PM: Jews unhappy to see us progress'. The ringgit, which is the local currency, had been down 18 per cent against the US dollar since July, and there were many voices blaming the crisis on the faulty financial policy of the government. It was time for diversion tactics and finding a scapegoat was in order. He may not have heard of the famous 300 bankers mentioned by Rathenau, but the time-honored practice of blaming a national crisis on an international consortium of Jewish financiers had worked before, and there was no reason it could not work again. Only this time the so-called 'Jewish Plot' was directed not against the Christian but, rather, against the Muslim states. He did not want to accuse them directly, the prime minister said, but he suspected that the Jews had their own agenda. 'Incidentally,' he added as if in an afterthought, 'we are Muslims and these people are not happy to see Muslims progress.' They didn't need to use pistols or knives, he said, they were using the currency market to rob Malaysia.

Not only was the international press outraged, some carrying the item on front pages, but even local opposition leaders were critical, warning the prime minister that he was 'treading on dangerous ground'.

Two days later he published a clarifying statement. He was not accusing the Jews, he said; he had said only that 'incidentally' those involved in the international financial manipulations ruining his country were Jews, 'and incidentally, we are Muslims'. He dared not accuse the Jews, he added. 'They are the strongest race in the world. We cannot make such wild accusations. They will twist our arms.' He said he hoped there would not be any attempts to cause him to be at loggerheads with the Jews. Turning to the press, he added: 'Please don't make things difficult for me. If I am in difficulty, I don't mind, but they make attacks to cause our currency to fall.'

The press carried his clarification in full. The *NATION* headlined it 'Clarifies statement on Jews', and in a subtitle 'No wild accusations'.

But it seems that Dr Mahathir Mohammed had not changed his mind. Addressing the Organization of Islamic Conference (OIC) on 22 October 2003, he could not avoid mentioning the Jews again.

Here is what he said: 'The Europeans killed six million Jews out of twelve million. But today the Jews rule this world by proxy. They get others to fight and die for them.'

On 1 August 1994 the UN Sub-Commission on Prevention of Discrimination and Protection of Minorities, which reports to the Commission on Human Rights, convened in Geneva for its 46th session.

In an address delivered on 3 August David Littman, representative of IFOR (International Fellowship of Reconciliation), warned that 60 years after the apocalyptic events of the 1930s the *Protocols of the Elders of Zion* were still widely disseminated, having been reprinted over the former decade in many countries, 'But it is in the Arab-Islamic world', he said, 'that the *Protocols* remain repulsive best-sellers of hatred.' He stated that Saudi Arabia was the largest producer and exporter of this document, which was also to be found in the centers of the Middle East and the Maghreb. He presented details of how the Islamic Republic of Iran was providing the needs of the Iranian market, spilling over into European languages for Western consumption. The journal *Imam*, published by the Press and Information Department of the Iranian Embassy in London, had reproduced parts of the *Protocols* in a series of articles from February to May 1984, stating that the key to all contemporary events was clear. 'The invisible hand of Zionism seems to have been at work for centuries everywhere, perpetrating crimes of unbelievable magnitude against human societies and values.' Only by studying the *Protocols*, they said, could one 'rediscover some horrifying realities of the corrupted Human Society as trademarks of Zionism'. 'Zionism is a plague that must be destroyed,' they said.

This was a clear directive, soon adopted by terrorist groups. As in the days of the Black Hundreds in Russia, and of the Nazi regime in Germany, the message was clear: the Jews were plotting to dominate the world; they were actually implementing their plan; they must be destroyed.

Not surprisingly, the August 1988 Covenant of the Palestinian Hamas movement, which openly takes responsibility for a large number of vicious terrorist attacks in Israel, states that Muslims are under obligation, by order of their Prophet, to fight Jews and kill them wherever they can find them. The Jews had taken over the world media and financial centers, the Covenant said, by fomenting revolutions, wars and such movements as the Freemasons, communism, capitalism and Zionism, B'nai B'rith, and so on. They were subverting human society as a whole, in order to bring about its destruction, propagate their own viciousness and corruption, and take over the world via pet institutions such as the League of Nations, the United Nations, and the Security Council. Their schemes were detailed in the *Protocols of the Elders of Zion*.

The *Protocols*, which had helped brainwash and incite the *pogromtchiks* in tsarist Russia and Hitler's butchers in Nazi Germany, were now cynically used to convince Arab suicide bombers that in sacrificing their lives to kill Jews they would be saving their country from Zionist domination, thus securing for themselves a place in heaven as *shahids*. Copies of the *Protocols* are often carried by terrorists for good luck, just as one would carry the holy Bible as a source of courage on a dangerous mission.

On one occasion, when Arab terrorists who had stabbed to death Israeli soldiers peacefully sleeping in their tents, were later apprehended, copies of the *Protocols* were found alongside the stolen arms in a cave that served as their hiding place.

On 11 November 1994, 21-year-old Hisham Ismail Hamad strapped explosives around his waist and rode his bicycle into an Israeli army checkpoint near Gaza, obliterating himself and three Israeli soldiers.

Six days earlier he had participated in a semi-clandestine meeting of a group of activists who claimed allegiance to the Islamic Jihad, one of the deadliest terrorist movements in the Middle East. Also at the meeting was Kenneth Timmerman, a journalist, whose report was published in the *Jerusalem Post* (on 25 November 1994), and in the *Los Angeles Times*, after the terrorist attack.

As reported by Timmerman, one of the participants in the meeting, Mahmoud Ahmed, had declared: 'Islamic Jihad considers that Israel, Nazi US, Britain, France and others are a cancer that must be removed. This is one of our central ideas. We would like to remind them that the Argentina bomb is only one of the actions of the

Islamic Jihad. We will continue this type of action. In fact, it is our main strategy.'

Hisham Ismail, the future suicide bomber, had added in a soft voice: 'Hani Abed [one of the former suicide bombers], peace be upon him, is blessed today in heaven. He is not dead. No, he is happy. That is why the women are ululating: they are happy because he has given himself to Allah.'

They had then explained the plot of the Jews to dominate the world. The Jews had stated their devious intentions in the *Protocols of the Elders of Zion*. 'They want to destroy the whole world ... we Islamists can never accept such a state .... our rejection is not just words ...'

Six days later Hisham rode his bicycle into the Israeli checkpoint. His family believes he has joined God in martyrdom.

I wondered if Hisham could also be considered a victim of the *Protocols of the Elders of Zion*, like the three officers whom he had murdered in cold blood. Would this young man have decided to sacrifice his life had he not been convinced by his fanatical leaders that he was battling a gigantic Jewish Conspiracy which threatened the Moslem world?

Over time the use of the *Protocols* in the Muslim world has become increasingly bold: not only are they published and sold in bookstores, taught in schools, serialized in official newspapers accompanied by *Stuermer*-style cartoons, quoted on numerous sites on the Internet, but at the end of 2002 a way was found to disseminate them to hundreds of millions of Muslims.

Ramadan is an Islamic holiday observed by Muslim communities around the world by fasting during the day, for a whole month, and gathering every evening for a traditional meal. It is during the month of Ramadan, which fell in November 2002, that Egyptian television chose to present daily a 41-episode series based on the *Protocols of the Elders of Zion*, entitled *Knight Without a Horse*. A large number of the most respected Egyptian actors participated in this series, depicting how bearded Jews connive to dominate the whole Muslim world. In one episode an Egyptian who plays a central role in the series explains to a group of friends how the Jewish conspiracy influenced and decided all major events in history, and how the Jewish serpent is winding its way through one country after another, leaving behind it total disruption, but no detectable marks.

In the last episode the Jews are seen toasting the announcement that their plan has succeeded and the structure of the Muslim Authority has been destroyed, its buildings burnt to the ground.

One year later, in the autumn of 2003, during the month of Ramadan, a new TV series appeared daily on the screens in Muslim countries, in which the *Protocols* are again prominent alongside scenes dedicated to the old blood libels, picturing a young boy being murdered, his blood used to bake matzos, which the Jews are seen eating on screen.

This time it is a Syrian production.

Watching these series I realize that, were I a Muslim, I would be scared. As a Jew, I feel a helpless rage.

On 17 November 2003 Gihan Hussein reported in the Egyptian weekly *Al-Asboa* that in the recently opened museum of manuscripts in the new Alexandria Library a copy of the *Protocols of the Elders of Zion* had been placed alongside the Torah in the display of the holy books of the monotheistic religions. This is the first translation of the *Protocols* into Arabic by Nuhammed H'alifa al-Tunsi, a Star of David surrounded by snakes on its cover.

Explaining his decision to display the *Protocols* alongside the holy books, the director of the museum, Dr Yusef Zeidan, asserted that the *Protocols* were probably more important than the Torah to the Jewish Zionists in the world, as they were their constitution, their law, their way of life.

UNESCO, which had financially supported the renovation of the Alexandria Library, received a number of protests. In a public statement condemning the *Protocols* its director-general, Koichiro Matsura, said that despite its widespread reputation, this book continued to exercise its terrible power as an instrument of anti-Semitism. It was instructive, she said, because it demonstrated yet again that, given the necessary mind frame, people can be induced to believe what has been formally refuted. This can then be used to justify the most unspeakable atrocities.

Asked by UNESCO to respond to the allegations, the director of the library, Dr Ismail Serageldin, issued on 6 December 2002 a statement, later posted on the library's web site, in which he explained that the first Arabic translation of the *Protocols of the Elders of Zion* had been briefly displayed in a showcase 'devoted to rotating samples of curiosities and unusual items in the library's collection'. He also stated that the book was well known as a nineteenth-century fabrication intended to foment anti-Jewish feelings, and that it had been promptly withdrawn from public display as its inclusion showed bad judgment and insensitivity. In a later interview on Egyptian television he called those who defended or promoted the book stupid and confused.

Dr Serageldin's statement led to a tide of anger among local extremists, who raised questions in Parliament, sent letters to the newspapers and published articles claiming that characterization of the book as 'a fabrication intended to foment anti-Jewish feelings' was a disloyal, unpatriotic act.

Sadly, at the beginning of the twenty-first century the *Protocols* have long ceased to be a bizarre publication distributed by fringe groups to discredit Jews. 'Jewish Conspiracy' and 'Jewish Domination' *have* become code-words used by certain societies, and by diverse groups and movements that have little else in common, not only to discredit Jews and Israel, but also to explain all the evils that plague human society in every corner of the world. The *Protocols of the Elders of Zion* have become a major item in public political discourse concerning the conduct of world affairs.

Select Bibliography

Aronsfeld, Caesar C., 'Protocols among the Arabs', *Patterns of Prejudice* 9, July/August 1975.

— *The Text of the Holocaust: A Study of the Nazis' Extermination Propaganda, 1919–1945*, Marblehead, MA: Micah Publications, 1985.

Bernstein, Herman, *The History of a Lie – 'The Protocols of the Wise Men of Zion'. A Study*, New York: Ogilvie, 1921.

— *The Truth about the 'Protocols of Zion' – A Complete Exposure*, New York: Covici and Friede, 1935; new edn Ktav Publishing House, 1972.

Black, Edwin, *The Anti-Ford Boycott*, Washington, DC: Midstream, January 1986.

Cohn, Norman, *Warrant for Genocide*, London: Eyre & Spottiswoode, 1967.

Curtiss, John Shelton, *An Appraisal of the 'Protocols of the Elders of Zion'*, New York: Columbia University Press, 1942.

Goodman, David G. and Masanori Miyazawa, *Jews in the Japanese Mind: The History and Uses of a Cultural Stereotype*, New York: The Free Press, 1995.

Graves, Philip, 'Truth about the Protocols', *The Times*, London, 16/17/18 August 1921.

Guggenheim, Willy (ed.), *Juden in der Schweiz – Glaube-Gesischte-Gegenwart*, Kusnacht and Zurich: Jewish Community of Switzerland/Edition Kurz, 1982.

Hans, Karmela, 'The Protocols of the Elders of Zion, a Secret Source of Nazi Ideology', FATPACKS – *Anti-Semitism, a Living History*.

Holmes, Colin, 'New Light on the Protocols', *Patterns of Prejudice*, Vol. 6, November/December 1977.

Institute of Jewish Affairs, *The Post-War Career of the Protocols of Zion*, 1981.

— *Anti-Semitism in Japan – Research Report*, London, 1981.

Iroshnikov, Mikail, Liudmila Protsai and Yuri Shelayev, *The Sunset of the Romanov Dynasty*, Moscow: Teppa Terra, 1992.

Johnson, George, 'The Infamous "Protocols of the Elders of Zion" Endures', *New York Times*, Sunday 26 July 1987.

Kadish, Sharman, 'Jewish Bolshevism and the "Red Scare" in Britain', *Jewish Quarterly*, Vol. 34, 1987.

Kohno, Tetsu, 'The Jewish Question in Japan', *Jewish Journal of Sociology*, Vol. 29, No. 1, June 1987.

Korey, William, *The Soviet 'Protocols of the Elders of Zion': Anti-Semitic Propaganda in the U.S.S.R. (August 1967–August 1977)*, Washington, DC: Public Affairs Division, B'nai B'rith, 1977.

Külling, Friedrich, 'Bei uns wie Überall?', Zurich: Jurist Druck, n.d.

Lacey, Robert, *Ford: The Man and the Machine*, Boston, MD: Little, Brown, 1986.

Lee, Albert, *Henry Ford and the Jews*, New York: Stein and Day, 1980.

Lewis, Bernard, *Semites and Anti-Semites: An Inquiry into Conflict and Prejudice*, New York and London: W.W. Norton, 1986.

Litvinoff, Emanuel, *Soviet Anti-Semitism*, London: Wildwood House, 1974.

Litvinov, Barnett, *The Burning Bush: Anti-Semitism and World History*, London: Collins, 1988.

Loosli, Carl Albert, *Die Schlimmen Juden*, Berne: Pestalozzi-Fellenberg, 1927.

Lüthi, Urs, *Der Mythos von der Verschwörung. Die Hetze der Schweizer Frontisten gegen die Juden und Freimaurer – am Beispiel des Berner Prozesses um die 'Protokolle der Weisen von Zion'*, Basle and Frankfurt am Main, 1992.

Newman, Elias, *The Fundamentalists' Resuscitation of the Anti-Semitic Protocol Forgery. The Tragedy of Tragedies and the Story of a Lie*, Minneapolis: Augsburg Publishing House, 1934.

New York Times, 'The Elders of Zion in Tokyo', 5 February 1995.

Raas, Emil and Georges Brunschvig, 'Vernichtung Einer Faelschung – der prozess um die Erfundenen Weisen von Zion', *Die Gestaltung*, Zurich, 1938.

Radziwill, Catherina, *The Last Tzarina*, Toronto: Longmans, Green & Company, 1928.

Rollin, Henri, *L'Apocalypse de notre temps*, Paris: Gallimard, 1939; new edn Paris: Edition Alia, 1991.

Samuel, Maurice, *The Great Hatred*, Lanham, MD: University Press of America, 1988.

Segel, Benjamin W., *Die Protokolle der Weisen von Zion – kritisch beleuchtet*, Berlin: Philo-Verlag, 1926; English trans. by Sacha Czaczkes, *The Protocols of the Elders of Zion: The Greatest Lie in History*; new trans. with introduction by Richard S. Levy, *A Lie and a Libel: The History of the 'Protocols of the Elders of Zion'*, Lincoln: University Press of Nebraska, 1995.

Streiker, L. D., 'Painful Tattoos', *Christian Century*, Vol. 84, 26 July 1967.

Sykes, Christopher, 'The Protocols of the Elders of Zion', *History Today*, 1967.

Taguieff, Pierre André, *'Les Protocoles des Sages de Sion – un faux et ses usages dans le siècle*, Paris: Berg, 1992.

Tsigelman, Yaakov, *The Myth of the Jewish Menace in World Affairs*, New York: Macmillan, 1921.

— 'The Universal Jewish Conspiracy in the Soviet Anti-Semitic Propaganda', in Theodore Freedman (ed.), *Anti-Semitism in the Soviet Union: Its Roots and Consequences*, New York: Freedom Library Press of the Anti-Defamation League of B'nai B'rith, 1984.

United States Congress Senate Committee on the Judiciary, *'Protocols of the Elders of Zion', A Fabricated 'Historic' Document*, report prepared by the Subcommittee to Investigate the Administration of the Internal Security Act and Other Internal Security Laws, Washington, DC: US Government Printing Office, 1964.

Wilson, Keith M., 'The Protocols of the Elders of Zion and the Morning Post, 1919–1920', *Patterns of Prejudice*, Vol. 19, No. 3, 1985.

Wistrich, Robert S., *Anti-Semitism: The Longest Hatred*, London: Methuen, 1991.

Wolf, Lucien, *The Jewish Bogey*, New York: Macmillan, 1921.

Index